THE VAN WYCK BROOKS
LEWIS MUMFORD LETTERS

The Record of a Literary Friendship, 1921–1963

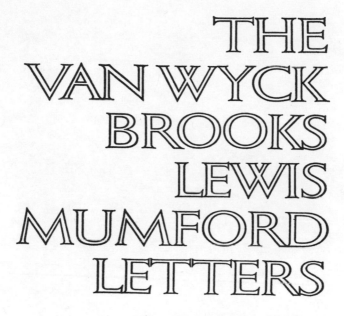

THE VAN WYCK BROOKS LEWIS MUMFORD LETTERS

*The Record of a Literary
Friendship, 1921-1963*

Edited by Robert E. Spiller

E. P. DUTTON & CO., INC.   NEW YORK   1970

814.52
B79v
14684
July, 1971

Published simultaneously in Canada by
Clarke, Irwin & Company Limited, Toronto and Vancouver

Library of Congress Catalog Card Number: 69-13355

Preface

Van Wyck Brooks died in 1963, having lived well past his three score years and ten; Lewis Mumford, almost ten years his junior, is still very much alive and has assisted his near contemporary, the editor of this volume, in the preparation of this unique literary correspondence.

It is unique in that it is so unliterary in the usual sense of gossip, incidental literary criticism, and the thrill of entree to the mysterious but nondescript world of literary and artistic personalities. It is literary in a deeper sense of recording the parallel experiences of two of the most germinal minds of their time in multivolumed attempts to relate the present condition of modern man to his cultural past and sift out the values which might have meaning and use for his future.

The Van Wyck Brooks bequest to the Charles Patterson Van Pelt Library of the University of Pennsylvania came in the form of a four-drawer steel filing cabinet bulging with letters of many people, from Robert Frost and Henry Miller to obscure authors of forgotten novels and poems. Among these letters, there were of course none from Van Wyck Brooks; but the folder of Lewis Mumford letters continuously covered the period from 1921 to 1963, and a query brought the reply that Mumford had been as faithful in preserving the letters of Van Wyck Brooks as had Brooks in preserving his side of the correspondence. Here was an important book, whatever its contents might reveal; a book that would write itself with a little editorial guidance.

It was a long but rewarding task to bring the two files of letters together, make typescripts of all but the incidental notes, arrange the interlocked result in chronological order, select and cut them to the moving essentials of the story, and put the resulting manuscript to press.

The story which is thus gradually revealed moves through dramatic stages with almost the structure and intensity of formal drama. An introductory decade shows Brooks in the ascendant at the center of New York's principal intellectual and literary group of which Mumford was a member. But Brooks's retreat to Westport and subsequent breakdown, with Mumford's growing strength and sympathy to lean on, brought both to a focus on the problem of the literary artist in America and the writing of three books each in a contrapuntal series of which Emerson, as it turned out, was the dominant chord.

Brooks's recovery in 1931 brought the story to a second phase in which each man was drawn into a major series of related studies of his own central theme, linked by a common concern for the meaning, origins, and future of modern man, and specifically modern man in America. This is the heart of the book, for the writing of these two mammoth works demanded consecration, mutual faith, long preparation, careful workmanship, and strength to withstand popular misunderstanding and neglect. It was in these trials that Brooks and Mumford meant so much to each other. The story swings back and forth from the creation of *Technics and Civilization* (1934), *The Culture of Cities* (1938), *The Condition of Man* (1944), and *The Conduct of Life* (1951), the Mumford series which was later titled *The Renewal of Life,* to that of the Brooks series: *The Flowering of New England* (1936), *New England: Indian Summer* (1940), *The World of Washington*

Irving (1944), *The Times of Melville and Whitman* (1947), and *The Confident Years* (1952), which was somewhat belatedly given the covering title of *Makers and Finders: A History of the Writer in America, 1800–1915.* That these nine books, based on an assumption of the integrity of Man and the value of life, could be produced, bit by bit, in an age dominated by literary disillusion and social and international dissent and disruption, is a tribute to whatever it was that these two men had in common and to what they gave to each other.

If the letters only revealed so much, it would be sufficient, even though perhaps the reading might not be easy, but the drama was heightened and enriched by the personal tragedies which both men endured and in which they looked to each other for comfort and support. Death always holds a recurrent and shocking role in any real-life drama, and the Brooks–Mumford relationship was sustained through two wars, a depression, the loss of closely loved ones, the failure of human hopes, and the unquenchable faith in life, by keeping an open channel of discourse. These are perhaps the letters that one will reread after the book is laid aside; but perhaps even more revealing are those letters which record the one real rift in understanding—when at last the minor circumstance of an award of a medal of distinction uncovered the deep differences in perspective, belief, and aim which had always been present but had been suppressed for the sake of more valuable human bonds.

That the correspondence moved out finally into the sunlight of reconciliation and enjoyment of the last chapters of life may turn the story for some into a mere sentimental romance, but it is comforting to know that the values of friendship can accomplish so much and endure even after the battles have been fought and the victories won.

As the dramatic story which these letters gradually unfold is therefore almost wholly one of the mind rather than one of events and action, the problem of editing them in such a way as to focus on the evolution of ideas, hopes, and plans and to eliminate or subordinate the *seemingly* petty details of daily life required somewhat greater editoral freedom than is normally allowed. Letters have been chosen, cut, arranged, and paragraphed in such a way as to allow them to tell the single connected story of the joint quest for the origins, meanings, evolution, and future of American culture as a rebirth of the heritage of Western man. Only enough of the personal annoyances, triumphs, discouragements, excitements, and even routines has been included to provide the human setting for this colloquy. Minor omissions, such as greetings, signatures, confidential references to living persons and institutions, details of daily family life, and conventional pleasantries have been silently passed over. Omissions perhaps important to a future biographer have been indicated by the usual sign (. . .), but personal crises which deeply affected the lives of both Brooks and Mumford have been sufficiently documented by letters to bring them into their context. Footnotes are kept at a minimum and are supplied where the information is most relevant rather than at the first mention of a name.

On the other hand, many records of moods, meditations, and confidences, as well as some events of personal life which seem essential to the underlying story, have been allowed to stand. The editor's judgment in all of these matters may always be tested, as the entire correspondence, either in originals or copies, is deposited in the library of the University of Pennsylvania where it may be consulted by qualified persons.

The editor has been fortunate in having the constant advice and assistance of Gladys Brooks, herself a writer of note, and of Lewis Mumford in interpreting difficulties of orthography, in identifying people, places, and times, and in advising on omissions and other matters of editorial policy. He is also indebted to Malcolm Cowley whom Brooks appointed his literary executor, to Neda Westlake, the indefatigable Rare

Book Librarian of the Van Pelt Library, to Suzanne Kirk, Susan Lowell, and others who made the typescripts from which this manuscript has been prepared; and to the Faculty Research Committee of the University of Pennsylvania for a grant which helped to make this work possible.

R.E.S.

Contents

THE VAN WYCK BROOKS
LEWIS MUMFORD LETTERS

*The Record of a Literary
Friendship, 1921–1963*

INTRODUCTION

The Beginnings of
a Friendship
by Lewis Mumford

Who can say when my friendship with Van Wyck Brooks
began? In the spring of 1920 Walter Fuller, the Managing
Editor of a new weekly, the *Freeman,* brought us together for
a hasty lunch in a white-tiled Child's to discuss the possibility
of my writing reviews for Brooks's department. But that
meeting mingles with an even dimmer memory of our being
briefly introduced a little earlier in the *Freeman*'s first office,
in the brownstone building on West Fifty-eighth Street which
that weekly briefly occupied before its removal to Thirteenth
Street. If those early meetings remain shadowy, it is perhaps
because I had already had a more vivid encounter with Brooks
in the pages of the *Seven Arts,* if not also in *America's Coming
of Age.*

But in spite of Brooks's constitutional shyness, which
neither of us ever quite overcame, I can recall the original
impression he made upon me: alert, diffidently humorous,
aloofly genial, with his close-cut hair, his ruddy cheeks, his
compact body, and the air of spiritual tautness, which one still
finds in his early prose. Brooks, almost ten years older than I,
was already an established critic, who always knew he was "a
writer born," while I, despite my brief associate editorship of
the fortnightly *Dial,* was still uncertain as to whether I would
become a sociologist, a dramatist, a critic, or a philosopher

until I found the coat of many colors that actually fitted me. Quite spontaneously we became fellow workers in the task of reclaiming our American literary heritage, too long neglected, or apologetically depreciated. In contrast to the disillusioned expatriates of the "lost generation" who were traveling in the opposite direction, we felt—as did Randolph Bourne, Waldo Frank, and Paul Rosenfeld—that this was an essential preparation for America's cultural "Coming of Age." For Brooks this remained a lifelong mission; and between 1921 and 1931, partly under his influence, I made it my main concern.

Immediately after our meeting, I sailed for London, and during the next half-year was faced with a momentous decision, whether to settle down permanently in the post I was then occupying, as acting editor of the *Sociological Review*, or return to America. Many factors entered into this decision; and not the least of them was the appeal of Brooks, in "A Reviewer's Notebook," his weekly column in the *Freeman*. That quiet but vibrant voice of his called me home.

What with short encounters in his cubbyhole of an office— the rear "hall bedroom" of a typical old red brick house—and occasional lunches, the ice between us thinned and melted: partly because we then shared many ideas, partly just because we liked each other in the inexplainable way that governs loves and friendships. With my marriage to Sophia Wittenberg the following year, our opportunities for meeting increased, for since the *Dial*, where she served at that time as editorial assistant, was on the same block, there were many occasions for casual meetings, all the more because in the fall of 1921 we set up a flat "around the corner," on West Fourth Street. I can't remember the details; and Brooks and I saw each other too often for letters of any consequence to pass: but by the winter of 1921 we were on solid ground together.

One animated and memorable night stands out—when Brooks and Fuller dined with us to discuss in detail plans we three had already sketched for publishing a new series of books, modeled after the French *Cahiers de Quinzaine,* with a subscription list, to ensure support for new work. This was only one of a series of similar projects that Brooks played with from time to time: like his earlier notion, startlingly like that which Leonard and Virginia Woolf actually brought to pass, for setting up "a small printing press, like Yeats's Cuala Press, to bring out essays and translations of writers whom we liked." That night we decided to call our series the *Scipian Pamphlets;* but though nothing came of this original plan, it actually planted the seed of the Literary Guild in the mind of the man who was then business manager of the *Dial;* and, by one of those coincidences that seem almost a deliberate rhyme, it was the Literary Guild's acceptance of Brooks's *Emerson* in 1931 that helped speed his recovery from the neurosis he himself has so poignantly described as "A Season in Hell."

In this early period I saw more of Brooks because of our propinquity, than I did later when he was in Carmel or Westport, writing his *Mark Twain* or his *Henry James.* During the winter of 1920–1921 we met every fortnight, too, in the basement of Harold Stearns's house in Great Jones Street, also "around the corner," to discuss art and letters and scholarship and life in general: a real symposium, usually accompanied by a gallon of domestic Marsala Stearns would manage to wangle from a neighborly Italian bootlegger; and if I remember the scene faithfully, the conversations were better, at least gayer and wittier, than the book we finally published, *Civilization in the United States.* It was during this same period, too, that Joel Spingarn invited Brooks, Ernest Boyd, and myself to take part in a more intimate weekend symposium at Troutbeck: an occasion I later translated into "Aesthetics: a Dialogue," first published in the *American Mercury.*

These meetings laid the foundation for our friendship, despite the differences in temperament, family background, and education. Brooks, as the readers of his autobiography know, came from a financially solid, if eventually shaky, upper middle-class background, established in one of the remoter Jersey suburbs, Plainfield. He had lived for a year in Europe before he reached high school age, and he had haunted the art galleries of Dresden: even that early he had drunk almost too deeply at the heady fountain that lured Henry James's desperate spinsters to Europe.

By contrast, I came from a very mixed family, the New York branch of which had sunk to the lower middle class. But I was emphatically a child of our great, multi-national metropolis, inoculated at birth against the glamor of Europe by feeling its vulgar but vital presence all about me. What was lacking in my immediate family pattern was abundantly supplied by my urban environment. Unlike Brooks, I was not, even as a lonely child, passionately bookish; and I never shared his exclusive, all-absorbing interest in the literary life alone.

At Harvard, Brooks had such a well-disciplined, indeed voracious mind, that he finished his course in three years: but his interests were so narrowly literary that, except for Irving Babbitt, he somehow remained unacquainted with the best minds that were still there in his time, perhaps because, as he confessed, he had no gift for either science or philosophy. Once past grammar school, where I was a model pupil, my interests spread out in many directions; and though the formal part of my higher education came mainly from the City College, it was reenforced and enriched by all that the city offered me in its museums, art galleries, and theaters: indeed so vivid and stimulating was this larger university, that never for a moment did I envy my friends who went to Harvard, nor did I feel in any way deprived.

Brooks, revolting against his genteel moneyed background, though fatally embrangled in it to the end of his days, admired his Plainfield friend, Randolph Bourne, who labored under no such handicap; and after Bourne died he transferred some of this feeling to me, as symbol of the monkish regimen he felt proper to the writer's vocation. Though my own poverty was somewhat softened by a small inheritance that fell to me when I was twenty, I was never thwarted by a plethora of bourgeois comforts, neither did my widowed mother feel it incumbent upon me to engage, for her benefit, in a more profitable vocation than the writing of books. In a word, I had no standard either to live up to or to live down. Brooks, on the other hand, was harried by his outer faithfulness to bourgeois traditions and by his inner need to escape them. For him poverty meant spiritual emancipation.

Though Brooks was exacerbated by his financial difficulties, even after he was a well-established writer, he was unwilling to achieve security by swerving ever so slightly from his life course, as the acceptance of the many offers of an editorship, after the *Freeman* days, would have caused him to do. He preferred to devil at ill-paid translations, rather than write a page of his own purely for money. That primal integrity, that inviolability, was I think what drew me most closely to Brooks, in the days when our friendship was forming: and it remained the basis of our lifelong mutual respect. This overcame our original differences in character and background, and offset those later divergences, occasionally sharpening into quarrels, which our correspondence discloses. If our friendship, however loving, never became deeply intimate, if some reserve and reticence always remained, we nonetheless could not part until death itself parted us.

Lewis Mumford

Amenia, New York
September, 1968

CHAPTER I

Bohemia vs. Utopia
(1920–1931)

By 1920, Van Wyck Brooks occupied a unique and quietly dominant position in the literary life of New York City. In the first of his autobiographical studies, *Scenes and Portraits* (1954), he tells of his birth and youth in the "Wall Street suburb" of Plainfield, New Jersey; of his early friendships and experiences there and at Harvard; of his Bohemian days of hack journalism and aesthetic self-discovery in New York and London; and of his gradual realization that America had "come of age" in literature and art as well as in economics and politics.

When Albert Jay Nock founded the *Freeman* in that year as a journal of opinion and offered Van Wyck Brooks the departments of literature and art, no one questioned his right to this central place as arbiter and judge of the mature culture which he both urged and announced. Quickly Brooks drew about him some of the best young critics of the time, among them the self-directed, learned, but then virtually unknown Lewis Mumford who, as he tells us, was drawn from a sociological post in London to share with Brooks the exciting reassessment of American culture that he, Paul Rosenfeld, Waldo Frank, Herbert Croly, Walter Lippmann, and many others had already undertaken. The four years of Brooks's literary editorship of the *Freeman* and his increasing kinship with Mumford are recounted in the second of the autobiographical volumes, *The Days of the Phoenix* (1957), as are the six or seven tragic years which followed. During this time, the roles of the two men were reversed and it was Mumford who supplied the vision and moral strength that helped to carry Brooks through his mental collapse and out, in 1931, to a literary life which the two men shared in continuous but sometimes uneasy comradeship for the next thirty-five years.

During this decade, 1921–1931, Brooks kept his connections with the New York literary scene, but had his home in nearby Westport, Connecticut, with his wife Eleanor (Stimson) and his two sons, Charles and Kenyon. After 1924, except for a brief connection with the firm of Harcourt, Brace, he had no regular employment and depended upon private income and earnings from his writings and translations for support. During this time the basic split in the American mind which he had first described in *America's Coming of Age* (1915) took shape in a trio of biographies of American writers: Mark Twain, Henry James, and Emerson: the writer who was destroyed by acceptance of "lowbrow" American culture, the writer who was alienated by flight to the "highbrow" culture of Europe, and the writer who—perhaps—might resolve the issue by a kind of Hegelian synthesis. The effort to project his problems onto the generic American writer became, however, more and more difficult as he sank personally into the same conflict within himself; by 1926 he sought psychiatric help, and the *Emerson* was laid aside until 1931.

Meanwhile Mumford, about whose early years little can be known until he has published his autobiography, continued his education in the arts and sciences in the rich resources of New York. During a brief editorial connection with the *Dial*, he met and in 1921 married his fellow worker, Sophia Wittenberg. After a few years in Greenwich Village and Brooklyn Heights, the Mumfords took up residence at Sunnyside in nearby Long

Island City, with summers at one of the "cottages" at Troutbeck, the country place of his friend J. E. Spingarn near
Amenia, New York.

A brief note from Brooks, asking Mumford to review for the
Freeman, marks the opening of communication between these
two so different and yet so similar creative minds. Both in-
herited the tradition of nineteenth-century British critical
prose from Carlyle to Arnold; both were profoundly disturbed
by the state of American culture and the dilemma of the
modern American artist and writer. From the start, they
seemed to realize that they shared a mission without being
able to define what it was. The story of their friendship is the
realization and then fulfilment of that mission.

Mumford's first book was *The Story of Utopias* (1922), and
in it can be found the germs of his entire future career as an
idealist and philosopher of culture. But close association with
Brooks provided an American focus for his inquiry, and a
series of articles in the *Freeman* on the history of American
architecture (see p. 23) formed the early chapter of *Sticks
and Stones* (1924).

With *The Golden Day* (1926) Mumford turned fully, not
only to American culture, but to American literature, and
explored the problem which he best states in his opening
sentence: "The settlement of America had its origins in the
unsettlement of Europe." Thus related to the dispersal of
classical and medieval culture into the Renaissance and Ref-
ormation, the American creation of a New World culture
began to make sense, and the Emerson which Brooks had
missed in *America's Coming of Age* became the companion-
seeker that he now so much needed; while in the life of
Melville (1929) the younger scholar explored the dark world
in which the elder scholar was then lost. Personal needs and
scholarly interests became so intertwined that the bond between the two men was signed and sealed.

The *Freeman*
32 West 58th Street, New York, N.Y.   April 2,1920

Dear Mr. Mumford:
   Would you care to review Count Czernin's *In the World War*[1] for us? I hope so. Let me know and I'll send the book to you at once.   Sincerely yours,
                                                     Van Wyck Brooks

B. W. Huebsch, Inc.
116 W. 13th Street, New York, N.Y.   March 25, 1921

My dear Mumford:
   I'm sorry—That was the Cole book which I had already sent out.
   Many thanks for the notes on the other books. By all means, drop Rees, and do with Mills what you like. . . .
   I took the liberty of showing your last paragraph to Fuller.[2] I hope it wasn't a liberty; for I did not know what you meant by the statement that your "Miscellany paragraphs have been increasingly unacceptable to the *Freeman*." As you know, I am not always closely in touch with the inner life of the first eighteen pages of the paper. I supposed that whatever you sent in went through without discussion. As you know, we have certain *difficulties* as regards sociology. In fact, I think Mr. Nock[3] is of the opinion that there is and should be no such thing; that there is nothing but economics, on the one side, and art on the other. But you are so versatile and your work is always so good, why not let us have a good deal more along

1 *Freeman* I (July 21, 1920) , 452–453. Mumford had written a letter of "Constructive Criticism" on the first number of the magazine, which was published on March 24, 1920, pp. 34–35.
   2 Walter G. Fuller, Managing Editor of the *Freeman*.
   3 Albert Jay Nock, Editor of the *Freeman*.

literary and aesthetic lines? I wish you would give me the names of books, for instance, that might start you off—not only for reviews but for articles as well.

May I see you one of these days at the office?

Sincerely yours,

Van Wyck Brooks

Peterboro, New Hampshire   July 29, 1921

Dear Van Wyck:

You have no notion how your two notes of the last fortnight have lightened up, in some inexplicable way, the tedium of this perfect physical existence: they have been like strokes of lightning in a dun sky, and you can fancy therefore how dun, intellectually speaking, that sky must be.

My work with the children is fascinating,[4] and it is deepening my comprehension of literature and human nature and the relation of the one to the other; but the hours when school is over are vacant of stimulus, and there is the perpetual distraction of play—and such jolly play!—to contend with.

The Colums and I are separated by long, hilly miles; but I have seen them occasionally, and I have delivered, to their pleasure and amusement, your cordial message. I welcome the books that you are sending me, and shall wrestle with them eagerly. Those that I have already on hand I shall review sooner or later; Tagore, soon I think; Carpenter's *Civilization, Its Cause and Cure* had better wait till I get home, for it is worth either a definitive review, with all his work under consideration, or nothing.   Gratefully yours,

Lewis

4 He was teaching in a small school in Peterboro, N.H., as a substitute for Padraic Colum who, with Mrs. Colum, was at the MacDowell Writers' Colony.

The *Freeman*
116 West 13th Street, New York, N.Y.   August 12, 1921

My dear Lewis:

We all telegraph our congratulations! As casually as I could I gave your news to W. Fuller and S. La Follette,[5] who were both delighted. It appears they knew or have seen your lady[6] whom they pronounce extremely charming.

In regard, by the way, to Van Loon—I should be only too happy to send you *The Story of Mankind*.[7] I have seen the new drawings for this and a good deal of the text and I think it a very important book— (Unless you have seen the drawings or some of them you will be surprised to discover how he has advanced). He also makes much, in pictures and text, of everything that Wells leaves out—i.e., Spinoza, Shakespeare, Goethe, Cervantes, etc. May I get a copy of *Ancient Man* to be reviewed with it? The *Freeman* treated this book rather shabbily when it came out—and the intelligent papers have been just the ones *not* to notice Van Loon's work—to which, if you agree, I think we should now attempt to give some space. Warmest regards and good luck to you both.

143 West 4th Street, New York, N.Y.   June 17, 1922

Dear Brooks:

I didn't get around to say good-bye to you; and after all that was only a pleasant formality; and I haven't written you in the meanwhile, although I have been very eager to be in

5 Susanne LaFollette, an editor of the *Freeman*.
6 Sophia Wittenberg.
7 "The Proud Pageantry of Man," a review by Mumford of *The Story of Mankind*, by Hendrik Willem van Loon. *Freeman*, IV (January 18, 1922), 449–450.

contact with you, because I have been working on *Utopia*[8] in a sort of fury of desperation; and at the end of a day there is nothing left in me to write with! Now however I am within sight of the end—there remains only some twenty-thousand words to be rewritten—and I can pause for a breathing spell. The book, as might be expected, is a very spotty and uneven affair; partly because of the fact that it was woven out of a mixture of silk and shoddy, and in telling the story of utopias it was a little difficult to rise above the level of the original utopian. In spite of all my efforts to show the contemporary facets of the classic utopias, I fear that there are passages which will clog the nostrils as badly as the dust on the southern route to California; and yet I dare not leave these passages out for fear of being convicted of a sketchiness that the book, at its best, is not altogether free from. Mere time would not have helped matters much; my instinct, when I have plenty of time, is to throw whatever I have written into the wastebasket; and it is obvious that no one can cling very long to a literary career when that instinct is dominant.

Lately I have been dipping into that book on education by Gentile,[9] which Spingarn is going to publish in the fall; and although I resent the jargon of Hegelian dialectic, I see plainly that this is exactly the sort of corrective that Dewey's philosophy ought to have, if all its real advances in educational method are not to be compromised by that amoeboid pragmatism which refuses to undergo the artistic travail of giving a shape and a form to ultimate values. Spingarn was very encouraging when I told him of your suggestion that I might write a book on Dewey and James; and if I get time to before July 26, when we are scheduled to leave for England, I shall talk the thing over with him; as it is more than likely that Liveright will be chary of dealing with the subject, unless *Utopia* has a success which no one looks forward to.

8 *The Story of Utopias* (1922) .
9 *I problemi della scolastica,* by Giovanni Gentile (1922) .

Our going to Europe is sheer madness: the plan began as a sort of "vital lie" which Sophie and I built up during a period this winter when our relations were rather strained and difficult, and we have clung to it, now that the Sturm and Drang is happily eased, partly out of inertia and partly because the trip will be a genuine adventure for Sophie. If we were going to remain abroad for a whole year, and if I could study a while in Paris and Montpellier or Grenoble I should be quite happy; as it is, however, we shall come home in November with but a few hundred dollars left to our names; and for the first time in my life I will face the world without the assurance of a nest-egg to plunder! This would be dismaying enough under the best of circumstances; but when I dropped in on Father Nock yesterday he was more frigid and remote than I ever before found him, and I gathered that for some as yet unfathomable reason I was no longer in favor at the *Freeman*. Is this due to some personal ineptitude, or has my work fallen off? You are a few thousand miles away, dear Brooks, and should have the courage of distance: please tell me what is the matter. In particular if my work is at fault, I would like you to speak out clearly; because it is hard to get a perspective on one's self, and the passive attitude that the *Freeman* now takes towards what I am doing is not in the least helpful.

Lovett[10] is back again on the *New Republic,* and will be as helpful as his position permits; but I gather that the plans which were arranged last December have gone awry, and that he is not to have a free hand with the work of rehabilitation; so my chances of contributing very much to the *Republic,* are dished.

Pach[11] was delayed in New York a week, and when he heard that Lovett was in town he arranged a dinner and meeting of the Civilization group, which took place last night: there were

[10] Robert Morss Lovett, novelist, critic, and Professor of English, University of Chicago.

[11] Walter Pach, painter, art critic and *Freeman* reviewer.

Lovett, Britten, (who brought along T. J. Craven as guest), Stuart, Lowie, Miss Anthony, Kuttner, Pach, and myself. It was not a particularly stirring affair; chiefly a jolly communion of faces; and inevitably the conversational incubus of Prohibition sat on our chests and smothered everything else: surely our constitutional amendment has caused more silly talk than wine ever did! We gathered that the American sales are already over 3,000 and still going strong; and that now the dissident Harold[12] is off the scene the corporate reality of the group is dubious. That's that.

My head has again been busy with our old pamphlet scheme; and as soon as I can get my own bearings straight again I should like to discuss it with you at greater length. Did you see Pierre de Lanux's article on the founding of *La Nouvelle Revue* in the *Evening Post* last week? I am quite sure that we could establish a fertile center of ideas in America, too, if we could only find two or three capable people who are not afraid to live on short commons and look physical destitution in the face. The American notion that nothing can be done without a gross subsidy is a superstition: what we need is a spiritual subsidy, and there is not quite enough capital in our Musical Banks to supply us with that! Fortunately, Sophie is quite willing to cramp our living quarters a little and wear some of the skin off her fingers if there is anything like the incentive of an adventure in letters to work for; and I think that within the next couple of years we might make a start, trying in the meanwhile to gather a group together and get it in focus. This of course is just the expression of my itch; the time to discuss plans will come later; and I shall not bother you now.

If you have time to write please address me at my permanent address: 100 West 94 Street, New York City.

---

12 Harold E. Stearns, editor of *Civilization in the United States* (1922), to which both Brooks and Mumford contributed.

Carmel, California   July 12, 1922

My dear Lewis:

I am horrified to discover, on picking up your letter again, that I have allowed so many days to go by without writing to you. I daresay you will put it all down to the California climate, and I shall not object, although the truth is that I have been fairly drugged with work—I mean with the effort to understand my subject and seize the form of my book.[13] I am not launched yet, in spite of two months of the hardest work I have ever undertaken. But no more of this. I am glad to see at least that I still have time to catch you before you sail for England.

And now about the *Freeman*. I have been completely out of it since I left New York—have had, in fact, virtually no correspondence with anybody. I am not posted, in other words, as to what is going on, and you know that at the best of times there is an element of the non-conductive in our atmosphere. I have never understood A. J. N[ock]'s feeling about the contemporary literary mind: but I do know that he has a certain specific standard of presentation and that he measures anything by that. You remember—it's an old story—that "sociology" doesn't exist for him, and that the whole terminology of modern scientific thought is for him a mere empty jargon. He has a severely classical mind, and I think his reserve in regard to your work has always been the result of a certain dislike of half the things that mean most to you and that have, in a measure—and this is the great point—influenced your style. His "coldness," of which you speak, is to me inexplicable on any other grounds. Style, to A.J.N., is nine points of the law; and when I say style, I mean the traditional style. He will accept almost any views if they are presented in the language of Arnold, Newman, etc., etc. But I admit—how is one to approach, *in* that style, the problems of modern

13 *The Pilgrimage of Henry James* (1925).

society, if one is not to ignore the thought (the *Expressed* thought) of the most interesting modern thinkers? It is certainly difficult. I never will understand how A.J.N. tolerated my own work, and have always, immensely as I admire him, found him capricious to a degree. Has Walter Fuller come back yet? He could explain the difficulty more clearly than I. I am quite sure that it all goes back to the "sociological" question, and that there is nothing personal in it. Many and many a time I have heard him praise your work when it dealt with purely literary and artistic subjects. But he cannot abide, I think, the names of Veblen, Geddes,[14] etc. or any of their words and ways.

I am delighted to hear that you think of writing the book on pragmatism. Do it—no one else will, and it should be done. You could undoubtedly say what ought to be said, and Spingarn will be certain to enter into your scheme and help you. Didn't you think his "manifesto"[15] exceedingly fine? Deeply I sympathize with your conception of a possible "center of ideas"—I think that in a sense we hold a strategic position—I mean a few of the members of the "Civilization" group, etc.,—*if* we can work out a new and clear idealistic basis. I am quite willing to believe that Spingarn is right in saying that Gentile, etc., might provide us with a point of departure. I am most eager to join you and shall hope to do so, if I ever finish, or even grasp, my present task. But I have a long, hard pull ahead of me, and my mind has been temporarily so disjointed that I cannot see anything at present in the proper perspective. It is quite possible that I shall not be able to finish this book in less than two years, and that I shall be obliged to come home with only a rough draft in my hands. I

---

14 Thorstein Veblen, Norwegian-American economist and critic, author of *The Theory of the Leisure Class;* Sir Patrick Geddes, Scottish biologist and town-planner, a major influence on Mumford.

15 "The Younger Generation; a New Manifesto," by J. E. Spingarn. *Freeman,* V (June 7, 1922) , 296–298.

shall publish nothing that is not, in some degree, a realization of the very complex but also beautiful *idea*, which I have in the back of my mind. In short, I am *hors de combat* for a long time to come.

It is very good news that your Utopian book is so nearly finished. And now my very best wishes to Sophie and yourself and all good luck for your summer in England. Don't take this apparent hitch with the *Freeman* too seriously. "Whim" is written over its door—but I think it is a wonderfully good school for us all. I have found it so, at least. And A.J.N.'s "remoteness" really something different from what it appears to be.

P.S. Incidentally, in my reading of H. James, I am discovering some rather interesting facts about the biographical origin of pragmatism. H.J. was the original of the "tender-minded" man, I'm sure. And W.J.'s philosophy was, in large part, a reaction against his bringing-up.

Aboard the S. S. *President Van Buren*   August 1, 1922

Dear Brooks:
     It was good to get your letter. I had attributed your silence to immersion and was prepared to write you again as soon as I had broken away from the maelstrom in which I was struggling. . . .
     The Story of Utopias as a whole stands up fairly well under the tenth reading—such limitations as the first ten chapters have were a condition of my being able to write at all; and I cheerfully embrace them. I had re-written the last two chapters twice, however, before I realized that they were out of key with the rest of the book; and, worse than that, were intellectually smudgy and evasive. The situation made me miserable.

I undertook this utopian inquiry because it seemed to me necessary to throw a rainbow into the sky at just this moment, if our generation, and the one that is on our heels, were not to become sodden in spirit as a result of the storm through which we've passed: on the other hand, if I undertook to put the last two chapters in any final form it would take a year, and possibly more, to think the matter through—if indeed I could achieve a satisfactory statement even then. So I resolved to publish the ms. as it stands and to take up the challenge of the last two chapters in another book which I shall do at my leisure during the next two or three years, if my thoughts ripen sufficiently. I am having B[oni] and L[iveright] send you an early copy of the book; and it will convey to you, I hope, a little of my gratitude and affection.

Your analysis of my relations with the *Freeman* had the warm effect of the sun cutting through a fog; and it cheered me not a little, in spite of the fact that the fog is not altogether dissipated. It will be easy while I am away, at any rate, to accept the position of a simple outside contributor; for at a distance A.J.N.'s (and S. LaF.'s) perfunctoriness and lack of interest won't have the power to hurt so much. Lovett tells me that unless the *N[ew] R[epublic]*'s circulation goes to the dogs, he will probably be able to carry out his plans to enlarge the civilizing portions of the sheet; and that there's still some chance that he and I may alternate in six-month periods—an ideal and wonderful arrangement which almost moves me to prayer. With the modicum of an income assured I should be able to give a good part of my time, gratis, to any publishing venture we may finally launch into. I sympathized fully with the spirit of Spingarn's manifesto; I am not so confident about his remedy; and my lack of confidence has been increased by a long tussle with Gentile's *Reform of Education*. Croce's humanistic position seems to me unassailable; but it does not differ, essentially, from that of any of the great humanists from Mencius or Socrates onward. The dialectic he uses to support this position—especially the Hegelian equation of the "ideal" and the historical, and the specious distinction between the "actual" and the "real,"—is as brittle as spun glass. It is altogether too easy for the Crocean to call the actual the "real," or the historical the "ideal," when it suits his purpose; and to deny them reality or ideality when it doesn't; I can't detect any canon of judgment except intellectual caprice. As for the Crocean conception of the spirit as an entity—I can make nothing of it. I have the sense that this sort of idealism tends to accept rather too easily the established institutions and practices, no matter how devoid of values they may be, so long as it is permitted to wrap them in a complex verbal shroud. The school, when Gentile gets through with it, is still very much the dreary institution it is today—only he has substituted "real" teachers, "real" pupils and "real" lessons for the "actual" ones. If this is all that Gentile's idealism can offer, why Dewey's naturalism, one-sided and incomplete as it now is, wins hands down. . . . This is a hasty preliminary judgment, however, and I have still to dig thoroughly into Croce himself.

I follow news of your book eagerly. How does your need for more time affect your return to the *Freeman?* It is needless to say how much you are missed there. You have the effect of making one perpetually stiffen one's spine and draw one's self up more firmly; you challenge where Nock, for all his charm and shrewd humor, frequently only irritates. I daresay I am not the first to tell you this.

I am dipping into Proust's *Sodom and Gomorrah;* and find it full of the influence of Henry James; and discover that I am more averse than ever to a method in which the solidity of things is perpetually being hammered out into the thin gold-leaf of a style. It is a sort of mental filigree work, in which an ingratiating craftsmanship attempts to take the place of three-dimensional sculpture.

The boat glides over a calm sea, and my pencil has been

unconsciously following it—alas! too glibly! We have changed
our plans, and shall first join a party of English friends in the
Austrian Tyrol, and then perhaps go on to Vienna.[16]

The *Freeman*   February, 1923
116 West 13th Street, New York, N.Y.   Wednesday morning

Dear Lewis:

So many thanks for the Lubin review.[17] You have done
yourself proud and I am a thousand times obliged to you. I
shall see that it goes in at once, in the first vacuum in our
schedule. I have made two or three slight changes in the text,
which I shan't insist upon but think desirable (if you also do,
on second thought). They are all of one kind—I feel that it is
a great mistake to use "American," "Americanism," etc. as
terms of opprobrium. It is, after all, fouling our own nest.
Isn't it better to substitute terms that signify local or temporary aspects of Americanism—i.e., "pioneer," "Westernism,"
etc.? Also I am fain to take issue with some of your references
to Mother Israel, i.e., as where you contrast Lubin with Robt.
Owen. It is rather paradoxical, after all, isn't it, and not the
reverse, that Judaism should have given birth to a Messiah of
agriculture? And it might be argued, mightn't it, that Owen's
agricultural religion was more strictly organic than Lubin's—
which concerned, after all, organization, prices, etc.? But if
you don't agree with me, you shall of course have everything
your own way.

I'm glad to hear that you are to summon the "Civilization"
group together again. I can't come on Sunday of this week,
but I should be free any other Sunday.

[16] They returned in November, 1922.
[17] "David Lubin," an article by Mumford. *Freeman*, VI (February 21,
1923), 570–572.

The *Freeman*
116 West 13th Street, New York, N.Y.   March 12, 1923

Dear Lewis:

Our good friend Spingarn suggests a party at Amenia for the week-end beginning on Friday the 23rd.[18]—to consist of ourselves, together with Geroid Robinson and H. L. Stuart. Do contrive to come! We are bound to have an exceedingly good time. I told Spingarn that I would send word to you— asking you in turn to send word to him. You *will* come, won't you?

Westport, Connecticut   [1923]
                                        Sunday morning

Dear Lewis:
This must be a hasty note. I hope to see you on Thursday or Friday—I can't do justice to your very persuasive and interesting letter. But the more I think over the proposal you make the more I realize that I cannot accept it.[19] I am really bound too closely to B. W. H[uebsch]—or have become so during the last few weeks. I could scarcely connect myself—with my loyal whole-heartedness—with another publishing institution. I shall explain this in detail when I see you, but meanwhile this must be my definite answer. In every other respect I am

18 According to Brooks, it was Spingarn's habit to hold "a sort of symposium now and then" at Troutbeck. "I remember one of these on the pros and cons of censorship, though who the speakers were I cannot remember; but in *Aesthetics: a Dialogue* Lewis Mumford recorded another that took place in 1921. . . . On this occasion Ernest Boyd, Joel, Lewis and I myself discussed our various ideas of criticism." (*Autobiography*, p. 397.)

19 A proposal to join the editorial board of the "Scipian Pamphlets" (see pp. 2–3) .

most enthusiastic about the scheme and I should be glad to join you *personally*—I mean if there were any suggestions I could make, etc.—

And now another matter. Waldo Frank and Paul Rosenfeld were here on Sunday and Waldo especially has a proposal to make in regard to a symposium on the censorship—to work out some sort of serious, philosophical treatment of the subject. I can't go into this in a note, but I think the question is an *interesting* one; and we propose to ask Spingarn, R. M. Lovett, Edmund Wilson and yourself to meet us and talk the matter over. Could you come next Thursday, 31st May? We suggest dining first at the Brevoort at 7 o'clock—Then to go to Paul Rosenfeld's for the evening. We want to take the question out of the mere journalistic and political sphere and develop its wider implications. Let me know if you are willing and able to join us that evening.

The *Freeman*   [1923]
116 West 13th Street, New York, N.Y.   Thursday evening

Dear Lewis:

We are sending your first article[20] to the printer tonight— heaven be thanked! for I like it *immensely!*—so do you suppose you could let us have another by Thursday or Tuesday? I should like to get them in a series, if possible—running continuously.

20 The series of five articles on "American Architecture" began with "The Medieval Tradition," *Freeman*, VIII (December 19, 1923), 344–346, and concluded with "The Realization of Industrialism," VII (February 27, 1924), 584–586.

Twelve Opossums Farm
Hackettstown, New Jersey, R.F.D. 1   April 30, 1924

Dear Van Wyck:

These months have been passing with ghastly speed; and I have precious little to show for it; except the completion of *Sticks and Stones,* with a *little* more architecture in the early chapters, and—I fear—a bungled last chapter. Somehow, the final chapter has a way of becoming a sort of last will and testament, and amid the dying gasps the whole sense and neatness of what has gone before is forfeited without one's having expressed any of the major things that are on one's mind. I am putting it in salt for a month; and will give it the benefit of a re-writing; but I shall be eager to discover what you think of the book as a whole, when it becomes a book.

Meanwhile, I am beginning to be engrossed in something else; a long philosophic excursus, with an apocryphal Geddes, a *quite* apocryphal Geddes, as the radiating center for all sorts of thoughts and experiences. The first chapter will detail the disappearance of the master and the beginnings of a dozen flatulent little cults, crystallizing and hardening and becoming, god save us: institutions. The master secretly reappears at one of the lustral gatherings of his followers; sees what has become of all his teaching, and begs the one disciple he has had who has fought against him and evaded him to write his intellectual biography since he had rather be supplanted by his follower, as Socrates was supplanted by Plato, and be raised into a myth, than be entombed as an effigy by those who passively "accept" him.

I have been reading the *Travels of Fa-hsien,* which Giles[21] has just translated, and have been more impressed than ever by the fate of Buddhism: the fate, more or less of every living idea, more particularly when the man himself has become

21 Herbert Allen Giles, British Orientalist.

more important and illuminating than the writings. Whether the rest of the discourse will live up to the introduction I shall try to find out during the next year.

So much for intellectual history. Spring has come gloriously out here. . . . This countryside is blasted and beautiful: a spent courtesan who has still some lingering marks of girlhood: swelling hills and the white patches of dead forest, growing beside the muck of abandoned iron mines. The landscape itself has a story that is worth telling. I don't like the sense of being buried and distant; but otherwise, if my purse continues to be lean, a retirement to the countryside will hold no terrors—and it's nice to be reassured to this extent by the experience.

What have you been doing or planning? I forbear to ask you about the Henry James book, except to plead, as ardently as ever, for its publication. I note in the *Literary Review*[22] that you've a hand in Boni's series; or rather, you told me about it, but I note the books announced. Wouldn't it be a good notion to have a collection of the mid-nineteenth century humorists, including obscurer men like "Philander Doesticks," carefully selected and weeded; with a very extensive introduction on their place and point? They would bear recovery if they had the same sort of editing that O'Shaughnessy has received.

Hendrik writes dolefully but bravely: he is the old Hendrik once more; but otherwise I have heard from no one. My vanity was sadly hurt the other day when Eva Goldbeck—do you remember her—to whom we've handed over our apartment told me that Mencken had suggested that she contribute to the *Mercury:* it hurt particularly because I have had much more respect for H.M. since the *Mercury* has turned out to be as good as it is: Did I say that I'd heard from no one? It isn't true. Walter Fuller broke his long silence with a copious letter and three copies of the *Westminster Weekly*. A wishy-washy

[22] The book section of the New York *Evening Post*.

sheet: but he is the same dear Walter, and, I gather from the
mood of the writing, a somewhat happier man at last. He of
course asked after you and wanted to know what had become
of Emily Macmillan. . . . .

Melba Inn, New Canaan, Connecticut   [April, 1924]
                                                Friday

Dear Lewis:

. . . I am living a preposterous life at present. My book
seems to be held up indefinitely, and I am casting about for a
job—for I must have one, and I am just about as helpless as an
infant when it comes to *finding* anything of that kind. Meanwhile, I am doing what miscellaneous work comes along,
translating, reviewing, etc. The future is a bit vague. What
isolated particles we all are! These economic questions should
so easily solve themselves if we could develop some sort of
group action; but alas, our New York groups, when they pass
beyond two or three people, seem destined to be hopelessly
artificial. I was sorry to hear that you were stopped in your
book, but that I know is only momentary. The chapter I read
was so awfully good. I remember it almost paragraph by paragraph, and that is a very good test after a few weeks. It was
nice to hear of Spingarn. . . . Every sort of good luck to you
and your work.

Westport, Connecticut   May 12, 1924

Dear Lewis:

It's so good now to hear that your architectural book is out
of the way—and that you are already making other plans.

Your fantasia apropos of Geddes sounds most marvellously appetizing, and I'm willing to bet anything that you will carry it through with flying colors—after much preliminary misery and oceans of doubt and half a dozen false starts. You have a beautiful big shining star over your head and your mind wasn't born last week (or "since the war")—ergo, and for a good many other reasons, you are cut out to do some of the reconstructing of the Reconstruction Period that most of New York doesn't seem to know is on the way.

Excuse me for indulging a prophetical instinct—but why shouldn't I when I can't help it? I am going through a little Reconstruction Period of my own just at the moment.[23] The *H. James* is to go on the shelf for (I think) a year, for the best and most unanswerable of reasons. It is finished in one sense, finished as a *tract;* but I haven't the heart to write tracts any longer. I mean to do the real thing, and can, with time. The *analytical work* is done, and it was a bit of a job—so much so that it wore me down most fearfully and convinced me that analysis is for me no longer. Another year of it and I should have killed what I have only temporarily benumbed. In another year I shall be able to return to the book and give it the right tone of feeling and be at peace with it. And meanwhile, having laid it aside, I feel all sorts of green shoots stirring again—oh, the blissful early morning sense of a new growth! I am going in for synthesis now, though it means fasting and prayers. (All this, about H.J., please, is between you and me. The first morbidity I have to live down in this rather nerve-shaking business of swapping horses in mid-stream concerns that ghastly New York whispering-gallery.) —And now, aside from all these matters, how much, *much* I should like to have a good talk with you. Hendrik says you and Sophie are going to make him a visit. Then you must make us one. Couldn't you contrive to spend the summer out here? It is really

23 Mumford notes on this letter: "Important. The turning point in Van Wyck Brooks's development."

touchingly lovely from May onward. I am shuffling off my interminable translation of Thoreau and going to town twice weekly to Harcourt's office: but one's roots here grow deeper and deeper and New York comes to seem more and more a personified and generalized *Algonquin*.[24]

Harcourt, Brace and Co., Inc.
383 Madison Avenue, New York, N.Y.   February 13, 1925

Dear Lewis:

Thank you so much for the charming dialogue.[25] I read it with the greatest excitement in the *Mercury* and the excitement endures—perhaps because I seem to see some of my own views expressed, far better than I could express them, in one of the characters. But even if I were wholly an outsider I am sure it would still strike me as a most delightful composition. Go on with these dialogues, Lewis. You have as happy a touch for them as Lowes Dickinson. I shall cherish this for many reasons. But is it possible that our conversations took place in *1921?*

We enjoyed so much your friend Liebowitz,[26] a most winning soul who was our neighbor for a few days at Westport. My wife and I are deep in a new translation of Romain Rolland's new novel,[27] but we hope to get our heads above water in another month.

24 The Algonquin Hotel, on 45th Street, was a luncheon gathering place for New York's literati for many years.

25 "Towers," by Mumford. *American Mercury*, IV (February, 1925), 193–196, a dialogue between an artist and a critic.

26 David Liebowitz, novelist, author of *Youth Dares All, The Canvas Sky*, etc.

27 *The Game of Love and Death* (1926).

135 Hicks Street, Brooklyn, New York, N.Y.   July 22, 1925

Dear Van Wyck:

The most admirable of babies has already begun to work his mild havoc in my life. . . . I've been aching to see you; and count myself seven sorts of fool for not making the effort to before the baby was born, when nothing stood in the way. Nothing, that is, except the fact that I have been almost standing on my head in a mad effort to get the lectures prepared. It has turned out to be a sort of general review of what I've been accumulating this last ten years or so; and although I find places where, unsuspected, my unconscious has been mulling over things industriously, there were also large blank patches, patches that I've been painting over with, at least, a first coat of reading! Zimmern[28] happily reduced the course to six lectures; so as it now stands, the first lecture will deal with the background of American culture, on which I have nothing to add to the familiar criticism, except a more detailed analysis of the breakdown of Europe. The next two lectures deal with American literature; and on looking over my first draft I am a little frightened at the fact that one is tempted to read a mission into, to give a special logical function to, our literature as a whole, which only a very few writers, perhaps only Whitman, can claim. The other danger that comes from dealing with literature before a foreign audience is that one is tempted to emphasize the importance of writers who deal with patently American themes, and to neglect those who don't fit so well in the general picture; whereas we've always had our Poes and our T. S. Eliots, who, whatever their faults and neuroses, have had as much significance as the Landors and Baudelaires in Europe.

28 Sir Alfred Zimmern, Fellow of New College, Oxford, had arranged for Brooks to teach in the Workers' Educational Association in 1913. At Brooks's suggestion, he also arranged these lectures for Mumford in 1925 at his new school for international education in Geneva.

Then comes a lecture on philosophy: its only particular virtue is that it treats John Dewey and Santayana at the same time, and indicates that something like a living synthesis of their philosophies would, for the first time perhaps, embrace the values of science and of humanism. In formulating the first lecture I found myself enormously helped by Santayana; and I think it's a mistake to consider the pragmatists the sole spokesman of the American spirit. This lecture almost looks to me as if it might have the germs of that book you suggested to me three or four years ago; but I shan't be able to tell until I'm a little more deeply saturated in it. The fifth lecture is in some ways the hardest; for it is on architecture, and it demands that I think freshly on a subject on which I've already, I think, been writing far too extensively, in proportion to my knowledge and preoccupation; but somehow, perhaps, I shall manage it; for I find, consolingly, that my standards in architecture and literature are one, so that the good life that hovers in the background has, at all events, a unity of interior and exterior. I come now to the sixth lecture; which is to deal with the prospects of American culture, with the criticism and appraisal of the last generation, and with such relevant issues as I myself can muster out of the void and make real; at present this lecture remains the sketchiest and most uncertain of the whole lot, and I can only hope that the holy spirit will descend upon me and enlighten me before I step on the platform in Geneva.

In all, these last three months have been hard and exacting and fascinating and delightful; and while my first flow of gratitude to you, dear Van Wyck, has turned at times into bitter self-reproach at my own folly, for attempting these lectures, or into black ingratitude at your not doing the job yourself—you are the only person who could do it with any sort of seasoned conviction: my work is mere jerrybuilding—in spite of all these mutations in my mind, I begin to see a little order in the mess, and I trust that everything will shake down into place during the tepid days on the water. I don't know what you'll think of this scheme, or the subjects themselves: I was a little tempted, at various times, to cut the development of American culture into periods, and treat literature and art and philosophy and whatever else I could muster together at one time; but my material is still too scrappy and badly organized to permit this; and I must leave such a treatment, if I ever attempt it, to a book. Someday I must write a real history of American civilization and culture; treated as a whole; but I don't want to have my hand forced until I can do it with a grand gesture, and with a firmness that will win the reluctant assent of the professional historians. What I feel most need for now is travel *in America;* in the back-country, in the older villages of the Middle West; in various out of the way places where a simulacrum of the older life remains. I might almost be tempted into lecturing if it would give me a chance to see a little. . . .

But I haven't had a chance to tell you half what I've been doing. After a very tedious winter of lecturing and hack-writing and hack-editing—all in a good cause and chiefly on architecture—I summoned up what energies remained, cleared nine full days free from all engagements, and at last wrote the play I had planned out and partly written eight years ago. It was a tremendous release, or rather, delivery; and I had some of the exhilaration that Sophie felt the day after Geddes was born. I was so amazed at my own capacities that I cackled about the prodigy all over the place; something I could only have done in the critical exhaustion of the period that followed; but in spite of the fact that I must re-write the last two acts pretty thoroughly, I think it will stand inspection, and as soon as I return and finish the revision I'd like to have you read it. I have called it: *Sumach and Goldenrod: An American Idyll.* Let the Sumach warn you of the poison and bitterness in it! It spans the period from 1859 to 1864; and enables me to project all our own interests and difficulties, at any rate a good part of them, through the clarifying medium of time. Unless I am quite deluded about the value of *Sumach and Goldenrod,* and I shall not remain deluded for more than a couple of years, I shall follow it with another theme that's burning in me, a little more heroic in proportions, centering around a counterpart of the brave invalid who built the Brooklyn Bridge! Don't think that I'm writing a pageant of American history in a bad medium: the situations are psychological and dramatic, but I find that I can load them more fully, and bring out the larger lines more emphatically, by placing them a generation or two away.

Sardonically enough, this impulse to write plays has at last come to fruition at the very moment when Sophie's financial independence has vanished and our burdens are greatest; but we're partly solving the difficulty by moving to a little four-room apartment at Sunnyside, in the midst of the swamps of Long Island City; and I have found this winter, moreover, that once one can keep the world properly at bay, one's expenses go down and one's capacity for work increases. I have known this before, of course, but until this last winter had let it slide into oblivion for a few years.

Well, this has been a copious spilling over. Please tell me something of your own White Whales.

Westport, Connecticut   September 13, 1925

Dear Lewis:

Your letter has been lying before me for weeks and weeks. I have given it a horrified, fascinated glance at intervals—it calls up so many checked impulses and occasions that I missed! I had you in my mind during all those weeks when you were agonizing over those lectures. I wanted to run to Brooklyn, run to the ship to wave you a happy farewell, telegraph, cable, swim across the ocean—and I did nothing. For four months I have been living in a dream, writing a life of Emerson. It has been a sort of religious experience: I never before knew anything like it; and it has kept me at my table, eight, ten, twelve, sometimes fourteen hours a day, reading when I was not writing. But why should I say any more?—I shall have so much to say when I see you. You may know I had a bad breakdown last spring—it really lasted about two years; and when it came to a head and burst—on May 20th, when I woke up—I felt as if I had expelled from my system the gathering poisons of years. I shall have more to say about this, too, when you come home, but I feel ten years older and ten years younger at the same time, and so conscious, deep down, of the value and meaning of all the things you have been turning over (in your letter, lectures, etc.) —about the "good life", and the "mission"—what other word is there?—of literature, and the necessity of re-asserting the idealistic point of view, with an energy and a faith our good country has not *known* for many years—though the *patter* too has a dim breath of life in it. Everything I have done so far has been a kind of exploration of the *dark* side of our moon, and this blessed Emerson has led me right out into the midst of the sunny side. I feel as if there were an army of us assembling to make war, as Campanella said, on the fraud-engendering schools of otherwise-mindedness—really *incomplete*-mindedness, the result of blind, partial, inexperiencing modes of living—all the things *you* feel, too, and have always been groping towards— (your baby is going to teach you a thing or two) .—We've got to turn the flanks of all their battalions; and what I seem to be discovering is that *all* the heavy artillery is on our side. (The deep *wishes* of people, which have always tantalized me so, because I didn't have the key of those chambers.)

I can guess what misery and chaotic excitement all this affair of lecturing, etc., has been for you, but it will all have been good for you, Lewis. You will have gained wonderful new perspectives—new responsivities, insights, energies, though you are probably *now* thoroughly heartsick. I have always felt that you had a great future, only needed focusing, a definite task—and, good heavens, what an opportunity we both have! It makes me feel the way Gibbon felt—have you sat in Gibbon's garden this summer?—when his great idea dawned on him in the Forum. All my dubieties about America and the twentieth century have gone into the dust-heap. Emerson was right when he said that it only needs two or three men to give a new turn to the public mind. But one mustn't eat rat's-bane, and think of matters in *this* light. All I mean is that we have a chance to use the small powers we have. Only come back, Lewis, safe and sound, and walk in and take what belongs to you.—I am afraid this letter will be too late to catch you. . . .

4112 Gosman Avenue
Long Island City, New York   [November, 1925]

Dear Van Wyck:
    I'm in the same wretched mess, too: that's one of the reasons I've been silent so long. The damned financiers who have been backing Zimmern have either bitten off more than they can chew, or on aesthetic grounds have decided not to take such big bites: the upshot is that they have insisted upon economizing expenditures, and since I am the heaviest item in this line on the American side, they have cancelled Zimmern's too cordial invitation to me. And all the while I've been resolutely turning down lectures and articles, and sweating myself sick over *Running Streams*,[29] in the fond expectation that heaven would allay my pains and reward my virtues by the jaunt to Geneva this summer. I've spent the last few weeks trying to

---

29 *Running Streams,* an early title for *The Golden Day* (1926) .

retrieve my carefree folly, doing much the same sort of devilling and grubbing as you've been forced into: so I can
sympathize only too well with you, in your plight, if I needed
any external aid—which I didn't—to make it real to me.
Spingarn has been nice enough to offer us the cottage that
Geroid Robinson usually occupies in Leedsville, a fully equipt
place; and if no hitches occur we'll probably spend the
summer up there. *Running Streams* flows a little more slowly,
it is true; but I think the book will improve by these impedi-
ments, which allow it a little more time to sink down into the
lower levels of the mind: at each step in re-writing it becomes
definitely more complete and thorough, and the various parts
are falling together better.

The *New Masses* disappointed me; or it would have had I
honestly hoped anything fresh and kicking to come from the
particular group that's running it; but I had a hunch, all
along, that their wish to create something new was a mere lip-
service to the ideas of the people they were trying to draw
along with them, and that at bottom they wanted nothing
different from the *Masses* of 1914, which of course is irrecover-
able, except as a corpse or a mummy; and this, I feel, is what
the *New Masses* chiefly is. I am sorry. They began with
excellent intentions; but they had not the courage to live up
to them. The difference between the old-fashioned revolutionist and those of us who have survived and kept our wits is
that they, essentially, were contented with an uprising, which
would transfer power from one class to another, whereas we
want, I take it, a revolutionary social change which will
displace a mean and inferior kind of life with a completely
different kind. An uprising merely means a new deal; a
revolution means a different kind of game. The old-fashioned
revolutionists are just as bitterly the enemies of our kind of
game as the financiers and rulers are; and the joke of it is that
in the confusion, the "revolutionist" lumps us with the ruling
classes, and the ruling classes think of us as "revolutionists".

The worst about it is that it places one in the dilemma of supporting causes in which one does not essentially believe, in order to defeat institutions and vested interests in which one believes even less!

I had planned a visit to Boston and Concord this April, to look over the ground, and recover my feeling for the place, which I know only by ferreting back almost a decade into the change-impressions I garnered when I was living in Cambridge, quite oblivious of my excellent opportunity for peering into the American past. . . .

Aren't you going to publish some of *Emerson* in the *Dial* or in the *Mercury?* I should think you had more than one chapter ready for publication, and the mere inspection of it in print is heartening—to say nothing of its financial advantage.

Paul Rosenfeld asked after you with concern, recently.

Westport, Connecticut

[December, 1925]
Sunday evening

Dear Lewis:

This is just the hastiest of lines to send you and Sophie a Christmas greeting and to thank you for your note. I wish I could see you, but I cannot seem to break away at present. My book is rather up in the air at present, as I found myself a while ago in a worse financial hole than ever, and had to go back to a bout of translating, to my unresourceful mind the only immediate way of assembling a few dollars. But I hope to be out of this in a week or two and ready to crack some of the metaphysical nuts that have stood in the path of my subject and reduced me to terror at moments. I was overjoyed to hear that you see your way clear now and have got your own book more or less in mind and hand. We are closing the house here about January 15th as Eleanor has to go West for three months. I haven't quite decided where I shall go; though I shall certainly see you by that time. Alas, my book was promised for the end of January, and I had to spend two solid months revising, entirely re-writing and reconstructing, what I wrote in the summer, and I am now still at the foot of the mountain! But courage! and we shall still come through.

4112 Gosman Avenue
Long Island City, New York   December 23, 1925

Dear Van Wyck:

What a miserable mess! I am kicking myself that I didn't earn enough for both of us, while I was grubbing! A little shrewdness in coming to terms, and a few more lectures might have done it. I shan't sleep easy till you can report that you have hit your stride again and have recovered your pace. My own book is growing portentously; it is even beginning to embrace religion, quite against my conscious will, and I find myself examining my own beliefs with a gusto that recalls the first stirrings of adolescence. If I am not quite daffy, I have discovered what the religion of a modern man may be; and it turns out to be something quite obvious and simple, which we overlook because we are searching for Messiahs or pragmatic justifications of the will-to-believe. But of that more later— unless I in fact turn out to be daffy. The Transcendentalists are just what I want to play off against the Pragmatists: my own instinctive Platonism vibrates to them, and since I was brought up, so to speak, on pragmatism my attitude to the first has some of the enthusiasm of the convert. I am still puzzling over what I shall exclude, because I am dealing with ideas in the larger sense—that is, as the *forms* of the race—and there are a number of sidepaths that tempt me to exploration. Once I am started this will probably however tend to itself.

4112 Gosman Avenue
Long Island City, New York   March 24, 1926

Dear Van Wyck:

I was, I think, in the act of caving in when you saw me last:
at all events, I have at last "caved" and am now committed to
spending the next month, more or less, in idleness. The book
was going nicely: I re-wrote that dreadful first chapter you saw
and made it quite decent: but I have postponed its publication date to next spring—and that in itself is a relief. Among
other things, I have been going through your *Mark Twain*
and *Henry James* again, and have realized, more keenly than
ever, how good they are, and how little they leave for any one
else to say. My chapter, which deals with the Gilded Age will
seem either piracy or abject discipleship! I saw Spingarn a
few weeks ago: the idea of using those houses in Leedsville[30]
to some better purpose has again occurred to him; and he
asked me for suggestions as to what might be done. Three or
four of the houses are very roomy and substantial: if he'd put
in a bathroom and a kitchen range, they'd be rather good to
live in. I gather that he's willing to sink some money into
it—with the hope of lending some little aid to the arts. . . .
If I'm fit for human company within the next month I'll run
up and see you. And if not—good luck with your work.

                                                    [April, 1926]
Westport, Connecticut   Thursday morning

Dear Lewis:

Good luck to you in Leedsville, but I wish you weren't so
far off. I should love to see you now we are back in Westport. I
knew you would soon emerge from your doldrums and find

30 Mumford himself soon settled here (P.O. Amenia, New York).

the book going well. Your account of it whets my appetite,
and I hope I shall have a chance to see your manuscript. I've
just been reading "Science & Sanctity" in the *Commonweal*
with many words of approval.—I have dropped my *Emerson*
as hopeless for a book; but I have salvaged six chapters that
make a good unit and will go well enough, I think, in a book
of miscellaneous essays this fall.[31] And I am now plunging
once more into Henry Adams. Paul[32] spoke of that as a possible subject for his year-book, and I had already been thinking of it as a subject for a small study. The only objections are
that the theme is so *political* and that Adams has so fully done
himself. Of course, he didn't quite know *what* he did or why
he did it; and that would have to be the angle of approach. At
any rate, the subject is well worth looking into. I am working,
by the way, three days of the week at the Yale University Press
in New York—a rather mechanical job, but that is the best
thing, I think, under the circumstances.

Westport, Connecticut July 26, 1926

Dear Lewis:

I have just finished the book[33] and I can't begin to tell you
how much I have enjoyed it. Don't take it for rank flattery,
but I don't believe there is another mind in the country with
such a grasp over so many different elements and aspects of
American life. You have beaten us all hollow. You know I
don't like your title, and I'm afraid it may fail to place the
book with the right public; but that is a detail, after all. You

[31] *Emerson and Others* (1927).
[32] Paul Rosenfeld.
[33] *The Golden Day; A Study in American Experience and Culture*
(1926). In the 1957 reprint, the word "Literature" is substituted for
"Experience."

have gathered so many different kinds of threads together and woven them into such a perfect pattern that I am quite speechless with admiration. Of course I admire most the things I can't do at all, and among these is your grasp of the philosophic stuff of the writers you speak of. That always astonished me—I was reading just the other day your old review of Santayana in the *Freeman*. How easily you ride through these breakers of abstract thought and how beautifully you present the gist of the matter! Then I am sure that no one else with this philosophic and sociological insight has such a feeling for literary and artistic values. In fact, you remind me in your universality of some man of the Renaissance; and I predict that before you get through you will have covered the seven arts and all the sciences as well. This book is certainly a great advance on *Sticks and Stones:* a greater perspective, a more comprehensive grasp and, I think also, a finer literary strain. It strikes me as the last word on all we have been thinking and writing about America during these last ten years. And one thing more. In your glowing appreciation of the *golden* age you have done the *positive* thing which the rest of us have mostly left out. Your treatment of Emerson, Whitman and Melville seems to me magnificent. (Incidentally, I have copied out, for my own reference, your whole passage on Henry Adams, in case I find I can do something with that gentleman.) Thank you so much, Lewis! I am ever and ever so grateful to you for having written this book.

The ms. goes back to you in a day or two, and I wish I might have a chance to see you in the next few weeks. But I am expecting to go over to England next month, sailing probably August 14th. I understood you to say that you were coming over in the spring, and in that case we must meet on the other side if I am still there. My address for the winter will be c/o American Express Co., London.

Middlesex [England]   September 29, 1926

Dear Lewis:

It is always so good to hear from you even when I haven't much to say in reply, as happens to be the case at present. I am laid up here for several weeks or months without the slightest prospect of getting away or seeing anybody for the present,[34] and with nothing to do but *translate* (which I am doing) while I undergo a "cure." Harrow is very nice, but rather like a South Sea island for me, absolutely out of the world. This will have to serve as an explanation, by the way, if I don't turn up for the *Caravan this* winter with anything about Henry Adams. I have a lot of notes about him and one of these days I think I shall be able to do something with the subject.

Well, I was most amused and interested to hear about your room. We are getting to be more like Leonardo da Vinci every day, with a new kind of fruit on every branch. I am perfectly sure that some of these fruits will turn out to be bad and that the branches will have to be cut off, but the bad ones have certainly not revealed themselves yet. I'm immensely curious to see the *Works and Days of Bernard,* and won't you *please* send me a copy of it when you've rewritten it?—I should so much like to look up Victor Branford[35] and shall do so when I can look up anybody. I have a line from Zimmern today saying that he is on his way to New York. One of the American lecturers at the Geneva School was on my boat coming over—an economist named J. Harvey Rogers.[36]

---

34 Brooks tells the story of his illness in *Days of the Phoenix* (1957) , pp. 437–445.

35 Victor Branford, Secretary of the British Sociological Society.

36 J. Harvey Rogers, Branford's colleague who invited Mumford to England as Acting Editor of the *Sociological Review.*

[England]   December 11, 1926

Dear Lewis:

It was so good to have your letter. Your book came several
weeks ago and I have browsed over it again and again, always
with fresh delight. How good it is!—so far the best thing you
have done and the clearest and most positive document in all
our literature of the renaissance, if it really in the end proves
to be that?

As for myself, "what has happened" is simply that I have
worked myself into a nice little neurosis, or rather re-worked
myself into one that I had before; but I am now busily
working myself out of it, and I hope to have it shuffled off in a
few months—these things are slow and not too pleasant—
certainly by the time your cheerful face appears again on this
hemisphere. I haven't been able to get into London very much
or to see anyone very much, though I am to have lunch on
Sunday with Walter Fuller and Crystal. I do hope that
Zimmern is succeeding in his "drive" for money and that he
can find a place for you again at Geneva.

4112 Gosman Avenue
Long Island City, New York   February 21, 1927

Dear Van Wyck:

Quiet days come so infrequently in New York, and in
particular quiet evenings, that I have been in no mood to
write to you. After the usual and always-to-be-expected and
nevertheless-exacerbating round of entertainment that I
suffered from during my lecture trip in January to Grand
Rapids and Chicago, I returned to what I hoped was peace
and the opportunity to do a little concentrated work; but
neither of them has been my lot. My Middle-Western hostesses

broke down my defences so abjectly that for the first month I was back in the city I was the victim of the same sort of attentions and solicitations, and succumbed. The only trick of getting back one's ground, I have discovered, is to decline automatically any and all engagements. As a result of this high resolve, I can have an evening's chat with you; and lord! it is high time. I have pretty well frittered away the winter; and have excused myself on the ground that it was a fallow period: but as a result of my lecturing and devilling I have a little money laid by, and now, after another round of lectures at Ann Arbor early in March, I intend to devote the spring months, which are always my best months, to a stiff bout of work.

The paucity of the winter was almost inevitable; . . . and before I could get back in stride the *American Caravan*[37] was deluged with mss. and ever since December Alfred and Paul and I have been busy, like the seven maids with seven mops, trying to dispose of the ocean of literature that came roaring in. We have selected some 300,000 words; and we must have rejected five times that number. It has been a curious business, and I wish you had been on hand to share it. We have turned up a lot of young people, and some good solitaries stranded in Virginia or New Mexico or Iowa, and have given them heart; we have opened up floodgates of poetry, and some of it has been very good; we have provided a stage for three or four quite actable plays; and beyond that the less said about us the better; for most of the stories are for me little more than interesting documents of the time: they will have little value five years hence except as history. And for some reason that I don't quite fathom we have attracted no essays. Constance Mayfield Rourke had just the sort of thing we should have

37 *The American Caravan,* a yearbook of new American writing, carried the names of Van Wyck Brooks, Lewis Mumford, Alfred Kreymborg, and Paul Rosenfeld as editors, although Brooks was unable to do his share or even to contribute. It appeared in 1927, 1928, and 1929; and then again in 1931 and 1936.

liked; but Harcourt is bringing it out this spring. (She is a dear, by the bye: she, and she alone, saved me from the lowest depths of boredom in Grand Rapids: we got on famously, for I discovered early in our acquaintance that she had a deep respect for you.) I wonder whether this is because the people who might have submitted essays think we are too *young*—which we aren't—and were afraid their pride might be hurt by rejection. An ungenerous notion; but almost every other explanation seems not merely ungenerous but absurd.

Has Paul written you, by the bye, to ask whether you are content to abide by our imperfect judgements and to appear with us on the title page? We want you; and, despite all the weakness and mediocrity with which we shall have to ballast the excellent work, we think you won't be disgraced by the act; but it is for you to decide. We count on you of course for next year; and it would be well to have you *there* from the first. The poetry bulks high in the contents; and I think our judgements in this department have been more true than else-where; at any rate, we have been more unanimous in dealing with poetry. In fiction we have made the best of a bad job; some of it is, as I said, execrable; but it serves the purpose of making the *Caravan* a complete exhibition. The job has been worth doing; and the people whom we have pushed along, as well as those who almost came in, will have gained something by it; moreover, we have planted something that may well grow, and become, like the Russian yearbooks, a definite influence.

That's that. My plans for the summer are still unmade; and much as I'd like to be near you, I'm afraid that Europe is a great distance away. The Zimmerns wanted me back in Geneva; but were unable to raise the amount I needed to enable me to go; and today I just learned that Spingarn is giving The Maples to his brother for the summer: so this definitely cuts off two possibilities we had been favoring with soft and languishing eyes. I favor looking for a cottage on the

Maine coast; but greatly fear that the four months I had
hoped to spend away will be reduced to two or three. There
are so many variables in my life! My only constant is literature; and even there I feel now I've wasted too much time in
journalism, when I should have been cutting straight through
to the things I wanted most to do. I am like an old-fashioned
merchantman whose course depends upon what goods it picks
up, what ports it can sell and unload at, what winds it encounters, and how successfully it manages to hold its crew
together. But I mustn't complain. *The Golden Day* has begun,
in the lowest sense, to live up to its name: it has already
started on the third thousand, and the other books have
picked up a little motion, from the mere wash of the latest.
Note how my mind runs on the sea!

Perhaps I *would* like to go to Europe—if Europe meant a
chance to talk with you, and a quiet cottage, and no telephones, and plenty of space to work. I don't mean Europe of
course but heaven. Waldo Frank, incidentally, is in Heidel-
berg now, recovering from the madness of a New York winter;
he wrote the only review of *The Golden Day* which gave me
anything I could chew on. You should hear the howls of
Dewey and the Deweyites; the book has shattered the Pragmatic Complacence, if it has not established a case against the
"acquiescence"! They are so damned smug and obtuse, these
pragmatists, and at the first hint that their Idols have feet, if
not also posteriors, of clay, they break into thinly disguised
vituperation. Leo Stein has sought, via the *New Republic,* to
draw me into controversy; but a bout I had there with Dewey
cleared off any obligation of honor that I might have felt—
and I have refused to be drawn on any further. Santayana
smiled on me with the most generous of letters—I hadn't
written him ever—and between the cheers and the sneers that
have greeted *The Golden Day* I have been much amused, and
a little heartened. Boyd, too, wrote a very generous and
sympathetic review, linking you and me together; and in

general, howls and execrations have risen from the very people at whom we have aimed, and who at last realize, thank heaven, that they are hurt!

With spring almost here, Van Wyck, read *News from Nowhere* and scull or walk along the Thames, and from the bottom of a good half-pint of ale, draw up a thought for me. Loud sing cuckoo!

Chilmark, Massachusetts   July 14, 1927

Dear Eleanor and Van Wyck:

. . . I have earned four months of quiet labor this summer; and this last fortnight I've spent in whacking my gay, sardonic, Rabelaisian confession,[38] which I told Van Wyck about last autumn, into shape: it began as an effortless poem, and there are still far too many effortless poetic patches in it, bad blank verse being, as Bernard Shaw said, the easiest thing in the world to write: but I am trying to compromise with fate by setting my stanzas into prose paragraphs, in the hope that parts of it will be forgiven as turgid prose instead of being damned as callow poetry. I faced it cold and still found it amusing, after a year's absence; and this either shows that there's a spark of merit in it somewhere, or that my critical faculties have a soft place in them for this kind of personal, or rather semi-personal and of course partly fictitious, revelation. I have just re-written the third draft; and with a final polish it will be ready—for what? I haven't the faintest idea. Liveright would doubtless take it; but his imprint would almost ensure its immediate suppression by the constabulary and the city magistrates: Harcourt might do it out of friendship to Spin-

---

[38] "The Little Testament of Bernard Martin, Aet. 30," *The Second American Caravan* (1928), pp. 123–169. See letter of September 9, 1962, for identification of characters (not included in this edition).

garn, who read it last summer and liked it in spots; but at the present stage of my existence, I hesitate to quarrel needlessly with Liveright. I'm in a quandary; and I have a foreboding that the "Little Testament of Bernard Martin, Aet. 30" may never be published; but the fun of writing it has been sufficient compensation; and for once, I have been an appreciative and sympathetic audience.

What lies in front is a little obscure. I've the definite job of writing a biography of Herman Melville for the Doran Murray Hill Biographies; and in September I shall begin gathering the materials; but for the moment I don't want Melville to plague me. Do you, though, know of any sidelights on Melville that Weaver may have forgotten? And have you, by any chance, the complete edition which includes *Billy Budd?* The New York Library hasn't got it.

Sam Ornitz tried to get in touch with Van Wyck to settle his relations with the *American Caravan.*

Did he succeed? Sophie has been reading proof on it; has read it and read it until she almost caves in when another batch of page proofs comes up; and to lighten the strain I've been helping her a little; and getting a more secure notion of the mss. now that they are in type. It might have been much worse; indeed, with the material at our command—and considering the limitations of the editors, it might have been infinitely worse. I've told you, haven't I, how I became a sort of devil's advocate on the editorial board, thrusting forth nameless nobodies for deeper consideration, and uttering recalcitrant noes on innumerable mss., sometimes succeeding, and sometimes being voted down. If Van Wyck had been in active partnership, heaven knows what might have happened; there would have been such a succession of two-to-two deadlocks that I doubt if we could have accepted a hundred pages before the year was out. I tremble for next year—if there is another next year. . . .   Affectionately,

                                                                 Lewis

Chilmark, Massachusetts   July 29, 1927

Dear Van Wyck:

When I got back I found a letter from Alfred Kreymborg, who is in South Dennis; we might have seen him the other day if I'd only known. I've just written him and given him your address. He had written a sonnet for the *Caravan;* and wanted the criticism of the editors; so I pass it on to you, herewith:

> For Van Wyck, Lewis, and Paul
>
> And now another unwinding caravan
> Moves foot by foot across the continent.
> Desert and mountain loom as each mere man
> Pries open the earth for enduring nutriment.
> Never did hearts conceive a madder scheme:
> America's new: she has now cosmic plan;
> But the liliputians strive and sweat, and dream
> Of the day Beauty will turn American.
>
> The men who scan the cosmopolitan
> Agree and disagree on what they find.
> One, like a bird, can see perspective span
> The next is radiant; cities haunt his mind;
> The third is passionate, warm with prophecy;
> The last and oldest is slow—he looks like me.
>
>   Alfred

My jest about a sinecure may turn out to be truer than I knew: Ornitz[39] writes me that there is the possibility of the Literary Guild taking over an edition. That would mean that it would be possible to make plans for next year at once.

I am sorry you are in such choppy seas now; I have been in them myself, and realize how little any one else can help. But I am sure better weather will break soon; a hundred people would hold out their hands to you, if they were only conscious

[39] Samuel Ornitz, Managing Editor for The Macaulay Co., publishers of *The American Caravan.*

of the need for it. You have many more friends than you perhaps suspect. At all events: courage! Remember the words of Foch: they are probably apocryphal: but they are none the worse for that. "My right wing has been routed: my left wing is falling back. The situation is excellent: I shall proceed to attack!"

Chilmark, Massachusetts   August 18, 1927

Dear Van Wyck:

I had expected to see you at New Bedford yesterday; for all the editors of the *Caravan* were there assembled to confer with Ornitz about the next issue. But I had counted on Paul's sending you the invitation, and he unluckily had counted on me; and between us, alas: you didn't get any. Our first $2000 in royalties is already assured; and so we made somewhat more favorable terms for the second year. Among other things, the editors are to divide between themselves 25 percent of the total royalties. We all naturally count on your remaining with us and taking an active part—as active, that is, as you care to. One of us, probably Kreymborg, is going to have the devilment of tending to the more grubby details.

Conrad Aiken[40] brought Kreymborg down in his car from South Dennis. He inquired after you; and among other things said that the English department of Harvard had been trying to get hold of you last spring. Aiken is taking a half-time tutorship up there: it involves very little work: no formal lecturing, most of it in the form of personal consultations. He thought you might be interested in it. It may be too late for the first semester, but there is a possibility for the second. Aiken gave me the address of the professor who wanted you:

40 Conrad Aiken had published some eight volumes of poetry by this time.

Dr. Harry A. Murray,[41] 508 Fairfax Hall, Harvard Square, Cambridge. The main thing is that it offers *much leisure;* the stipend, if I remember rightly, is $2000. Aiken, you will remember is at South Dennis.

My beard has come off since you saw me last; otherwise nothing of importance has happened.

Chilmark, Massachusetts   August 25, 1927

Dear Eleanor:

Your letter was a double pleasure: for when you sent "The Little Testament" back I feared you had found it just too dreadful for words. . . . Of course it is emotionally immature: I left out everything that would make it seem otherwise: but that isn't what makes me hesitate about publishing it: what makes me hesitate is that everyone who knows us will identify the empty huzzy Tanya[42] with Sophie: while the truth is that they are interesting characters only, and part of Tanya is someone else. Bernie is a fragment of me: but I can stand that! I have been rather too kind to him in fact.

What I am now working on—an epic play in 15 scenes, which will take about 3½ hours to act—is much more mature and well-rounded: I have been sketching it out, day by day, ever since I left you, and I am as much surprised with this as I was with the "Little Testament"—which literally gushed from me! It will take me another year to finish the play however: one doesn't do an epic overnight!

You are good to think of the little cap: we missed it for an hour and then forgot about it. I absolve Van Wyck from answering my bombardment of notes—and you as well.

41 Henry A. Murray, Jr., Professor of Psychology at Harvard; a Melville scholar.
42 When published, the name was changed to Eunice.

4002 Locust Street
Long Island City, New York   October 14, 1927

Dear Eleanor:[43]

I was glad to hear through the Pachs of you and Van Wyck: and I wonder if you are settled and how your affairs are arranging themselves and whether in any way I can be of help. Please call upon me: my time is mostly at my own disposal this winter. True: New York is a maelstrom: but now that the first month is over we have become "adjusted" to these funny currents of activity, and one's work goes on. I am now deep in Melville, and find him something less of a mystery than I had anticipated. Is *Billy Budd* among the collected pieces of your edition of Melville? It is not in the New York Public Library and I don't know where to lay my hands on it.

Have you seen the nice things that Desmond McCarthy has been saying about Van Wyck in the *New Statesman*—two pages, one week on the *Henry James,* and another on the *Emerson and Others. The Golden Day* has been coupled with the *Emerson* in various reviews and I am very proud of the juncture: I am glad that people recognize all the Van Wyck in Lewis, and wish there were more of it.

Our affectionate greetings to you both.

4002 Locust Street
Long Island City, New York   March 13, 1928

Dear Eleanor and Van Wyck:

Sophie and I have been wondering how you both were and whether you ever got down to the City for a visit, and whether you wouldn't come to see us? We greet you heartily and hope

43 During Brooks's illness, Mumford kept communication open by corresponding with Mrs. Brooks.

you'll come soon. I've been infernally busy—with the Second *Caravan*—and *Melville*—and the revision of the "Little Testament"-and-and-and! But spring is in my bones and the will-to-power oozes away.

I have a favor to ask! I lack complete copies of the *Poems, Pierre,* and *The Confidence-Man,* and I wonder if you'd entrust these to me till I'm finished with Melville: sometimes one's notes, no matter how ample, miss an important passage. Weaver[44] has put me to a great deal of work: his book is such a wretched mess, not even *academically* adequate: so that I dare not trust it as I originally fancied I could.

The Second *Caravan* looks good: I hope we'll lure you back to the Third! Sophie and I are going to spend the summer in Amenia.

Amenia, New York   July 2, 1928

Dear Van Wyck:

. . . I wonder where you are and what you have been doing? Since I can only speculate dimly about this, I must fill you with more gossip about us. Sophie has been busy seeing the *Caravan* through the printers. It is, by the way, a good *Caravan:* not quite as adventurous as we should like it to be; but at all events it is solid. It contains a fully revised version of "The Little Testament" which you saw last summer: it wasn't in final shape then, but it approximates it now. Macaulay is already beginning to talk about the Third *Caravan:* so you see we have started an institution going: our days of fun are over: it will move along on its own momentum, with ourselves like so many dusty coaches and empty baggage cars in the rear! The people who damned the first *Caravan* certainly never expected a second to appear: mark you: we shall be greeted

44 *Herman Melville, Mariner and Mystic,* by Raymond M. Weaver (1921).

this time with respect! Merely to come again, they will think, is an achievement.

My little criticism of Melville, to be done in 35,000 words has turned into a ponderous book more than twice the size. I had only to read all of Melville's works, especially his later poems, to see that what you suspected in your *Freeman* review of Weaver was true: he had been misled completely, overlooked the material for the last thirty years of Melville's life, which was lying around in buckets and bushel baskets, and created, instead of a man, a romantic tailor's dummy—making of Melville the very South sea "character" that would have nauseated him. I am happy to be able to report that Melville had at least twenty years of peace and three years, at the very end, of fulfillment: wistful and sad he may have been at the end, but not bitter or harassed. The book as it stands will have equal parts of biography and criticism, *Moby Dick* being the peak that dominates the parts that taper away on each side. I have based all my interpretations of Melville so far upon his own words, just filling out here and there with extraneous data; but in August I shall go up to Edgartown[45] for a couple of days to consult Mrs. Metcalf about her grandfather, and possibly to see some Melville memorabilia. As for the rest: the days will be Melville, Melville, Melville, till at last I can say Done.

Are you doing anything now that might have its first publication in the *Caravan*? If the new one goes well, we should be paying at least two cents a word next year; so it will not just be throwing the stuff away, particularly if you can use it in book form later. You know how we all want you.

Spingarn hasn't got back from Europe yet; but the Pachs have a little old ramshackle cottage nearby which, by dint of much labor and courage they made habitable for themselves: so we have not lacked companionship and conversation.

45 Edgartown, Martha's Vineyard.

Geroid Robinson[46] will come up later. As for us, we live in the sumptuous Dutch cottage just across the river from Spingarn; and all three of us are, for the moment, as content as so many well-fed Alderneys, placidly drunk on green meadows.

Amenia, New York   July 31, 1928

Dear Eleanor:

I have been thinking about Van Wyck steadily since you left; for what you told me about his treatment in London has changed considerably my notions as to what ought to be done. Someone must undo the work that those criminally stupid physicians did: I do not think that this can be left merely to Time and Nature, although both Time and Nature are better doctors than most of the people who put up their shingles and practise. I have also taken the liberty to consult with both Walter[47] and Mr. Spingarn; and in doing so I have at last come upon what seems to me a more promising path than any Van Wyck has yet tried.

You know, perhaps, that Mrs. Spingarn has been in Zurich, where she has had consultations with Dr. Jung. Spingarn has met Jung, too, and has formed a high opinion not merely of his abilities as a psychologist, but of his culture and his understanding of art, literature, and philosophy. Jung is a man who could appreciate Van Wyck as a personality and a writer, not merely as a patient. He speaks English fluently; and his patients come from all over the world: in short, he is not a provincial horse-doctor with a bias in favor of pecuniary respectability and mediocrity: he is himself a great personality, with a distinct philosophy and point of view of his own.

---

46 Geroid T. Robinson, a colleague on the fortnightly *Dial;* then *Freeman* editor; a Russian historian.

47 Walter Pach.

Jung does not impose this view upon his patients; he seeks rather to discover the sort of philosophy and way of life that is in temperamental agreement with the people who consult him. If anyone could counteract the virus acquired in England, and lead Van Wyck out of the morass that impelled him to go to England, it is, I think, Dr. Jung. There are doubtless other physicians of broad culture, and still others of wide experience in psychology: Jung stands alone in his combination of these things: he would appreciate Van Wyck's value, as well as see into his predicament; and no one can really get to the bottom of his predicament without appreciating his value. Jung will recognize the soundness and integrity of Van Wyck's life, instead of reinforcing those fears and doubts that come over all of us in our weaker moments—even Walt Whitman had them. Jung has no sanitorium; he is more like the conductor of a private seminar. Within a few miles of Zurich, reached by bus or riverboat, is the village of Kusnacht, where Mrs. Spingarn lived, as you will see from the enclosed bills, for between $12 and $15 a week. Van Wyck could live here, and yet have all the advantages of a culture-city, when he cared to use them.

So I put this to you now as a definite suggestion,[48] drastic though it may seem in its threat to all your existing household arrangements: spend the coming winter with Van Wyck in Zurich, and let Van Wyck consult with Dr. Jung. The first thing is to consider whether this is the *best thing that it is possible to do*. I think it is; Spingarn and Walter think so also. If it is, and you thoroughly agree, the next thing is to ask Dr. Jung if he will accept Van Wyck as a patient. Jung's time is so precious and his calendar is so full that we shall have to act very quickly about this. These two considerations come before

---

[48] This suggestion seems to have gone no further than a letter to Jung, who diagnosed Brooks's symptoms as "chronic melancholia." (*Autobiography*, p. 441.)

any others: money and household convenience are quite secondary.

As for the expenses involved, please remember that Van Wyck has many friends, bound to him by both affection and respect, who will consider it an honor to be allowed to come to his assistance. We all owe a great debt to him; as America owes a debt to him; if he never wrote another word, that debt would still be heavy. . . . Van Wyck doesn't belong only to his family: he belongs to his country, and his friends exist to acknowledge this tie. What is good for Van Wyck is the only thing that should guide your decision here. Everything else can be arranged; and what is more, everything else is distinctly secondary. . . .

Amenia, New York   September 12, 1928

Dear Eleanor:

Don't make me weep for your apologizing about mentioning any words of mine to McRae [sic]:[49] I would proclaim them from the housetops, if I could, so that the rest of the world might hear, too. My debt to Van Wyck is too deep to be repaid in any adequate way; and I can only acknowledge it, and proclaim my admiration, in one feeble way or another.

Now then: I went carefully through the whole ms. It is complete as it stands except for the missing chapters that have been published: but it is more than complete, for it contains some additional material in longhand which is excellent and which should be incorporated with the existing chapters. There lies the chief, indeed, the only difficulty. I doubt if anyone should take this responsibility except Van Wyck. Without this material, however, the book would lack a little

49 John Macrae, President of E. P. Dutton and Co., Inc., publisher of most of Brooks's books.

of the body that Van Wyck intended it originally to have. The portrait of Emerson would be complete; the sense of his work, his vision, would be incomplete. Why not show the ms. as it stands to McRae, if he is interested; and then, if he wants to publish it—and is eager about it—put the matter up to Van Wyck, with McRae's comments and my own. You will have to take your own time and opportunity about this, of course; and as an alternative, there is always the possibility of using some of it in the *Caravan,* if circumstances do not permit of any decisive move during the next couple of months.

I trust Walter and Magda carried our loves to you. I am still busy with Melville, and shall be till October, alas! But Dr. Murray, my rival, has been the most chivalrous sort of fellow. More in a little while.

4002 Locust Street
Long Island City, New York   November 1, 1928

Dear Eleanor:

I must go up to Boston next week to see some Melville documents I couldn't see during the summer, and, incidentally, to give a lecture in Worcester on the twelfth; and I shall stop off and have a few hours with you and Van Wyck either on the way up or the way down. Will it be all right if I just telegraph in advance?

Without committing Van Wyck about the Emerson ms. I think it would be just as well to show it to Macrae: his innocence about the *American Caravan* is amusing, since that volume has been on display in Dutton's window, in all pomp and circumstance, for a whole month! Macrae has a prior claim; and if he is as impressed as I think he will be with it, Van Wyck may banish some of his reluctances. The Boswell would be a marvellous thing for Van Wyck to do: there are so many interesting strands in that fellow's character and his connections. Coward-McCann is a new firm, with a good list: they are generous and Coward is a rich young man: if Van Wyck doesn't shy at advances, I am sure they would give him at least $2000 without a murmur.

The American Caravan
257 Fourth Avenue, New York, N.Y.   December 16, 1928

Dear Eleanor and Van Wyck:

I haven't done any work for a month; but I am at last beginning to feel the ice break and the stream of ideas and notions is beginning sluggishly to move; so presently, perhaps, I shall be working again. Thank heaven that I imitated the ant, and not the grasshopper, during the past year: the last scorpion's bite of illness, namely, not having the money to pay for it, was spared us. In the midst of it all, I had numerous last moment changes to make on my Melville galleys, and there was the tedious business of correcting the galleys themselves: so more than once I felt more like my hero than myself and became almost as beautifully "Timonized." The book will be out late in January, I think, and I shall be eager to have your opinion of it. Zimmern has asked me to lecture in Geneva next summer, and Sophie and I have half a mind to assuage our disappointment over the events of this autumn by spending a couple of months abroad; but we have made this resolution so often, and broken it, that we fear to make ourselves ridiculous by announcing it publicly once more.

Paul and Alfred and I are now busy on the next *Caravan*. You perhaps saw some of the scurrilous criticisms we received in the press: and these alone have made us stubbornly decide to get out a Third, although the eagerness and elan, which bore us through the disagreeable details of the first Two, have

now considerably lessened; and, unless some sudden turn for
the better occurs—like discovering a young genius—it will
probably be the last. . . .

The American Caravan
257 Fourth Avenue, New York, N.Y.   [January, 1929]

Dear Eleanor:
. . . Tell me: have you broached the publication to Van
Wyck, or are you awaiting my visit for that? I am glad to have
all my enthusiasm confirmed. Van Wyck must consent (1) in
justice to his genius (2) because there is every likelihood of
the Book-of-the-Month Club using the book—and that could
mean complete financial independence. Before closing with
Dutton I would make sure that they are on good terms with
the Book-of-the-Month Club and The Literary Guild: if they
are not, I should choose another publisher who is—you would
be able to pay Dutton for all past advances out of additional
royalties, and have more left over to boot.

4002 Locust Street
Long Island City, New York   January 3, 1929

Dear Eleanor:
. . . Van Wyck's improvement may at first be slow; but the
fact that it is beginning seems to me a great encouragement. I
am still a little shy about writing him, for fear of giving more
pain than pleasure, but if you think either a letter or a visit
would please him the slightest bit, please tell me; or if there is
anything else I can do, command me. Maxwell Perkins and I
have been conspiring, as you know, to achieve a literary coup

d'etat with the Guild; but Van Doren hasn't answered yet; and I labor under a disadvantage in dealing with that gentleman since, despite his kindness in accepting my Melville, our relations have always been icy. . . .

We have bought a house up in Leedsville, not the one we were living in, but one at the end of the village; and we expect to have a lot of fun in the spring making it liveable. . . .

The American Caravan
257 Fourth Avenue, New York, N.Y.   March 21, 1929

Dear Van Wyck:

Last summer, as a result of my pleadings, Eleanor let me look at your manuscript of Emerson. From the first chapter on, I was enthralled and delighted by it; and ever since I reached the last chapter I have been troubled by only one thing: the fact that you had not published this great book, your true masterpiece. It is a life-sized portrait and it diminishes to miniature inches every other American biography, even that of Henry Adams.

Eleanor tells me that you were troubled over the fact that you could not, somehow, add a last chapter on Emerson's philosophy. I know how easy it is to lose one's perspective on a work whilst one is in the midst of it: I am only now seeing the flaws in what I originally thought the completest chapter in Melville, that on *Moby-Dick;* and I think this must have happened as you drew towards the end of *Emerson.* Do you know why you could not add the last chapter? The reason is that the book is complete without it. The portrait as you have presented it is a unity: Emerson's philosophy is embodied in every word and embedded in every page; and your literary instinct told you truly that it could not be treated as a sepa rate thing. You doubted your instinct; but I am glad that it triumphed: for the work is done, magnificently done.

In justice to yourself, in justice to Emerson and to our American life, I urge you to publish it. . . .

4002 Locust Street, Long Island City, New York   June 1, 1929

Dear Eleanor:

You have had so many hard decisions to make during the last few months that I am loath to begin again to discuss a matter you now regard as settled: but I am still a little troubled in the matter of the Emerson ms. and I feel that I should be doing justice to neither Van Wyck, yourself, or to myself if I kept silent about it. I feel the responsibility all the more because, ever since you showed me the ms. last summer I have been urging its publication. Now I am as enthusiastic about Van Wyck's *Emerson,* as confident in its merits, as I ever was: but since he would not consent to its publication I do not think the issue should be forced. That was my intuition after my walk with him the last time I was up; it was confirmed by Dr. Murray's judgement, that the ms. might prove an excellent tool in the hand of a physician, to hasten Van Wyck's cure; and, now that the chances for Van Wyck's improvement seem to be good, I think it might prove to be an unbearable humiliation to him later on, if the ms. were published in a form not altogether just to his original intention. There does not seem to me to be any urgency that would dictate immediate publication; you have taken no steps that cannot easily be retraced. Do, please, postpone the matter. Everything he has written will be as sound, as valid, as important five years from now as today. The ms. will keep. And as long as there is a chance that work on the ms. might improve his health, or its publication prove an embarrassment to his complete cure, I

am strongly against going on with its publication. I have every
confidence in Van Wyck's recovery; and so long as that possibility is real, it seems to me he retains complete rights over his
ms. It is not necessary to cancel publication; it would be
enough to postpone it, assuring Dutton that they alone will
have the privilege of publishing it. I know how hard it is to
make or rescind decisions, when one is under continuous
strain; but I feel I bear a little of the onus of this burden, and
that what I am urging now is what you yourself decide in a
less harassed mood.   Ever yours,
                                                        Lewis

87 Kings Highway, Westport, Connecticut
[from Eleanor Brooks]   July 7 [1931]

Dear Sophie and Lewis:

After all these years I have at last persuaded Van Wyck to
read *Emerson*[50] over again and lo, he thinks it is not half bad
and is quite willing to have it published.

You can imagine how pleased I am, half on account of the
book itself, which I feel is too good to die, and half because of
Van Wyck. You know he is so much better that he came home
this spring and if the book comes out and is well received I
believe he may be encouraged to go on writing once more.

A great deal of the credit for this happy decision I think
goes to Lewis, for all his urging and encouragement, that
seemed wasted two years ago, is bearing fruit now. Thank you

50 This letter is dated merely "July 7th," but the year is presumably
1931, as Brooks states in his *Autobiography* (p. 451) that he emerged in
that year "from the shadow of the mountain." The *Emerson* was published in 1932 and was, through private action by Brooks's friends, adopted
by The Literary Guild.

again, Lewis, for this and for all the other items in your long
list of kindnesses! . . .

And now can't you, won't you come and visit us for a
week? . . . Van Wyck has got a driver's license and his driving has become most expert and is distinguished by caution.

Ever affectionately,
Eleanor

Oh, there is also a very good new little theater, Dorothy Gish
and Co. We have subscription tickets.

[V.W.B.] We will drive up and get you. I'll drive!

CHAPTER II

The Challenge of the Past
(1931–1936)

The year 1930 was the low point in the career of Van Wyck Brooks. Unable to conquer his malady, he had spent four years in and out of hospitals in this country and in England, and despite all that his friends and the doctors tried to do for him, he seemed to make no appreciable improvement. Dr. Hans Zinsser, author of *Rats, Lice, and History* and professor in the Harvard Medical School—an old friend from Stanford days—; Dr. Henry A. Murray, Jr., the Harvard psychologist who was, like Mumford, a student of Melville; as well as Mumford himself made various suggestions to Mrs. Brooks, but the manuscript of *Emerson* lay in his study at Westport, completed but unedited, as a kind of symbol of his failure to resolve, in a final chapter on Emerson's philosophy, the dialectical crisis of his own personality—so much like that of Emerson himself and, in the minds of both men, the chronic malady of the American mind: the apparent impossibility of achieving an idealistic cultural unity in a complex, volatile, and violent civilization.

The book could not be published while the unwritable last chapter remained unwritten, even though its author's very life might depend upon it; and, without recovery, its author could not see that such a conclusion to his dramatic narrative was unnecessary. Mumford's two-pronged suggestion that they drop the last chapter on the grounds that Brooks had already resolved the issue in his narrative, and that the Literary Guild be persuaded to adopt the book in spite of its publisher's unwillingness to submit it, seems to have provided the way out of the shadows. Mumford had earlier suggested to Eleanor that Brooks apply to Jung to become his patient, without success; but Brooks now was freed from the necessity for a philosophical statement which was not native to his genius, and he was relieved, by the book club adoption, of both financial worry and doubt about the book's reception. Brooks himself once said that all he knew about insanity was contained in the elementary tract by Bernard Hart on that subject, but it is hard to believe that he did not, somewhere in his psychiatric treatment, come strongly under the influence of Jung's method which Mumford thought was the therapy he most needed (see letter of July 31, 1928). Judging by results, it would seem that Brooks was saved from his own inner schism, not as he had previously tried to do by projecting it onto other authors like Mark Twain, Henry James, and Emerson, but by translating it into a problem of the general American culture, which he now at last had learned how to treat historically and objectively. He was thus able to translate the subconscious experiences of the individual into an objective literary perspective and method by which he could once more take up his search for a "usable" past for the American writer and artist.

With the publication of the *Emerson* in 1932, aided by Mrs. Brooks and Mumford, Brooks could thus leave his former literary life behind him, a completed whole, and, with his new cultural rather than personal focus, plunge vigorously into the career that lay ahead. A long-cherished dream of writing a full history of the literary life in America was reawakened when he returned in 1931 to "our little white cottage in the village of Westport." The next five years were uneventful except for his total immersion in the new life; and the publication of *The Flowering of New England* in 1936 marked, by its enthusiastic public reception, the first major step on the way. Hereafter he would seek the meaning of culture in the panorama rather than in the problems of human experience.

Meanwhile Mumford had reached almost as sharp a turning point in his intellectual if not in his personal life. Since 1922, when he had, in *The Story of Utopias*, spread a wider canvas, he had narrowed his focus, as had Brooks, to the study of the American cultural past. But the larger problem had always haunted him. Now settled at Sunnyside in Long Island City with his wife, son, and later his daughter, with summers in the farmhouse at Amenia, he took the occasion of a course of lectures at Columbia to return to his early interests, which he had touched on already in his plan for his Geneva lectures. He had done books on American architecture and American literature, as well as on Melville, but his real concern was not so much with the American cultural tradition as with its larger frame of the culture of Western Europe since the Renaissance and with the prospects that these foundations had laid for the destruction or the welfare of future Man. *The Brown Decades* (1931) cleared up some leftover problems in his view of the American past, but Brooks rightly sensed, in his letter of October 25, 1931, that "all these sketches and ideas are properly fragments of the great book that has to be written." But even he did not envision it in the proportions it was already taking in Mumford's mind. A Guggenheim fellowship the next year gave Mumford the opportunity to prepare for what was to become the absorbing commitment of his major phase as Emerson's "Man Thinking"—an analysis of the effects of the technical revolution on human culture from the tenth century to the present and beyond. At first conceived as a single work, this project, like that of Brooks at this time, developed into a series of which *Technics and Civilization* (1934) was but the first step. For some twenty years (1931–1951), the two men worked in parallel on related projects, each in his way attempting to recapture from the past the sources of those values that he treasured in the present and to project them into a "usable" future. Each of them, isolated by his refusal to accept his own times on its own terms, found strength and consolation in the other as the one became more deeply involved in the past and the other in the future. The letters of 1931–1936 mark the first phase of this relationship, the completion by each of his first and shaping volume.

Amenia, New York   July 26, 1931

Dear Van Wyck:

I am happy to say that the re-writing of my first draft has gone on fairly solidly and I have every hope of earning a few days' rest at the end of another three or four weeks. Fletcher[1] came up yesterday and was sorry to have missed you last week. I am eager to have you see especially the first chapter of my present attempt to unite a *concrete* philosophy of art:[2] but it may have to undergo a third revision before it is ready to meet even your kindly and sympathetic eye.

P.S. Fletcher, too, thinks that the published chapters of *Emerson* are the high-water mark in biographical portraiture: he was happy to learn that the rest of the book is of a piece with them.

[1] John Gould Fletcher, imagist poet from Arkansas, was in London when Brooks first met him, but he later settled in New York.
[2] *The Brown Decades* (1931).

4002 Locust Street
Long Island City, New York   October 5, 1931

Dear Van Wyck:

Forgive my long silence. My book kept me busy till the third week in September: then I had to run up to Dartmouth for a week to open a course in city planning and now we are finally back in Sunnyside with all the rigors of a *schedule* and a *program* staring us in the face, and we still haven't planted our spring bulbs in the country or taken the gladiolas out of the ground! I fear that a full weekend at Westport with you is now impossible, dearly as we would like it: but the first week in November I have to lecture at New Haven, and if I may, I should like to stop off and see you on the way up or down.

Don't bother to say anything about *The Brown Decades:* it is a very minor book and no one knows it better than the author! At best, it will remind the historians of a few worthy names they have forgotten.

87 Kings Highway, Westport, Connecticut   October 25, 1931

Dear Lewis:

I have just finished *The Brown Decades* in such a mental ferment that I shall have to get some of it off my chest. Of course your subject-matter alone so excites me that I would read a book half as winning as yours with enthusiasm; but you are, as usual, such an engaging guide and you inspire so much confidence in regions where I have to follow you blindly that I was enchanted all the way through. I kept wanting to ask you questions and urge minor objections; but it seems to me that you carry the day beautifully at almost every point. The sketch of Ryder, for instance, is a masterpiece; and if you can discourse in this fashion in virtually every known field of

expression, *where* are you going to end up? Nobody else can
do this that I know of in this generation, and to me the always
delightful thing is that your aesthetic sensibility, which is so
amazingly comprehensive, bears just what seems to me the
proper relation to a general sense of those even greater things
—the "Great Society" and the "Good Life."

I must make my little points of objection before—if you'll
bear with me—I dwell on this latter. As an ignorant outsider
in regard to modern architecture, I am still not entirely
convinced in regard to some of your judgments in this field.
Every one of your books has educated me and opened my eyes
to realms I had never thought of. Roebling, Richardson,
Olmsted are three men of genius of whom I first became fully
aware in your pages. (We have one of Olmsted's parks here in
Westport, which I'll show you the next time you are here.) I
have studied your photographs of buildings, and they have
literally dawned on me while I looked and read. But I can't
see the Schlesinger building at all—can't *believe* it; and while
I *do* see the Chicago Auditorium, I asked myself in what sense
it was a new creation if, for instance, the Hotel Langham in
London (do you know it?) is not?—for I always supposed that
buildings like the Langham were just part of the "day's work"
in Victorian British architecture. But I am so truly unin-
formed in this field that you could probably meet with ease
any objections I might offer.

The main thing is that you have made people conscious of
modern building; for I remember very well when I was a child
that while one always thought of contemporary books as
written by "authors" and pictures as painted by "artists," one
never thought of buildings as built by "architects" and seldom
of plays as written by "dramatists." At least I didn't: the
buildings and the plays "just growed." My grandfather's house
was built when I was a boy by an architect who was at that
time famous in New York, but it never occurred to me that he
was an "artist" in the same awesome sense as our neighbor

George Wharton Edwards who painted bad pictures but somehow belonged, in my own childish imagination, to the apostolic succession. I merely mention this because, if it was true for me, it must have been generally true for the children of that time. And in this line alone I am sure you are educating great numbers who were in the same case as myself.

Two or three other minor points. I feared you might have gone too far the other way in the matter of Sargent. Have you looked *hard* at the portrait of Major Higginson in the Boston Museum? Surely that is magnificent and represents a great and permanent phase of his genius. (Though even there, allowing that the portrait was *meant to be seen* in the great hall of the Harvard Union, his tendency for display leads him to occupy too much canvas. It amused me, not long ago, to compare, in this respect, that great showy portrait of the Wertheimer sisters with Reynolds' Mrs. Siddons in the Public Library (N.Y.). If you cut off the bottom *yard* of the Sargent you would lose nothing in the way of *painting,* however much you might lose in the way of *composition.* But the Reynolds is superbly *painted* down to the last inch.) As regards Trumbull, whom you mention only incidentally, do you happen to have noticed the four battlepieces in the Yale Gallery? They're *wonderful,* both in color and in breadth of treatment. As regards Winslow Homer's West Indian water-colors, you had no occasion to dwell on them, but it seemed to me, when I saw them collected once at the Century Club, that they beat all creation in that line. And one question, in case I forget to ask you when I see you; where can I get hold of that mysterious Charles Peirce? I have wanted to read him for years. And then come your *omissions*: for instance, that admirable Timothy Cole. But there the fat's in the fire!

What bowled me over all the time I was reading was the thought that all these sketches and ideas are properly fragments of the great book that has to be written and that nobody in the world but Lewis will ever be able to write. I mean, the History of American Culture, in six volumes, on the scale of Gibbon's *Rome,* also written in the grand style and from a point of view that is absolutely and everlastingly *central.* Parrington's point of view was not central *ever,* and his line was too narrow, as mine would be if I had attempted such a work. I would neither have wished nor have been able to comprehend anything outside of literature; and Parrington's "man" was always too instinctively the "economic man." But you, by some miracle of birth and early adaptation, stand in the centre of the field and comprehend the whole circumference. You have a head (which I utterly lack) for abstract philosophy and economic and political thought. You have the sensibility for all the fine arts and the sympathy for all the industrial arts; and you know how to find your way about also in religious thought. I used to be afraid that this general aptitude of yours, coupled perhaps with economic necessity, would cause you to scatter your energies too much, in the American way; but your writing grows in depth, or suggests a growing depth in yourself, with every book. And what makes *The Brown Decades* so vaguely unsatisfying, in a sense, is because in reading it I found myself instinctively relating every new fragment to this more comprehensive work that must be written to give all your intuitions their proper value and setting. This is a defect inherent, it seems to me, in your conception. You discuss (always admirably) "neglected" figures like George Fuller. But it is pertinent to ask, By whom are they neglected? Not by half a dozen people in this neighborhood who have always known Fuller's work. No, but by some "central," hypothetical audience, which in your mind you assume *should* exist, but which really doesn't exist and will not exist (in the sense in which a central audience exists in France or England) until it has been created by some critical historian, by some such work, for instance, as the great, grand and immortal History of American Culture I have spoken of, a work that rehandles all the *centrally accepted*

figures (Howells, Whitman, etc. in all lines) and so provides
the right angle as every point from which to study the lesser
and "neglected" figures, etc. Good heavens! What I imagine is
a work like a great river system articulated along some main
current with all the branches indicated, etc., etc.

Lewis, read, if you haven't read it, Gibbon's autobiography
and see what a wonderful thing it is to have a life occupied for
years with an immense work like this that possesses all your
thoughts, reading, etc. But I mustn't go on this way. Your
"neglected" figures suggest to my mind so many others whom
no historian has really mentioned: Thayer, who got ahead of
the Germans and wrote the great book on Beethoven, H. G. O.
Blake, Thoreau's friend and editor, Charles C. Perkins, the
grandfather of Max Perkins, who wrote "Tuscan Sculptors,"
etc. and might be called, along with Jarves, the first American
art critic, and dozens of others. I have some interesting old
letters, papers, etc., that I'd like to show you along this line.

This is a very long "thank you" letter, but the thanks are
sincere.

Westport, Connecticut   October 28, 1931

Dear Lewis:

We have just heard from our old and dear friend John Hall
Wheelock[3] that he is coming out to spend Saturday and
Sunday with us just after your Thuursday and Friday; and I'm
writing to ask whether it wouldn't be possible for you to stay
over with us an extra day or two in order to see him. We have
plenty of room and we feel so confident that you and he would
like and enjoy each other. If you don't know his best poems
which have not had at all the recognition they deserve, you

---

[3] John Hall Wheelock, poet and editor; friend of Brooks from Harvard
days; coauthor and publisher of *Verses by Two Undergraduates* (1905).

have missed something! But aside from all such questions, you would hit it off, I know, as human beings; so if you *can* spare us a little extra time—which we don't expect—you would give us a lot of pleasure.

4002 Locust Street
Long Island City, New York   October 30, 1931

Dear Van Wyck:

Your letter has been booming through my head like a prophetic bell, for the last day: it is the most acute and the most encouraging criticism I have ever received, and one realizes, not for the first time, that the existence of one understanding mind makes the rest of the world possible—which I suppose is the moral of the relations of the good Lot with heaven. What you say on the negative side, only supports my own dissatisfaction: matters like Sargent's exact place in life are nice things to weigh, and when one leaves but a sentence or two to do the weighing in, one is always in danger of grossly tipping the scales to one side or the other: this is equally true of Homer, and I have no doubt it would apply even to some of the others where I am not yet so acutely conscious of having swerved too heavily in the opposite direction of common opinion. I tried deliberately to reduce the dimensions and the scope of the book, so that I would not have to give too much of myself to it, since the book that I am now still dwelling on was all the while my main preoccupation: but there are no in between places, in writing: it is either neck or nothing, and in *The Brown Decades* I feel that, despite its *usefulness* to the historian, it is too often nothing.

Not altogether nothing: how quick you were to detect that it was only a preparatory argument: all the quicker because I had not even hinted to you that during the last few years I have begun to look forward to writing such a complete and rounded account of our culture as you have magnificently sketched out. If only the book could be as thrilling and persuasive as your sketch. I must put off the work itself, I think, for at least five years, and the actual doing of it will require easily five or ten more: for in the meantime, I have one or two babies that have to be born, and one of them beyond my present one—it is a very unphysiological metaphor—has begun to clamor and kick and call attention to itself: but in another five years these particular matters will be settled: if the works are not born, they will be at least out of the way, and then I hope to be ready for the book you have described.

Partly as a result of my adolescent illness and disability, my whole life has been arranged, more than half consciously, on the assumption that I would die before forty: so that every work was conceived and finished on a limited scale, with a short breath, as it were, as though it were to be my last! It is only now that I have begun to look beyond forty and to feel the sufficient assurance of physical ruggedness—barring all the possible accidents and fatalities of life—to carry through a book of more epical dimensions. You can't imagine how your letter has heartened and stimulated me. It is a heroic demand: and even failure on that particular errand would be better and more satisfactory than most kinds of success. But I look forward to talking this and a dozen other things over with you. Yesterday I had lunch with Lee Simonson[4] and gave him the gist of your criticisms and suggestions, and he, who is now working on a very comprehensive critical history of the theater, was enthusiastic about it: one of us alone, he said, might have no effect, but the three of us, each working in his own field, might have a concentrated effect, multiplied far beyond the mere addition of our powers.

4 Lee Simonson, stage designer and drama critic.

Westport, Connnecticut   November 1, 1931

Dear Lewis:

It didn't require any particular insight for me to feel that you had, in the back of your mind, the grand and glorious notion that filled *my* mind as I read *The Brown Decades*. I saw it all, instinctively, as a group of related fragments that seemed to imply, as if by the nature of things, the conception of such a work; and the more I think of you in connection with it, the more it seems to me that the stars in their courses had you in mind from the beginning of creation for just that work; and the thought of you *thinking* it, and ultimately *doing* it, as you can and must, gives me a feeling of joyful satisfaction that I can't put into words. And it reassures me now whenever I see you reviewing a book on science, on town-planning, or any dammed thing whatever that is truly related to *culture,* that you are always exercising your muscles in new directions, gaining always a more comprehensive understanding that will serve you well when the time comes. It makes me fairly dance with delight to contemplate the picture. For you are a mighty hunter before the Lord. I always knew it, from the first moment when I came across your trail.

I have reason to be grateful to you, for you have done more to educate me than any living person (except the demigods, AE, Gandhi, Romain Rolland and two or three others) by arousing my unwilling curiosity to *look at* buildings, parks, painters I had never really looked at, even poets I had never really read—to remain always more or less a stranger among these things, for I cannot really get outside of literature, but at least an initiated stranger and not a Philistine. And you are just the one American living who is really capable of the monumental, the classic thing such as the old fellows used to attempt and carry through: Prescott, Motley, the Carlyle of *Frederick the Great,* etc., who had their minds filled, as we have not in these last generations, with heroic and classic models. And that Lee Simonson also has his mind on a similar undertaking adds to the joy of it.

In fact, Lewis, I have taken your letter so much to heart, as a sort of vote of confidence, that it has recreated in my own mind an idea that I have cherished for years—twenty, I guess—and that Eleanor is always driving me to carry out—of a History of American Literature in two or three volumes which I can spend the rest of my life writing!

Nov. 9th. Dear Lewis, I broke off here because we have been snowed under with a translation. It has to be finished tomorrow and delivered on Friday by hand at Tuxedo Park; so we are wondering if you couldn't manage to come out *earlier* on Thursday, in time for lunch—so that we can have a good 24 hours with you. . . .

Hanover Inn, Hanover, New Hampshire   January 14, 1932

Dear Van Wyck:

I have been thinking of you often, despite my silence this last six weeks or more: and I would have written you before Chistmas, but for the fact that I was at loss for words, and knew that you could rely on my sympathy and fellow-feeling, even if it were silent. I am here again in Dartmouth for the last time this year; and, though the trip is always pleasurable and rewarding in various ways, I find myself resenting the break and I am glad that the rest of the winter will find me pretty close to New York. How I have been gallivanting about! I gave a lecture on Melville at Union College last Friday, and breathed a little of that timid and austere Presbyterian atmosphere: merely by geographic propinquity, the James family and the Melville family both seemed very near. You doubtless know how that rich rascal, Grandfather William James, kept Union College going in the early days by quite munificent loans: they take a little pleasure there in the thought that William and Henry *might* have gone to Union. Another local note: when Mussolini seized power in Italy he had an interview with an American newspaper correspondent in which he justified his action in terms of the American philosophy of pragmatism. One of the Albany papers, I was informed, printed this with the caption: HomeTown Boy provides Slogan for Fascist Dictatorship.

What news of the *Emerson*:[5] Is it coming out this spring? I am playing with the notion of publishing my opus on Form and Civilization in three little volumes, united by a common title, but appearing at intervals: this will ease the task of rewriting them, and for once give me the opportunity to finish up a book and put all the final touches on in another state than the breathless and exhausted one which usually characterizes them. I shall be back in the city after the 23 January, and . . . if you will appoint a day and an hour, I will invite Paul Rosenfeld and whoever else you may care to see. Thomas Beer,[6] who is a great admirer of yours, is very anxious to meet you; and when I saw Ernest Boyd[7] a short time before Christmas he inquired eagerly after you and said that he should like to see you again: but we can let Beer and Boyd wait till a second visit if you want to. Don't hesitate to say what you would like best.

4002 Locust Street
Long Island City, New York   March 23, 1932

Dear Van Wyck:

Your *Emerson* has been fizzing like champagne in my veins: it is so warm and humorous and poignant and complete that a draft of it would give a dying man a new lease on life. It is not

---

5 Published in March.
6 Thomas Beer, author of *The Mauve Decade*, etc.
7 Ernest Boyd, Irish-born critic and biographer.

merely your best work, but the best biography any American
has written, and you make me proud of you and proud of my
country all over again. . . .

P.S. Fletcher is coming back from England *for good:* he sails
on the Majestic today!

Westport, Connecticut   March 27, 1932

Dear Lewis:

It was nice of you to say all over again that you liked my bit
of *Ancient history.* I meant to spare you even a word of
comment, for, truly, Lewis, if it hadn't been for you *and*
Eleanor it would have gone into the furnace and I would still
have thought it a mud-pie. We were happy that you got the
Guggenheim award and are really off for the other side, as you
hoped—happy, that is, if you don't stay away from us too
long. . . . Would you have it on your mind to tell me
Fletcher's address? I am eager to see him when he comes.

[Long Island City, New York]   April 10, 1932

Dear Van Wyck:

. . . I am enclosing the Manifesto,[8] not to plague you to sign,
but just so that you may look it over at leisure. It doesn't more
than half represent my own political philosophy: how could
any manifesto? One or two of the phrases still stick pretty

8 An unpublished effort to formulate a non-doctrinaire view of Communism, drawn up by Waldo Frank, Edmund Wilson, and Mumford. The
manuscript is preserved in the Brooks Papers.

badly in my gullet: but I think it is worth signing just to make clear what side I am on.

Political action by itself is insufficent: it must be accompanied by a moral and spiritual regeneration: and I don't think the old-line Socialists can do the job. Neither, of course, can the Communists, with their silly animosities and materialist superstitions: but their interest in a passionate and disciplined minority makes me more sympathetic to their *tactics*—though I am just as distrustful as you of the philosophy on which they are based.

P.S. Would you mind writing frankly what you think about the Manifesto to Waldo? I shall not see him before I go. (41 West 83 St.)

87 Kings Highway, Westport, Connecticut   April 18, 1932

Dear Lewis:

We were too disturbed over the week-end for me to get down to the Communist Manifesto, so I will write about it fully to Waldo in a day or two. This is just to wish you a *bon voyage* and a mighty good one, and I hope you will have a gloriously good three or four months, and come back filled to the brim with fresh ideas. I was sorry to see the account of Patrick Geddes' death. It will be a grief and disappointment to you, as I know you counted on seeing him this summer. Will you have the task of publishing his papers? I have just been asked to do this for Mrs. Gamaliel Bradford,[9] and am going up to Boston next week to talk it over. I think I shall undertake it, for it will involve me in reading great masses of old New England diaries, etc., which are just in line with my

9 Gamaliel Bradford, professional writer of brief biographies.

plan for the *New England Literature*. In fact, as I was planning to give up a year to reading, it is providential. . . .

P.S. I hope you received the *Italian Literature,* which I returned. It is very fine, of course, but, for *method,* not within
shouting distance of Brandes' *Main Currents.*[10]

Verlag Max Lafargue, Hamburg [Germany]
[Postcard from Mumford]   April 30, 1932

I never asked you if you had read *The Magic Mountain:*[11]
it towers above everything else this last ten years for me. It
comes to mind—or rather Mann does—because I am travelling to Lübeck[12] tomorrow and will probably stop in the
"Stadt Hamburg" where Tony Kroger stayed. The last fortnight in New York was chaotic but now the knots begin to
unravel. The Germans I've met are fine: but the people in the
streets are sad, white, pale—all the old North Sea floridness
gone.

87 Kings Highway, Westport, Connecticut   June 7, 1932

Dear Lewis:
    It was a joy to have a line from you and to know that you
are having such exciting days. Well I know the feeling! It used
to seem to me in "Europe"—which never quite meant England—that one lived every second at ten times the intensity of

---

10 *Main Currents in the Literature of the Nineteenth Century,* by Georg
Brandes, the Danish scholar (1872–1875) .
11 *Der Zauberberg* (1924; English translation, 1927) .
12 Mann's birthplace.

one's normal existence. And it was a continual crescendo as one went southward: at Naples I had to pull in my belt to keep from bursting like a shrapnel bomb from sheer inflammation of the brain. In such conditions it is all wrong to have letters on your mind. The most you should be expected to do is to shoot off an occasional postcard.

Things go well with us; and I am trying to reduce my work on the Bradford papers, interesting as it is, to a minimum in order to make progress towards the new book. Even so, we make numerous visits to Boston. I have met all the literary lights there and will tell you about them, those you don't know, when we meet. New England of 1812–1914 interests me more every minute as my reading advances and I have the sense—not illusory, I trust—of discovering now and then valuable secrets that have only to be given another life in our new terms. . . .

87 Kings Highway, Westport, Connecticut   June 27, 1932

Dear Lewis:

We have had the usual June whirl, with all New York pouring over us, and we have been longing to fly for the woods. Of course, we'll drive to Amenia the first day you will have us. . . . I'm longing for a good talk with you. I have been working hard every day for an endless stream of months, but I've made good progress, and I have so much to talk about. Your Oberlin speech sounds like the real thing! and I want so much to hear about vol. II. Also to see Alison Jane.[13] The Pachs were here on Sunday for the afternoon and evening. Walter was in his best form, in spite of the last reviews of his show, which I hope he didn't see.

13 Mumford's new daughter.

Amenia, New York   September 14, 1932

Dear Van Wyck:
 . . . Please remember me to Newton Arvin.[14] I am eager to know what he is working upon now. I have just been running through Calverton's *Liberation of American Literature*[15] and find it superficial and pedantic: as for the economic interpretation of literature, it takes me back to the salad days of 1916. It seems as if the war generation would have to tunnel backwards to the point from which we began, in order to make any headway forward: but if I didn't think that I had a more adequate and applicable philosophy than Marx, even in the economic realm, I would dig six feet of earth for myself and get buried. I have finally written, in response to a request from the *Forum*,[16] a concise statement of where I stand politically which satisfies me much better than the abortive statement Frank and I sent you. I cannot help calling myself a communist, for that points to the fundamental demand: but I am certainly post-Marxian, and I wish Arvin and Granville Hicks and the rest would get through their growing pains and catch up. Does this sound like an old roué talking indulgently about the wild oats of his nephews, at the very moment that he is boasting about the virtues of his established mistress? Perhaps it does.

You doubtless received the regular nomination blank for the National Institute of Arts and Letters.[17] Don't you think

14 Newton Arvin, Professor of English at Smith College; critic and biographer of American literature.

15 V. L. Calverton, *The Liberation of American Literature* (1932), a Marxist interpretation of American literary history.

16 "In Our Stars: The World Fifty Years from Now, II," *Forum*, LXXXVIII (December, 1932), 338–342.

17 Brooks was elected a member of the National Institute of Arts and Letters in 1925, Mumford in 1930; Brooks became a member of the American Academy of Arts and Letters in 1937, Mumford in 1955, and was its president (1962–1965). He subsequently resigned.

we should do something about it: do something, that is, to keep them from electing the inevitable list of mediocrities and nonentities, whose presence there gives us a black eye, the mere threat of which, too, is enough to keep me away from the dinners and elections. Why shouldn't we put our heads together, in partnership with a third member—perhaps Robert Frost—and nominate a few congenial spirits. What do you say to Paul Rosenfeld, Alfred Kreymborg, Waldo Frank? Or who else? Time presses. We must act. Please take this weighty matter under your wing and let me know the result of your thinking.

These days have been heavenly up here, and the Mackintosh apples were never plumper or juicier. My notion of heaven is an apple-orchard on a warm mid-afternoon in September: apples should be eaten close to their birthplace: another argument for regionalism against metropolitanism. A divorced, a dissevered apple—faugh!

Amenia, New York   September 28, 1932

Dear Van Wyck:

You have been with me all week—the memory of you mingling with the pages of your *Critical Sketches*,[18] more than one of which, in turn, reminded me of the glowing and fateful hours when I first read them. It was one of your *Freeman* notebooks, that I read on a journey to York in 1920, that sent me back to America, instead of continuing as a sociologist in England—and I have never regretted my choice! Your words are today more vigorous and robust and eloquent and persuasive than ever, a tonic for heart and soul as well as food for thought. No one has ever dealt with more awful

18 *Sketches in Criticism* (1932), many of them reprinted from the *Freeman*.

justness with Mencken, Sinclair, and Eastman: no one has ever more *infectiously* presented the case for literature of an heroic order. You leave me with a sense of humility and courage— which brings me back to 1920 once more!

[Amenia, New York]   December 27, 1932

Dear Van Wyck:

I have used the season of peace and cheer and goodwill to begin a murderous attack upon Mr. Bernard De Voto;[19] and I am having a great deal of fun with it, more I fancy than Mr. De Voto will have if and when he reads it. I can discover some of his errors by myself in his attack upon your *Mark Twain*, but it will give me a new sense of greater security if you will send me the list of the ones that you discovered, if you still have it. It has taken three months for me to make up my mind about writing it at all: I know there are plenty of good reasons for not doing so, including the one that De Voto is, fundamentally, a jackass. Unfortunately jackasses live for years in our society, treated as pedigreed horses, and surrounded by all our outward marks of respect and admiration, and even their long ears are praised as an evidence of originality in horses: so I have decided, at last, to give him a few medicinal pellets which will perhaps make him a little more careful of his citations and his tactics in future. I wished that someone else would step forward and spare the effort: but no-one did, and in some ways perhaps I am the one in the best position, among us three, to give him the sort of treatment he deserves—humane, nay humanist, but quite deadly! Hurrah for the holiday spirit!

---

19 *Mark Twain's America*, by Bernard De Voto (1932), is a reply by a native of the West to Brooks's *Ordeal of Mark Twain*.

87 Kings Highway, Westport, Connecticut December 30, 1932

Dear Lewis:

I agree that De Voto is an ass, but I don't think he knows his own mind. He says in his article in the January *Harper's*[20] that "literary men should not be allowed to write biography," for reasons he enumerates. But that is a position he could not substantiate in the face of a child's objections. The only thing that makes him worth attacking, or adversely analysing, is the general point (as it seems to me) that, along with Max Eastman and so many others, he has tried to invalidate the literary or critical approach *as such.* His point of view seems to me a recrudescence of that of the Western "he-man," the Red-Blood of twenty years ago, and as to this perhaps I mentioned the rather funny but probably unquotable fact that all Utah is out for *his* blood because of the saucy things—in the spirit of Sinclair Lewis, I imagine—he wrote about them. This was told me by the Browning boys, the gun-making Brownings who are Utah ranchmen and who know De Voto's name as that of the man who had poured vitriol over their West. Of course this couldn't make a point unless it were substantiated by a glance at De Voto's stories. In that case, it might be your deadliest point of all—but it would only serve to show that De Voto is very immature and doesn't really know what he thinks. (Which is also, as I have gathered, the case with our other "enemy," Seward Collins, the editor of the *Bookman*.)

As for his attack, specifically, on me, I haven't kept the citations, and can't refer to his book, which I read in a borrowed copy. But he was very unscrupulous in his dealings with me. I benefitted to the extent of about a dozen corrections, which I was able to make in my new edition. In about as many more he was simply mistaken. I remember only one point important enough to fill one whole page in his book. I

---

[20] "New England, There She Stands," *Harper's* CLXIV (March, 1932), 405–415.

spoke of the American people as "homogeneous," a point that
became important for me in a later chapter where I was able
to quote Howells as saying, in a connection where Howells
spoke with authority: "We are doubtless the most thoroughly
homogeneous folk that ever existed as a great nation" (*The
Ordeal*, p. 210). Howells, of course, meant, as I meant, homogeneous in *feeling and experience*, not in race. But De Voto
simply wiped me off the map for making such an abysmally
ignorant statement. And he then went on to say that I specifically referred to the period *before* the Civil War in the
quotation from Georg Brandes, etc. (page 65 in my book)
the whole point of which was that it referred to the "Gilded
Age." All this to prove that I knew absolutely nothing about
American history. But all this seems to me of importance only
because of a much more general point, the point where De
Voto has scored in people's minds (as Canby's review
showed):21 that De Voto "knows" about the West and we
don't know about it. This question of what "knowledge"
consists of, in the matter of criticism, is a very serious one. A
critic with any intuition would be able to understand Sir
Walter Scott with very little experience of the old border life
of Scotland. And what in the world has "knowing" the West
in De Voto's sense got to do with fully understanding the
effect which the West had upon Mark Twain? Surely my
quotation from John Jay (page 30) justifies my treatment of
Mark Twain's early environment, for John Hay was both a
writer and a Westerner of just that place and time whose
views on such a matter Mark Twain himself would have
accepted. And even more to the point is a quotation I have
incorporated in my new edition from Hamlin Garland's *A Son
of the Middle Border*: "I shall always insist that a true musician, a superb violinist, was lost to the world in David Mc-
Clintock—but as he was born on the border, and always

21 *Saturday Review of Literature* (October 29, 1932).

remained on the border, how could he find himself?" All the "knowledge" of Western life for which De Voto has been credited weighs very little, surely, against these two quotations from two intimate friends of Mark Twain, whose life-experience almost paralleled his, *in regard to this question at issue,* the relation of Western pioneer life to the psychology of an artist. As for the general question of East and West, in regard to their relative "freedom," you might look up the rather long passage in Mark Twain's *Letters* (vol. I, 289) where he says that he now lives (1876) in "the freest corner of the country," Connecticut, where people can break bread without "offering impertinent interference in each other's political opinions," and describes himself and the St. Louis he had known twenty years before. "And that is what the average Southerner is at 60 today": "I think I comprehend the position there—perfect freedom to vote just as you choose, provided you choose to vote as *other* people think—social ostracism, otherwise." But this is the old story we all know so well.

As for my book, I am well sick of it, and am glad to think I shall never again have to psycho-analyse an author. The method is too clumsy and paralyzes one's intuitional sense, the one that really counts in criticism. And I'd love to see a real book on Mark Twain, written from a literary point of view. I had no chance to do him justice, since my point of view was consistently psychological. I made about 2500 revisions, and the new version is better than the old—that's the best I can say. There will be copies ready about January 13th; it will be published at the end of the month, and I have asked Dutton to send you one.

87 Kings Highway, Westport, Connecticut   January 8, 1933

Dear Lewis:

I hate to bother you with any suggestions that might interrupt your work, but I do want to say a little more about our
friend here, Richard Ellis the printer. He is most enthusiastic
about the idea of "Work in Progress"[22]—of course we should
have another title: and I really think that something might be
done that would not involve much time on our parts. Here is
this beautiful press standing idle, and Ellis a really unsurpass-
able printer—I enclose specimens of his work—eager for something to do. And it strikes me that unless you are willing to
undertake the job yourself, you and I jointly—and perhaps,
Lee—might constitute ourselves a duumvirate or triumvirate
and carry the thing through. With *one* long essay each month,
of the kind we spoke of, and with one woodcut or other
illustration (together with a typographical supplement supplied by Ellis himself) —what would the work amount to?
Simply rounding up our twelve writers and postponing the
initial publication until we have the mss. in hand (or else
reliably promised for definite dates). And as the element of
literary style would be a prime requisite for any publication so
beautifully printed, the "editing" would be reduced to nil.
Nothing would be submitted; we should invite our contributions, from authors selected by ourselves, whom we could trust
completely in the matter of style *and* substance. We spoke of
Thomas Beer and Thomas Craven, along with ourselves. I
should propose Stark Young. Ellis can get good contributions
from his friends H. M. Tomlinson and Wm. Mc Fee—our
neighbors here—both of whom are collector's authors and (I
think) always good. We should have no difficulty making up
our list. In short, *I'll* say yes if *you* do! Ellis has worked out an
estimate, which I enclose on a basis of 1000 and 1500 copies,
which might be shown to Harcourt, and he feels pretty

22 Mumford note: "Another of our abortive plans."

confident that he could get the greater part of the issue into
the hands of collectors. He suggests a type-page similar to the
one I have marked, but no doubt the page should be fuller—
something like Eliot's *Criterion*. Of course he would be awfully pleased if he could see you, and especially if *you* could
see his press; . . . and perhaps on your next journey to Dartmouth you could stop here for a night with the Glintenkamps[23]
and meet him. . . .

4002 Locust Street
Long Island City, New York   January 20, 1933

Dear Van Wyck:
. . . I have at last written Richard Ellis. I told him that I
thought it would be easy and cheap to get together a subscription list with the aid of half a dozen bookstores of the type of
Hallidays in New York. What is needed for this is (1) an
editor (2) a list of the first six contributors (3) a Georgian
Press prospectus. The editor is obviously *you*. More than one
editor for a publication of this kind would be ridiculous.
None of us believe in window-dressing: so why should we
practice it? With the booksellers to act as subscription agents
—and they know the "right" and likely people—the expenses
of the whole scheme would be reduced to a minimum; and
there would be no need to bring in a publisher. (Publishers
aren't usually *set* to circulate magazines.) The plan seems to
me flawless, provided that there are any bookstores left in our
Deserted Village. (One of the *New Yorker* boys suggested the
other day that 1933 would be known as the year *before* the
depression!)

23 H. Glintenkamp, an old *Masses* artist, better known later for his
woodcuts.

I am still having fun with my book:[24] but I am still abashed at its Aristotelian pretentiousness. It is either *very* good or quite empty; and for the next ten months I shall have the privilege of continuing to bet on the more favorable alternative.

29 Shenandoah St., St. Augustine, Florida   February 20, 1933

Dear Lewis:

I hope you don't think I've been eaten by sharks, but no, though I've had it in mind to write to you every day for a month. The truth is, we are having a heavenly time! Never have I been able to work better, and there never was another such place for work. We have rented, for nothing at all—for there isn't *any* "standard of living" here—a huge old Southern house that was used as a hospital in the Civil War (there are still blood-stains on the parlor floor), with great airy bedrooms ten paces long, with up-stairs balconies at front and rear, over-looking a half-acre of forsaken garden, filled with palm and orange trees, with the old Spanish fort just beyond, and the ocean beyond that and overall a vast magnolia tree, in leaf and almost in blossom, that covers us like an umbrella. The weather is like the best of June at home, and the only thing to disturb one's mind is the *numerous* note of the mocking-birds—or the far off murmur of a lawn-mower. For sheer mental absorption there never was anything like it, and as I read and write these old New England authors I begin to see why they did such good work, and so *much* work: they lived in these old-fashioned country settings. Really, Lewis, the South is a great discovery, for a Northern writing-man. I'll tell you a lot about it when I see you. Of course the South is

24 *Technics and Civilization* (1934) .

pathetic, and mentally stagnant, and the chain-gangs one sees, yes, really sees, only without the chains, show you that they are living still in the old slave-days. But we see very little of people, and, while these evils get into one's blood, they act as a kind of stimulus, and make you feel that writing *has* a function, and that everything you say about *anything* has its connection with the chain-gangs and can help in its way to make such things impossible. But for *writing conditions,* the South is beyond comparison, and we hope now to come down every winter. No interruptions, no telephones, no casual encounters, nothing to spend money on, rent, say, $30 a month for this birthplace of General Lee (as it might have been), and bungalows in proportion, excellent meals for $8 a week—we cook our own breakfasts of coffee and toasted rolls—and your soul is your own for 24 hours a day. The town, of course, is purely old European, unbelievably Spanish, in spite of all the efforts of the Rotary Club—and just further north are Savannah and Charleston, just as charming and just as quiet and cheap. But I shan't say anything more until we see you—except that I am working at the top of my bent.

I wrote Ellis a day or two ago, having heard from him that he had heard from you. I told him that I couldn't be editor, for the same reason that you can't: each of us has a whale on the end of his line, and each is trying to drag the whale ashore. I am resolved not to be interrupted by anything short of death and taxes. . . .

He should get his friends McFee and H. M. Tomlinson, both capital writers. His printing is so fine that I am sure he will have no trouble rounding up his authors, with four good names to start with; and, that with twelve good names with which to approach the public, the practical questions will soon solve themselves. . . . I suggested only two additional names, those of Stark Young[25] who seems to be prolific and might give him a charming essay on the South, and J. Brooks Atkin-

[25] Southern playwright and critic.

son,[26] who keeps (I think) a kind of Thoreau journal from which he has published three delightful books (I wonder if you know *East of the Hudson* and *Skyline Promenades*) and would probably be able to give him other selections. . . .

Dear Lewis, I hope things are going well with you and our dear Sophy! I always think of you both as just having stepped out of Utopia, and as if you were looking around for a few of your country people who had somehow got astray on this sad planet and only wanted a chance to get home again. Please regard your humble servant, together with his wife, as worthy fellow-passengers!—also our son Charlie, who is on his way South, we have just heard, and would send his love, if he could, along with ours.

4002 Locust Street
Long Island City, New York   March 26, 1933

Dear Van Wyck:
. . . Another dithyramb such as you wrote from St. Augustine and Sophie, Geddes, and I will spend the next winter within a stone's throw of your Southern doorstep, making you regret that you had ever taken the first step to ruin your solitude. (And after that other writers will come trooping down: there will be a colony and an Art Shoppe and gossip about it in Mrs. Patterson's column and the prices will go up and in desperation we will all flee to Labrador!)

Do you gather from these caprices that I am writing? I am: writing steadily, firmly, relentlessly, crushing ahead as slowly as a glacier descending under the vernal sun from Greenland's icy mountains, slowly but with the feeling that nothing can stop me, and that at the end I shall have a very powerful and

26 J. Brooks Atkinson, for many years drama critic of *The New York Times*.

important book to show for it. Even in the shapeless first draft, about half of which is now done, I can feel the richness of the material itself. Better still, the book has taken charge of me, and it drives me to work harder than anything I had ever attempted before. It may be another year before even this first part, *Book One: Machine,* is finished; but time doesn't matter either: I refuse to be hurried so much as an extra minute: it would not matter if I ended my days with the manuscript unfinished: the fragment would still be important.

I know that this cockiness and egotism will be succeeded by less pleasant sensations when I finally have to organize and conquer the mass of words that are now pouring out: but the inner conviction is indisputable, and it will carry me through. It is good to hear that your own work is coming on steadily, too: so let's meet soon and shake hands. . . .

87 Kings Highway, Westport, Connecticut   June 20, 1933

Dear Lewis and Sophie:

I am still staggering in the chaos evoked in my mind by the events of two weeks ago. We have no engagements for the rest of the summer, after July 2nd, and can come to Amenia any time, but I wouldn't have missed Paul for the world. He is as slippery as an eel, and I would dearly love to see him, at least once a year! How it all happened, I simply don't know. I looked up your letter afterwards and saw that June 10th was plainly indicated. We couldn't, in any case, have come on that day, as that was the day of Kenyon's graduation, and we were scheduled to go to Windsor. . . .

I am travelling along in my work at about the speed of an inch-worm in the Alps, but my subject is so glorious that, for once, I never lose hope. . . .

Amenia, New York   June 21, 1933

Dear Van Wyck:

I am writing by candlelight at the end of one of those perfect hot days when one seems capable of swimming a thousand miles and actually feels a little exhausted after twenty feet. Like you I have been working steadily along: sometimes with a feeling of exultation, and sometimes with a dread for all the long weary months of revision and correction which must crown the happier part of my labors: but on the whole, the more exuberant emotions prevail, and I justify them to myself, when they would otherwise make me feel a little sheepish and doubtful and adolescent, by remembering what an adorable fellow Kepler thought he was when he was developing his observations about the planetary motions—and how right he was after all!

By now my book has expanded into three books: one on machines, which covers incidentally the major problems of economics, and of politics and morals as related to that: the second on cities, which will cover politics, and to no small degree include also culture and art; and the third on the Personality, which will bring everything together, but which will mainly be concerned with philosophy and education and marriage and what not.[27] In one sense, all my life has been a preparation for writing precisely these three books: everything else that I have attempted has been a side-issue, or rather, has been like a spring or a brook or a rivulet, significant only in so far as it has converged on this main stream: and yet of course neither I nor anyone else for that matter is really competent to write any one of these books properly, let alone all three of

[27] *The Renewal of Life* series: (1) *Technics and Civilization* (1934); (2) *The Culture of Cities* (1938); (3) *The Condition of Man* (1944). Mumford notes: "The historical treatment had become so extensive that I realized while writing Vol. 3 that a fourth would be necessary." (4) *The Conduct of Life* (1951). *Values for Survival* appeared meanwhile in 1946.

them, and to even imagine such a series is a piece of unmitigated and unpardonable impudence.

It was bad enough for Plato to write the *Republic* in eight short dialogues: what chance have I of doing half as well in three bulky books? Well, sufficient to this summer is the evil and the glory of writing the first book, on Machines: it is a book to out-Bentham the Benthamites, to out-Marx the Marxians, and in general, to put almost anybody and everybody who has written about the machine or modern industrialism or the promise of the future into his or her place. I am just in the act of making my second draft of the historic section, which is the prelude to the whole theme—how our Western society came to be in a *mood* for mechanization and how the will-to-power came to take precisely the channel that it did. Waldo set himself to answer this question in *The Re-Discovery of America,* but what he did there in a somewhat cavalier fashion, I am now doing with utmost exhaustiveness and scholarly investigation: it will be a grand broadside at the mechanists and the mammonists from within their citadel, by one who knows how to use their own weapons for exactly what they are worth. Or so I hope and pray: the delirium and the doubt are equally real, but one knows that the delirium is a little more productive. . . .

I shall be anchored here, through gale, hurricane, fire and earthquake, until my second draft is finished; and only God knows when that will happen: alas! not by the fifteenth of July!

Amenia, New York   September 3, 1933

Dear Van Wyck:

How goes it? A fortnight ago I committed the pious fraud of writing "The End" at the bottom of the last page of my second draft. Actually I am a good half a year of hard work away from the end, and by now I am sufficiently relaxed and recuperated to be fit for human society again. In the meanwhile my calendar reminds me that you and I must conspire presently to deliver the National Institute from the Dodos by nominating new members: so attention! Whom do you propose? And where is our third seconder? Frost? If so, where is he?

4002 Locust Street
Long Island City, New York   November 24, 1933

Dear Van Wyck:

Paul and Waldo have asked me to join them in editing a symposium in honor of Stieglitz' 70th birthday. I've been too deep in my book to meet with them: but they've produced the usual outline, and we'd all like very much to have you do an "Essay on Stieglitz and the American Tradition," or some such theme. (Much tradition and little Stieglitz, if you're inclined that way!) Can you and will you? It's all very indefinite—for a publisher has still to be found, and I am not so very sanguine about that. At all events, the essay needn't be done till next March or so.

Norton writes me that he's asked Macrae if he could reprint your *Emerson* in his new White Oak library of contemporary classics. (He's doing *Sticks and Stones* and the G.D. to start off.) Norton seems a very decent fellow and the idea is excellent: no effort to push or find the drug-store counter: just to keep a book quietly and conveniently alive.

I'm now on the latter half of my book: the gasoline is oozing out of the tank but I still hope to make the other side by January if I can keep my course charted! But I go around muttering the refrain of Tennyson's "Mariana."[28]

28   —"I am aweary, aweary,
      I would that I were dead!"

November [1933]
87 Kings Highway, Westport, Connecticut　　　　　　Friday

Dear Lewis:

With the best will in the world, I couldn't write the Stieglitz essay. I work so slowly and painfully! And the amount of reading I have to do, while something less than infinite, sometimes seems appalling. At the rate of ten hours or more a day, I am still lucky if I get two pages written, and I simply cannot undertake any miscellaneous writing. I'm really sorry, but it's the old story. Whatever I write has to come from the innards, and everything that is prompted from without seems to me inadequate after having cost a fearful waste of time and work. Of course, I am very much pleased and complimented that Norton wishes to reprint my *Life of Emerson.* A popular edition seems to me the height of flattery and I hope it can be arranged.

Dear Lewis, don't miss the next meeting of the Institute! It was as good as a town-meeting. As a student of the American mind, you cannot afford not to be present at such an exhibition. I learned more about New York in the '80's and '90's—in the Stedman celebration—than ten weeks of reading could have taught me. So many amusing side-lights. But I'll tell you all about it when we meet.—I'm so happy to hear that the book is really in the home-stretch. I hunger and thirst to read it. I blunder along in mine, always entranced with the *subject,* and that is the main thing. The rest is only a matter of tears and groans.

P.S. As for the Institute dinner, the election of Carl Sandburg ought to have been recorded in the Goncourt Journal. You should have heard poor old Mr. Johnson[29] rising to read aloud a poem of Sandburg's, on shaving in a pullman car, to

---

[29] Robert Underwood Johnson, Maine poet, was a member of both the National Institute and the American Academy.

show that the election of such a man would represent the ruin of the ancient faith. It was a great scene.

87 Kings Highway, Westport, Connecticut   January 3, 1934

Dear Lewis:

. . . I saw the Zimmerns for a few minutes just before Christmas. I understood them to say that they were in New York for 48 hours only, or less. They spoke most affectionately of you, and perhaps you saw them also. They did not expect to return next year and made a visit to Oxford seem pleasant. It would be pleasant and most amusing. The last time I was there, with Zimmern, in 1913, our principal occupation was jumping over gates at night with the present Archbishop of York. . . . My book goes well, but is going to be very large and will probably take the whole of the year to finish.[30] I am so happy to hear that your big job is almost finished. You know how eager I am to read it. I'm sending back today Granville Hicks's book,[31] which we borrowed.

87 Kings Highway, Westport, Connecticut   January 8, 1934

Dear Lewis:

So glad to hear that the book is finished—and also that we may see you in Washington. I am a little frightened of the latter. It will be a great temptation to waste valuable afternoons listening to the Senators from the gallery. Do come down and rescue us. I don't want to get "political-minded." I

30 *The Flowering of New England* (1936).
31 *The Great Tradition* (1933).

wish we might see you before we go, but we shall have to spend one night in Plainfield and another (I think) in Philadelphia, and I am desperately anxious to get to work on Channing and the Unitarians. Every one of my chapters requires a liberal education, and each on a totally different line. It's awful but exciting.

4002 44th Street, Long Island City, New York   March 3, 1934

Dear Van Wyck:

Where are you? And how goes everything? Except for a trip to Dartmouth, I've been anchored to my desk, putting the final touches on my proofs. The bout is almost over now: it is just one year ago to the day that I sat down to write in good earnest.

The book should come out on 19 April: an auspicious day! It is the battle of Lexington for *my* revolution. I'll send you a copy—or, better yet, deliver one unto your hands when you return.

87 Kings Highway, Westport, Connecticut   March 14, 1934

Dear Lewis:

. . . I am so excited to hear that your proofs are finished and that the book is coming out so soon. Dear Lewis, I know it's going to be as good—almost, as you deserve it should be! And if we can't meet before the date, do let me have one of the first copies—for you won't find many more sympathetic readers! I have a thousand things to talk about—partly about Washington, where we had some interesting encounters, but much more about the "internal" things. We hoped to see you down there. It would have been fun to go about with you.

I am writing my book much as you did, or as I imagine you did, getting down to business just now, after I had floundered for a year. But however it goes, the *subject* is always enchanting! And I come down every morning with the same zest.

[March, 1934]
87 Kings Highway, Westport, Connecticut   Friday

Dear Lewis:

The great book arrived yesterday noon, and I sat me down and read it for seven hours straight. I was really stumped and stunned with admiration. However you organized such a mass of learning and made it fairly *swim* beats me, and it is not only monumental but alive in every phrase. I read as far as about page 170, and my mind has been humming with it since, and it opens up the most exciting vistas not only for your own work to follow but for *my* salvation! It seems to me an absolute triumph, from any point of view, style, thought, feeling, organization. I've never quite known what you were driving at—I mean since you told me about the book, but I almost think I see it all now. Let the Philistines beware! They will pick your book up in large numbers, and possibly make your fortune, in French and German also, I have no doubt. But the adroit way in which you pack your train of dynamite *right through* this story of the dear machines will give them a jolt before they get very far. This book comes from a great mind, and if you carry it out through the rest of the series, you may have written the great book of the epoch. It will be your fault if you don't. I can't wait to sit you down and get the rest of the story in detail. But first I must finish this volume— which I shall do and write you again early in the week. It

looks to me as if you were going to do for this generation—
which God knows needs it—what Ruskin and Morris left
undone for theirs. But I must keep hold of myself for a real
letter, when I have had time to digest it all. Meanwhile, Dear
Lewis, you don't know how grateful I am to you. You make all
the other critical writers look like Lilliputians. You are the
only one who has ever dreamed of the first-rate thing!

I was in Cambridge the other day and met a great admirer
of yours, Frederic Carpenter,[32] who heard you lecture in
Chicago and takes you for gospel. He gave me the manuscript
of an interesting book, of which I should like to tell you
something. This must wait. But one practical question I must
ask you. John Cournos[33] and his wife and two children (step)
are going to leave New Haven and want to come to Westport
or Sunnyside. How can I get information about the latter? If
there is a renting agent, who has *illustrated folders, etc.,*
would you mind asking him to send me some? The Cournoses
are coming here next Friday, a week from today, and I
promised to get them some information. If you could get the
"literature" in my hands I should be mightily obliged.

Eleanor hasn't read the book and is waiting for me to
finish it.

April 24, 1934
Hanover Inn, Hanover, New Hampshire　　　　Tuesday

Dear Van Wyck:

Your letter came tonight, and I have been dancing around
with it, and hugging it to my bosom, and mixing it, like some
fine wine, with my food at dinner, and altogether having a

---

[32] Frederic Ives Carpenter, author of *American Literature and the
Dream* (1955).
[33] John Cournos, Russian-born novelist of immigrant life.

good time with it. Even if only a tenth of your praise is deserved, that tenth was just what I needed at the present moment; for, with the work done, and the book itself, cold and resistant, in front of me, I can see all the weaknesses, all the soft places, all the nasty little errors—like the horrid one of thoughtlessly writing down Uncle Toby, poor injured Uncle Toby, for Tristram Shandy's father—that now rise up to greet me, when they can only be partly rectified by some future printing, if at all. Parts of the book, I can see now, were re-written too often, so that the clear truth has become confusedly qualified, the stock fault of academic writing, and there are other parts, in the argument itself, where I see now perhaps for the first time what I was really trying to say. This lowness is real enough, natural enough, justified enough; but your letter, like some great friendly wave, has loosened the hulk of me, bogged in the sand, and lifted me into deep free water again: for which, in all affection and friendship, thanks. You stirred me up to the writing of these books, perhaps partly without knowing it, a long time ago, just as before that one of your *Freeman* essays made me determine to return to America instead of throwing in my lot with the English: and by the same token I should never had the courage to think of a task like this in three volumes, unless you yourself had set the example and enjoined the discipline. If I do the next two books I think they will be better: for they will be on more familiar ground to me than the machine was, and in addition I have learnt much in the act of writing this.

4002 44th Street, Long Island City, New York   May 24, 1934

Dear Van Wyck:

I have been dipping into the three essays—always with a quick renewal of the excitement and fervor they originally filled me with, and always with renewed delight in your clean and forceful and apparently effortless prose.[34] Those three books, now one, are still the sturdiest monument anyone has created in our generation: they carry on and complete the great work Emerson opened in the "American Scholar." (Of course I mean "complete" for our generation: the work is never completed.) . . .

[June, 1934]
87 Kings Highway, Westport, Connecticut   Sunday morning

Dear Lewis:

I can't believe that you are going to loaf, but it's mighty good news to me. I should think, from the reviews of your book, that you ought to be able to bask on your capital, taking in money like a movie-author. I have never seen such reviews! And they make me so happy. Everyone seems to have noticed that something has happened, and I gathered from Paul, who spent last Sunday with us, that in his circle, as in ours, the book has made a tremendous impression. I could not see the point of Waldo's objections—as to the mediaeval mind, into which you were not obliged to go deeply. *How* the thing started was not your business, beyond the circumstances that you described, but *that* it started. As for his objections regarding the future, I think he was on firmer ground. But I take it that you will answer all these in your volume 3, in which you discuss the personal life. Of course, that's the volume I'm waiting for. If you can carry it out with the richness and fullness you have brought to this first volume, you will have written, as everyone will say, the great book of our generation. I am honestly thrilled to think that you will really have time this summer to see something of us. Do let's meet often! . . .

34 *Three Essays on America* (1934), a reprint of earlier work.

Amenia, New York   June 24, 1934

Dear Van Wyck:

The days have wings on them: no, six hundred horsepower motors and triple propellers. I used to think that it was the writing of books in the summer that made them go fast: but pottering around in the garden and really doing nothing at all seems to have the same effect. . . .

The book has gone very decently, despite the original apathy and inertia at Harcourt's: about 2500 copies so far. Having had a grand quarrel with Harcourt over their lack of faith in the book as a commercial possibility, I am now reaping the reward of my temerarious challenge in renewed activity on their part: so with luck, before the year is over, I will not merely have paid off my advances, but may have enough put by for a modest trip to Europe. In another month, I shall begin my reading for the second book.

The reviews, as you say, have been all that even a vain author could ask; but I confess that I have been a little distressed at the superficial reading that it has got from people like Waldo and John Gould Fletcher; who in more than one instance have quarreled with it for not containing the very things that it does contain. This may be due to literary ineptitude on my part: but I think it is even more due to the fact that they found what they looked for. I knew the risk of showing unfinished work to the world at large, and so was at particular pains, not alone to put in passages that I might have held over for a second or third volume if they were coming out simultaneously, but also to warn the reader that there was more to be said, which would necessarily further modify what one so far had stated. In vain! The race is impatient; so are even one's friends: and it makes no difference, of course, except that it gives one a temporary sense of loneliness, a sense which was increased with me by the curious picture of myself I found in the mind of another friend,

Horace Gregory, who reviewed the book for *Common Sense*. Good heavens: if a friendly eye sees one in such and such a fashion, what distortions and caricatures must not appear in the mirror of an enemy?

I have been re-reading *Anna Karenina* in small doses, probably was doing it when I wrote you last; and have been delighted with the healthiness of it and the deep human penetration; and for the first time since 1928, I have begun to re-read *Moby Dick*. In both cases, I have been discovering new things, even whole passages that I had completely forgotten.

87 Kings Highway, Westport, Connecticut   July 2, 1934

Dear Lewis:

I have been having some distracting weeks, or I should have written to you at once. Really, Westport is a complication! . . . I seem to have lost the thread of my book, although of course I know I shall catch it again, but this is to explain why we haven't been over and haven't written.

We have to go up to Boston tomorrow, to finish up the business of the Bradford Letters. By Thursday we shall be back again, and after that things will be quieter. Then we want you all just as soon as you are willing to come. I know you won't mind if I work in the mornings and the rest of the time will be the sheerest pleasure. . . . I may inflict upon you a few short passages of my book, in the hope of winning a few kind words—much needed in my despondent state! We can have some grand talks, some good swims and some good music. The Sokoloff concerts will be in full swing. Also I want to show you some of the mural paintings in nearby buildings by some of our local Riveras.

It's grand to see your book swimming ahead—as I judge from the advertisements it is. I didn't see Gregory's review and would like to see it if you will bring it over. We have had a long letter from Hendrik Van Loon, in Dorset, Vermont, writing a Life of Beethoven. He seems to be in good form.

Amenia, New York   July 3, 1934

Dear Van Wyck:

Suppose we come on the twentieth or the twenty-first, if that suits you. This will give *you* a little pause, too. Your morning's preoccupation will be taken for granted—likewise any other hours that you need for brooding by yourself: we'll recompense ourselves with the promised slices of the book.

How well do I know your present symptoms: they explain perhaps the desperateness with which, despite admonitory resolutions to go slow, I attempt to rush a ms. to its conclusion, as if one's inspiration were a patched tire that might bust!

Amenia, New York   July 30, 1934

Dear Van Wyck:

Ever since coming home Sophy and I have been idiotically happy; and we are both conscious of the fact that our peace and joy and exhilaration all stem from the perfect days that we spent with you and Eleanor—altogether the most satisfactory five consecutive days we have ever spent outside our own home—and how often are there five such days within one's home?

The chapters from your book gave me a new appetite to go on with mine. I would have plagued you for more; but for the fact that I know from my own experience how one hates to be plagued; but the fact is that I can scarcely wait to see—or hear!—the whole work. The texture of it is so sound and close, and the wool itself comes from such thorobred sheep: altogether it is like some fine tweed, woven of home-dyed wool, deep and rich in tone, with flecks of color on the surface that dance like the markings of a rainbow trout. A good book, and a true fulfillment of your youth, I can already see. In youth, the sketch: weak in detail, but with the main lines in the right place. In maturity, the main lines get slightly rectified as one alters one's position and takes a wider strip of horizon for background: but one adds to the composition something youth does not possess, because it is ignorant, because it has not the instinct for accumulation: in maturity comes richness of detail. And once the main lines are right one is justified in filling every inch of the canvas: or, to change the image, one happily, without abandoning the first violin, adds to it the full orchestra. I have that sense of fullness and richness, and therefore sonority, in your book. All this means a heavier tax on one: how heavy I well know when I swung from the 45,000 words of *The Brown Decades* to the 200,000 of *Technics;* but in compensation, the larger thesis, I think, tends to take care of itself, so that one can spend one's dull weeks and one's tired weeks on what are still valuable stretches of detail, or preparation for detail. And all this is a roundabout way of pleading with you *not* to cut out too much detail when you come to the final draft: it is essential, not merely as the boat's ballast, but as its component pegs and timbers. You will overwhelm all the carpers and critics by the sheer immensity of your knowledge.

I found an enormous pile of correspondence here when I got back, and I am still plowing through it. . . . I long ago discovered the futility of going agin one's nature to please someone else: the result is that one mars the beauty of the sacrifice with cussed ill-nature! Meanwhile I hope to embark at last on the reading for my second opus. The further I go the greater the difficulties: hurrah!

The candle is flickering in the wind. Thank heaven the rain finally drenched us here and the soil is sweet, with even a touch of dank September, and the autumn, in it.

87 Kings Highway   [September 1, 1934]
Westport, Connecticut   Monday afternoon

Dear Lewis:

Bless you! what a wonderful letter! all about a book that I haven't written. But you have given me an impulse that will last all the way through—and all you say about my own task I prophesy is going to return on yours. It's a fine thing to have a pacemaker, and I honestly think, without conceit, that we're both doing work that is going to count, provided we can keep the stroke and keep war out of our back yards. It was such a joy to have you here. I'm afraid that many summers will pass before you will have such a free mind again; but, busy or anxious as we may be, we must not lose touch with each other. Good luck to you for your second venture!

I hope you have seen the August *Atlantic Monthly.* You are the man of the month in the book-section, with words that ought to give you a thrill, and I see that the book has reached the third printing. . . .

Westport, Connecticut
[Postcard from Brooks]   October 10, 1934

Thrilled by your Orozco article![35]—and how I wish I could see you. We think so much about Sophie and hope she is well. I

35 *New Republic,* LXXX (October 10, 1934), 231–235. As Visiting Professor at Dartmouth from 1930 through 1934 and occasionally thereafter, Mumford had watched Orozco doing the library murals from the start.

am still buried alive under the Amiel translation, and would feel wrong if it were not a grand book. But it is taking a three-months' hole out of my own book and will not be finished before November 20th—at earliest. I can't budge till then, but about Thanksgiving time, if you will have us, we shall come to Sunnyside *en bloc* and *en masse.*—This last article of yours is a wonder and makes me mad to run up to Dartmouth.

4002 44th Street, Long Island City, New York   October 11, 1934

Your letter, dear Van Wyck, came like a blue bird at the end of a miserable April thaw. . . . Have you read Ignacio Silone's *Fontamara* yet? He seems to me a writer of the first order: a more acrid Tolstoi of the *final* period, with the dramatic power and insight of the earlier one. Waldo Frank's novel[36] I'm half way through with: it seems better than any fiction he's written, except perhaps parts of *City Block*. Did you hear the grand joke about the Stieglitz book? It's being published by Doubleday, Doran—plus the Literary Guild!!! And thanks for your words about the Orozco article: the ominous silence that's greeted it in Hanover makes me think I did wise to abandon my visiting professorship *voluntarily* this year!

Westport, Connecticut   November 3, 1934
                                              Saturday A.M.

Dear Lewis and Sophie:

Mrs Gamaliel Bradford is coming down from Boston to go with us to the Academy luncheon. Won't you join us at a

---

[36] *The Death and Birth of David Markland* (1934).

table? We always feel lost among the great and celebrated and would appreciate two good timbers to cling to. Now come along, Lewis and Sophie! It's as good as the annual visit to the zoo which I hope you make. How can you appreciate all these books on evolution unless you see man Rising and Descending at these annual exhibitions?

Westport, Connecticut
[Postcard from Brooks]   November 7, 1934

So sorry you can't come. And I am a fool to go, too, only I can't help it this time. And oh, dear Lewis, I don't know when I shall see you. This Amiel is proving to be a four-months' job—inescapable now and undertaken for the best of reasons. It is a great book, but I am desperately stalled by it—till Dec. 15, at earliest—and then I shall have to bury myself alive for six solid months to get my own book done (possibly in the South). I mean to be as rigid about seclusion as a decent regard for Eleanor will permit. And I shall not be diverted again, please heaven.

4002 44th Street
Long Island City, New York   December 22, 1934

Dear Van Wyck:
. . . I begin to feel my next book knitting together inside me, although I fear that, like yours, it may turn out to be an eleven months' baby. I've had good luck with *Technics:* it's sold 5000 copies to date in America: even Harcourt (I've never been at ease with him or he with me) relaxes a little when I encounter him in the office. I was delighted the other day by an English review of your *Sketches in Criticism:* intelli-

gent and appreciative. I trust your book makes headway once more: selfishly, I want to read it; so don't be too captious in your self-criticism. You set yourself a standard of performance higher than most people's *ideals.*

87 Kings Highway
Westport, Connecticut   December 26, 1934

Dear Lewis:

The endless job of Amiel is not yet out of the way but there are only forty more pages. It will be finished in a week. I am curious to know what you will think of this book.[37] Do read it when it comes out. Amiel had the kind of faults that nobody forgives nowadays; but he was a keen psychologist, and you must reckon with his point of view when you come to write your volume III.

Of course, for me all this has been a grievous interruption, five months out, and when I get back to my own book next week I mean to live like a prairie-dog in his burrow. We shall stay here this winter and I am not going anywhere. . . . The practical success of your volume I is a joy to think of. I smiled when you said you never felt "at ease" with Harcourt. I never did either. . . .

[1935]
87 Kings Highway, Westport, Connecticut   Thursday

Dear Lewis:

Winter in Westport is a dreary business, and my book looks stale, flat and commonplace, with no go or life in it—but

---

[37] A translation.

when some good days come, everything will seem quite different. There is nothing to do but stick here, and I don't expect to go to N.Y. again, even to the *Freeman* party, so you must come here in April, if you can. Did you see the *Spectator*'s review of your book in England?—the "most important work of its kind of the 20th century." That ought to sell an extra thousand copies. I have had several messages from Llewelyn Powys, who seems to be desperately ill. He sent me a number of clippings about a libel case in which he has had a rough deal—or so it appears to me. I am enclosing one—don't return. We had a lovely time with the Kreymborgs and Paul, who came out here a month ago, and we wished for you all day.

4002 44th Street, Long Island City, New York   April 12, 1935

Dear Van Wyck:

. . . How have things been with you? I trust you are back in stride, with more to show for the last few months than I can. At least you have not been spending your time in aimless Pullman cars, like a Thomas Wolfe hero, have not been dispersing yourself in unimportant lectures to vacuous people, have not been showing, as I have, latent capacities for mob oratory in addressing groups on War and Fascism. One is damned in one's work, not by the cohorts of Satan, against whom one is on one's guard; but by all the little Children of the Light who bait one with their good intentions and make one surrender one's proper virtue in the interests of *their* virtue, as if, in the long run, that could be more important. Henceforward, I shout to the heavens, I shall deliver no more lectures on behalf of good causes: I am the good cause that denies the need for such lectures. Avaunt! importuning world! Back to my cell. . . .

87 Kings Highway, Westport, Connecticut   April 15, 1935

Dear Lewis:

. . . With you whirling about and me sitting still, things appear to be about even—except that you'll have more to "recollect" when you have "tranquillity." I haven't the least idea what my work comes to. I have about 130,000 words written and copied, but I fear that half of it is trash and will have to be done all over again. This is the first long book I have ever attempted, as well as the first history, and the difficulty of organizing grows—not to mention the keeping a stream of continuous movement—in proportion to the size of the whole. How successful I've been, I don't know; but if I can write at all, I should certainly finish the book by the end of the summer– God knows, I hope so! . . .

P.S. We have formed a Socialist local here in Westport—or rather, Ray Anderson—Sherwood's brother—has. But I fear it's mainly a sop to my conscience for not doing anything else with or for the Children of Light—who load the mail heavily these days! . . .

Amenia, New York   June 24, 1935

Dear Van Wyck:

We're here at last: settled at last: the garden planted at last: and now we can breathe and look around us and watch Alison Jane keep time to the burgeoning and the blossoming of the other perennials. I've just come back from a jaunt to Oberlin, where I made my first and last commencement address— indeed, witnessed for the first time in my life the whole ceremony of graduation, and felt my bosom expanding imperiously like Hitler's when I walked at the head of the procession with the President, reviewing all the fine, sober, characterful faces of the faculty, to say nothing of the giggling, sheepish, self-conscious faces of the female graduates. My talk was on the recovery of the American Tradition, in which I turned myself to the insidious task of equating our old Americanism with communism, showing how free land and a fresh start and equality must now be read, not in terms of individual audacities, but in collective plans toward a better and more stable life. I took a lot of things for granted that must have infuriated the conservatives there; but the President was very sporting about the whole matter, even though he admitted that it was the most revolutionary commencement speech he had heard in his long academic career. (Naturally, it was NOT reported in the Times.) . . .

Amenia, New York   July 19, 1935

Dear Van Wyck:
. . . Your going from here was the signal for my departure: then five dismal days at Syracuse. The weather was hellish: floods of heat after floods of water: the only bright spot of the days was what I could make of my lectures, and, thus goaded, I managed to deliver one respectable first lecture, on the Post-War Mood and its challenge, and two brilliant ones, on the Modern Concept of the Personality, and on the Modern concept of society, in which latter I dealt with regionalism, humanism, and communism, and finally ended up, for illustration, with Jules Romains' Men of Good Will, as in effect bringing together all three paths of social action. The best lecture was that on the Personality: I am tempted to put it down on paper: but to offset this temptation I have resumed preparation on my book, and I don't know quite how to pack everything, including the gardening and the swimming that

will make me fit for next winter, into the usually cosmically limited day.

The one thing Syracuse did for me was to show me in detail another fragment of the American landscape I had not known —and I was as deeply impressed with its beauty as I had been with that of Northern Ohio: really, no one has done justice to the more commonplace physical aspect of the country: we have been so set upon admiring our Niagaras and Yellowstones that the finest sweeps of cultivated landscape roll past us without causing more than a murmur of response, if that. No wonder the robber barons have so easily taken the land from us: we don't really deserve it. . . . Already I can see an edge or two in the general blur of my new book: which whets my appetite for further thinking.[38]

Round Pond, Maine   August 4, 1935

Dear Lewis:

Your lectures sound thrilling, and I hope you've kept all the ideas so that I can read them in your book, which, I hope, is progressing. These ideas excite me terribly! I want to break away from my somewhat restricted subject, although I am not going to do it, and swim out into these deep waters. (I have some plans for doing so this winter.)

I want to see the country you have been seeing, and *get at* the South and the West. There are much deeper things about this latter than I have understood hitherto, and I shall have to wait five years, till I have finished two more volumes, before I can do anything about it! This is still an age for explorers in all things American, and how wonderful to feel that you and I are sailing more or less on the same ship,—wonderful, I mean, to me.

[38] *The Culture of Cities* (1938).

At present, I am entranced with Maine, which has such a steady life of its own, although it does not reach to the higher intellectual centers! This coast is wonderful in its wild, crisp, fresh beauty. And the people are alive with character. The other day, almost by chance, we stumbled on Edwin Arlington Robinson's birthplace and were taken to call on the people who live in the house, a tragic sort of family, a vain old D.A.R. mother and a lovely young girl, dying of consumption—everyone mad over *authors.* *"Do you know any authors?"* the young girl said in a hectic whisper. I did not dare to say that I scarcely knew anyone else, for fear she would die of excitement.

My work is going well, but I have got into the deep places, and it may stretch out for weeks longer. I am reading Spengler, really for the first time. I am not sure of the general thesis, for I am only half-way through; and there are limits to my capacity of belief in any German *welt*-historical scheme. I have read others before, from Hegel to H. S. Chamberlain; and I will never surrender my inborn feeling that every day is a day of new creation. One gains something, anyway, by belonging to the "younger races," and even illusions have their value. But Spengler is a great mind and gives one thrills along the spine.

I stopped to see Packard at Dartmouth and was greatly stirred by the Orozco frescoes. Packard was away, but he writes that he will see what he can do about the Prendergast[39] pictures. I have suggested his talking to you about them, and I feel sure you will back me up. The Prendergast pictures gain so much by being seen together *en masse;* and he was a New England painter, and surely a New England college would be the right place for them. I have so much to say, dear Lewis!— but must keep it *all* till we see you. Much love to you, *one and all!*

---

39 Maurice Prendergast, an Impressionist painter.

Amenia, New York   August 17, 1935

Dear Van Wyck:

Your last letter bore down on us like a white cloud of sails and a spanking wind and a shower of spray: so that we wanted to cheer, it contained so much good news and had so much of the electric energy that's going into your book. With that energy and that health all things are possible, even in a wicked world and a dissolute civilization.

Spengler, curiously enough, I was re-reading about the time that you were reading him for the first time: for all his Prussian obfuscations and obscurantism and his intolerable intellectual manners he has moments of deep authentic intuition which make most of his contemporaries in history sound like mere adolescents, who had never heard about love or reckoned with death; and I found that the things that I valued in Spengler originally I hold to more strongly than ever, although as time goes on and my own knowledge broadens and my own philosophy becomes better articulated I am more conscious than I was originally about the weak and even jerrybuilt portions of his imposing edifice. On technics he is very unsound indeed, unsound and careless; but on cities, and on their relation to the country, as well as on the contrasts between the organic and the mechanical in thought, I find him very satisfactory. (Incidentally, the more I think about the machine the more I find myself appreciating Bergson. The dilettantes who flocked to him before the war discredited him with their facile enthusiasm and the same breed of nonentities, flocking to Neo-Thomism or Pareto or what not, embarrassed by the memory, have sought to discredit him during the last decade: so that he is a seriously under-rated thinker in France, and probably everywhere. My own philosophy could be treated as a modification of his, for whereas he draws a distinction between intuition, which is vital, and reason, which is mechanical, and lets it go at that, I go on to point out that the mechanical itself is a creation of life and only when it is perversely divorced from all our experience, including our feeling and intuition, does it become dangerous, that is, antivital. But this is a parenthesis.)

Recently I have been preparing to review a three volume Study of History, by Arnold Toynbee. It is a colossal, super-Spenglerian effort, with ten more volumes to come; and it has the best of Spengler's thought, plus the balance and sanity and the tough empirical reference to fact that distinguishes the English; and much more than Spengler's book it indicates, I think, a new turn of thought in history, as revolutionary in its way as Einstein's is in physics. Unfortunately, the man has given himself too much space and he makes us climb all the stairs before he will show us the vista from the top story: the books, even though packed with fact and theory, are alas! prolix. Nevertheless he is important; for he redefines the nature, and therefore the task of civilization and its component units. More about him in my *New Republic* review.[40] . . .

Amenia, New York   September 5, 1935

Dear Van Wyck:

You and Eleanor must think Sophy and me a fine pair of churls: just because I economically waited to hear from Crawford about factory whistles[41] before also writing you, as I was moved to the moment we returned here, to tell you what a fine spark our visit to you lighted in all of us. And your book,[42] the very thought of it makes me go around with my chest out,

40 "Civilized History," *New Republic*, LXXXV (November 27, 1935), 63–68.

41 See reply from Brooks, September 8.

42 *The Flowering of New England* (1936).

as if I had written it myself, proud to be a citizen of the country and a weak link in the age that has produced it. Among all the many things the book will do, it will teach the next generation of historians, as Walter Scott taught the good nineteenth century scholars, how to write history. As for my own book,[43] I began putting down the first words last Sunday: and I feel as though I had been committed, to a cloister if not to a prison, for the next couple of years. Unfortunately the introductory chapter is the hardest in the book: it breaks new ground even for me: so I feel like a mountain climber having to scale the most difficult rock early in the morning, before he has digested his breakfast. I miss the exhilaration; but I already feel the bulldog grip tightening on the subject! The fun will come later!

Now about the bells. Crawford tells me that the first cotton mill, the Slater Mill in Pawtucket—in the 1790's I think, but I don't trust my memory—had a bell. "The mill," he says, "is still standing. Nautical people accustomed to navigation would naturally use a bell, particularly if they were church people, as they were in New England." He adds that he doesn't believe the whistle was introduced until the steam engine came, and the first steam cotton mill was the Naumkoag Steam Cotton Mill in Salem in 1847. The need for bells may not have been great originally; for the cheap Connecticut wooden clock had become pretty common in America, whereas the English operatives just didn't have anything to tell the time with, and so incidentally were at the mercy of the manufacturers, and the rascals used sometimes to start the day early and shorten their lunch periods without being caught.

In the matter of the anecdotes about Prendergast, I must reluctantly confess that I am of Eleanor's opinion. The piece doesn't bear your signature, and only your love for the Prendergasts and your desire to brighten the memory of one

---

43 *The Culture of Cities* (1938).

and the days of the other could for a moment blind you to that fact. If I may be so bold, I'd even say that I don't think you ought to print the piece anywhere: in its present form it is really too external, too outside the subject, for all the intimacy and authenticity of the data. I'll keep it and show it to Paul if you like; but my own vote would be against it. So when you get your book finally off your hands, please put together some of the items from your journal: I'd be willing to say yes, with a confident heart, to any part of that, the selections to be made blindfolded!

Westport, Connecticut   September 8, 1935

Dear Lewis:

Thank you for the note about the bells. I had a feeling there was something wrong. It was good of you to point out the howler.[44] Half one's readers only read for howlers and feel as pleased as little Jack Horner when they pull these plums out of one's pie. Dear Lewis, how good it was to have you here, all, young and old! And of course I purr over all you say of my book. I feel just the same way about yours, the same confidence and the same delight, and I know it will go grandly once you get your timbers fairly gathered.

I have been sadly interrupted these last few weeks, and have only been able to work in the mornings, when I needed afternoons for reading. However, we have had interesting times. J. G. Fletcher was here four days,—days of solid rain,— and Eleanor's brother Frank Stimson has turned up from Tahiti, to spend two weeks. It has been like listening to Melville in the days of *Omoo* and *Typee*. Frank turns out to be the most exciting *scholar* I have ever met. He has a vitality

44 Mumford note: "His having early N.E. workers summoned to work in their water-mills by steam whistles!"

and power like Agassiz's, and he has put them both behind his Polynesian studies. It is evident that he has no rival in his field. He is writing the *Tuomotoma Dictionary,*—50,000 words, and is just publishing his fifth monograph on Polynesian folklore. And he has, with an intensity of accuracy, such a grand, poetic and humorous feeling for the whole subject. Fletcher said that Frank reminded him of Sir Patrick Geddes, and I think it must be so: I have only met one American scholar, Professor Marshall Perrin, who is so commandingly convincing. It's all a great thrill to me, for I have scarcely seen him for 20 years. He had become almost a myth to me. . . .

Now about the Prendergast business. Please send it back. Eleanor quite agrees with you, and I don't want to have any doubts in anyone's mind regarding a contribution to the *Caravan;* and as it isn't really mine at all, but an almost literal rendering of Charlie Prendergast's verbal stories, I have no personal feeling about it. I should rather substitute bits from my journal, and I shall do so, if you wish it, if you will give me till mid-winter. Tell me how much you want, and I will send you twice as much: then you can cut out half of it. Would not that be a good plan? I still say that, for myself, I like the anecdotes. They are exactly in the vein of Vasari's Lives, which I have enjoyed rereading for thirty years. This latter is parenthetical.

4002 44th Street
Long Island City, New York   December 21, 1935

Dear Van Wyck:
. . . I have never spent so consistent and *concentrated* a winter in New York as the present one. I am now about two-thirds through with the first draft; which means that during the last six weeks I have written over a hundred thousand

words: scattered inconsecutive words, the mere building stones of the book that is still to be shaped. Yet, as you know, it is something to find a quarry with good stone in it, and to be able to extract some of it and hew it in the first rough blocks: so I have had a great deal of satisfaction, even though the pace has been a little wearing. After the middle of January, I hope to rest; and I don't think I'll pick up the second draft till I have been to Europe in late spring; so there will be time for visiting presently, and I look forward to it. . . . We are now making preparations to remain in Amenia all through next winter. . . .

87 Kings Highway, Westport, Connecticut   January 12, 1936

Dear Lewis:

I had promised myself to finish my book before the middle of January. That's my explanation, and it seems to be coming out well. Five more pages, and I'll have it all out of the house next week. It reads well, too!—far and away the best I've ever done. In about two weeks, when I have shuffled it off and cleared up various odds and ends, Eleanor and I are going to Charleston. We shall probably spend two months there, and I hope to get some fresh ideas and find out something about the South.

I was simply stunned by your report of yourself! It sounds a Gargantuan feat, and I know what it means when one's ideas flow at the rate you describe. You must be on the top of the world. It feels to me like a grand book already. I wish I could hear a little of it,—for there must be a few parts where you have said your final word. . . .

Your trouble at Sunnyside sounds very disturbing, still more disturbing (though not for us) the prospect of your American winter. Of course, you have thought about the South; but, with a car and all, and the warmth and cheapness of living there, I wonder if you have thought enough about it. When I think of our old ranch-house at St. Augustine, under a flowering magnolia, and the stillness and the sunniness and cheapness, I shiver at your heroic resolution. However, more of this when I see you,—which I must do before you go abroad, at least. We have had a crowded winter, and I've scarcely been to New York,—but, on second thoughts, taking you at your word that you are letting down a little, about this time, I must and will come over to see you.

Long Island City, New York
[Telegram]   February 16, 1936

VAN WYCK BROOKS
WE SALUTE YOU ON YOUR FIFTIETH BIRTHDAY KNOWING THAT THIS IS BUT A HARBINGER OF THE SALUTE THAT WILL GREET YOUR WORK AND YOUR NAME ON FUTURE BIRTHDAYS DECADES AND CENTURIES HENCE STOP . . . LENGTH OF DAYS TO YOU AND INCREASING POWER TO FINISH THE TASK YOU HAVE BEGUN STOP AFFECTIONATELY

SOPHY AND LEWIS

CHAPTER III

The Heritage of Culture
(1936–1940)

The friendship between these two men went through its most rewarding phase and survived perhaps its most severe test in the five years before World War II. Circumstantially these years were comparatively uneventful. The Mumfords moved to Amenia, New York, in 1936 and spent their summers and winters there almost continually until 1942, interrupting the quiet routine by occasional lectures or lecture series at Dartmouth, Harvard and elsewhere. Brooks continued to live in Westport, Connecticut. As Mumford's children were still young they occupied much of the time and attention of their parents; while Brooks's two sons were away from home most of the time. Literary and artistic friends from New York were frequent guests at both homes. Mumford went to Hawaii and the west coast, usually to lecture; Brooks to South Carolina, Maine, and California on what were mainly vacation jaunts. The personal lives of both were relatively settled and serene.

The force which made these years especially meaningful in themselves and for the friendship was the sharing of similar and all-engrossing long-term writing objectives. Each man had published what he considered to be the first of a series of books on cultural history which each considered his major life work. Whatever else they did, the book currently in preparation was always the center of absorbed interest and shared hopes and discouragements. Both series were launched with a missionary zeal to dig deep into the moral consciousness of Man in America and save the spiritual values of the nation in a time which seemed increasingly materialistic and disintegrative. As the shadow of the war darkened and drew nearer, their zeal increased. These years tell the stories of the successes of *Technics and Civilization* and *The Flowering of New England* and of the efforts to cap those victories with even more ambitious quests for some ultimate verities in *The Culture of Cities* and *New England: Indian Summer*. By the close of 1940, these second books had been published and each man had begun his preparations for a third in a systematic and all-engrossing long-term writing objectives. Each man had Church fathers; Brooks in the American thinkers of the post-Revolutionary period, the age of Washington Irving, as he was soon to call it.

The tensions which developed during these years were caused by no new developments, but rather by the revelation of basic temperamental differences in the two men, as they reacted to outside events, in this case the issue of whether the United States should or should not enter actively into the struggle of Britain and France to stem the rapidly developing absolute dictatorships of Germany and Russia. Both had espoused, as "liberals," the Socialism so popular in the twenties and went along with Communism and pro-Russianism in their early idealistic phases; both withdrew from association with leftist extremism when the issue became sharply defined, first within the League of American Writers and then in world politics at large. But Mumford, a man of strong passions and activist impulses, became more deeply involved in causes as an anti-isolationist when he was involved at all, and either worked hard for or resigned from the activist groups with which he was from time to time associated. Brooks, on the other hand, had left emotional commitment behind him in the mental hospitals from which he had so narrowly escaped and, although he was intellectually almost always on the same wave-length as Mumford and he continued to support movements and to sign manifestos, he kept a tolerant detachment from any militant action and advocated a similar attitude for the nation.

The issue between the two became clear when each took time out to write a book which would define his basic attitudes and convictions. Mumford produced the passionate *Faith for Living* and Brooks the coolly detached *Opinions of Oliver Allston*. Although each book was accepted in its turn by the friend with the usual enthusiasm, the real differences in temperament came out in Mumford's attack on isolationism in his letter of February 1, 1940, and Brooks's somewhat short and defensive reply of the 7th. For a moment it seemed that the bond might break, but a few words of understanding and appreciation on both sides moved the issue aside without resolving the basic differences which had been uncovered. As in the case of Emerson and Carlyle, the friendship had reached its crisis by over-reaching itself and from then on sought a level less demanding on both sides and more suited to endurance than to intensity.

Meanwhile, Brooks in these years had become increasingly absorbed in his effort to make the National Institute of Arts and Letters a vital force in American aesthetic life rather than the elite reward for conformity that it had become. Mumford was one of the early nominations in the interest of revitalization and he joined in the largely successful campaign by nominations of his own. The tradition of Henry Van Dyke and Charles Dudley Warner was successfully challenged by the election of such people as Robert Frost, Carl Sandburg, William Faulkner, James Gould Cozzens, Paul Green, Sinclair Lewis, Eugene O'Neill, and John Steinbeck, many of whom were elected also to the inner circle of the American Academy; but Mumford soon made clear that his involvement in the campaign was half-hearted, and Brooks's election to the Acad-

emy in 1937 further emphasized the difference. It is a tribute
to both men that their friendship survived to contribute
creative mutual support for another quarter of a century.

Summerville, South Carolina   February 18, 1936

Dear Lewis and dear Sophy:

  What a lovely message to receive on a birthday. Of course, I
know it's blarney, you dear good friends, but just the same it
feels *awfully good,* like a whole box of precious ointment
spilled on my ageing and sciatic limbs. That is to say, I know
they are ageing, and I must pretend they are sciatic, if one is
to live up to being fifty. It will long act as a dye for my
whitening locks and stop the increasing cavities in my teeth;
and when the rheumatic twinges become too dire I shall take
your message out and rub the joints. In short, I pity Father
Time if he has to concern himself with a friend of *yours.* We'll
give him a run for his money, we two and you too! I bless the
day when I found you in this complicated world, and scarcely
a twenty-four hours goes by that I don't rejoice because you
are alive. It's grand to think we can go on, as I hope we can,
together, and perhaps in another twenty years we shall have a
more respectable world to live in. If we do, I shall know who
has cut the pattern. It will be the two of you almost more than
anyone else.—Dear Lewis and Sophy!

  Such a funny time as we are having. South Carolina is no
place for the *impecunious literary;* but here we are, and
therefore here we stay. There's no middle way, known to me,
after some exploration, between living in dilapidated gran-
deur and living in unsanitary squalor that makes one shiver to
think of. In Charleston, you either sleep, at six or eight dollars
a night, in the room in which J. C. Calhoun was born, or you
sleep with professional gamblers in a lurid red light and an

imminent prospect of seven or eight diseases. At least, so it appears, and we fled to this village, where we are living in the works of E. A. Poe. We found quarters here in a lovely, shabby old plantation house, which I call the House of Usher just before it fell. Great dying oaks and pines surround it, dripping with trailing Spanish moss, and the alleys in the moonlight from our windows, all ashen and sober, save for the blossoming camellias, are for all the world like "Ulalume." You could never know Poe if you had not seen it.

I am working in the mornings, at a little book which may be only an experiment but it keeps me from dropping to pieces with this mild air and too much ease; and here we stay for another month. We have a card to Miss Josephine Pinckney,[1] and I also hope to see Du Bose Heyward.[2] How I wish we could all be here together.

4002 44th Street, Long Island City, New York   March 23, 1936

Dear Van Wyck:

As Alfred, Samuel Butler's clerk, said to him after Butler had given him a long lecture about the phases of the moon: "That may be true sir, but please to never mention the subject in my presence again." The monstrous days have swallowed me: mornings at my typewriter: afternoons at the library preparing for work next summer on my book:[3] endless evenings doing committee work on the Board of Higher Education,[4] holding hearings on the slithering worm of a Robinson, always with the sick feeling that all the time will be wasted for

---

[1] Josephine Pinckney, Charleston poet and novelist.

[2] Du Bose Heyward, Charleston novelist; author of *Porgy* (1925).

[3] *The Culture of Cities* (1938).

[4] Mumford was a member of the Board of Higher Education of New York City.

lack of a majority to vote with one when the time comes. But John Flynn,[5] the other people's money man, is as good a fighter as his name indicates; and though he sometimes wastes energy in fighting over trivial points, it is fine to see him in action. He has the reactionaries cowed. They have never before been sassed back by a person who wears a clean collar and pressed trousers and buys the same kind of whiskey as they do. I play a quieter part only because I find myself too often troubled by an excess of emotion when I speak: after twenty placid years I find myself getting angry again, feeling a kettle boiling in my stomach and hot lead coursing through my veins: so all my philosophic calm, when put to the test, proves a sham. Every night, after losing my temper, I say to myself: This will never do: when the time comes to cross-question Robinson you must be as cold as ice and as sharp as steel, and anger blunts the edge of the weapon one wishes to use. Well: perhaps when the time comes I'll be ready. Don't think that I am not enjoying my public duties: quite the contrary. It forces me to see people whom I never otherwise would have spoken to: people who have never heard of literature or philosophy, and who call me Professor because the thought of such a lowly beast makes them less uncomfortable than the notion that they harbor a writer in their midst.

And I have dipt into the affairs of the college at first hand, too, talking to the Anti-Fascist League of City College (composed of members of the Staff) and discussing a whole variety of educational problems with my old Professors. The latter are fine: I realize how lucky I was, at a critical moment, in having such a good lot of men to start me off. There are plenty of more brilliant scholars and thinkers than these men: but I would match them for character against the best that Harvard or Yale could show in their palmiest days.

In the middle of May we'll be going up to the country: so if I am immersed now, it is partly to compensate in advance, like

[5] John Flynn, economist; contributor to the *New Republic*.

a gold-star mother of Future Wars—*wasn't* that a sublime bit of satire?—for my absence next year. . . .

We are all inconsolable over the failure to get a juicy part of your notebooks for the *Caravan:* Paul was so much so that he couldn't bring himself to write you. But at the first drop of the hat, if there is another *Caravan,* we will appear in formal deputation before you, and if necessary bind you and chloroform you and walk off with whatever manuscript we can find lying loose on your table. It may be only your cheque-book: but I warn you: we'll publish it in full over your authentic signature! The editors of the *Caravan* had some doleful disagreements among themselves before the last pieces were selected, partly because Paul was averse to applying our old and wise scheme of letting each editor accept one piece over the heads of the other two: and it will take a little time even with continuous application of ointment, before we will be over our wounds.

The family here has been fine, all of us; and I trust things are sprouting inside you. But don't push yourself after finishing your book: remember that one is in a sort of drunken state and is tempted to tax oneself beyond endurance, just because one has dangerously lost for the moment the saving sense of fatigue. Whatever your new work is at the moment, I trust that most of it is routine.

Westport, Connecticut   April 8, 1936

Dear Lewis:

I have been here for ten days and I have not answered your letter. This was not for want of thinking about it and thinking *much* about you; but I have been in some confusion and am only just getting straightened out. Now the thing is to see you! I feel as if we could talk for a year and I'm hungry for the chance. It's only a question where to begin. I do think it's grand, to begin at *that* point, to see you in the mêlée of educational politics. When you recollect *that* in tranquillity you will have something to talk about; and I long to sit in the front row and hear all the details and the generalizations. Also I think America should seem like heaven after such a winter as you have had. You say you are coming up in the middle of May. I scarcely dare to hope that you are not going abroad. But in any case you won't stay long, and we must have some real times this summer.

I have just sent back the proofs of my book—608 pages; and meanwhile I'm launched in another one, the only one I've really *enjoyed* writing, since I can remember, I mean continuously enjoyed it; for it involves none of the drudgery that most of my books involve. It's the sheerest fun every morning. I am calling it *Opinions of Oliver Ashwell,*[6] and henceforth nobody will have to ask what I *think* on any question! I'm getting everything in, or hope to, and, believe me, the Ashwellian *weltanschauung* is a great *surprise* to its creator. I had never thought out what I have to think on most human topics, including some on which I have thought much; and all of a sudden, at the age of fifty, I find that I have a point of view. It was all there, all the time, and I *kann nicht anders!* It simply tumbles out like one of the spring floods, and I put down what I cannot *not* say. For me, it's been a strange experience. It's a question of "looking in one's heart and writing"; and I have the oddest sensation that I am holding a pen and setting down what I am told to write. But more of this anon!

I have been reading the 8 bound vols. of the *Freeman,* with astonishment at all the good things I find there. The history of those four years, 1920–1924, seems to me assembled there as one could find it nowhere else. Have you any idea, Lewis, how

6 Later changed to "Oliver Allston."

well *you* wrote in those *Freeman* papers,—for instance, your paper on Bishop's *Roosevelt,* and so many, many others? Well as I should have known it, I am amazed by the quality of this work, and so much else. Dozens of volumes of capital essays lie in that tomb, no doubt forgotten; and more than once they say the last word—for instance, Macy's review of Woodberry's essays—on subjects of large and almost permanent interest. I have gone through it all specifically to gather suggestions for my vol. II, on the Decline of New England. But I think that in preparation for any book, concerned with any phase of modern thought, one could not do better than to run through the *Freeman.* It brushes up your knowledge of almost every subject, revives your forgotten impressions and gives you hundreds of clues for investigation and thought. I mean to do this periodically before each new book I write.

Charlie Prendergast has just come in with your *New Yorker* article on the Cubists.[7] He thought it very fine; and I don't see how it could have been better if you had written it as a chapter in a book on Aesthetics. How do you keep up this brilliant writing in a weekly *causerie?*

Prendy was delighted by what you wrote of his Exhibition. He is doing some more lovely panels and is looking forward to seeing you.

87 Kings Highway, Westport, Connecticut   [1936]
                                   Saturday morning
Dear Lewis:

I had lunch with Middleton Murry the other day, and he told me he was going to have lunch with you. I talked to him like a Babbitt,—one hundred per cent *all-rosy,* but I told him not to believe a word I said, for that, being fatuously cheerful, I was probably all wrong about many things,—espe-

7 From 1932 to 1937 Mumford covered art galleries for *The New Yorker.*

cially the state of the U.S., which puzzled and depressed him. However, I said I thought that you would agree with me in certain matters, perhaps because you were fortunate also. I wonder, but you and I are fortunate.

About *Oliver Ashwell*, I'd rather not bother you with it now. But I wish to ask a double question: 1, will you let me dedicate it to you, and 2, will you glance through the ms. when it is finished—it won't be more than 200 pages—sometime during the summer. These two requests are connected. I want to put your name on it, because what you think about what I think is something very special in my mind. My feeling about you in some respects is a mighty queer thing. I somehow feel that, in any given connection, if you don't agree with me I can't be right. I don't feel this way about any other man, and it rather puzzles me at times: for I know you wouldn't agree with me about all sorts of things unless I did a lot of explaining, and meanwhile I disagree with you, or with many things you say and write. What's at the bottom of this? I have my own theory, and meanwhile I accept the fact. Therefore I crave your indulgence in reading my brief ms. when it is finished—for one sole purpose, to punch holes in it. I know when I'm on firm ground *for me;* and I know it's important for me not to let anything pass that doesn't get by with you—I mean, that needs more explanation. But this can all go over till one of our reunions in the summer. . . .

P.S. I met another Alison the other day. I asked her if she was named after yours, or after "Alison-on-Taste."[8]
P.P.S. I have found a remark of Blake's that throws some light on the "Puzzle" mentioned in this note:—"Truth cannot be uttered so as to be understood and not be believed." That we both assent to this may be the explanation.
P.P.P.S. Have you heard of John Gould Fletcher's marriage?

---

[8] Archibald Alison, Scottish philosopher, author of *Essay on the Nature and Principles of Taste* (1790). Mumford claims that his Alison was named after Chaucer's "naughty lady."

4002 44th Street, Long Island City, New York   April 29, 1936

Dear Van Wyck:

. . . You can't possibly guess how proud and excited your letter made me. To have my name on your book will probably be as good a passport to posterity as I shall acquire in this mortal life;[9] and to have, in addition, the privilege of reading your manuscript before it goes to press will be like knowing what one is going to get for Christmas the week before it happens. All the more because, as I have often told Sophy, I have an identic feeling toward you: it is not that we agree or disagree about this or that, but that beneath all such relatively superficial matters there is a rock-bottom respect that is more important than agreement or disagreement: something that will make me for one feel forever reassured that, no matter which way the battle goes, or how quickly one is blown to pieces, the flag will still be waving. To have that assurance about one or two people is sufficient to keep me confidently at work, no matter how many Hitlers and Mussolinis make their appearance on this benighted planet. . . .

87 Kings Highway, Westport, Connecticut   June 28, 1936

Dear Lewis:

. . . It seems so long since we've seen you. I have been quite worried about your Board of Education business, which we have followed in the papers. It suggests a lot of nervous wear and tear, and I wonder just how much you can stand it. But I am keen to hear about it.

9 Eventually *New England: Indian Summer* was dedicated to Mumford; *Oliver Allston* to Edward Sheldon.

I am rather disturbed and have been marking time, or wasting it, trying to do two books at once, and a bad cold has rather pulled me down. I dropped *Oliver Ashwell*[10] in the middle and went back to my history, vol. II[11]—wrote a chapter on Parkman and began with Henry Adams. I've been shilly-shallying over the latter, and wondering if I shouldn't go back to *Ashwell*. A typical *silly reason* state of mind, which results in bad temper and general desperation. I need a blow in the solar plexus and lack the energy to administer it. Kenyon has gone to France for the summer, and Charlie is at home . . .

How good to hear your book is going ahead! Will you be ready to read us a little of it? *The Flowering of New England* is in print—at least I have the sheets and will try to get a copy to bring you. It looks very smooth and harmless, considering the chaos it came out of.

Amenia, New York   July 24, 1936

Dear Van Wyck:

I feel such a duffer at not being able to tell you either to your face, or even I fear in a letter, all the thoughts your *Flowering of New England* gave rise to; and I didn't give you a hint of the enthusiasm it roused in me, and keeps alive, from hour to hour and day to day, when I forget my own book long enough to think about it. I finished the book finally within two days after you had gone, and marvelled at the way that you topped off the period of the great burgeoning with

10 *The Opinions of Oliver Allston* (1941).
11 *New England: Indian Summer* (1940).

Lowell—without making it a literary anti-climax that it might have been. Those are the weightiest and justest words on Lowell that anyone has written: the Archangel Gabriel and the Devil between them couldn't have done better by the man, couldn't have given him so completely his deserts, such deserts as the honest man would rejoice in, applied to himself, even whilst he suffered! Your various discoveries and re-discoveries are enough in themselves to make anyone green; but when you top them off by unearthing Longfellow and putting him where he really belongs you do something that shows how many miles higher you are in moral stature, in understanding, in penetration, in magnanimity than any of the rest of us. You have executed so many masterly portraits, in a sentence, a paragraph, a page, as you go along that I can scarcely say which of them seems best, since they are all so good: but the ones I find myself returning to most often, with a smile of pleasure on my face, such a smile as I remember to have had all the way back to the Hotel in München after meeting Thomas Mann, were the portraits of Prescott, of Dan'l Webster, and of Hawthorne with Webster. In a half dozen strokes you turned a Rogers figure[12] into a masterly Audubon-study of the American Eagle. And how deeply saturated you were, how much you have packed into it: I can tell by the texture of the parts I am most familiar with how much of the very flesh of what you have read has been crammed into these pages: they pump richly with a double life, your own, and that of the authors whose history you are following.

It is a great achievement; a very great achievement; and as I told Macrae it will probably usher in another era in American life and letters, in much the same fashion that those first fragile pipings, *The Wine of the Puritans* and *America's Coming of Age,* did twenty or more years back. It is good to be alive when such books can be produced; I feel as Emerson

12 John Rogers, American sculptor of popular small genre groups.

must have felt when he read Whitman, as Melville felt when
he read Hawthorne. If there is any life in the dull pages I have
been typing these last three weeks, I have you to thank for it;
they live by such transfusions as have passed from your pages
to mine. Thank you for the gift of the book; thanks for the
book itself. A half dozen of us, firing steadily from behind our
book-barricade, may yet keep off the fascist hordes!

Thanks to the rains, our garden has been thriving since you
saw it in its searness: the escarole leaves are as big as cabbage
heads, and the long green cocozelle is all ready to be picked.
There have been other changes: Geddes kept his temper for a
long week at a time, and thereby earned (for the household) a
twenty-two calibre rifle: we went on our first murderous
expedition against nature today, taking pot-shots at derisive
crows and finally—thanks to Geddes's good eye—intercepted a
woodchuck, that grubby little vegetarian Cain, in an effort to
reach home plate. Some lurking savage in me shrinks at
nothing about this but the final scene of slaughter; as for
Geddes, the savage in that hardy bosom dances rather than
lurks: and I try to keep myself from wondering openly
whether this innocent rapine is but the preparation for such
strife as is taking place in Spain—which at least has an
element of human reason in it—or perhaps for the emptier
and more dastardly strife that would mark another world war.

Really: you and I grew up in an innocent world. Soldiers
then were all of the tin variety: they liked drums and music
and such innocent displays of brass buttons as colored people
used to like at a cakewalk: they still thought of war in terms of
manly encounters on galloping horses, indeed, only as a more
spectacular exhibition than a hunt or a horseshow. Now war is
as grim as the assembly line of a Ford factory and as relentless
as a financier: the morals of the rattlesnake[13] are everywhere.

13 "Unfair to the rattlesnake? He at least gives warning and tries to
avoid a deadly encounter!" (Mumford note.)

Sometimes I am tempted to stand up on my two legs and preach: one last desperate sermon to my friends and brothers: one frantic gesticulation toward safety before some putrid fool touches off the dynamite. When we were young we could ask ourselves: what can we conquer? Now we can only ask: what can we save? That shrinkage of ambition is not due to age but to the times we live in.

Well! work apace, apace, apace! A touch of this grimness inevitably will get into my book, since the last two chapters sway back and forth across the contemporary stage: but every ounce of energy I have, every atom of hope and confidence, will go into it too: for at the end the only thing that can save us is that a sufficient number of people will, thanks partly to our example, love life dearly and desperately enough to prefer it to death, and to find the way out—to life—that courageous souls may still find. And that, dear Van Wyck, is what your book does: it is an exhibition of life, and life flows through it, with signs of visible growth almost under one's eyes, as it flows through the meadows and woods on a fine spring morning. We can never have enough of that: so I pray that your history will pile up into many books, each one a monument, each one to serve as a cornerstone to the America of our dreams. In friendship, and in deep admiration, I embrace you.

Pleasant Point, Maine   August 26, 1936
—not so pleasant—

Dear Lewis:

What must you think of your Wandering boy,—namely, the undersigned? We asked you to visit us in August,—not asked, but begged, insisted, pinned you down; and then we absconded to Labrador and silence. Well, I was frantic in Westport. The telephone, the highbrow Coney Island, etc., etc., etc.

I wasn't getting a thing done, and hadn't been for months, and finally Walter and Magda Pach said they would take our house for August, and we simply cut and ran. Then my *Oliver Ashwell* went to pieces. At least I got bogged in the middle of it, and then suddenly Charlie[14] took it into his head to *get married—!!!*—and, what with one confusion and another, and, what with heaving wood and drawing water, and struggling with kerosene lamps, and trying to keep the seals out of our Bedroom, we have had a most unprofitable summer. I shall have to Re-Organize from top to bottom when we get home on Saturday.

Today we are having lunch in a camp in the woods with the great Professor Whitehead,[15] and on our way home, on Friday, we are spending the night with Paul at York Village. These are the two high-lights or spots of a year that has been wrecked beyond redemption. But I reflect that our troubles— and yours—are nothing beside Llewelyn's[16] and Theodore Maynard's.[17] I have just heard from the former that he and Alyse have had an "atrocious" summer, although he is better than he was a year ago. Theodore Maynard, with *eight* children,—the last one born this spring,—and with next to no money, came down with tuberculosis two months ago, and is now in another hospital for a nervous breakdown. So I count my blessings even at "Pleasant" Point!!! where a teepee would look like a palace.

Let me add a solemn warning in regard to Maine, if you still think of coming up. Don't go an inch further than the River Saco,[18]—unless some friends from Wall Street with a yacht take all the responsibility for your existence. . . .

Now, Lewis, I can't begin to thank you for all the things

---

[14] Charles Brooks, Van Wyck Brooks's older son.
[15] Alfred North Whitehead, English scientist and philosopher.
[16] Llewelyn Powys, English novelist.
[17] Theodore Maynard, Catholic poet.
[18] Saco, south of Portland, Maine.

you've said about my book. Your letter was a godsend to Mr. Macrae, although he has taken your name in vain. I mean, he's made publishers' copy of it, and sent out a Mumford first edition with every blessed copy of the book. I hope you have NOT blushed over this shameless publicity. You appear to have made me a best-seller. Somewhere at the bottom of the list; but your own letter to me was the one that warmed my heart; for if the book really pleases you, I don't care too much for other opinions; and, if one can make New England appeal to the rest of the country, I have little doubt of other subjects and periods. The *New England Afternoon*[19] will be harder to write, or at least harder to bring to life. I'm struggling with this at present, or shall begin to struggle when we are settled next week.

Meanwhile, your book is closer to the firing-line than mine, and you will have a real chance to influence opinion in this country. I hope you've been making grand strides. I was thrilled by the parts you read to us and am waiting for more in September.

We are having daily heart-attacks over the news from Spain, and one finds oneself instinctively expecting the worst! Of course, this war *may* turn the tide; and in any case I can't see how the fascists can prosper in an all-fascist world. The more power they get, the more they are bound to prove that their ideas do not work, and they will have made their countries into "corporate" bundles that can be socialized over-night. But I'd like to go to sleep for twenty years and have the rest of my life postponed a little. . . .

[19] "New England Afternoon," early title for *New England: Indian Summer.*

Amenia, New York   October 12, 1936

Dear Van Wyck:

How horribly fast the days have been flying! I have gal-
livanted around, too, the last two months: Marthas Vineyard,
Cape Cod (with Waldo), Washington (to speak at a Power
Conference) and Boston: to say nothing of the worst killer of
time, my now-weekly trips to New York. By now I have had
enough of the Odyssey and would like a dose of Walden—or
even Cranford. . . . I trust that all the rumors of the book's
success are true, and that you are well-settled in your next
task, whether it be Vol. II or *Oliver*. Let's have a word from
you soon—or better, your presence.

87 Kings Highway, Westport, Connecticut   October 25, 1936

Dear Lewis:

Two nights ago, in New York, I made a speech at the
Norman Thomas dinner, neither bad nor good, but at least I
had 1000 hearers, which gave me a taste of blood and the soap-
box that may be somewhat useful on future occasions. Otherwise I have done nothing but read dull books for *The Decline
of New England*,[20] and, not having written a word for
months, I feel like a good-for-nothing. A very futile year this
has been, mostly waste-motions, for me; and, according to Mr.
Macrae, my book is only selling well because you gave it such
a send-off. But now I'm going to get going again, and plan to
start writing tomorrow morning. Eleanor has been writing to
Sophy every day for a month, although I don't think it has got
on paper. . . .

I'm running for the Connecticut Legislature on the Socialist
ticket. But I'm not running very fast, and I'm sure my neigh-

---

[20] The title is still unsettled.

bours love me too much to vote to send me away. Ray Anderson and I are running together, though perhaps I had better say *standing*. We had an invitation to the *Caravan* party, but I don't think we will go. Many thanks, however, and best luck. . . .

Amenia, New York   January 8, 1937

You see by the above, dear Van Wyck, that I can't let 1936 get away from me, although why I should want to prolong one of the most painful years in my life is beyond reckoning. . . . Our experiment up here has not worked out quite as we thought it would: the country itself has been far better, and Sophy has not had time to be lonesome, although we have had no visitors and few diversions: but my devilish job and my thrice devilish Board of Higher Education have been taking me down to the city every week for from three to four days; and that disrupts everything: it ruins domesticity, health, equanimity, and work: so what it leaves is hard to figure, except a few dishonest shekels in one's pocket. The alternative is to quit the *New Yorker* or to quit Amenia next winter; and that leaves only one answer: chuck the *New Yorker*.

But in some ways these disrupted days have been fruitful. I have been surrounded, all these last months, with the whole sum of my written works, most of it hitherto buried in the cellar at Sunnyside; and I have had an opportunity to take a line on my past, to see where I have come from and where I have been going to (or not going to) and it is all very edifying, if painful, too, with a sense of missed opportunities, wrong turnings, futile beginnings, and untimely abandonments. I have a feeling that, if a dozen more years are given me, I may be able to redeem some of the early waste and blight: at all events, a first step is to tighten my belt and go back to a more rigorous life of writing.

My reading has been mixed and inconsequential: tardily I have been going through *The Last Puritan,* and I still don't understand what Santayana was doing there or why he did it or why anyone else thought it very important; although one of my very dearest friends, a woman whose mind I value highly, found it a sort of key to the universe when she encountered it. Maybe it is; but I have not found the lock. I've read Sullivan's critical biography of Beethoven; and found it very penetrating and sound and exhilarating, too, perhaps as much as anything because of the life it dealt with: such a colossal statue carved out of such a mountain of pain! I've had another curious discovery: that of going through Shakespeare's sonnets after many many years absence from them as a whole sequence, only to be pained at discovering how superficial and mechanical the great majority are—the ones that are not, being the great ones that are always on one's tongue. Whether this shows the sterility of flunkeyism or of homosexuality I don't know: but I confess the run-of-the-mill sonnets seemed to me lacking in all Shakespeare's great qualities. . . .

87 Kings Highway, Westport, Connecticut   January 14, 1937

Dear Lewis:

I feel like a voice from the tomb addressing another, for the silence between us of late has been positively noisy. We had such a racket for two weeks over the holidays that I have simply pinned myself in my work. It grows so well when you don't hear the telephone, and my book makes good progress and should beat the other one hollow. But I am so troubled that you should have had a bad year. The first year of a new book is always bad with me, and probably with you; but all these interruptions you have had and the problems of primitive country living are enough to spoil any year, and we long to see you and Sophy and talk things over. . . .

What you say about looking over your own old books comes home to me, much more than it ever can to you. So much of your writing is so solidly objective, so much of mine, alas, is merely opinions. There is little I can take for gospel now, as I seem to grow beneath and behind it. (You are right about the influence of the garden, the presence of these natural facts, botanical, biological, gestation, germination, efflorescence, has the deepest effect on one's work. Country living and good writing certainly go together, which explains a lot of the trouble with our city-authors.) We feared you were having difficulties this winter, where the country living is so unrelieved, or too much relieved, under your conditions. Would not this region really suit you better? And the question is of pulling out of some of these N.Y. engagements. Of course, in the end your work will immensely gain from them all; but when one reaches forty one has to take in sail and substitute intension for extension. Then all one's old extensions begin to count. I am sure your second volume will be better for all these tribulations. I have so many things to speak about. I have my theory about Santayana. The queer little Spanish boy is getting back at the overwhelming Sturgis[21] family. But what I don't like is the treachery of his Epilogue. I have known plenty of Olivers,[22] rather distasteful prigs, but Santayana seemed to take his side. And then to build his future on that little squirt of a Mario! Oliver, at least, was a fairly good building-block, but to build on Mario is to build on rotten eggs. I have had a distressful letter from Llewelyn Powys, who seems to be getting better, however—however. He and Alyse are at Davos-Platz. Then I meant to speak about

---

[21] The father of the Spanish-American philosopher, George Santayana, married into the Boston Sturgis family.

[22] Oliver Alden, hero of *The Last Puritan*, by Santayana.

Harold Stearns, whose new book is interesting. Max Perkins[23] told me the other day that Harold is a new man, confronting life with confidence, and isn't that good? I think his plan for another *Civilization* is capital[24] and will be a great success. I am only not contributing myself because I'm damned if I'll do anything until my second volume is finished. We are staying here this winter, not going anywhere. It is beautifully rainy and muddy and good for work.

Amenia, New York   May 28, 1937

I was on the point of writing you, my dear Van Wyck, when your letter came—and then I had to run down to New York to elect a President for Queens College, and now it is a week later: that is how life goes. As for Shuster,[25] I wrote him at once to give him the right bearings about the post he would like: although my influence or that of any of the other members of the Board will count for nothing in the selection of the staff. Dean Klapper's good sense will; and I am sure that Shuster is just the man he is looking for in his English department. The whole business of selecting a president was, by the bye, very amusing: the citizens of Queens, in their mother's club, kiwanis, and chamber of commerce capacities, bombarded us with demands for a Queens man; and since no educator has ever been known voluntarily to settle in Queens, they lighted on a self-nominated high school teacher, whom we wouldn't have trusted to run a shoe-blacking parlor. We had to go through the motions of politely listening to their indignant protests over what they quite justly suspected were our intentions: they knew exactly whom they wanted—somebody paro-

23 Editor for Scribner's.
24 *America, A Re-appraisal* (1937) .
25 George N. Shuster, author and educator.

chial and patriotic—and whom they didn't want—an enlightened and able and progressive administrator who would give their children a valuable education. The clash between the Queens citizens and our Board reminded me a little of Chesterton's *Napoleon of Notting Hill:* my favorite Romance; and it brought my political career to a climax, for I am now on the point of resigning from the Board of Higher Education. . . .

The third draft of my book will be finished in another week, I think; and then I have to make the hard choice between running over to Europe for six weeks and mulling over the final draft in the sweet air of Dutchess County. I think Dutchess County will probably win out; for I have determined to put the book behind me by the end of September: if I keep it too long it may turn sour on me, and I have been more or less living with it for seven years.

87 Kings Highway, Westport, Connecticut   May 29, 1937

Dear Lewis:

I've promised to make a Commencement Speech!!! and have thought of nothing else for weeks, except to call myself an ass, which doesn't get the speech written. In fact, the academic world is suddenly too much with me. I have never seen a Commencement, not even my own, and I don't know what the natives behave like; and now I am being doctored all over the place and have to go to three. I give you my word that all I *want* is to write another book before I die, and next spring I'll escape to Vermont before the migration begins. My little dose of limelight has simply wrecked my brain, and until this speech is written I shall be lost. No chance to go to Amenia! The next three weeks are sold and ruined, and *then* we are going to Vermont to "begin life over." But we shall be back in

August, and then, if you don't go abroad, we must have a really truly visit. It's grand that your book goes so well, and I long to hear some of it. My own belongs to ancient history. I haven't been able to touch it for weeks. Thanks so much for writing to Shuster! What a time you must have had with the new Queens president, of whom I've read something in the papers. But how glad I am you're resigning! We are going in next Friday to the Writers' Congress mass-meeting, and I hope we shall see you there. It sounds like something one ought not to miss, and we may as well be shot for sheep as lambs. I love you as much as I can in a panic!—and we'll all hope to meet soon—"when the war is over."

P.S. Robert Frost was here last week. He said grand things of you.

Amenia, New York   October 5, 1937

Dear Van Wyck:

I am writing you now at the first sign of a break—the handing in *next* week of my manuscript. There will still be two solid months of work on the galleys and the illustrations and the bibliography; but at least the worst part of the travail is over, and one is entitled to relax a little and think about other things than one's thoughts! We have had the sort of summer you can perhaps guess about; and what you fail to imagine, Eleanor will. Since June, except for a week's break with Sophy at Marthas Vineyard, I have been deep in my final draft, grasping for the first time, in its fullness, what I had written and in what direction I was going: the goal along my much travelled road toward *The Culture of Cities* did not, curiously, become fully visible till a month or so ago, and might not have been visible at all but for this final period of

brooding and reflection. The result is that the last three
chapters are, to speak most favorably of them, a little bulky
and clumsy, and they still lack the perfect ease and finish of
the first four. But that is as it is: who ever said that even with
plenty of time I could write a *perfect* book? Gardening teaches
one the limitations of perfection: life is always "never quite,"
and when summer's flowers are most brilliant the iris gives the
show away by looking a little sere. But I have the sense of
having written something big and solid and possibly even
juicy: perhaps the best, if not the most brilliant book, I have
yet turned out. . . . Is your book done, too, and are you in a
state where relaxation is permitted? . . .

87 Kings Highway, Westport, Connecticut   January 26, 1938

Dear Lewis:
   How lovely to hear from you. The little bird tells me that
we're not going to drift apart, but I've seen enough of dear
friends whom absence makes fonder. It's the living interests
that keep us going, along with all the other things. . . .
   I'll save for your private ear my own reflections on publishers. I shouldn't have thought Harcourt was stupid, but,
after all, does April make much difference? I supposed the
May and June sales were most important; and perhaps you
know something of my relations with E. P. Dutton. But I
understand your feeling, with your own book and its special
problems. However, it will probably be selling well next
Christmas, and meanwhile how good to know that all the
family thrives. My own book is going well at last, and I think I
am getting down to fundamentals. I want particularly to
finish before I see you, and to show you then, *The Younger
Generation of 1870.* It is only chapter IX, and I've spent a

whole year doing these chapters, but I think I'm breaking the back of the problem and ought to finish the book next winter.

I have been absorbed since September but have had some interesting days in N.Y. and must tell you something about them. You should come to the Institute meetings. The Institute is waking up, and you learn all manner of things about the country.

How exciting that you have seen the West, which I can hardly wait to see—I mean the Mississippi region. But I give up hope of catching up with you unless, some day, we can all take a boat and sail away for a summer in Sweden. Why shouldn't we do it? These little exciting meetings for a day or two leave everything unsaid! We ought to have at least a month together. I'm glad you read O. W. Holmes. Of course, he is far from being the pearl of wisdom, but I'm more and more convinced that the weakness of our intellectuals comes largely from their not knowing the native writers. We all began, and rightly, with the European end of things, but we can't understand our people unless we know what has really expressed them; and the old writers got under their skins and really made them largely what they are. . . .

87 Kings Highway, Westport, Connecticut   March 30, 1938

Dear Lewis:

. . . I meant to tell you that I met Harcourt in a Child's restaurant about three weeks ago. If he has put the book off, it is not for any lack of enthusiasm, for he touched the ceiling in his excitement when he spoke to me about it. He couldn't say enough about your "top-flight" mind and all the rest of the current cant that pictures a publisher's gold-mine. He evidently expects it to have a mighty sale and means to push all his resources to assure this event.

And now, to get down to my *real* business, I don't see how the book can fail to make a profound impression. I finished it last evening, with all my usual feelings about you touched off to a regular Fourth of July display, for the book is tremendous in its intellectual grasp of the subject and inspiring beyond all words in its implications. You know that ever since I read Spengler, two summers ago, his dreadful logic has seldom been out of my mind, and, although I didn't really believe it, I have never yet found a counter-logic, outside these books of yours, to set him down; and there simply isn't anyone else, so far as I know, at least in this country, who suggests or begins to suggest your absolute *vision*. For of course there is sheer poetry behind all this writing of yours, a poet's vision of the future, and it has the logic of history as you convey it; and if your third volume is up to these others, you will be a world-thinker, friend Lewis. I don't wonder that you have such a following in the colleges, for you stimulate the will while you picture the goal so clearly. I hope that a hundred years from now this country will have saved the world—no other country surely, is going to do it unless all manner of changes take place in Russia. Well, if we are saved from chaos, you will have had a pretty large hand in it. I shall watch the papers feverishly to see how the reviewers catch what you're driving at and back your intentions. But this book is sure to work slowly as a ferment in vigorous minds and bring forth fruit all over the country.

I'm a little overwhelmed at moments by the total impression and can't go into details, although there are so many points that I'd like to mention. But in all your remarks on region-alism, on small communities, local interests, and a hundred and one other matters, you have certainly caught the secrets of the younger people. The book is extraordinarily intuitive and prophetic, and your final chapter especially is so packed with ideas that a whole generation might live on the crumbs from your feast. Wonderful and logical your statement that Louis

XIV is "provincial." I have just transferred to the page I was writing this morning your observation about Tolstoy's "unfurnished" sainthood.

(I have only one little question: I don't see the force of your objection to mural painting—page 420; although, come to think of it, there is another. I was troubled now and then by a certain abstractness of style that made the book in passages heavy sledding. Take the phrase on 416—"determinable coefficients of expansion"—as a case in point. This is rather formidably scientific, though I know that the subject often determines the language.)

I want to read the last chapter over before I write again, but I want at least to get this off at once. The book has rather stunned me at the moment, it is so packed as well as so masterly, and I fear these few remarks are not very coherent. I'll write again before long. Meanwhile, congratulations on this grand work accomplished and health and strength to you for your next great tussle.

P.S. I have the temerity to enclose a few suggested errata, which you may have overlooked. I have made about 70 of these changes in my last book—after spending 2 whole months correcting the proofs.

Amenia, New York   April 7, 1938

Your letter, dear Van Wyck, has been warming the cockles of my heart ever since I received it; it was the shadow of a rock in a thirsty land. Even when I discount, for friendship, half of what you say about *The Culture of Cities,* what remains is still very precious: it has helped offset that horrible feeling of humiliation one has when a task is finally over and when one realizes, more clearly than one's most rigorous critic, how far short one has fallen of the mark one has set oneself. I have been in that cursed mood for the last six weeks; and am only now, thanks to the further demands of new tasks and to such words as yours, beginning to crawl out of it. What you say about the sandy jargon that managed, despite my efforts to prevent it, to creep into the book is all too true: I wince at phrases like the one you mentioned even more than I winced when Hendrik [van Loon] discovered that I had called the town of Naarden Middleburg, although I know quite well what they look like and had even labeled Naarden correctly in the picture I used in *Technics*.

For your corrections—and any more you may find—I am deeply grateful: I hadn't caught one of them. (Arrows of the Chace, however, is Ruskin's spelling, not mine; and the Fitz-Stephens I referred to is a medieval writer quoted by Stow, not Leslie Stephen's brother.)

As for the new tasks that have occupied me, one in particular I should have liked to discuss with you while in the midst of it: it is an article I have been pondering the last year and have finally written, on what we must do to really meet the barbarism that is going to engulf us unless we build our dykes high enough to keep from breaking in. What prompted me finally to do this, though desperately tired, was the Defense Supplement of the *New Republic* which, by ignoring Fascism, seemed to me to lurch onto a plane of unreality which was defensible only in 1932, but which is criminally careless in its optimism today. I don't know if I can persuade them to publish it; but if they do, and if you should agree with my argument, I earnestly entreat you to rally to my side with a letter to the editors at the very least. I shall not lie easy on my bed nights until this "call to arms" is published.

Did I tell you, or did Sophy tell you, that I rose from my sickbed in March to run up to Harvard on a wild goose chase. Gropius, the new German professor in the architectural department, asked me up to his place and suggested a day on which Conant would be present for dinner. I misinterpreted this, misled by false hopes, as an effort on Conant's part to find out what I was like without committing himself; so, much against my basic common sense, which told me that a sick man couldn't possibly make a good impression on anyone, I went up. Well: I met Conant and his wife at a very intimate dinner and had a fine evening's talk with him: was very favorably impressed: keen, well-balanced, modest, confident, authoritative, all that a good college president should be. But it turned out that the initiative had come entirely from the architectural department, which has vague and insubstantial dreams of perhaps making me a professor two years from now when the road is clear: so it was a double disappointment, since I don't look forward to spending the rest of my life as a professor of Regional Planning, and since, for anything else, my wan coughing presence was not precisely the sort of thing that would charm Conant into looking upon me as one of the great minds of the age!

(Pace Van Wyck!)

87 Kings Highway, Westport, Connecticut   April 12, 1938

Dear Lewis:
. . . The burgeoning life outside increases one's impotent feelings. We have been planning to go to Tennessee in May,— because it sounds so far away and green, and now I rather think I may disappear next week if I can find an inn at some place like Sharon. All the problems of my book still lie ahead, and I simply must press on till I solve them. For the subject is wonderful. I feel this more and more and I must, if possible, finish the book next spring.

But I really began this letter to say that I've been re-reading your book and am more and more convinced that you have done something great and for all the world. Your mind is so powerful and healthy, so altogether beneficent and your vision so unique in this time of darkness! You take it so for granted, as all great minds have always done, that the world is in its first day and only asks to be made into something. You make every other mind look *tired,* a remark that may strike you as amusing, when you are so tired yourself. No wonder, after this gigantic effort. You give me the impression of a real creative force that I don't know where else to look for. But you always did remind me of Adam, naked, under the morning sun!— with the feeling that life is a grand and a primal adventure. Only complete your series and give us Adam's philosophy, and the whining shades of Eliot, Joyce and Spengler and the other false poets who have cursed our time will vanish like acrid smoke with the bats and the owls. You are certainly one of the great builders, as everyone will see when the rubbish of our time is cleared away. I felt this more strongly than ever as I re-read your last chapter, with its wealth of new and fundamental thoughts.

I want to see your "call to arms" and should probably be glad to back it, though my mind is still confused over some of these questions. I have been in a turmoil myself over political matters and have lately had sleepless nights over a question that bothers me much, "Political Catholicism" and what should be done about it. For the Catholic Church is growing so bold in this country. It defeats every measure for decent living. I think this is very important and that we ought to combat it. But how? What's the best method?—short of raising the Ku Klux bogey and the latent hatred of popery all over the country. Anyway, keep this in mind and let us discuss it.

I am glad you saw Conant and thought well of him. I have not met him but have heard much good about him. He is a relief from the "big shot" college presidents who, let us hope, in another twenty years, will be as extinct as the dinosaurs.— We have been seeing old friends, and much I enjoy it, al-

though I am so tired that I am snappish,—the Pachs this last
Sunday, next Sunday the Lee Simonsons. We have wanted you
and Sophy most of all.

Amenia, New York   April 26, 1938

The generosity of your praise, dear Van Wyck, would
keep on mounting to my head like wine were it not for the
sobering remembrance that my next book at least must prove
more fully worthy of it: so that your words may be justified as
prediction, if not as description. What you have said about
The Culture of Cities, both privately and with such public
magnanimity, too, has had the effect of hastening the return of
my energies, and of making me eager to be at work again: for
the night cometh when no man can work. I have kept reviews
at a distance; won't even let Sophy, poor girl, discuss them
with me, though she is itching to do so: but what filters in to
me, through Harcourt's advertisements, which I do read with
lynx-eyed vigilance, and above all through letters, has filled
me with quiet delight: this is a sort of double spring for me,
and I feel as if I were putting forth rosy buds, like the maples
around us here!

Of course I know the stage that you are in now, and your
need for seclusion, so that the various fragments may have a
chance naturally to knit together in your book; but I do hope
our meeting will not be postponed till my return from Honolulu. . . . I have been wrestling with the earth in the garden,
which is almost as rewarding as wrestling with an angel; and
all the grime and sordor of the intellectual life has been
sweated away in this manly struggle.

During this last week I have been reading the ms. of Waldo
Frank's new novel,[26] which I think is far and away the best

26 *The Bridegroom Cometh* (1939).

thing he has done: it is a strong, sinewy piece of work, with all the vaticinal writhings and effortful orginalities eliminated: it is indeed as if his whole style had been purified by fire. The Markand book[27] had good spots in it; but this seems to me to have the same strong texture through and through; and I am very happy about it. He seems to me by now a man very near the end of his rope: deeply disappointed in what life has offered him on every hand: without a publisher, without a secure position in life, passed over perpetually in favor of people who are not fit to typewrite his manuscripts. If the publishers are not too leery of him now, this book should help towards his remaking; and he is too good a man to be thrown on the dust-pile.

Another book I have been reading is *Joseph in Egypt;*[28] and I must say I am still as aloof from this as I was at the beginning: it does not seem to me the masterpiece everyone has been proclaiming it: alas not! There is something irretrievably wooden about this resurrection of ancient time; the same sort of woodenness one finds in Salammbo. Plenty of archaeological detail; too much; but the characters are at once too much and too little like us to be convincing; and when Joseph, to show his pretty intellect, talks Einstein I am incredulous. One can deal with ancient mind by allusion and suggestion, as happened in the case of such a relatively contemporary account as in the Bible itself: but as soon as one becomes explicit, one tends to describe, willy-nilly, one's own contemporaries, one's own state of mind. Try as he will, Mann does not escape this: indeed, half the time one believes that Joseph is just Hans Castorp, he of the Magic Mountain, in Egyptian fancy dress. Which reminds me: shall you be in New York for the Mann lecture on the sixth? I have to be down that day to see Hudnut of the Harvard Architectural School; and Sophy and I thought of going, seats on the platform being

27 *The Death and Birth of David Markand* (1934).
28 by Thomas Mann.

offered. And why in heaven's name hasn't the Institute ever had a reception to him?

Amenia, New York   September 29, 1938

Dear Van Wyck:

I put off writing to you in Hawaii because there was too much to say; and I haven't uttered a peep since coming home. . . . No matter what the storm and the destruction, the important thing to do is to trim our lamps, not so much like the wise virgins as like the lighthouse keeper, who sticks to his post and waits for the dawn. What a world! And what a combination of knavery and stupidity! Today probably decides everything,[29] and I shudder to think about it as I remember that the two most important men at the meeting, Daladier and Chamberlain, will have traveled a long distance, be frayed and tired and edgy, while the maniac who threatens us will have had a smooth night's repose and a leisurely morning breakfast. Knowing what mistakes and blunders I myself make after a night's travelling and a strange bed, I tremble for the world! Come over soon.

Westport, Connecticut

[September, 1938]
Sunday morning

Dear Lewis:

. . . You have all been in our mind almost every day this summer, and we've been so happy to think of you in those *hopeful* regions. (There seems less hope than ever anywhere

[29] The meeting with Hitler in Munich.

else, after this week of betrayal, except for at least a gleam of light in Spain.) And there have been evidences that San Francisco is eating your book alive and will probably have a bronze effigy of you at the gates of the coming World's Fair. Imagine how eager I am to hear your impressions of Palo Alto, as of the Northwest and Honolulu. Sophy was ecstatic about the latter, and we have resolved to go there on her say-so. I have a notion that your discovery of the Pacific will have a great effect on our future thoughts,—and everyone else's under fifty.

I've scarcely lost a day with my book, and I'm advancing steadily, though it may well take another year. I was discouraged a year ago, but now the subject seems to me better than ever. No move at present, except to say that we saw the Kreymborgs twice this summer. They were at Stamford at the Knudsens' house. Do try to hear Alfred's broadcasts.[30] He has invented a new kind of radio-play. We have heard two,—*very moving*. Let's leave no stone unturned to get Alfred into the Institute. It is a scandal that he wasn't in long ago. I see by the enclosed that your old friend on the *Spectator* is on your trail again.

87 Kings Highway, Westport, Connecticut   December 7, 1938

Dear Lewis:

I said my say about politics for good and all on Sunday night. I have since had *your* requests to print the speech, so I suppose it will be printed somewhere. Now I am back at the *serious* business of writing on Mary E. Wilkins, and I think this hitting on the surface will help me down in the depths.

I suppose you have *your* theory about the immediate future. *I* think Mussolini will make or break within two months and

---

30 *The Planets*, a radio pacifist allegory by Kreymborg.

perhaps a fortnight. The Germans will come tumbling after, but slowly as befits Germans. I think they are all going to crash within, and then we'll have some fun in this world again. But everything is going like lightning this month, and to-morrow's papers may show I'm entirely wrong. Anyway, three cheers for Mary Wilkins!

Amenia, New York   February 3, 1939

Dear Van Wyck:

. . . Now that *Men Must Act* is off my shoulders, I have two or three things on the fire—including a project for revisiting *Sticks and Stones,* fifteen years later, with a fresh point of view and a maturer set of values: this will probably be the six lectures I'll give at Harvard next fall. I wanted a theme that wouldn't require a year's special research and yet wouldn't just be a re-hash of something I had said many times before; and I think I have found it. Up to the moment I made this decision the winter had been a nightmare, just because this unsettled matter of the theme for the Harvard lectures hung over my head. The real purpose of this note, however, is to say that I am going to be in Boston next Thursday, to talk at an anti-fascist rally at Harvard; and that I should like to stop off to spend an hour or two with you . . .

Westport, Connecticut   February 4, 1939

Dear Lewis:

This is a case of mental telepathy, for I had just finished *Men Must Act* and was setting pen to paper when your letter came. More about the book in a minute, but now of course we shall be here. We haven't been anywhere else and shall not be, and I didn't even go to the Institute meeting. I am dead to the world henceforth till my book is finished. (It is going well!) . . . I want to hear about the Harvard lectures. Yes, we are all "myths",—or moles,—but we are covering ground down there in the darkness.

Now your book is a perfect model of intelligent thinking, and I don't have to say that it has enlightened me. Almost more than anything you have done, it made me feel glad that you are alive; and I thoroughly agree with all the measures you propose, except in the matter of immigration,—I mean as a settled change of policy.[31] (I think we should take an army of refugees, but that is another matter.) Your analysis of fascism is wonderfully fresh and true, and I back all your seven points in the matter of non-intercourse, and I wish every member of Congress could see your statement of them. Also what you say about conscription and the greater effectiveness of voluntary service,—all very true and convincing to me. I have seen nothing about our relation to the fascist menace that seems to me to hit the bull's-eye so; and I hope it will be read very widely. (It should absolutely be read by political people; and in this connection I wonder if Harcourt would care to send a copy to Henry L. Stimson. I doubt if he ever makes comments for publication, but Eleanor and I feel sure that he would read this with interest and probably mention it to others.) As for the composition, it is superb, lucid, persuasive, intelligent and generously felt. It adds a big stone to the structure of *your* American culture, in which I usually feel like your gold-dust twin. But more of all these things on Friday.

P.S. I am having grand and glorious times with my book.

[31] "I feel we should have a chance to *shake down* at least for a generation." (Brooks's note.)

Amenia, New York   February 7, 1939

Your letter made me rejoice greatly, not merely over what you said about my book, but over the good news of yours. Occasionally it may be necessary to write a *Men Must Act:* but such books are like whisky or aspirin: they presume a normal organism, if they are to have any effect. It remains to be seen if *Men Must Act* will have any influence on a country that has been *living* on whisky and aspirin! . . .

Westport, Connecticut   April 12, 1939

Dear Lewis:

We are just starting off for a ten days' journey, but we expect to be here again by April 23rd. We are going to Richmond and Williamsburg, etc., which we have always wanted to see in the spring; and Miss Ellen Glasgow has kindly arranged for us a sort of royal progress through the State,—visits at all the grand houses and lunch at William and Mary with President Bryan. I believe we are also to meet Dr. Freeman and dine with James Branch Cabell; so when you see me you must expect to find me riding high and dry in a world that knows none of our mortal troubles. . . .

P.S. What do you suppose has fallen from the sky? A grant from the Carnegie Corporation! Just like that, and I didn't ask for it. Our good LEE must have told them that I was bankrupt.[32]

---

[32] Mumford arranged the grants for both Simonson and Brooks.

Amenia, New York   August 3, 1939

Dear Van Wyck:

    Last week I was forced to spend a few days in torrid New
York; and I wandered about the city, on the night of Joel's[33]
death, pondering his life, all that he had done and all he had
failed to do, and becoming more keenly conscious, in that act,
of all the weaknesses, flaws, and omissions in my own. I even
spent some time at the library reviewing his published work;
and was surprised to find how blind I had been at times to its
very real intent and its effective purpose. Quantitatively, his
writings are small; but that makes all the more surprising the
impact they had. Because I knew it would have pleased him, I
sat down and did an essay about his work for the *Saturday
Review:* it should be out presently, perhaps in the next number. I even employed the method he advocated in criticism in
assaying his life and work; and though the essay is by necessity
merely an opening one, it makes me think I shall perhaps
some day do a more extensive piece. . . . Amy came directly
over here after the funeral and was well enough recovered to
see us for half an hour on Monday. She rose to both Joel's
illness and his death with real nobility: deep feeling but poise.
We were in some doubts as to how she would feel about returning to Troutbeck; but by taking the plunge immediately,
I think she overcame her inhibitions against returning to a
scene so completely saturated by Joel's personality; and I
understand he made the request that the place itself should be
kept up and used; so that will probably be done.

    My reading has been desultory this summer; but I have
gone back to Coleridge's lectures on Shakespeare with keenly
renewed delight and deepened respect: they strike me as getting closer to the heart of criticism than any other English

    [33] Joel Elias Spingarn, critic and historian of criticism. In his later years,
he became completely immersed in his life-long interest in the Negro and
his problems.

critic, Matthew Arnold not excepted: and one only wishes again that there had been more strength and consistence in that poor fellow's life. Paul recommended Robert Penn Warren's *Night Riders,* and it turns out to be as excellent as he said; and I have had great pleasure out of Helen Waddell's novel: *Peter Abelard:* an historical novel with the air of a contemporary narrative and not a touch of Wardour Street reconstruction. I have done about a hundred and fifty pages of my own novel; enough to assure me that some day I shall have to finish it: it will be probably my one and only essay in that form. Now I have to get back to my Harvard lectures soon, for they will begin next November, and I'd like to make them reasonably fresh, even though I no longer believe that they will in any way increase the likelihood of my being taken in there.

Westport, Connecticut   August 21, 1939

Dear Lewis:

. . . I was so touched by what you said about Joel. Villard's article in the *Nation* is quite good, but there is scarcely a line about his writing; and the paragraph in *Time,* which summarized all his other activities, did not even refer to him as a writer. I have sent for the *Saturday Review,* to see your paper. It was so fine that you were stirred to write it. It always seemed to me a pity that his *Creative Criticism* should have been made so prominent, the weakest of his writings, for you are certainly right about some of his essays. Some of them,— the one on the "Younger Generation,"—were among the best of our time, beautifully conceived and felt; and I regret so much that we didn't *keep at him.* He had to feel the demand from without, and he was so glad to respond. I remember how happy he was to join the *Civilization* group, after the right pressure had been brought upon him, and some of those finest essays of his were written for the *Freeman,* though only after repeated and urgent proddings. He had a beautiful mind, and I shall always think of him as a beautiful person. I am so glad that he had that active and useful *other* life of which Villard makes much, but I know that his heart was in critical writing. He might have done so much, and he must have felt bitterly about it. One of our friends in Westport who knew him well, E. C. Richards, said that Amy told him, on his last visit to Joel, during his illness, that he could talk about anything else, but he must not mention *literature.* But what he did was fine. It was all distinguished, and how it would have pleased him to have you say it!

I am plodding along with my everlasting book, and really mean to finish it by Christmas. I have twenty chapters written of the twenty-five. But some of these latter-day Yankees are baffling to me, and I shall be happy to say good-bye to New England. If you have done anything on your Harvard lectures, won't you bring that over too?

Amenia, New York   August 13, 1939

Dear Van Wyck:

. . . If you have had as much difficulty in getting your copy of the *Saturday Review* essay as Amy has been having, I'd better send you on a clipping. And while I think of it, I must correct a piece of misinformation in my last letter, which was due to the working of the folk mind up here. The story that Joel was buried in a *Jewish* cemetery is entirely apocryphal: that would have suited the folk-fancy apparently, but it isn't true. It is true, however, and not a little strange, that they had selected Joel's final resting place only last summer, when he seemed in perfect health: had come upon it on a jaunt around

the country, visiting gardens and estates, and liked the place
because of the ancient trees and the view looking across the
Hudson. It is also significant that Joel in his will apparently
left two injunctions for Amy to fulfill: one was to conceive a
memorial which would testify to their common love for
Dutchess County, and the other was for another suitable
bequest that would perpetuate his interest in *aesthetics and
literary criticism*. This entirely confirms your own intuition
about his life: that this part of him was central. As usual, I
have learned a lot about Joel, now that he is gone: one of the
things that seemed unbelievable, and yet was entirely characteristic of the man, characteristic of his insurmountable pride,
is that he had never actually visited Croce, though he had
more than once been in his neighborhood. And the reason?
Joel didn't feel that his Italian was good enough. He hadn't
visited Vossler, either, when he was in Europe in the late
twenties and the reason for that, I surmise now, is that his
German wasn't entirely adequate either. Poor Joel: his pride
cut him off from his center and made him spend too much
time building up the periphery.

I am gladdened by the news that your book is within sight
of the end: that last effort of the will always takes most out of
one, I think; and I have never yet been completely happy
about the final chapter of any long book I have written. On
my next, I am going to try to circumvent the natural results of
fatigue by writing my concluding chapter first! The *New
Yorker* is going to print the prelude, in verse, to my novel;
but, after reading the novel itself, in large chunks, to Paul
Rosenfeld when he was here, I have concluded that it is still
too crude, still too much a matter of intentions and outlines,
to be imparted to another ear, no matter how sympathetic.

393 Bleecker Street, New York, N.Y.   November 3, 1939

Dear Van Wyck:

My Harvard lectures kept me so infernally busy all last October that I have scarcely had time to look at the clock. . . . I have no confidence about my *prospects* at Harvard; or perhaps it would be better to say no interest; for the next three years I shall have to devote wholeheartedly to my book, and if I did succeed in bowling the authorities over sufficiently to make them come through with an offer, that would only increase my embarrassment. I did not feel this way in March 1938; but then a lot has changed since that date.

Your letter to the League of American Writers came this morning: a noble document, and I concur in every word of it.[34] Presently, I shall join with you; the only thing that makes me hesitate is that I should like to make my own resignation public, in order to clarify the position we take: I don't want to make it easy for the more unscrupulous fellows who are left to make it seem that theirs is a noble and disinterested and liberal position and ours is a reactionary one. What appals me is the moral debasement that subtly has made its inroads every where: white is black and foul is sweet if you happen to think it so. I had some caustic sentences on this subject in my original notes for the *New Republic*'s anniversary number; but, as usual, these were precisely the words that were cut out when they reduced my sentences to fit the space they had allotted me.

It is high time that I started work on my next book[35]: decay has already eaten deep, and we must work and build, in the way that men on a sinking ship work the pumps, if we are to even keep hold of what we already have—to say nothing of

34 Many liberals resigned from the League at this time because of a take-over by the Communist faction in it, as disclosed by their justification of the Stalin–Hitler pact.

35 *Faith for Living* (1940) .

advancing it further. In a time like this, salvage is almost creation. I reproach myself for having remained so long indifferent to the fate of Communism in Russia and so silent about the villainies of its dictatorship: the period of suspended judgement lasted too long, and the suspense has now proved almost a noose around our own necks. For many years I have feared this alliance of Stalin and Hitler; it was one of my standard nightmares; but I never breathed a word about it in print. Well: it is too late to cry over that: but I shall at least perform the only remaining act of reparation that lies within my power, and that is announce, if I can find a place to announce it in, the reasons for my resignation. Sheean's first article in the *N.R.* seems to me to say exactly what should be said. . . .

Westport, Connecticut   November 7, 1939

Dear Lewis:

I was so glad to have your line, and good luck with the Harvard lectures. I know you will hit the bull's-eye every time.—And how I agree about your book!—ditto, ditto about mine.—As for the Communist revelations, I think they will have a good effect. They will destroy the myth of a universal Communism Mill on the ruins of national psychologies; and I think this should result in a rapid growth of socialism, along the line of the psychologies of the various nations. This aims at the same objective, organically achieved.

About the *League,* perhaps you are right in the matter of making your statement public. (My dread is that the Dies Committee will stick its nose in and iron out the subtleties that prevail among writers.) Elmer Rice feels as you do and is sending me a projected statement; and everyone to whom I sent my letter seems to agree with us both. So wait a few days. We might get up a joint statement, signed by a large list of members, that would differentiate us from the politicians and *sketch and even necessitate* a new League. (My apparent tenderness is owing to the fact that I want to *save the League*.) —I met Elmer Rice at one of the Anti-Nazi luncheons connected with the organization you spoke of. You mentioned this to Eleanor, and if you can get her into it you will find that she is a *Dynamo* for this kind of thing. I should stand behind her but must act through her. She has a great force for this work that is ready to be called into action.

P.S. In suggesting a joint statement about the League, I do not mean to imply anything against your individual statement.

393 Bleecker Street, New York, N.Y.   December 19, 1939

Dear Van Wyck:
   During the last fortnight, I have been settling down to that long communion with other books which is part of the incubation period on my own; and I can only too well sympathize with your reluctance to break into your own work by a visit to New York. I am still excited by our removal to the city; and I wander around the streets, peering at the faces and attempting to read them, as I might if I were in a strange city in Europe for the first time: I feel that I have so much to learn; and that at any rate, every sight, every person, every building, has something fresh to say. It would be marvelous, in a mood like this, to begin the preparation of that interpretive book on the development of New York that I have long planned to write; but that was a task that beckoned before the evils and catastrophes of the times began to press upon me; so, with a sigh, I put it aside; and instead I have started to flounder about the vague literature of a subject that won't be

fully defined until I have succeeded in writing about it: which means that I am reading practically everything about human life, from books on psychology and costume and medicine to the *Imitation of Christ*[36] or the *Paradise of the Heart*. It is really great fun; if anything can still be called fun in a civilization that shows so many signs of disintegration, and in which our fellow countrymen have reached such a desperate point of moral apathy.

Nevertheless, as you know, I never completely despair; just last night, facing a wealthy Philadelphia audience, telling them that civilization could not be saved unless they were willing to resign most of their status, their privileges, and their wealth, instead of losing everything in the general onslaught of barbarism, I met with an unexpected reaction: One of the audience challenged me to name a class that had ever voluntarily resigned its privileges anywhere; and when I cited the abolition of serfdom in Russia by the aristocracy, and the renunciation of the much more complete power of the Samurai in Japan, the audience loudly applauded. There is always a ray of hope flickering somewhere through my mind; but certainly the treachery and moral obliquity of our time has reached the point of creating an almost physiological nausea. I have it still on my conscience that I haven't yet resigned from either the League of Writers or the *New Republic;* but the only thing that has prevented me from doing both is the fact that I must frame a letter to accompany my act.

I have seen Waldo Frank lately, likewise Paul, likewise Lee Simonson; and find that they are all more or less in the same state as I am in, except that Lee is still buoyed up by enthusiasm both over his task and over his own courage in attempting it; and if only he doesn't overweight his cleverness, for in the manner of the nineties, he poises like a bombing plane over his victim, waiting to drop his devastating epigram,—if

---

[36] *Imitation of Christ* by Thomas à Kempis; *Paradise of the Heart* by John Amos Comenius.

only he isn't *too* clever he will produce a challenging and important book, I am quite sure. At the moment Lee regards me as a hopeless renegade because, despite his earnest approval, I have decided not to print my Harvard lectures. My immediate reason is that the lectures would need a month's work before they were ready to appear, independent of the visible lecturer, as a book; but perhaps my ultimate reason is the fact that, despite large and steady audiences, my visit to Harvard was a very disappointing one. I gathered almost immediately, without anyone's saying a word, that the reason originally given for having me give these probationary lectures, had vanished, and that the chances of my getting a post there were nil: nothing that happened since has in any way falsified this original intuition of mine. And apart from that— though in the circumstances it sounds like very foxy sour grapes—I did not feel at home with the people I met there, nor was I pleased with the atmosphere of the place. (This despite good talks with Murray, Matthiessen, or others.) The Oxford complacency surrounds Harvard like a layer of protective fat; and it isn't good for the spirit's exercise. Count me out. Some of the Middle Western state universities are much more to my taste!

I met your young architect at the School of Design and had a good talk with him: he seems to have the right stuff in him. You and Eleanor should pay a visit to the house that Gropius[37] built for James Ford, out at Lincoln. Gropius is beginning to conquer the Brahmins: a nearby Adams visited him and was completely captivated, although he had almost disowned his son for becoming a modern architect; he had thought of the modern as vulgar and flashy but in Gropius' work he recognized something restrained, sober, even Puritanical—in his own tradition!

37 Walter Gropius, founder of the Bauhaus at Weimar and Dessau; later Chairman of the School of Architecture at Harvard University.

Westport, Connecticut   December 22, 1939

Dear Lewis:

. . . How I wish that I could walk about the streets with you
and share some of your cogitations. I spent most of my youth,
as it seems to me, wandering about the streets of New York,
Boston or London, though usually alone, and how wonderful
it would be to recapture the feeling that one had all the time
in the world ahead! When I finish this book—by the first of
May, I hope—I am going to recapture it for a while, and
couldn't we have some times then, real old-fashioned spend-
thrift times to commune and invite our souls together? I
should like to hear you talk for hours about your new book—
and I will talk for hours about mine—for I have my *Oliver
Ashwell* in mind for next year; and this, thank heaven, will
not require reading. It will leave me a margin of time. This
letter of yours suggests a marvellous mood, and how good it is
that we both feel that we have everything to learn and have
not *begun* our life-work yet! That is my feeling every hour.

I won't go into the state of mind of the country. But when
was it *not* morally apathetic?—except at a few great moments
of revolution and crisis. And as for the unity of thinking
minds in the days of abolition, it was nothing to the unity of
writers today. (The poor old League was only a segment of
them.) They are all "on the side of the heart and not of the
liver." And that is something, dear comrade-in-arms. And
what you said about the Philadelphia audience interested me
very much indeed. I have a deep impression that our fine
people, rich or poor, are only too eager to withdraw from a
plutocratic world—if they can feel behind them a reasonable
security. I think they would gladly give up their status and
privilege and wealth if they could have this, and the feeling
that the under-privileged did not hate them. I have heard that
the German military people are really quite friendly to communism, because they find that it rather flatters their *prestige,*

which is all they really want in the way of power; and you remember that Henry Adams made a similar statement—and these are the mundane of the mundane! They are beginning to feel that *wealth is vulgar,* as the really fine people have always felt, and that's a line that you and I can work on. I am an incurable optimist and always shall be, but I hope I shan't stop working for my optimism! Nor shall I ever forget the volume of baseness that our times have revealed on this poor planet. (As for the *New Republic,* you surely should not resign from this! All things considered, it is a candle in our world.)

And, to take up other points *seriatim,* you are right about Lee—that his cleverness alone might undo him. He needs a kind of reassurance that would put an end to this clever business, which is a form of whistling in the dark, but from all that I gather he is writing a really great book. As for the lectures at Harvard, I am astonished at what you say. Our young Westporter Billy Linde said you were an enormous success—firstly, that a multitude came to hear you and, secondly—but these were his words: "Mumford made a tremendous impression. I can tell you how they felt behind the scenes. The whole architectural department, every man in it, was enthusiastic over Mumford." Linde came to see me especially to say this, and I am quoting his actual words. He was radiant with conviction as he said them, so you must be mistaken. But as for the contemporary and *general* "fat," there you are certainly right. I have seen it on my actual visit as one of my visiting committee in the English Dept. I wouldn't live in that region for any reward, but is it not better than *other* university atmospheres? (It was ten times worse at Leland Stanford.) You and I could not breathe in a world of professors, after spending our lives among writers and artists. And, if you'll forgive me, I think it is one of your delusions if you have ever thought you could. Universities are places to deliver your *results* in, and to retire from rapidly to your world of *causes!* But, as for printing the lectures, have you properly thought this over? Would you let me see them and discuss them with you? Could you spend a month better than in putting them in shape? They must have been grand lectures—anything else is unthinkable.

393 Bleecker Street, New York, N.Y.   January 21, 1940

Dear Van Wyck:

The Hapgood book came back,[38] and I agree entirely about his essential immaturity, which comes out also in his failure at self-criticisim. When I read the first four or five chapters I thought the book awfully good; but it petered out before it was half-way through; and after a while he made one seriously dislike the hero, which is the worst thing one can say about an autobiography; though certainly it is true of Rousseau and true, with how shocking results, of Havelock Ellis's self-revelation. . . .

My days have been well-filled; I have been reading the early fathers of the Church, as the first step toward launching myself into the spirit and the culture of modern man. About the *Shadow of Tomorrow*,[39] which has so many of the shadows and reflections of our own thoughts, I have mixed feelings: the critical and analytical parts of it seemed to me finely done; but I felt that the end was weak: that Huizinga didn't know where to look for sustenance; that he didn't recognize the bread and wine of his own culture and so looked backward, and sought to fill his stomach with dried husks from which the nourishment has been sucked out by now. My review of it

38 Hutchins Hapgood, *A Victorian in the Modern World* (1939) ; leftist journalist and novelist.

39 *Shadow of Tomorrow* by Johan Huizinga, Dutch-born cultural historian.

came out in the *New Republic* a few years ago; and I should like to look at it now in order to see if I have drawn closer to Huizinga since then, for my ideas about the world, though not fundamentally changed during the last couple of years, have deepened, and that is bound to have an effect even on one's surface thoughts. Do you know his *Waning of the Middle Ages?* It is a masterpiece of cultural interpretation; and I am reading it for the second time, after almost ten years, with renewed pleasure and admiration. He has had a very direct influence on me, not so much by bringing me fresh thoughts as by confirming, sharpening, backing up thoughts I already had.

I have been shocked at the belligerent tone that the State Department has been taking with Great Britain over the matter of examining our mails at sea; and I wasted some of the family substance today by sending telegrams of protest to Hull and Roosevelt. I know these telegrams are futile; but they lower one's blood pressure a little. Were you equally perturbed? We are turning upon our best friends and most-needed allies, giving confidence to the Coughlins[40] and their crew, and behaving exactly as if our chief concern were to advance Hitler's interests—or, what is quite as bad, behaving as if no one in authority had the faintest notion of what interests were at stake in the present war. It is a shocking display of ignorance, provincialism, and loose emotion on the part of Mr. Hull and his cohorts. I wired Roosevelt that this legalistic impatience ill-beseemed us, when we had so defiantly violated international convention and our solemn treaty obligations in the putting an embargo on the Spanish Republicans, unless we purposed to aid Hitler and Stalin as he had then aided Franco. I simply do not trust the man; the longer he stays in office the less I like him. . . .

40 Roman Catholic Father Charles E. Coughlin of Detroit preached Fascism openly between 1936 and 1942.

Westport, Connecticut   January 27, 1940

Dear Lewis:

Your letter is reassuring about your general state of mind. I am in one of my periodical frenzies, with my book promised for April or May and Eliot and Cummings and others still to be dealt with. I have to describe the whole modern world apropos of New England! And I shall probably be in a nervous panic for the next three months. I am redirecting the book to you, so I expect some "absent treatment"; though only in the form of benevolent thoughts.

I was sorry not to see you at the Institute dinner. God knows such affairs are shallow, but so is the circus; and I regard these dinners as a small annual circus. It is fun to see our fellow-animals performing. I sat with Sherwood Anderson (who was disgusted), Thornton Wilder and Stephen Benét and had a rather amusing time. Yes, I think Calverton's book is wonderfully good.[41] Do you know him? I don't, and I never liked his *literary* writings. But this was full of amazing facts, mostly new to me, about early communities, etc. Two or three days ago, we saw Rudolph Ruzicka, a great friend of ours, the wood-engraver, whom I wish you knew. He is a tremendous admirer of Lewis Mumford. He quoted at lunch something you wrote in the *Freeman,* and later knitted his brows and said, "Mumford has a *great* mind, it seems to me." I have never heard him use the word about any other American writer, and he is a man who chooses his words with care.

Do you observe the stamp that adorns this letter?[42]

[41] *The Awakening of America* by V. L. Calverton (1939).
[42] The Writers' Series.

393 Bleecker Street, New York, N.Y.   February 1, 1940

Dear Van Wyck:

The thought that you are dedicating the new book to me
fills me with a great elation, with which is mixed a great
humbleness: I have a hundred reasons for wanting to see your
book appear at an early date, and now pride is added to them.
When one writes a book of one's own most of the thrill of
anticipating its appearance vanishes in one's weariness: but
appearing in a dedication has quite as much glory, and none
of the disadvantages of authorship. If I had not made a resolution, when I wrote my first book, never to use the dedicatory
form, because it was a surviving badge of the writer's degradation at court, I should have asked the privilege of dedicating
The Golden Day to you. But I shan't try to even up accounts;
it will be good, even in this, to remain eternally your debtor.

My life these last few weeks has achieved an almost monastic
simplicity, which harmonizes very well with the work I am
doing at the library not alone on the Middle Ages but on the
period of confusion, so much like our own, which preceded
them. I have been deep in the early Church fathers; and
found myself full of admiration for Tertullian, who felt about
Roman amphitheaters pretty much the way I feel about
modern ones. I would like to enter a monastery for a few days
in retreat, just to get the savor of the life; but not in America:
it would have to be some little known place, mossy with the
past, on some high hill overlooking the Adriatic! Meanwhile,
my due feet never fail to walk to the 42 Street library almost
in time for the opening each morning; and I keep right at my
desk till two or three in the afternoon, not even pausing for
lunch. (I have something to learn about fasting!) I am struck
by the fact that I am haunted by fewer devils than St.
Anthony or St. Jerome: all of us seem to have capacities for
concentration that those holy characters lacked. Their diet
may have made them irritable: at all events I can't imagine

plucking the feathers off a bothering little sparrow because I was sure he was a demon sent by the devil. A sparrow is a sparrow for us, which is a comforting thought, especially for sparrows.

Today I put the final touches on my resignation from the contributing editorship to the *New Republic*. The reasons that prompted me to do this are very much like the reasons that make me wish to wrestle with you, like Paul with the men of Corinth, over your heretical belief in isolation. For it is a heretical belief for you to hold: it denies all the things that make you what you are and that make all your thoughts, not just a gift to your countrymen, but to the world. How can we be isolated? Men are suffering by the million in Europe; our whole civilization is likely to perish there. Whole patches of Europe are already dead; the flesh is covered with gangrene; the putrefaction and the poison will spread. I would not bother to remind you that our physical isolation is gone; that Berlin is closer to New York than Boston was a century ago; nor would I awaken a very legitimate fear over what may happen to us *if* Hitler wins. No: the real reason to be concerned is that humanity cannot be divided off into isolated parcels: for good and ill we belong together; we must live or suffer together. We Americans are not the chosen people, precious though our own experience is, unique though some parts of it have been. If we withhold ourselves in this crisis, we shall only create that philosophy of insane national pride and self-adulation out of which fascism grows to fuller stature, and by fostering this attitude we will make the pacification of the world impossible, for a true world organization, without serious sacrifices of privilege and power on our part, just as much as on the part of the British Empire, would be impossible.

I know as well as anyone the insufferable attitude of the English toward other peoples; I know their long series of crimes and blunders in fulsome detail: the horrors of the cotton industry, the iniquity of the opium war, the human desecration in the Sepoy mutiny, the terrible brutality at Amritsar: symbols of a score of other acts not so easily remembered. But if I take England at her worst, in her rule in India, and if I add to it every crime, misery, and brutality she has committed, I still see in the English, taken as a whole, the unmistakable signs of a civilized people that is capable of self-correction and self-improvement, and that even in India has created by her own example, her own ideas, the very power that is capable of challenging her regime. I had rather be a low-caste Hindu in British India, than a respectable middle-class man in Nazi Germany: in every way, the chances of improvement would be better, and the degradations that would threaten me would be less in India. The accumulated miseries of British rule during the last hundred years have worked less harm, directly and indirectly, than the bare eight years that the Nazis have ruled in Germany. There is a vital difference between barbarism and civilization: not a difference in degree, but a difference in kind, and a difference in destination. To remember the terrible crimes and blunders that England and France committed in the remote and the recent past seems to me a stultifying attitude today; for a crime a thousand times worse is being committed by the Nazis, the crime of denying civilization itself; and if we remember only those that England and France have committed we shall be worse than the Bourbons, who forget nothing and learn nothing. The thing for us to learn is not to repeat the errors that France and England made, in not sensing the danger soon enough and not taking sufficient measures against it. When England and France are beaten, it will be too late for us to wake up: by that time, the only course left to us will either be to submit, or to fight, to fight without a clear purpose or a universal objective, to fight for mere survival, under odds so desperate that we ourselves would succumb from the effect of the war even if we were technically the victors. No: *life* is not worth fighting for: bare life is worthless.

But justice is worth fighting for, order is worth fighting for, civilization is worth fighting for. Are we too completely debunked to fight for a universal idea? If we are, we are already dead and our carcasses are not worth the effort needed to keep them from putrefying.

I have a feeling, dear Van Wyck, that I am only saying back to you those things which you, in other situations, at other times, have said to me or to the world. But I can't withhold my words; for the thing that makes me despair of the world, even more than its worst barbarisms and brutalities, is the fact that at a moment when—as in a shipwreck—there should be only men, those who best embody our manhood should think of themselves and their countrymen as *Americans*. We are men: other men are dying, other men are being tortured. Their governments are dishonest, infirm of purpose, given to cheating? I admit it: so was our own government during the crisis of the Civil War: Honest Abe was surrounded by rogues, cutthroats, timeservers and autocrats far worse than Chamberlain's friends. But these obstacles are of no account. Men suffer; they need us; and we should go to their aid, to the Spaniard, the Pole, the Finn, the English or the Frenchman, simply because they are men, and men have a call upon other men when they need succour or love. One might as honorably keep out of Europe today as a doctor out of a stricken home.

Westport, Connecticut   February 7, 1940

Dear Lewis:

It is fine to think of you reading away at the Public Library, and good luck to you in your enormous enterprise. You are sure to pull a big fish out of the waters. But I wish I hadn't uttered the word "isolationist" in that unfortunate letter of mine. Of course I feel as you do about these questions, and I think we only differ over the practical matter of our participation in the war. I think we should help the allies in every way, short of immediate participation, that we should be strongly armed (much as I hate the thought of it) in order to participate, if need be, and that we ought to go in decidedly if there is any real chance that Hitler and Stalin are going to win. England and France want nothing more at present, and it remains to be seen if they will want more. I cannot yet believe that Hitler will survive a year. Everything depends on what happens in the spring. The test is to come then, I suppose: but it seems to me you take a good deal for granted in saying now, "*When* England and France are beaten." If this seemed to be impending, my feelings would change nothing about Huizinga. You see how I keep up with things!

As for the British question, dear Lewis, I remain an incurable isolationist. I don't welcome *rapprochements* with England, and all the less because I have been reading a most moving book about India and the Empire. I think we should be strong enough to help *in case* Germany seems to be winning; but otherwise I welcome anything that reduces British prestige in our population. (I don't think anything will ever *raise* German prestige.) Well, at least I agree with you about everything else!

393 Bleecker Street, New York, N.Y.   February 10, 1940

Dear Van Wyck:

I never doubted for half a moment that we agreed about the human fundamentals here, and always will: and perhaps I am unnecessarily worked up about the immediate application of those fundamentals to human affairs. But an inertia as massive as that of America is not something to be overcome in a few days; and I fear that if things go badly for the English and the

French—and I don't see any ground for thinking that they are going well, when it is obvious that they are being opposed by the combined force of Germany and Russia, and the latent force of Italy—it will be too late for us to do anything effective, unless we have been getting ourselves ready, intellectually and morally, a long time in advance. A last moment intervention, as in the first World War, may prove as disastrous, in its final results upon peace, as our first was: an outburst of unconditional idealism, followed by an outburst of unconditional disillusion. And the thing that needs emphasis now is that there is neither health nor safety for us alone: our fate is bound up with the world's, and all men are our brothers.

Maybe I am vehement on the subject now, out of all reason, because I feel deeply my own guilt during the past twenty years, when, despite my extreme skepticism of the totalitarian tyranny that was being built up in Russia, I said nothing and did nothing to counteract it, because Russia was Russia, and because the conservatives were against Russia because of the virtues (i.e. vices in the capitalistic sense) they thought Stalin's regime still possessed. I made the mistake of thinking that Russia could work out its own salvation, and must therefore be protected from hostile criticisms: forgetting that a poisoned political system transmits its infection, by subtle carriers, all over the world: compare the timid brutalities of Mussolini before 1925, with his arrogant villainies afterward, and the absolutely unscrupulous violence of Hitler after that. Russia, with its contempt for democracy and its open persecutions, had made the path easier for these later dictators. I feel now, if I was ignorant of it then, that our only chance for salvation consists in creating a universal society, moved by a common set of human ideals: a society wider than Christendom, and big enough to contain all the creeds that war within it. Isolationism, as practiced in America, as conceived in America, is opposed to the spirit and to the end of such a society; and the sooner we realize that the obstacle to peace lies in ourselves, not alone in Hitler or in Stalin or Chamberlain, the sooner we will rectify the difficulty. . . .

P.S. The idea behind the writers series of stamps was a noble one. I have written Farley to congratulate him on it; and to ask him why he partly spoiled the gesture with such ugly frames for the portraits! Why not a scientist and an artists series, too. It is something if the populace even knows such people by name, has heard of their existence.

393 Bleecker Street, New York, N.Y.   April 14, 1940

Dear Van Wyck:

Here is my miserable little contribution to the discussion: I hadn't time to think out anything fresh, and I fear I have thumped on this chord too long a time to amuse even myself. But I was almost as appalled at Allen's contribution as I was at that of our publicity man at the National Institute a couple of weeks ago; and I can't imagine what on earth made Keppel invite him to take part in this shindig. As for the Institute, I was discouraged and depressed for a whole week after that meeting: I don't know which was worse, the hiring of a publicity man in the first place, or the drivel which he uttered, and of which apparently some of the people there, including the reverend Hendrik, approved. When Canby first asked me to join this committee I told him frankly that I didn't see how I could, since in the ten years I have been a member of the society it hadn't given the faintest indication of life. I finally let Train,[43] of all people, persuade me to take part, because I felt that if I resigned from the Institute, I had better at least have a little ammunition, to be obtained only by participation

43 F. L. Allen; F. P. Keppel; H. van Loon; H. S. Canby; Arthur Train.

in these dreary affairs, to justify my action. I still haven't had the faintest intimation of why I shouldn't resign—of why we all shouldn't resign. . . . Have you read Waldo's new book yet? It seems to me a true continuation of Our America; pithy and well-done in the main, though lacking the sense of support from and high confidence in his contemporaries which the earlier book had.

Westport, Connecticut   June 5, 1940

Dear Lewis:

I have been worrying and wondering about you, for Stanley Young told me he had seen the jacket of your new Book.[44] Waldo, with whom I had a most simpatico meeting last week, had also heard nothing about it. Now it appears that you are just writing it. Dear Lewis, all good luck with it! And I should say that we sadly need it. As for ourselves, not regarding the war, which feels like a cancer in my liver, we have had the usual over-burdened spring. Eleanor, who should have been resting after her pneumonia, has been working like a cart-horse; I have just yesterday shuffled off my proofs, and our Polynesian brother[45] has been here since March, a really extraordinary man—I long to bring you together—but a dynamo of energy over whom the roof of the house trembles. Add to all this, the usual problems of Westport in spring, the comings and goings that cannot be evaded, and you will see, etc. We have rented the house for July and August and are going to Maine about June 20th. My new book is really good, I think, and I have new plans for writing, which would be

44 *Faith for Living* (1940) .

45 John Francis Stimson, Mrs. Brooks's brother, a student of Tahitian language and customs.

defeated if we stayed in Westport. Such, more or less, is our story.

The war feels to me like a fatal disease inside myself, but, just the same, dear Lewis, this book will not be your last. You will write fifteen others, each one more necessary than all the others.

I much liked Waldo's chart,[46] and I understand how you feel about the mealy-mouthed *New Republic.* I feel much more at home with the good old *Nation,* which still has some of the ancient fire.

Amenia, New York   June 6, 1940

Dear Van Wyck:

I am in splendid shape, and already in the last five days, have done about a third of the first draft of my pamphlet— although not all of it is new material. I should be finished by the end of June. The most painful days were the days of frustration I experienced before the temper of the country changed and the sense of danger stirred us. Now, at least, I feel that I have escaped from the deaf and dumb asylum in which I lived these last five years. As for the *New Republicans,* they are really sublime: their reply to my resignation gave me the sense of a document jointly penned by Messrs. Chadband, Pecksniff, and Uriah Heep.

The news of your own work is altogether happy; and I am eager to see both what is now well done and what is in prospect. It is physically impossible for me to get my book finished and drive over to your place, even for the shortest of visits: but can't you and Eleanor and your Polynesian brother-in-law run over here for a middle of the day session? It won't interfere in

46 "A Chart for Rough Waters."

the least with my work; on the contrary, it will give it the lift
it sadly needs in order to temper its formidable message.

Westport, Connecticut   June 17, 1940

Dear Lewis:

I am going to be in N.Y. tomorrow, but I know you have
gone there to work, and on the whole I think I had better not
interrupt you,—although I have so many things to talk over
with you. I have a feeling that our time doesn't belong to us
any longer, and we'll have to postpone a meeting till September. I want to get at my own "faith for living" and am going
to Maine to have the quiet to work it out. Meanwhile, I
wonder if you would second a few of these nominations.
Hendrik was here yesterday and signed seven of them. Don't
bother to comment or explain where you don't feel like
signing them. Good luck till I see you, and I hope the book is
coming well. I feel that we are all at the point of a pistol and
have got to stand and deliver.

Amenia, New York   July 14, 1940

Dear Van Wyck:

My private Blitzkrieg is over: or at least the first campaign
is. Last Friday I turned in the last batch of page proof; and if
the printer keeps to the schedule, a copy will be in your hands
by the middle of August, if not before. The writing of that
book has been one of the most interesting psychological experiences of my life; for I started work still feeling the effects
of my exhaustion and nervous heart in the spring, and the
harder I wrote, the more strength I gathered, like the fabulous

Antaeus himself. I never spent six such intense weeks before, in my whole life; for the book, which began as a mere pamphlet, has turned out to be a sort of last will and testament, about 75,000 words long. The other day I went down to Washington to speak to a small group of progressive politicians and civil servants, called the Cooperative Forum; and I found their pulse still lamentably weak. If we are finally wiped out during the next year, it will not be for lack of armaments but for lack of guts; our cowardice is unspeakable, and our poor disoriented youth merely reflect the state of their parents and teachers. My one hope for the world now lies in our capacity for voluntary organization: there is still life and zeal left among a saving remnant.

I daresay that McRae has approached you for a contribution on America, to be syndicated in our newspapers; and I trust you have written it. *We* must become the national propaganda department: a worthier, if more amateurish one, than the old Creel Bureau.[47] How goes Oliver Ashwell? This is but a brief note till I recover breath.

[Maine]   July 19, 1940

Dear Lewis:

How good to hear that you have finished your trumpet-call, and you may guess how eager I am for it. (Our books should meet halfway in the mail, for mine will go to you in the middle of August also.) It looks to me as if you had written the first draught of the third volume of your series; and at any rate, from what I gather, it will be at least the first sketch of the most important thing you've done. I am doing the first

[47] Mumford note: "These contributions duly appeared—all but mine which was quietly suppressed because I openly advocated getting into the war at once on England's side."

sketch of mine, for I am hoping that *Oliver Ashwell* will be able to contain my *weltanshauung*. (If this is not properly spelt, so much the better, inasmuch as the word is German.) I have been living in rather a pitch of excitement, for I came to the conclusion this spring that I had to work out *what I really thought,* not about American Literature but about life. I shan't know for a month or more just what the results will be, but the attempt has kept me on pins and needles. So in some ways we are again in the same boat, and even as regards our reading; for, as you went back last winter to fundamentals, I am reading other fundamentals, for the next volume of my history, the age of the Revolution and the generation after.[48] It is a tremendous experience, in the light of this moment, to read Franklin, Jefferson and Thomas Paine. And I shall be a duffer if I cannot convince our coevals that America has *a monopoly of Revolution,* that we really started the whole thing and have our chance *for the last word also,* if we are able and if we prove willing to take it. If you have not read Paine and Jefferson recently, do take a little course in these two worthies. I am reading Dos Passos, etc., in their light, and trying to occupy all the space between. But now you give me a very guilty feeling when you ask me what I am writing for the present moment. I am not enough of a Pharisee to fall back on these plans, and say, Am I not writing for the present? If I can find a focus for something more immediate, I shall certainly do so. For I know that we need for the moment thought as action, and I mean immediate thought for immediate action. I am only handicapped by habits of long-range thinking, and a challenge for anything else is apt to scatter what thoughts I have. I have to be prompted from within and shall hope to be so prompted. Meanwhile I seem able only to sign petitions. (I have not heard from McRae[49] and don't know who he is, but

48 *The World of Washington Irving* (1944).
49 A misunderstanding of Mumford's misspelling of the name of Brooks's publisher, John Macrae.

I should be glad to do whatever I can.) This must be a hasty line, for I must get back to work. All the conditions here have been perfect. We haven't spoken to a soul in the three weeks we have been here, except the fine Maine people; but I foresee interruptions in a week or two. It seems to be impossible to have solitude for more than a month. We shall be back in Westport on September 1st.

Amenia, New York   August 9, 1940

Dear Van Wyck:

Your noble book came this week while I was down in New York: but though I have read only the first chapter I am sure already that you have repeated, or more than repeated, your first triumph. Not merely does our literature for the first time really live in these pages: but America lives, too, as it has never before lived in the works of any of our historians. What a man you are—and with what skill you make this prodigious marshalling of ideas and events seem *easy!* I need not tell you how deeply gratified I am by the dedication: I cherish it as a sort of knighthood, excited and humbled by it, in the mood I first met you when Walter Fuller introduced us in the old *Freeman* office!

This week—not having your address at hand in the city—I sent *Faith for Living* to Westport. Don't bother to read it while you are working on *Oliver*. I have much more to write about: but this letter will not hold it. Take my congratulations to your heart.

Amenia, New York   September 1, 1940

There is already, dear Van Wyck, a touch of orange atop the big maple down the road; and this incredible summer, which for us never had the taste of summer at all, is now almost over; the tomatoes still unripened in my garden, the squash still in blow—and young Geddes, in another week, making his first break away from home, out into a world which is bound to get much more foreign and much more formidable to all of us, and most of all to still untoughened youth. Already, our personal and domestic life has shrunk to the vanishing point; we have had no visitors all summer; and I have spent my time between New York and here, helping to develop the theme for an exhibition on what America is and may be. I hope I shall be able to get your advice and counsel once our first bare outline is accepted by the trustees. Meanwhile, at odd moments, I have been devouring your book; and last night I reached the last chapter and the deep, quiet, sustained note that so beautifully rounded off the whole work. You should pride yourself even more on this second achievement than on the first; for some of the flow and energy and joy of the first book came from your subject; while here, for the most part, it is you who have given the animation and order that make all those days live again, with fresh meaning both for the original work and for ourselves. Your pride, too, should bear some proportion to the humility you awaken in your reader; for by the sweep of your reading and by the depth of your explorations you make all other views of the period and all other criticisms of the literature seem meagre and superficial: even those of us who thought we were reviving the American past had no suspicion of all that lay buried until your searching eye began to bring to light what had been hidden in the far corners of the attic, shoved away by contemporaries and never looked at again.

I am eager to get at John DeForest—just as in your first

book you converted me into reading, with growing delight, old Holmes. Nobody has ever written our history before with this density, this amplitude of detail, this living accent and color; and what you have touched no one, in a sense, will have to write about again; just as no one ever had to repeat Thucydides's work. May you live to be a hundred and fifty, until every part of our America shall be, through your insight and imagination, as familiar and dear as our own living rooms. But do not work too hard on *Oliver* after such an effort as this: though one gets keyed up in the act of writing, and often has something very precious to say—nevertheless every fibre and pore need a rest, and the mere fact that one wants to write in such a semi-intoxicated state is no sign that one really should!! Every book is a battle; and it is part of the wisdom of war to follow such strenuous bouts with equally full relaxations. I speak by the book!

[Boothbay Harbor, Maine]   September 2, 1940

Dear Lewis:

I ought to have written you long, long ago, but life has been too exciting for me. No more of this except to say that I have written or rewritten 45000 words in a month, something that never happened with me before. It is my *Faith for Living*, and you have been feeding it. In fact, I am astounded as I read and reread your book to find myself stumbling into you at every corner in my mole-runs. We are certainly in telepathic communication, or, rather, we have certainly some blood-strain in common, for the same stimulus has produced the same effects in both. Your book is written in my native language, and chapter by chapter you have said what seems to me the most important thing to say, the thing that has to be said and shouted from the housetops. Amazing to me that this should have happened (though my line of approach is wholly different from yours), and yet it is borne in upon me that your whole past life has absolutely necessitated your saying this. That's the reward for integrity. And now I see why I was drawn to you,—we were nurtured at so much the same intellectual fount,—at least, we had Ruskin, Whitman and Morris in common. Also I see already that your third volume is going to be far and away your best, the straightest expression of your deepest self, and the self that goes all the way back to the first germ-plasm. How I wish that my next volume might deal with the theme of my *sixth* volume and that I might write of you in your altogether,—which is going to be one of the joys of my old age!

But now about this book (which I shall quote *ad lib* in mine), it may very well not be understood at this moment. At least, your addressees, the liberal intellectuals, will be the last to understand it,—and this has also given me some furious thoughts. For you are striking down now into the *folk* mind, and you have the reputation of a highbrow writer. (The same thing is happening to me, and it indicates already one of the new alignments that are going to throw our literary map into confusion.) When you amplify this sketch in your third volume, I predict that you will be quoted in every American pulpit.

I can't seem to get my thoughts in order (we are in confusion here, packing to leave, and shall be in Westport next Friday). But everything you say is a superb formulation of the deepest things necessitated by our whole American history and life. Only it will come as "such a surprise,"—and the intelligentsia will not know how to take it. What, talking of love, family, sacrifice, talking of first and last things, when everybody knew there wasn't such an animal,—and, worst of all, talking of "roots" not as a literary concept but as of something that actually grovels in soil. (All you say of regions is perfectly extraordinary, but your documentation here is of course unique.) This will all tease some of our friends, who will later arise and call you blessed. Some of your readers will fight with your political premises and then wholly miss the rest, and they will not be prepared to see that you have presented a vision of life in the only possible terms at the moment that could make for survival and triumph. When I get home again, I am going to read you through again and take careful notes from the book,—this is only a preliminary salutation,—but thrills go up and down my spine whenever I think of what you are doing.

Amenia, New York   September 14, 1940

Dear Van Wyck:

The words of your Boothbay Harbor letter left me walking on air for days; and the sense of our working together, tramping forward side by side, using the same maps, heading toward the same objectives, makes me feel that we will, before it is too late, gather around the ideas for which we stand the force and vitality they need to make them real. There are latent resources in our tradition, and indeed in human nature itself, which we have not yet tapped. One of my English friends[50] has written me a letter which sums up the possibilities that will soon open before us, as they have already manifested themselves in England. She says: "The incredible exploits of our airmen are in a way symbolic of what's happening. Personality, which has been coming to birth slowly during the age of democracy, is born, matured, and giving place to a super-personal ego consciousness. It is as though the Jehovah, 'I am the I am' is now consciously being transformed to the Pauline,

50 Gladys Mayer.

'Not I, but the Christ in me doeth it.' The first stage is the consciousness of democracy as a whole, which we with the States and our own Dominions had to some extent reached. But to found a new world order the further stage of an all-human sense of brotherhood, based on the consciousness of this second *super*-self must come. Those boys for the time of their exploits at least seem to have achieved this. Complete masters of their own personalities and their machines, completely super-personal in the way they give themselves, but with no sacrifice of individual initiative or any of the qualities of free men. It's a sort of living picture of the next stage of the human race, and in that sense religion is being born again not so much as faith but as deeds directed by the Spirit of Man."

Westport, Connecticut   September 20, 1940

Dear Lewis:

Will you read the enclosed, and will you join this Conference?[51] It is a thrilling affair, I can tell you. There is a report of it in this week's *Time*. Dr. Finkelstein wants you, and I am nominating you. (You wouldn't have had to be nominated if you had answered the first call!) This is not *just another damned thing;* and Dr. Finkelstein is one of the most remarkable men whom I have ever known. Now be good and behave yourself, dear Lewis! You are the one man the Conference needs.

We are still devouring and re-devouring your book, and Eleanor says that I am a black traitor for not shouting our praise from the housetops. Between snatches of sleep I have

[51] Conference on Science, Philosophy and Religion. Brooks encloses a form letter calling for an annual conference in September. He was very active in this, but Mumford never attended.

composed letters for Harcourt to use, but every hour of my days has been eaten alive, and I have a barrel of letters still to answer. Well, no more excuses, but your present train of thought is the most exciting thing that is happening in America.

Amenia, New York   November 11, 1940

Dear Van Wyck:

I daresay that you felt the same relief that I did when the election returns came in. Not that I have complete confidence in Roosevelt, for I dislike his somewhat shifty ways; and not that I couldn't have survived his defeat with a better sense of humor than most of the Willkie supporters. But on the whole, the equability of the majority of our countrymen, their calm decision, in the face of the most outrageous threats, seemed to me to argue a certain health in our democracy. By God! as one of our neighbors said on election day, this is the one day in the year when the Boss has nothing to say that you have to listen to. We even seriously undermined the prestige and strength of Ham Fish[52] up here; with another week or so to go we might have taken the election away from him.

Now that the tumult has died down, I intend to devote the next two months to the first draft of my book. It will give me a better notion of what I have done, where I am going, and what remains to be accomplished, by way of reading and reflection. I shall only do a part of the whole book this winter; for it is too big to bite off at once; and the period from the 18 century to today, the era that I know best, is one that requires

[52] Hamilton Fish, U.S. Representative from New York, was defeated in the next election.

much further digging into in a systematic way before I attempt it. *Faith for Living* dodders along; a good way behind Mrs. Lindbergh's insidious book; but, if I am not mistaken, with the slow even pace of a long distance runner who knows that he has a long way to go.

How have you and Eleanor been, and how fares Oliver? I am very eager to see those thoughts of yours in print. It was a great joy to find that you consented to put your name to Borgese's Manifesto[53]; and I only regret—no fault of mine needless to say—that you weren't at the original Atlantic City meeting, which was a sort of milestone in my life, and which gave me back the energy to write *Faith for Living*.

I have been reading all sorts of odds and ends, whilst busy for the most part with the philosophers and legislators and prophets of the sixth century B.C., which is the point where I am tempted to begin my present book: the age of Isaiah and Solon and the great Ionian thinkers. One of the books that I have read, with surprised interest, was Hagedorn's little brochure on T.R.'s beliefs and opinions during the last war[54]; he stands up far more creditably than I, a very prejudiced contemporary, remembered. Still another excellent work was Foerster's *Europe and the German Question:* a book that sails into the maudlin errors and myths that have been built up around Germany's guiltlessness and the sins of Versailles. (After all, the worst mischief done to Germany after the war, worse than the occupation of the Rhineland, was the inflation: a domestic trick.) Some of our history professors begin to feel sheepish about their interpretation of the post-war period, and well they might be. The college students I talk to have a fantastically biased picture of post-war events; and at the present moment that may well do decisive mischief. But I

---

53 *City of Man*, drafted by Borgese with the help of Herbert Agar and Mumford.

54 *Roosevelt in the Bad Lands*, by Hermann Hagedorn (1921).

talked to a group up in Williamstown the Sunday before last, giving a sort of political autobiography of our generation, and they were surprisingly full of approval: One of the professors told me that six months ago they would have filed out of the hall before I was half through. . . .

CHAPTER IV

The Valley of Shadows
(1941–1946)

The war years and the years immediately following were filled, for both Brooks and Mumford, with personal illness, sorrows, and tragedy as well as with the tensions of national and international violence. Both men suffered serious heart disturbances which made them take long periods of rest, and the wives of both were stricken with illnesses from which Mrs. Mumford happily recovered but which proved to be the prelude to the terminal illness of Mrs. Brooks in 1946.

The war was brought home to both men by the absences of Geddes Mumford and Kenyon Brooks in the armed services, and by the death of Geddes in action in 1944.

Nor were the times auspicious for the kind of deeply considered and long-term reappraisals of human culture in which both were engaged during this entire period and after. Mumford became increasingly impatient with the isolationist policies of the United States during the early war years and translated his impatience into both participation in protest movements and vigorous writing for the issues of the times. The more detached Brooks was inclined to seek refuge in his study of the American literary past and to exercise a maximum of tolerance in his attitudes toward both people and nations. Elected to the American Academy of Arts and Letters in 1940, he thereafter devoted much of his thought and effort to transforming this honorary body and its larger parent, the National Institute of Arts and Letters, from an elite group of elder literary statesmen to an active association of the artists and writers most vital at that time. In this effort Mumford offered only token accord which broke down later and led to his own resignation from the Institute on the issue of awarding the medal of distinction to the isolationist historian Charles A. Beard.

There was no significant change of residence of either man in these years although both spent time on the West coast: Brooks at his familiar resort of Carmel in a vacation mood and Mumford as Professor in the abortive School of the Humanities at Stanford University.

All of these circumstances were, however, collateral to the continuing strong friendship and shared commitment of the two men. Differences were wiped out and irritations softened when they spoke to each other of what had now become the dedicated life work of each. Mumford moved his "trilogy" on Western culture into a third major work on *The Condition of Man* in 1944, and Brooks moved his study of the literary life in America back to its sources in *The World of Washington Irving* in the same year. Brooks carried the narrative forward on a national canvas (excluding now New England) and published *The Times of Melville and Whitman* in 1947, the year in which Mumford took time out to revisit the early years of his son in a self-evaluative memoir, *Green Memories: the Story of Geddes*. Writing, as it were, above rather than against the destructive currents of the times, both men thus kept their literary vision focused on a far horizon which they continued to share.

Amenia, New York   January 24, 1941

Dear Van Wyck:

. . . I have been compelled to cancel all my lectures engagements. In Baltimore, where I was in bed four days with the
flu, I discovered that something much worse had overtaken
me: that my blood pressure was kiting upward again, as it had
done last spring. There is nothing structurally wrong with my
heart or blood vessels as yet; but if I went on at high pitch for
any length of time, the vice would become organic.

So the problem that has always been devilling me more or
less—how much time to apportion to lectures and "people"—
is now more or less automatically solving itself; and I don't
mind saying that it gives me a secret sense of relief; although I
will have to keep my eyes open, to see that I do not turn into a
smug and benign and more-or-less fatuous hermit, as I would
become if I lived up here steadily, without knocking and
brushing up against people in New York.

In Washington, I met old Justice Brandeis for the first time;
and was mighty glad I had the opportunity. The pure sap of
New England runs in his veins; I don't think I have ever met
a better man, so strong, so sweet, so simple, so straightforward,
so free from minor foibles: a sort of Abe Lincoln with the
backwoods cow-dung brushed off. Do you know him well? I
sent him a copy of *The City of Man,* and hope that it goes as
well with him as *Faith for Living* did. It is silly that we should
find ourselves halted in our plans for going on with the *City of
Man* project by a paltry thirty or forty thousand dollars. And
though the book has scarcely been noticed or advertised, it has
sold over four thousand copies on its own momentum; which
shows that there are other waves besides Anne Lindbergh's.[1]

I am still pessimistic about the immediate future of England; for I believe that just as Germany staked everything

---

[1] *The Wave of the Future* (1940) advocates isolationism and accepts
totalitarianism.

upon the success of u-boat warfare in 1917, she will stake everything once more upon the use of poison gas in her final attack upon England—and though that might bring us to England's side openly, and decisively in the long run, it may nevertheless result in a temporary victory, since England can't produce the same weapon in anything like the amounts necessary for hitting back. But my English publisher wants me to write about the Future of the City in England; and I have enough confidence in their ultimate recovery and restoration to be tempted to say Yes!

I shall read both the books you left me; and in particular, of course, the one about the Conference. It is a worthy enterprise; although I confess I have more hope for synthesis by way of the route we chose in *The City of Man* conference than by way of monster conferences that provide no effective point of focus and that give opportunities to Mortimer Adler,[2] to perform on the high trapeze. But in any enterprise that engages your love and interest, dear Van Wyck, please count automatically on me, as your sergeant or waterboy, to be marching at your back.

I have been re-reading Montaigne lately, in the course of plowing through the sixteenth century for my book; and I have been cursing myself for letting the impatience of youth, when I first read him, keep me from having him as a constant companion these last ten years, when I was ready for him, as he was for me. I understand Emerson's adoration now. Incidentally, the English style of Florio's preface to the translation entrances me; I don't think the language ever crackled with so much vitality before or since as it does in those sentences; it gives the impression of champagne foaming over the glass!

My book is overprepared in the early parts: I know far too much about the origins and early development of Christianity. This will undoubtedly make my pages on medieval culture all

2 Mortimer Adler, popular philosopher; author of *How to Read a Book* (1940).

the richer; but I feel a temporary embarrassment over my learning, so much of it directly unuseable, and nothing short of an invitation to deliver the Gifford lectures will salvage all the work I have done in this department. For once I had plenty of time and means—and wasted it instead of getting on with my main thesis.

Sophy tells me that *Oliver* is coming out in the *New Republic*. I am so eager to see it that I shall have to become a subscriber!

708 Wolfe Street, Alexandria, Virginia   March 2, 1941

Dear Lewis:

I haven't tried to write or think since I saw you last, but have plugged away at dusty reading, hoping to get my new subject[3] under my skin. All reading and no writing reduces my tone to zero, but I hope to come up again with the bulbs in the spring.

Now about the "blood pressure." At least it doesn't seem alarming, and I hope it will never prove to be so. But it might well be alarming, and I can't help wishing that it will keep you to a quiet life of writing. We so need your thoughts and we can't spare any of them, and I can't bear to think of your squandering your energies in these exhausting lecturing tours. We have everything to gain from your keeping quiet, as quiet as you can keep when your thoughts alone are so exciting. . . .

Beyond that I have been thinking of another plan that we might carry out in the future. Why should not you and Sophy and Eleanor and I run down to South America one of these days? Don't you think we might have a grand productive time? I have been seeing something of the Pan American Union here

---

[3] *The World of Washington Irving* (1944).

and have met some fine fellows from those regions. It opens up to me a new horizon as exciting as Europe used to be; and now I am trying to get an appointment with Nelson Rockefeller to find out why they haven't invited Waldo. It seems incomprehensible, or would seem so, if the Rockefeller projects were not such a mess. I could tell you stories about it that would be comic if they were not tragic, and everyone seems sure that Waldo is the one person to send. More of this when I see you.

I have been so buried in reading that we haven't seen much of Washington, except for innumerable casual encounters. But MacLeish seems to be doing wonders at the Library,⁴ in the way of making it an active center. I am going to speak there today.

Amenia, New York   May 2, 1941

Dear Van Wyck:

Last night I came back from the South, and though the trip was a remarkably good one, perhaps just because it was a good one, I find myself this morning buried under seven layers of fatigue. It will be quite impossible for me to come down for the meeting next week: my lectures, which I thought to have done before going away, need drastic re-writing; and I must finish an important paper for the Stanford conference before 1 June.

Have you joined the Fight for Freedom Committee, or—we have only had a few press announcements as yet—been aware of its existence? Our purpose is to get people to recognize the existence of war between us and Hitler and throw all our weight into it immediately. It seems to me that the next

4 The poet Archibald MacLeish was Librarian of Congress at this time.

month is critical—perhaps the next few weeks: the situation has not been worse since last June and July. We need money, and even more, we need moral support. Both are coming in, in an astonishing way, from all parts of the country; but that is just the reason why I hope your support will be forthcoming, too. Our purpose is to press the President into taking a more courageous and confident stand: to meet events with a bold front instead of letting Hitler decide what events we are to meet, and then attempt to handle them in a sidelong fashion. I regard the present crisis as so terrible that I would drop everything I am now doing to make my voice or my pen heard. If we fail to act now, we may never have the chance to act again.

Westport, Connecticut   May 4, 1941

Dear Lewis:

I had not heard of the Fight for Freedom Committee, and I hesitate to join any more of such. I am in four or five more or less similar things already, and I am only a deadhead anyway, as far as active help is concerned. But I approve of this and should be quite willing if the Committee wishes to use my name.

Your statement for the Institute is fine. I am sure it is much more fertile than any of the others will prove to be. I have not got round to making any sort of statement myself.

My work goes well, and I think I'm writing something that will really count. Meanwhile during the next three weeks, we are moving into the new house.[5] We shall take it slowly because I can't miss a day's work; but by the end of May we must see you.

5 A larger house in Westport.

Amenia, New York   September 13, 1941

Dear Van Wyck:

. . . What a life I have lived this last three weeks: ever since
we said good-bye to you. In part, it has been a very satisfactory
three weeks; for I got started on my book, with less trouble
than I had anticipated; and have done a rough approximation—and sometimes more than an approximation—of the
first three chapters, some two hundred pages: in fact, I have
meditated and moralized on the fate of man between Jesus
and Dante; so that a good third of the historical portion is
already behind me, and the method of treating the material
has pretty well defined itself. In some places I am overprepared; in other places, my resources are skimpy; but the
main thing is that it flows, and begins to gather volume and
power. I have a long way to go still, so I am deliberately
putting on the brakes and not going full speed unless I find
myself effortlessly coasting: there are three solid months
ahead; and I must not exhaust myself after the first spurt!

Your speech this week, which I had previously read in
extenso, sounded doubly brave in its newspaper setting; and I
was proud once more to have such a man to call my friend.
Bravo to all that you say: I am going to return to the analysis
in the final historical chapter of my book, where I hope to deal
with Joyce, Proust, and Picasso as symbols of our moral state
during the last thirty years. . . .

Westport, Connecticut   September 21, 1941

Dear Lewis:

We have missed you, but I well know how confusing these
days are; and I see you are speaking again in New York. I am
to have another session at Columbia on the first of October,

and then I must go to Washington; and I'm struggling to begin my *Washington Irving,* which simply doesn't wish to be written at all! So it goes.

And now I have read your little book with delight.[6] I don't quite see why you have kept it so dark: for as *writing* it seems to me clearly your best. To you it may be elementary, but your absolute mastery of the subject gives it an ease and flow that are perfectly delightful. Besides, nine-tenths of it is altogether new to me and I've pilfered a dozen notes from it. You must have given those Southerners thrills of joy; and I'll wager that Alabama felt like a peacock after those so skillfully chosen bouquets. I had scarcely realized, and I'm sure they did not know at all, how much they had run our show in architecture. It is a lovely composition, chockfull of nuggets; and the South should buy it—and won't—but the North will.

By the way, when you speak of the Renaissance and say the architects were amateurs who were simply masters of *drawing,* do you happen to know the house the Italian-American painter Fabbri built for himself just off Fifth Avenue? Walter Pach pointed it out to me last week, and it is a modern case in point. It is a superb house, and Fabbri was not an architect. As he told Walter, he only knew how to draw! It is worth looking at and thinking about.

Amenia, New York   December 23, 1941

Dear Van Wyck:

I have thought of you often these last weeks; and I've been wondering where you are and what your plans are. The first draft of my book was within a couple of chapters of being finished when, toward the end of November, I stopped work-

6 *The South in Architecture* (1941).

ing on it; and I was lecturing up in Dartmouth the afternoon that the war broke out into its active phase—a surprise only to the dunderheads and pro-fascists in the State Department, and to the Rip van Winkles who were in charge of the army and navy in Hawaii. Since that time, I have been taking counsel with myself as to how I could use myself most effectively. My instinct now is to remain silent, and to get on with the preparation of my book: this in spite of the fact that one of my main reasons for getting a place in New York was the thought that I could be more effective there, giving occasional talks and lectures, and consulting with people. But at least we have an apartment there now: 56 East 87 Street. . . . Have you looked lately at Whitman's poems written just before and just after the Civil War; they are prophetic of our own state, too; for we have not made a single mistake as a nation that the North did not make before and during the Civil War. (I wish I could be certain that we had our Lincoln, too.)

321 East 43rd Street, New York, N.Y.   January 15, 1942

Dear Lewis:

You see we are in New York—in two rooms in Tudor City—in clover for the last 48 hours. . . . As for me, I have had the scare of my life. I sat down to work here the first morning and suddenly felt my left side paralysed—arm, hand, leg and foot useless. The doctor says, however, that it wasn't a stroke and indeed on the third day I'm getting up and the arm and the leg are virtually well again. It was what they call a "spasm" in a blood-vessel in the brain, and just a sort of pleasant warning. But no more smoking forever—for which I thank and curse God, and apparently I can work as usual.

We have these rooms for 3 months. Living at home was impossible and our adventures there were almost comic. We

were snowbound, actually, for 36 hours, almost frozen for lack
of fuel, and the car slid over the ice and got its axle twisted
and ploughing through the snow broke the clutch. We might
have been living in the Laurentian mountains, and a winter
in N.Y. looks like heaven, with everything and everybody ten
minutes' walk away and all so simple and easy. Even the
biggest of all the libraries just down the street, and things here
in Tudor City arranged like a village and for people who
haven't too much in their pocketbooks. It's too wonderful to
get used to in a minute. (Dear Lewis, I'm writing in bed,
which explains the wobbly script—but I'm getting up to stay
up this afternoon.)

On April 1st, in time to start the garden, we'll be going
home again and I can't help rejoicing that you will perhaps be
in Amenia, though it almost might be California, now we
have no cars. I am sure this lack of cars will have made a big
difference to you out West. There can't be any state where a
car makes so much difference, although to be sure we never
had one there; and, as for the other conditions of the school,
while I'm not surprised about some of them, I am ever so sorry
they haven't gone better. But I don't quite see how you can
buck this army programme, with many colleges closing up
altogether and the so-called "liberal arts" everywhere pushed
into corners. (Of course I'll say nothing about your possible
leave of absence, etc.) What a pity that the school should have
had to start at just this time, or rather that just these conditions should have surrounded its birth and cradle; but teaching for you must after all be a secondary matter, and you've
probably lost no time or energy for your thinking or your
writing. And I'm glad that Sophy and you like the people;
there was always something disarming and winning about them.
I must say we were counting on finding you out there, and so it
may be when we can go—But when will that be? We put it off
from year to year, and our San Francisco grandson is almost
three years old.

I have no gossip to give you, for we have seen no one as yet in N.Y., though we're dining with the Simonsons tomorrow. My book has begun to go well again, though the old South and West are complicated subjects, and I'm hoping to finish it by next August. It's about three-fifths done, and I expect to profit by the neighbourhood of the Public Library.

A letter just comes from Hendrik who says he never leaves home any longer and we must go out and visit him there. He is now going to write a 3-vol. history of the Netherlands and sends a photo of himself with a new dog 8 months old that looks much like his Hansel and is just as big. . . .

P.S. The conference on Science, Religion and Philosophy,—I should have sent you the details about this. You should send a line to Dr. Louis Finkelstein, c/o The Jewish Theological Seminary, Broadway at 122nd St., N.Y. I believe the dues are $5, but this includes the book which contains the papers read at the meeting. You will not regret meeting Dr. Finkelstein, who is a rare person. I feel sorry to have badgered you so about this, and you won't have to renew your membership if you don't think it worth while.

Last night we had to dinner Honor Spingarn[7] and her husband, who is in charge of the District P.W.A. Honor looked quite lovely and seems very happy. They are living round the corner.

Dutton is making a little book of my Hunter College speech. I'll bring you a copy when we come home.

7 Daughter of J. E. Spingarn.

56 East 87th Street, New York, N.Y.   February 3, 1942

Dear Van Wyck:

Last Saturday afternoon, for me, justified our whole removal to New York—an act which at other times during the
last two months has seemed altogether disruptive, not to say
calamitous. I am glad you felt the same way about the afternoon. How carefully our whole civilization is arranged to
postpone or circumvent such quiet, uninterrupted, unharried
hours of friendship. We must find a way of repeating it—or we
set ourselves down as unbelievers who, having heard the
Gospel, callously turned their backs to it!

P.S. I saw Paul in the Library today—looking *very* fit and
alert and "integrated."

56 East 87th Street, New York, N.Y.   March 28, 1942

Dear Van Wyck:

I got back from my five week trip to the West coast, just last
week: much revived in energy by what should have been a
thoroughly exhausting experience. . . . From the time I
reached Los Angeles I was busy, from morning to night, with
conferences, discussions, committee meetings, lectures, first at
Claremont, then at Palo Alto, San Francisco, and Los Angeles:
I got little sleep and no exercise, scarcely ever had a moment
to myself for enjoying the spring landscape; and yet, day by
day, I got stronger within, more confident about the future,
and more sure about what I wanted to do with my own life
during the next few months; so that I came back here completely refreshed! Officially, the work I did out there was on
behalf of my Commission on Teacher Education; but unoffi-
cially I had a profitable time in Palo Alto sitting in on the

work of the Committee that is directing the New School of the Humanities they have just started there; and if the offer from Stanford finally comes through, there is a good chance that I will go out there for a limited period as a full-fledged professor. It happens that all the work I have been doing on my present book is just so much found gold in relation to the Humanities program; so that lecturing and teaching will not be nearly the distraction from my main work they might otherwise have been. But I won't have any definite news about this till the end of April.

Meanwhile, all that I saw going across the country and on the coast has increased my alarm over what is likely to happen this spring. The country is still not working with the concentration that the immediate dangers we confront command; and instead of raising us to the pitch of effort needed, Roosevelt and his aides have been administering soothing syrup: coddling us into defeat instead of fortifying us sufficiently to ensure victory. Roosevelt has handled the whole forty-hour business as dishonestly as he handled the Supreme Court issue; and if Germany and Japan succeed in doing during the next couple of months what I expect them to do—conquer India and make bold sorties against the whole Pacific coast—the popular reactions against his leadership may become dangerous in the extreme, since it would be used by the traitors and appeasers to promote their own undisguised ends. Once more I hope I am mistaken. Meanwhile I am going back to the preparation of my book, and hope to spend the next couple of months down here, working at that, with a few intervals at Amenia for planting the garden. . . .

Amenia, New York   May 26, 1942

Dear Van Wyck:

The teasing glimpse I got of you at the Academy junket was scarcely better than that I had of Frost before the grand procession began; but I have been wanting to compare notes with you about it. . . . As to the new members and the awards, there was such a distinct improvement that I feel at last driven to make an effort, next year, to see that some of the few remaining neglected ones get into the Institute: Paul, Lee, Waldo, all surely belong there: Alfred Kreymborg, too. Did you hear about the colossal faux pas, or worse, I came near to making that afternoon? The best and strongest page of my whole address was one that I did not give: it cited the Bill of Rights Day radio program as a dreadful example of the vices we are ridden with. As I glanced idly over the program, when I got on the Platform, I noticed that Norman Corwin[8] was getting an award for work done in radio; and some guardian angel—I am sure it was not knowledge—prompted me to ask Canby if Corwin had written the Bill of Rights day program. If I had given that passage, everyone would have regarded it, inevitably, as a malign insult to both Corwin and the Academy; and since I didn't get my speech finished till that very morning and did not send up an advance copy, the circumstantial evidence would have been very strong against me. I escaped that pitfall by the skin of my teeth; and I should have been more chagrined over involving you in the mess than I would have been over my own plight. The Corwin award was, I do believe, a mistake: his stuff is false and flatulent, and doubly bad because it imitates cadences and lifts thoughts from nobler works. But in general the going out to youth was splendid: in a sense, even Bloch,[9] in his sixties, can be included in that category.

[8] Norman Corwin, early experimenter with radio-drama.
[9] Ernest Bloch, musician.

Our plans were at sixes and sevens for many weeks, because the Stanford appointment had not finally come through; but confirmation came ten days ago, and now I am Professor of Humanities with a three year appointment. It is a great challenge, and I leap to it with joy; I only wish that my present book were not an equally great challenge and that I did not have to finish that *and* to block out three new courses before we leave for the West at the beginning of September. Did I tell you anything about the contents of those courses? The first quarter is on The Nature of Man; the second, on the Development of Greek Culture, from Homer to Plutarch and Plotinus; and the third is on The Making of Modern Man. The third is that on which I am best prepared, for it partly corresponds to my present book; and I hope to deal with a succession of Ideal Types, or Archetypal Personalities, from the Christian to the Revolutionary. I have even more than a faint notion of what should go into the second course; for there many other minds have blazed the trail for me, and I am sufficiently saturated in Greece, have been since I was eighteen and read Plato and Zimmern, to make at least a creditable stab at it. But the first course—that is a poser. One's temptation is to treat the contents of it scientifically, to give a second hand report about what the biologist and the anthropologist and the sociologist and the psychologist have said about man's constitution. But to treat the whole subject from the standpoint of the humanities is to throw it into a quite different focus. Has anyone done it yet?

Have you any hints or suggestions? I want to deal with the role of religion, ethics, philosophy, literature, art, drama, and music, and I at first thought of doing this largely by means of original texts; but I don't believe that this can be done in twenty lectures; and so I must find some other way of tackling it. If you have a glimmer of inspiration, please pass it on; I will need every crack of light I can get. My last days in New York—I came up here on Sunday, after three days chasing wild geese in Washington—were spent at the Library reading Calvin's *Institutes of the Christian Religion:* a book well worth study. An unpleasing character but a remarkable mind; and I thank my stars that our country grew up under his guidance rather than Luther's, for the mixed form of government, which the fathers of the constitution so carefully wrought, corresponds exactly to his conception.

Westport, Connecticut   May 31, 1942

Dear Lewis:

. . . I thought your speech was grand and I am eager to see it again in print. As for Norman Corwin, that was a lucky escape, no doubt, but, although I probably should have known, I actually knew nothing of Corwin, nor do I know now who he is—or what award he got if he got one. I guess I must have been thinking of something else!

But now about the news of the Stanford appointment, you can just guess how happy I am to hear it, and all the more because it seems probable now that we shall be following you to California in October. In the probable absence of fuel-oil we can scarcely inhabit our house, and we are eager to see our grandson,—now two years old, and we have not had a glimpse of him. So, if other things are equal, we shall certainly make the long trek, and you know we have always thought of ourselves as half-Californians, since we were married at Carmel and lived there four years. We are both homesick for it and haven't seen it for 20 years. . . . For the atmosphere out there is so totally different, or, rather, I mean the circumstances. You really cast off a hundred and one responsibilities when you leave this part of the country (I find that I'm actually a member of 9 committees!), and seeing friends, so impossible here because of the pressure of living, is something that really happens in that blessed region. Here I am jealous of every hour, and all the more if we're going away, because I'm so eager to get my reading done. My book[10] has been going like a dream for the last three months, and I can get this reading all done by October. . . .

Meanwhile, about your book and all the thrilling questions you raise, I must look to you for my education. I doubt if I can offer you any suggestions, though much would come up if we could *talk,*—and in California we can surely do so. You don't know what I would give for an afternoon at Stanford, which I used to know so well and where I suppose we probably still have friends.

About the Institute, it is indeed looking up, but because the candidates are seriously discussed; and there is little use in making nominations unless one is prepared to speak up for them. They are discussed at one of the fall meetings, and this discussion settles each question and it works! Of the last five elected, I nominated four and got them elected by arguing for them. It is the only way in the new system. . . . A candidate has twice as good a chance if he has a new book before the public. There are many new and unusual talents in the country now. But I doubt if anyone can be elected unless there is someone present to speak up for him.

Amenia, New York   July 12, 1942

Yesterday, dear Van Wyck, I finished my book,[11] or rather the second draft of it: thus averting the very real possibility that the book might finish me. I drove myself at an inhuman pace; but now I can be sure, as I was not when I finished the

10 *The World of Washington Irving.*
11 *The Condition of Man* (1944).

first draft, that I really have a book: something that holds together and makes sense: a book that, with a little more brooding and nursing, I could probably get ready for the printer with a month's actual work. I am glad to be able to lay it aside again for a decent period; for I will not return to it, probably, till the Christmas vacation, possibly not till that in spring.

Its publication can wait: the spring of 1944 will probably be the earliest date, and 1948 would not surprise me as an alternative; for I am perturbed at the lack of grip and toughness and relentless energy that both Washington and London reveal: "the corruption of liberalism" was no local phenomenon, but the general disease from which our civilization was dying. If I had suspected how deep it went, I would have given up all thought of pursuing my literary career in 1937 and turned seriously to politics: because it is for lack of political fortitude that we are now in such a desperate condition. But it is too late for tears; and it is probably good for me that in this juncture, instead of eating my heart out, I can push on with a quite different kind of task: that of giving the young the vision and discipline they will need to lift themselves out of the muck and the chaos that their easy-going elders have created. . . . California may be that dreamed of heaven where you and I will lie on a cloud and discourse at our soul's ease; but I hardly dare believe it; and at all events, though it is great news to hear that you and Eleanor will be coming out there next winter, I want at least a few hours of seeing you and looking at you before I go. The village school teacher, about to be married, will probably take over our house while we are gone; and our Lares and Penates will rest a little easier if that happens; but I've found myself, all this early summer, going about with an elegiac feeling, as if I had to see for the last time, and take in completely and intensely, something I might never see again: a feeling that alternates with visions of returning, say five years hence, to a wilderness of burdock and mullein and wild grape, where once order had reigned.

I have been using my spare moments to put my monstrous accumulations of letters, manuscripts, notes, memoranda, and what not in order; and of course that has only added a little to the dismal hollow feeling. It is curious to compare this mood with the quite desperate sense I had of the future in June 1940. At that time, before England had shown her latent courage and spiritual hardihood, our prospects for survival seemed so bad that to pay the slightest attention to what might become of my manuscripts seemed to me a sign of mental weakness: my past never played a smaller part in my current life or my calculations than they did then—and if England *had* gone under, I am sure my reactions would have been right. Now our situation is, despite all the setbacks of the last six months, and all the probable setbacks of the next six, less terrible than it was then; but in the meanwhile I have had a chance to gauge the inertia, the callowness, and the pitiful weakness—what Waldo calls sleaziness—of our leaders, and I have less hopes for either a good ending or a gallant recovery than I had in that blacker period. . . .

Amenia, New York   August 5, 1942

Dear Van Wyck:

. . . For the last dozen years, I have warned young writers regularly not to plunge into new work until they have had a chance to recuperate from the book they have done; and now I am under the necessity of giving the same good advice to myself. I rejoice in the news that your own book goes forward: there seems but a handful of us who realize the importance of what we are doing and the necessity of keeping on with it; and if I even half earn your confidence, dear Van Wyck, I shall consider myself a fortunate man. Your words made me come back to America when I read them in London in 1920; though they were written in the *Freeman* they seemed directed personally at me, and I can still remember the train journey from London to Scarborough on which I read them and realized that they settled my fate for me and made only one decision possible: to return. Ever since then, at intervals, I have gotten my own bearings by taking you as a fixed landmark, as a sailor takes a church tower when he is standing off from a shore and must fasten to some durable landmark in order to be sure he avoids the rocks. Like you, I have at last discovered where all my preliminary explorations lead to, and I only hope the world spares both of us long enough for us to leave the mark we are now prepared to make. Already, we have been luckier than was poor Constance Rourke, who took too long in assembling her material before setting to work on it; and at the moment I am temporarily depressed because I realize that on my present book I became the victim of the same weakness, with the result that even in my second draft I have not yet shaken myself free of the preparatory research sufficiently to be able to handle it freely and imaginatively: so that all the good work I spent on it this last year, if not wasted, at all events will not come to anything until I have another year of brooding and reflection to counterbalance the three years of assiduous reading and analysis. The fact that during the last fortnight I have cast aside the illusion that I was "practically finished with the book" has only made me, for the moment, a little more tired.

P.S. What a brave fellow Waldo has been again: I am proud of him and think the country should be proud, too. I wonder how well our wishy-washy State Department is backing him up.

Westport, Connecticut   August 9, 1942

Dear Lewis:

The books have come and many thanks. I had forgotten all
about them—and I was delighted with your letter to John
Chamberlain.[12] (It goes into my archives.) I had been struck

12 Full text of the letter to John Chamberlain:

Amenia, New York   August 6, 1942

Dear John Chamberlain:
I was delighted with your warm-hearted and generous appreciation of
Constance Rourke's book: you did justice to a writer whose work was
always rather under-valued; so much so that it took endless struggles to
get any of the foundations to give her even a modest backing for the
writing of the now-unwritten book.
But in giving her the praise that is due her and more than due her, you
fell quite naturally into an error which I am tempted, for the sake of
history, to correct: this has to do with her influence upon Brooks. He had
known her back in the *Freeman* days, if not before, and when he was at
Harcourt's he was zealous in getting them to take her first book (*Trum-
pets of Jubilee*). That came out in 1927; and if one didn't check oneself on
dates one might easily take Brooks' affirmative attitude toward American
culture as the result in part of this and later books by Constance Rourke. I
have no doubt that he was affected by her, as was I: we all maintained a
fairly close relationship by correspondence. But the fact is it was not Miss
Rourke, but Emerson, that effected the great change in Brooks: it was in
the midst of writing the *Emerson* in 1925 and 1926 that he fell in love
with America, as his letters to me then, ecstatic, glowing letters, plainly
show.
In giving Constance Rourke a formative part in Brooks' change you
have merely overlooked the actual dates. But I think you do something a
little less just in your suggestion that she turned "the Brooks-Mumford
generation from an increasingly sterile pre-occupation with American
artistic failure"—at least if by that you mean Brooks and Mumford
themselves. It is probably a long time since you looked at *The Golden Day*
(published in 1926—a year before C.R.'s first), and the chances are ten to
one that you remember it, not for what it was, but for what unsympathetic critics like Farrell and DeVoto have sought to make of it. If that can
happen to you, dear John, it must be even more true for the young who
have never even heard of *The Golden Day;* and for that reason I call your
attention to the injustice of this sentence.
The Golden Day is not preoccupied with American artistic failure: its
central chapters are devoted to just the opposite theme, to an unqualified

by his very loose statements but supposed it came from his writing in a hurry. Of course Constance Rourke did not influence either of us, though she was a fine companion on the way. My own reorientation came with my breakdown, when I cleared a huge neurosis out of my system, and recovered my original temperament, which was not "recessive." As for your dates, they are clear, and you are perfectly right in saying that *The Golden Day* was the first book in the positive line that we have followed since. You found Emerson, Cooper and Haw-

---

assertion that the great writers of America were among the giants of world literature and in some ways had gone farther than any other group of writers in Europe. I did not get this perception from Constance Rourke, whom I barely knew at the time: I got it directly from my own reading and my own experience of life. As a sailor in the navy I had carried Emerson in my middy blouse, and as a lad of nineteen, three years before, I had bayed Whitman's verses to the sands at Ogunquit: Cooper and Hawthorne were part of my living consciousness from Childhood.

Though I think I understand and would even justify Brooks' negative feeling, in his early essays, toward the great American writers of *The Golden Day*, I never shared it; and you will find, if you should dip into critical literature for the twenty years before *The Golden Day*, that this is the first large affirmative expression of interest and pride in what we had done, apart from parts of Frank's *Our America*. Brooks and I did not affect each other directly during 1926; but during that year we found ourselves paralleling each other, in the course of our natural growth. Even on the interpretation of the pioneer and the puritan you will find, in the face of De Voto, that I gave full credit to the positive elements in their characters: note the passage on pages 65 and 66. In her *Audubon* Constance Rourke paid tribute to my interpretation of the effect of terror and cruelty on the imagination of the pioneer generation; and in alluding to De Voto's remarks on the absence of sex themes in Mark Twain, you are only picking up a thread I had dropped in tieing up Paul Bunyan and Walt Whitman. Rereading *The Golden Day* recently, I have been struck once more with how little I would change—although much has been uncovered during the last fifteen years that I would be happy to add. I don't object to your taking De Voto at his own self-evaluation; but I do object to your following him blindly in your references to me. By now you probably believe that I was one of the querulous, nay-saying spirits of the 1920's. Constance Rourke, who backed me up in 1938 on my publication of *Men Must Act*, when all the clever people knew I had gone crazy, never made that mistake about my contributions to our cultural history.

thorne long before I did; in fact, I had read them only in a perfunctory way in 1925 or '26. All my early positive influences were quite remote from America although the theme of America obsessed me from the first. All these matters become very interesting when we see them in perspective but I never could see this popular notion of a "Brooks-Mumford school." Who started it? What does it mean? Has it any basis? I think not. I have felt for years now very much closer to you than to any six other American writers, yet we've always worked in strictly *parallel* lines. As for our friend De Voto, I really doubt if in the end he will appear to have made any contribution.

Do you mean to live *steadily* in the West for the next few years? Of course, if you do, we shall soon be out—if not this year, next year—still, I shall feel exiled here without you. On the other hand, perhaps California would be just the place to live for a while. I am sick with curiosity to see it, and Lee said the other day that he would throw everything up for a chance to go and live there for good.

Westport, Connecticut   August 27, 1942

Dear Lewis:

So many thanks for sending me your pamphlet on the new school, which is truly stirring. I can see how symptomatic and timely it is at the moment, and no doubt California is just the place for it. I remember when Alfred Zimmern came to see us there, when we first met in 1913. He was just off the ship from Greece and he stayed with us at Palo Alto, full of the striking resemblance between Greece and California. Everything, he said, seemed alike!—the bare hills, the wild flowers, the air and the handsome young people; and I am sure that in these thirty years all manner of exciting things have developed in the *foreground*. Then it seemed only a *background*. And now,

with our new feeling for the planet as a whole, it means much
to be facing the Orient as they do out there. Your new school
somehow reminds one of John Davidson[13] and his hopes, and
I trust you will not suffer from the jealousy of professors. Also
that you will not have too much administrative work. But you
will know how to keep out of these professional pitfalls.

By the way, have you seen Nehru's *Glimpses of World
History?* It is elementary, of course; yet it gives one an extraordinary feeling of the planet as a whole, with Europe only
a peninsula sticking out from Asia. It might be worth recommending to some of your students. (Thanks, too, for the fine
review of Constance Rourke's book, which I picked up at
Brentano's, a burning wick in the tallow of the *Saturday
Review*.)

694 Alvarado Row
Stanford University, California   [September, 1942]

Dear Van Wyck:
. . . My first lecture went well; the students have flocked
around; and, though there is an outer fringe of antagonism
and suspicion in academic circles here, it has been more than
overcome by the cordiality, the friendliness, and the helpful-
ness of both faculty and students. My days are committee
bound and pretty monotonous: apart from a couple of picnics,
"enjoyed" while we were still under a heavy strain, we have
seen nothing of the surrounding country. . . .

What probably appals us more than anything is the suburban respectability of these immediate surroundings. Stanford itself is surpassingly beautiful; but this residential section, though near to the open fields, is smugly, elegantly

13 John Davidson: perhaps Thomas Davidson, founder of the Fabian
Society.

suburban, like the garden; and we all rebel against that, as being foreign to our nature and what is worse now, representing a distasteful and outmoded standard of living. You can't think with what sadistic satisfaction we ordered the gardener, who willy nilly goes with this place, to dig up some ugly annuals and prepare the soil for a vegetable patch, which I have just planted. We have a deciduous oak tree on our side lawn that has turned a rich crimson during these last three weeks and has made us very homesick; the plane trees and the elms are yellowing slowly, too; and the poplars are quite vividly yellow; but otherwise the climate remains the same: tropical at noon and Londonish at night. I have had no intimate contact with the students yet; there is of course a disproportionately large number of girls; but the class, which began with 85, has risen to a hundred, so it would seem that the course we are offering has something for which the students have been looking. My real task is to persuade my colleagues to break their comfortable academic mold; and that is a harder job.

Geddes had a stiff summer of ranching. . . . It is good to have us with him again, however; indeed these days, weeks, and months, precious in any case, are doubly so because he has been so long away from home that we have long arrears of time to make up for; and in his relaxed moments he is exceedingly charming, and I think he has enjoyed the experience almost as much as we have. . . .

Westport, Connecticut   November 9, 1942

Dear Lewis:

How I wish now that we could join you all at Stanford, as I'm confident we shall if you stay. It doesn't sound like old times there with "residential sections" and (as you give it) a

hovering aroma of Scarsdale. It was still somehow idyllic when
we were there, with picnics under the eucalyptus and old
ranch-houses half-decayed and a faint fragrance still lingering
from the Spanish days. . . .

I was a little afraid of the jealousy of some of the faculty,
who have their own peculiar kind of neuroses. But you have
certainly started with a bang if your class has risen to a
hundred students. I'm only wondering now what will become
of the men when they begin to draft the 18-year olds. I dread
the committee-business for you too. But there must be all sorts
of compensations that you would not find in an Eastern
college, and I can't wait to see you in this new incarnation.

Here winter is really setting in and we long for a taste of
California, though we may have a few months of New York
instead. I rather hope so, for we are isolated here with
everyone afraid to use a car. However, Lee was here yesterday
and last week the Maxwell Geismars[14] came up from
Mamaroneck and spent a day. They are charming young
people, eager and intelligent and Geismar has made a mighty
impression on me. I don't know whether you got round to
reading his *Writers in Crisis,* but he is something quite special
in the critical way. He is working on a second series of essays
on the novelists of the Dreiser–Anderson time. He is a very
slow worker and spends two months over one of these papers,
and I hope he has some little income of his own for I think he
has a rare talent and shouldn't be harried and hurried,
though he certainly *thinks* better than he *writes.*

Lee is in a conquering mood and says it's too good to be
true (as I hope it isn't), for he paints better than he ever did,
speaks better French than ever, has the whole plan of his book
clear in his mind, and he is producing besides a play that is
going to make his fortune and has two other small books
almost finished. I never saw anyone so on the top of the wave,

14 Maxwell Geismar, literary critic and historian.

and, what's more, I think he is going to stay there. He has got hold of all his vitality and knows how to keep it and use it, or at least I really think he has, for keeps. I went in two or three weeks ago to a dinner he gave for Louis Untermeyer to celebrate a new anthology. It was a grand party—with champagne flowing from the faucets and I looked around for Madame Recamier. Then I went to another dinner for Waldo; to celebrate his return from Argentina. There were six or seven hundred there, with six or seven speakers, including me, del Vago and Charlie Chaplin! I sat beside the latter and had an amusing talk with him, and such inexhaustible energy I never did see. After the dinner we got a little room, with Jo Davidson and Art Young, and consumed a pile of sandwiches and several pitchers of Ballantine's beer, with Charlie Chaplin acting all round the table. He was just getting started at 11:45 when I had to leave to catch a train. Waldo spoke wonderfully well and had a great reception, though I know he is saddened and puzzled by the general indifference to him here. And it's nine-tenths the result of his mannered style, which I can't feel easy with either. He has gone away to write a new book on South America and perhaps prepare another book of his speeches.

For a little more gossip, we met the Kreymborgs at the Soviet–American Congress last week—exactly as they were ten years ago. Alfred was the delegate of the Poetry Society and I of the Authors' League; and we heard a really superb speech from Senator Pepper, a first-rate man, whom I shall watch, as you must, in the future. A strongly marked Southerner, with the deep South written all over him, and a statesman of real calibre, intellect and heart. I have seldom been so moved by any speaker, and I hope he will [have] something to say when it comes to making peace. . . .

My book *drags*, but I do my page every day, only I fear that this time it is going to be dull. Most of those early writers are so thin and pale that I am at my wit's end breathing life into them. However, that remains to be seen.

P.S. Walter and Magna tell us they are having glorious times in Mexico and seeing much of Diego Rivera.

School of Humanities
Stanford University, California   January 1, 1943

Happy New Year to you and Eleanor and your children and grandchildren, visible and yet to come—dear Van Wyck. . . . Your homesickness for Amenia and for your friends in the East may be destined to be removed at a much earlier date than seemed possible a little while ago; for the Army program for technical training is bound to wipe out most of the liberal arts program; and even the students under eighteen will probably sidestep what I have to offer. If by March it looks as if we would not have enough students to be worth staying here for I shall probably apply for a leave of absence for duration of war. Please keep this last item confidential. I am not quite as sad-faced over all this as I might be; looking backward I can now see that I was foolish to come out here last September instead of giving myself and the school six months more time for preparation. We might not have gotten started at all, as things stand now; but that would hardly have been worse than a false start, and in the meantime, if we had gone on, we would have had a better chance to pick a good staff. . . .

I don't think I shall ever quite lose my heart to California, or lose the sense that Amenia, or at least Northern New England and Dutchess County are my real home: at forty-seven a voluntary exile, to be tolerable, must also be a short one: at least for me! But this change of scene has other good things to its credit, despite all the harassments: I now see my ms. in better perspective and have a pretty sure sense of what must be done to it to make it the book I had originally planned: to this end, my lectures have been a great help. What I really object to about teaching right now is that I am forced to prepare my lectures on a week to week basis, without having had a year's preparation: hence I feel like Eliza on the ice-floes with the hounds' breath uncomfortably near my ear. Another year, it will be different. My giving the course on Greek Civilization which opens next week will be nothing short of impudence: I tremble at my own audacity, because I simply am not sufficiently saturated in the material—though occasionally I have a glimpse of something that will not perhaps be found already in the books, as in my perception that the Greek character, with its overemphasis of the rational, is defined in its three great heroes: Odysseus, Prometheus, and Socrates. One other effect of teaching is also good: it keeps my mind temporarily away from the war, and gives me a chance, I trust, to store up a little strength against the day when it will be profitable to talk it out again. . . .

For a time I had a bad conscience over the fact that I, who had put all efforts into making people face the inevitableness of the war, had taken so small a part in the actual organization of our military effort; but as time goes on I get more and more reconciled to this passive and apparently impotent role; for the more deeply we become engrossed in fighting, the more likelihood there is that the wolves, the vultures, and the jackals will come out on top again, unless there are dozens of independent people left, like you or me, to speak up once more on behalf of the things we are fighting for. I am carefully hoarding my own ammunition for the moment when I will be in a position to deliver a broadside: that is why I have taken no pot-shots at the administration's weaknesses, though I have occasionally written a private letter to MacLeish or Frankfurter or Elmer Davis to let them know how a friend of the government feels and thinks about its actual conduct of policy.

How does your book go now? And where do you expect to be next June when, if my plans go forward, we hope to be moving back East? . . . .

Stanford University, California   February 13, 1943

Dear, dear Van Wyck:

The grievous news in your letter[15] was a stab in my own heart; and I hope and pray that, now the fear of God has been drummed into you, you will gain a new lease on life through this premonitory accident. The main thing is quiet and moderation in everything: probably you would do well to take the advice the wise old Baltimore physician I must have told you about, a pupil of Osler's, gave me: namely, to spend at least two or three days every month in bed, to give oneself a complete rest. It will add years to your usefulness and length of life, he told me. Maybe Mark Twain had discovered this principle for himself, when he spent so much of his time in bed. You simply can't over-exert yourself too much when you are lying on your back. . . .

I am champing at the bit in my eagerness to get back to my book, for I have at least discovered the central theme of it, which I almost muffed in my preoccupation with details; and I want to spend three or four months re-writing it, above all simplifying it and developing more clearly my own contribution. How easy it is to become a victim of one's own industry or of one's own pride of acquisition: to depend too much on one's notes, to get smothered in details, and to forget the deeper more important things that oneself alone can say, and

15 A minor heart attack.

that all the pack-donkeys of scholarship would never, with all their diligence, even get a smell of. In preparing this new book I have made all the possible errors one can make in letting facts take precedence of ideas; and now I want to rectify this mistake and turn out the real book. . . . There are moments this winter when life itself has seemed one long chronic ailment: but of course I know better. What is one's philosophy for except to tide one over these moments? Having the Greeks at one's elbow this spring quarter has been a blessing: particularly Hesiod and Aeschylus. Some of my lectures have been thin and weak; but occasionally I have given one, on Tragedy, and on the Greek polis, that was adequate enough to make me sorry I have not had time to make adequate notes of the lectures, to say nothing of writing them out.

Your being in Tudor City brings you and Eleanor very near, somehow; for when I was living up in the country and attending the meetings of the Board of Higher Education and writing *The New Yorker* art reviews, I used to camp in the Hotel Tudor regularly; and those windy open spaces and high eerie vistas have become an indelible part of my New York background: though the WPA workers have vanished from East 42 Street. What a mess you must have gone through this winter in Westport: no wonder it brought you low. It was probably more of a strain than you suspected. I am full of misgiving over Roosevelt's and Hull's policy in North Africa: it is capable of undermining the very basis of peace, for it will help establish Catholic fascism in both Europe and South America, as the legitimate successor of Nazism—and heaven help all we have dreamt of and sweated for then: I wish a more persuasive tongue than mine could bring Roosevelt to his senses; but if it does not attempt to, I shall be driven to make an attempt by the end of spring.

321 East 43rd Street
New York, N.Y. (until April 5th)   March 13, 1943

Dear Lewis:

You were still doubtful, when you wrote, about your plans for returning home and whether or not the army-training might perhaps involve you. Of course I long to have you back again in June, but I have such happy memories of California that I also long to have you see it at its best. You have seen too many of the drawbacks of it.

As for myself, the disability never returned, and they say it may never return or not for years; and meanwhile the cutting out of smoking and the cutting *down* of food have raised my physical tone a hundred points. I never felt better, never did better work than I'm doing, and never had such a sinfully good time, for, when I stop to think, it seems positively wicked to enjoy life in war-time as I am doing. Yet the cause of this enjoyment is nothing more than innocent talk with a great number of good people, old friends and new *young folks* who have delighted me with their spirit and with whom I feel ten miles more congenial than I felt with the "post-war" question. (Odd to think that is *your* generation, as well as Dos Passos's and Edmund Wilson's—those permanently negative and slightly cynical minds.) Of those, besides Maxwell Geismar, I have seen a number, and they're so reassuring with their faith in fundamentals and such a fund of pure good will. We've dined with enough of them to give me a taste of the new generation which I was predisposed to believe in and find altogether delightful. We've also seen Robt. Frost three times, the Ralph Bates,[16] Hamilton Basso, the Third,[17] and (a dozen times) Jo Davidson.[18] The latter I had not seen for 28 years (when we saw each other every day in London) and we

---

[16] Ralph Bates, British writer.
[17] Hamilton Basso, novelist and biographer.
[18] Jo Davidson, sculptor.

fell into each other's arms and have stayed there ever since. I don't know whether you know him but you would love him. Then we've dined with Paul twice and find him in good form and keen to talk about his present work, a sort of auto-biography;[19] and Lee was here yesterday and read aloud to me two hours. By all odds the best thing he has ever written.[20] It is a group of discursive essays, reminiscent and critical, to serve as text with the photographs of 90 of his settings. The book, to appear in May, will be a triumph, and what pleases me is that Lee has struck an even keel at last and seems to have got out of both his manic and depressive phases.

We have not seen Waldo since he set out on his southern tour—and I dare say he has been with you in Palo Alto. I could write a dithyrambic poem about our N.Y. life. I had forgotten all the wonders of it, and now I'm determined that we'll have no more country winters, which seem to me both positively and negatively so wasteful. (I mean when your life begins to be short, and you have to choose between pictures and talk *and* chores.) We have kept rather late hours for me, and it's been a continuous picnic, but we are going home in 3 weeks with a prospect dull enough to make up for it: no cook (presumably), no gas for driving, no food to offer friends— and therefore solitude and silence. Not that I mind in the least. My work continues to go well, and it is fun to think that we shall be finishing our books perhaps together.

Stanford University, California   May 12, 1943

Dear Van Wyck:

Three or four weeks spent in writing regularly every morn- ing did more for my health and general happiness than all the

19 This was never completed.
20 *Part of a Lifetime: Drawings and Designs, 1919–1940.*

doctors in the world could have done: no small part of my malaise and fretfulness all winter has been due to the fact that I have been absent from my desk. That is fatal to me: that is, in fact, why I shall never be a professor, even though my colleagues should hail my success at the job. Now that I have almost a year's distance from my manuscript I can see how good it was, in essentials, and I am less daunted by the problem of re-writing it than I was when I put it temporarily behind me. . . .

I have received a leave of absence from June to January and shall spend it in Amenia. In January, I come back here to teach a course on World Unification in the army school and to take part in the planning of the post-war curriculum. That will settle me for the duration, I am afraid, except perhaps for a trip to England, to consult with various authorities there on the rebuilding of Britain! (That invitation just came through from an old associate of mine, Farquharson, with whom I gave a course on the Principles of Social Reconstruction at High Wycombe in 1920. I am excited by that prospect) . . . .

Westport, Connecticut   May 20, 1943

Dear Lewis:

Your arrangements for the future seem very happy—both the return to Stanford in January and the journey to England. You will be dealing in both with *ultimate* things, and this atmosphere of the essential and general is bound to stir your imagination. I have distrusted your giving so much of your energy to other work than writing, and how good it is to hear that you'll have six months for the book. I am sure you will finish it and that it will be superb.

I am getting on well and hope to finish by October. We are living in all but absolute solitude and might be on Mount

Ararat for all the people we see. But Westport no longer seems to attract me as Amenia attracts you, and I fear that New York has completely spoiled me. It has taken me back to the feeling of my twenties,—that only life in cities is the life for me. But of course any life is good that enables one to work.

Amenia, New York   July 30, 1943

Dear Van Wyck:
    The days have glided through my hands like quicksilver: but yesterday I was spading the garden and today the string beans are ready for picking and the cabbage almost headed: but a minute ago I was sifting through old notes and resurrecting forgotten portions of Draft I, now I am almost half way through the final re-writing, moving as confidently through the water as a tug-boat pulling an ocean liner behind her: at an even pace, unpressed by time, with plenty of assurance that, barring accidents, I will have both plenty of steam and plenty of time left when I am finished.
    The book has made the homecoming marvellous; and the homecoming has helped the book: as for me, I feel sounder and fitter than I have felt for a good five years or more; so that all this blessed news from Italy seems merely like a belated echo of a freedom and a hope I had achieved within myself. The book will be the better because the spectres that prompted it and that accompanied it, through the early stages, may be fading into the light of common day by the time I reach the final chapter: not banished for good and all, not completely eliminated, but at least reduced to human dimensions, instead of threatening to cover the world with poison and wrath like some evil genius out of the Arabian Nights. Our place here showed little signs of the terrible winter: only two bushes, Kolkwitzias, lost, but to offset that minor mischief,

some of the bushes and trees that had been doing poorly were shocked into a more intense life. Sophy, though she has had a backbreaking household on her shoulders, is better than she has been for many a year; her old reserves of energy seem to be building up again; and we both have been so warmed by the cordiality of our old country neighbors that California is no longer a problem to us: we know that for good and all our die is cast here. Alison and Geddes both share this feeling: for Geddes had two weeks up here before—ten days ago—he left for the Army; and the taste of his old fishing and hunting haunts, the greeting that even the old men gave him, gave a sweetness to all his memories here, at the very parting of the ways; . . . Whatever happens, we have all come to the end of a definite period as a family; and he knows that as well as we do. Coming back here and putting on my harness made me realize at once that there is no comparison between a professor's life and a writer's one: I had rather live lean in the latter state than wax fat in the former. The only thing that mars the news from Italy is the apparent fact that Roosevelt, with a terrible consistency he has shown no where else, is ready to follow up his African policy with an even more fatal deal with the Darlans of Italy, abetted by the house of Savoy, and excused over here on the ground that it will "save American lives." His speech the other night does not allay my suspicions: for I have learned to watch his actions, not listen to his words; . . .

The Italians did not perhaps descend to the German level of baseness and servility; but there was enough popular fascism to warn us against accepting at face value the overnight democrats that will soon be popping up there, as saviors of the people and allies of the United Nations. In our impatience to win the war, we will be like a clumsy surgeon who removes the visible tonsils and lets the roots remain, to grow again worse than ever.

The Conference on Science, Philosophy and Religion

tempts me this year; if I can possibly manage to, I hope to be down for the Friday and Saturday sessions; but alas! I must say No to the informal meeting you are arranging on Thursday, though the very fact that you are arranging it makes me want very much to attend it. . . .

If all goes well my book should be finished between 1 and 15 October. What about yours? We must arrange for a meeting to celebrate their completion!

[September, 1943]
Westport, Connecticut   Friday

Dear Lewis:

Your good letter warmed my heart, and we were both so happy to hear that all goes well with you. I wish I could send you an equally cheerful report, but the devil has got into me this summer, and after swimming along with my book, which had entered the home-stretch, I became suddenly mentally muscle-bound. I've been going round in circles for weeks, as far from the end as ever, but things will probably straighten out and what I have done I think is good. I discovered a few points about the "Southern mind" that are wholly new, I believe. The Southern critics are always saying that the South has been ignored, but it has never occurred to them to do their own spadework. I shall never finish by October 15th, but shall always be ready to celebrate anything with you.

As for the Conference luncheon, I shall probably give it up, because there have been eight refusals. I had grave doubts about it anyway, but Finkelstein's heart was set on it and I am so fond of him that I went ahead against my better judgment. Writers will not come to these academic festas, and anyway I am quite sure that the upshot would have been something quite alien to the purpose of the Conference. As *their* contribution to an enduring peace, the writers could only have agreed on some kind of programme of revolution. And that would scarcely have been a thing for the Conference to sponsor. . . . Perhaps I made a mistake in arranging such an ill-assorted list. I thought they would all agree that writers could do *something* and that because the theme is vague the more they differed among themselves the more they might turn up concrete suggestions.

I won't say anything about the war, but I am haunted by a feeling that we are headed for a sadly disillusioning peace. There isn't a statesman big enough in the US or England. And there never was a time when the whole world was more plastic. Something really tremendous might be done. Personally I would rather see Willkie making the peace (on the basis of *One World*) than the obviously tired and cynical FDR. But as for Italy, I was struck by something I saw of Walter Lippmann's, that whatever govt. makes peace there will be discredited by events and therefore it would be better to have the underground come in *after* the dirty preliminary work of getting the Germans out of the country had already been performed by some makeshift group.

Amenia, New York   October 24, 1943

Dear Van Wyck:

I handed in my manuscript the third of October, as I had promised both Morley and myself. . . . The book as a whole, however, is pretty solid, I think; and if I didn't know you were probably in the throes of a similar effort now, I would beg and beseech you to read it in galleys, so that I might have your balanced judgement and insight to guide me in places where I cannot be altogether sure whether I have hit the mark or overshot it. I have had something of a problem to suppress my very pessimistic view of the present sufficiently to permit my fairly hopeful vision of a farther future to come out: I could not repress it altogether without being false to myself, nor permit it to come out with full force lest it obscure the only thing that will be left to any of us when the war is over: hope. That has been a very delicate problem. I have borne in mind all along your very just criticism of *The Culture of Cities:* its too technical and specialized language; and I think I have mastered that weakness in *The Condition of Man,* partly because the nature of the material made it more easy. (Dare I say something now that I felt when *Indian Summer* came out but withheld because it was a minor item; and that is to pray you either to leave out footnotes or to put them at the end of the book. They are terrible distractions; and sometimes they are only a sop to people whom you are in a position to ignore!) I have seen no one all these long months since coming home: not even Paul. Lee I met by chance the last afternoon I was in New York, while I was scouting around for illustrations for my book: we had a doleful half hour together, for he is alas! in a pretty bad mood, not made less desperate by the fact that he has a very clear and objective picture of himself now, and I lacked the resources in myself at the time to cheer him up or to make him see all the brighter sides to both his life as a whole and his immediate situation. I came back here with the thought of seeing a dozen people, and especially, of all people, yourself, dear van Wyck. . . .

According to our present plans we will return to Stanford at the end of December and stay there till June. . . . My reading dropped almost to zero as the summer drew to a close, for the mere act of typewriting my 215,000 words put a strain on my eyes; but for the last couple of weeks I've had time to read for the first time in years it seems, for sheer, indolent, self-indulgent pleasure; and that has helped to relax the tension. Some of the essays in D. H. Lawrence's *Phoenix* gave me great pleasure; for his tastes and instincts were often quite sound,

sounder than his conscious expression of them; and there is
one essay in that book, a letter on Germany he wrote in 1924,
interpreting the turning of the German soul back to its bar-
baric past *at that moment*—the moment when everyone was
talking about Germany in just the opposite terms, as with the
Locarno agreements, that makes the shivers run up and down
one's spine, so deeply right have his intuitions proved.

Chatham, New York   October 29, 1943
[From Mumford]

You've brought it on yourself: I am sending herewith the
first slice of my book—one of those Swedish hors d'oeuvres
that completely destroys the appetite! Please criticize it
ruthlessly: I have time to make drastic revisions.

Westport, Connecticut   November 7, 1943

Dear Lewis:
I'm returning the first 43 galleys today. It is truly magnificent, and you couldn't have thought seriously that I
would have any suggestions to make (except a few indications
of printers' errors) or any feeling in reading it but excitement,
awe and gratitude. All I want is More, more, and I hope to
find more at the post-office, for of course it grows more exciting
with every galley, and as you are certainly dealing with the
most important of all subjects, and your treatment is important as well as your theme, the book should lead all others in
1944. It has the spaciousness of Taine and the great 19th
century men, and it strikes me as absolutely masterly thus far.
The style, too, is moving and flexible, always concrete, with a

powerful flow, with something impressively massive as it carries one forward, and I am astounded by your classical and
historical learning. You have rung all the bells this time, but I
wish I could see it all at once. However I'm grateful to have it
in any form. Just let me have more, more and as much as you
can.

I should have sent it back sooner, but I have had to fit it in
with a good deal of final reading for my own book, I have only
a few days' work to do on this and was hoping to finish it
before we go to town. This isn't quite possible, but I'll turn in
the MS this month, and I think it is fully as good as either of
my New England books. (With much more of the nature of
discovery in it, of course.) . . .

I am dreadfully sorry that you have all been ill, but there
are truly no signs of haste in your MS, which suggests an
amplitude of learned leisure and all the tranquillity of Gibbon. I can't imagine any rewriting in these opening 43 galleys.

This is a very jerky letter, and I don't know where I am, but
let me say right now that I'm ever so glad you are going back
to Stanford only for the spring. Life is too short for you not to
be writing all the time, and there must be for you much waste
of energy in teaching. . . .

Did I say we are going to town next week Monday or
Tuesday. We are to be at 307 East 44th St., but it would be
better not to use this address until you hear from me again. I
read all your letters aloud to E. except the part about my *notes*,
for that is a sore matter between us. She agrees with you, but I
cannot (for positively *mystical* reasons). My publishers ob-
jected too at first and loudly, but there seem to be as many
readers who agree with me as those who feel that the notes are
too distracting. Anyway, on that head, after long ponderings
and arguments, I take my final stand on the precedent of
Gibbon who has even more notes of the same kind than I and
who is yet popularly reprinted every year.

Amenia, New York   November 9, 1943

Dear Van Wyck:

Your letter was like a great glass of sparkling wine at the
end of a tiring journey: I once had such a glass when I came
to Berlin and know how it tasted. Even when I allow fully
for your usual generosity and sympathy, I am greatly elated
over your words about *The Condition of Man:* not less
because they openly support my own secret sense, as I read
these galleys, that almost in spite of myself I have written
the sort of book I should have wanted to write for these times.
I am afraid that it is too overloaded with learning to be what I
originally wanted it to be; yet part of its impact is derived
from that kind of authority, which our age still respects; and if
the book were but half its present size—as I was often tempted
to make it—it would have but half its weight and convince
only those who were already more than half convinced. I hope
the last three-quarters of the book lives up to your expecta-
tions: perhaps it will—though I am still wrestling with the
problem of the introduction, which I didn't send you, and the
conclusion, which still makes me sweat. Lee wanted to see it so
badly that I sent him a carbon of what you read a month ago;
but it was bad medicine for him, since it only aggravated his
depression by picturing a whole civilization in his own state:
so I sent him the later chapters as antidote and asked him to
send them on to you as soon as he was through. I think he has
the next sixty galleys or thereabouts, and what remains at the
moment is in the hands of the *Menorah Journal.* The news of
your own book excites me; and I'll see you soon after you
return to New York.

[December, 1943]

Westport, Connecticut   Saturday A.M.

Dear Lewis:

The galleys went back to you by special delivery yesterday and I hope they will reach you today. I am very, very sorry to have kept them a week, but I only got my ms. off my hands on Tuesday and had to fit the galleys in with other pressing things. I found only a few slight typographical errors which you must have caught. I had throughout the impression of a great book and was deeply thrilled by your general introduction, which is extremely moving. Still I can't feel that I have really read the book—the business of looking for errors is so distracting—and I look forward to this as one of the real experiences of next spring. The book is sure to make a profound impression.

They have put me off to next August—autumn 1944—a little discouraging at first, as I have to live on borrowed money. Then one always feels—or I do—impatient about a new book. Still I am already deep in plans for my next.

307 East 44th Street, New York, N.Y.   [January, 1944]
[From Brooks]

THE CONDITION OF MAN

Someone told me the other day that you were not satisfied with this title, and I only want to say that I think it's a title in a thousand. I said to your great admirer Rudolph Ruzicka that it had the ring of a *classical title*—and I feel this strongly. I should feel *heart-broken* if you changed it.

I have been laid up with a bad cold here—but yesterday I finished my book and I think it is good too.

School of Humanities
Stanford University, California   March 2, 1944

Dear Van Wyck:

I came out here, in the teeth of all my instincts and inner remonstrances, to fulfill my obligation to the university, deliberately ignoring the fact that I had a more pressing duty to myself, since my book had exhausted me and I badly needed at least a three months rest. Because I did not ease the outer pressures as drastically and as decisively as I should have done, my heart has been misbehaving, and finally, last week, the doctor put me to bed. Nothing organically wrong: just fatigue and tension. But I won't be able to go on with my spring quarter, since no short rest will really put me in shape: so I might better have scraped along in Amenia than have added to my burdens by coming out here- only to have to retreat ignominiously anyway. Well: there is no help for it; toward the end of April we are going back to stay back—hooray! If I try teaching again it will be only on my own terms, when I am fully rested, when the war is over, and when I can say exactly what, how and when I shall teach. But it is not my vocation: even at its mildest it takes too much out of me: far more than writing does under normal conditions. The worst blow is that I must give up my English trip, too; and I do that with extreme reluctance, even though this week the State Department declined to give me a passport. (It would have been fun to have fought it out with Mr. Hull's gentlemen. With the aid of the British Local Govt. Board and Foreign Office, I think I would have won!) . . .

The correction of my book kept me busy till the end of January: by now I wouldn't know if it were a botch or a masterpiece. It won't be out till May at the earliest—at which moment, I suspect, the eyes and mind of the world will be occupied with the Great Offensive. What of your own book— and what of your life? . . .

307 East 44th Street, New York, N.Y.
(until April 10th)   March 9, 1944

Dear Lewis:
. . . I always knew that teaching would take too much out of
your life and hope this phase is over, though I am grieved
about the loss of your English trip and the astonishing action
of your disgraceful State Dept. How far can they carry these
things, I wonder?—and do you think there is any chance of a
serious reorganization with the new election? My opinion is
that the whole State Dept. ought to be replaced by foreign
correspondents, who know the sort of world we are living in
and really represent the people of the country. I have been
hearing them talk this winter and am much impressed by their
tone *in general*. They really give one hope for the U.S.A.

As for your book, I can't wait till May to see it, for I feel
that I haven't yet read it really. Mine will not be out before
October. Meanwhile I'm reading for the next volume, but this
has been a distracting winter and we have seen few people too
and accomplished little. One doesn't know where the time and
energy go, and now, speaking of hearts, it appears that I have
hardening arteries and can walk only a little way without
feeling it in my chest. I don't know what this portends—nothing too serious I hope beyond a severely restricted diet. It is
very common I suppose and only means that one must comfort
oneself like an elderly person. A rather dreadful prospect, say I.

Kenyon has just been here on leave after a year in Bermuda
and has now gone to Miami to prepare for another assignment. . . .

694 Alvarado Row
Stanford University, California   April 9, 1944

Dear Van Wyck:

What a confounded frustration these physical infirmities of ours are! The one sure thing, in my observation, is that they respond to two things: a good regimen and the will-to-live. We both have the second; and the first is largely a matter of watchfulness and discipline, which might be galling in its pettiness did we not have good thoughts to accompany us—once called angels and ministers of grace. So submit to the further rigors of a careful routine, dear Van Wyck: and strength and length of years will, I am sure, follow. My own mother, now almost 80 was more active at 75 than at 55!

My own ills and follies have heaped up so high this year that I have begun, privately, to call it my *Moby Dick* year; but though this abrupt move back to New York with no visible means of support may prove the worst folly of all, I remain sanguine about it.

Westport, Connecticut   April 18, 1944

Dear Lewis:

We are just out from New York to stay and here is your letter. I am just reading now for my next book and hope to begin writing in four or five weeks. I'm also expecting *The Condition of Man* early in May, isn't that right? You are very wise on the subject of these illnesses and the effect on them of a will to live. My loss of an artery mainly means that I can't do any longer what I do not want to do, push lawnmowers, carry trunks to the attic and climb cliffs and peaks, which I think should reinforce the philosophic mind.

Amenia, New York   May 5, 1944

Dear Van Wyck:

It is good to be back: to be near my books and notes, to be near my friends, above all to be near you: there is something in mere physical contiguity that no merely platonic passion can equal; and the compost of one's past lives is nourishing to one's soul. What is a writer without his notes, his very house? not a proud snail but a mere slug.

I am glad to learn that you already give such evidence of improvement as to be reading for your next book. Heavens: I wish I had such powers of recuperation and such capacity for continuous industry. My own plans are for three solid months of untrammeled day-dreaming and irresponsibility: once I have the garden planted I shall take no thought for the well-being of the family, but shall live like the lilies of the fields. I am as full of books as the belly of a hen is of eggs; but I refuse to think seriously about the next one till I have gotten over the lacerations produced by this one.

By this time, I trust, you have received *The Condition of Man;* which I shall inscribe when we meet. . . . Don't bother to read *The Condition of Man* now: your own work is more important.

Westport, Connecticut   May 29, 1944

Dear Lewis:

You have only not heard from me because for the last few days I have been deep again in *The Condition of Man,* missing not a single moment that I could spare from anything else. It is overwhelming, and, while I have seen no reviews except the two in the *New York Times,* I should scarcely

expect any real comprehension of it until the quarterlies begin
to have their say. One can't take in such a book for newspaper
reviewing, and I still have not got my mind around it. What
I'm looking forward to is a rereading of the whole series, with
all your other books, in three or four years now. I scarcely ever
remember encountering such a bewildering array of ideas or
so *many* of those occasions, between one pair of covers, when
one says "I never thought of that before." It is prodigious in so
many ways, in the range of your portraits, for instance, the
studies of Loyola, Rousseau, Geddes, etc., and I marvel at your
use of the illustrations as supremely articulate symbols. What
a history of *art* you would write if you set about it, with this
wholly new approach and breadth of vision. Like every really
great book, it leaves one hungry and thirsty for *more,* and am
I not right in feeling, don't you feel yourself, that your series
calls for a fourth volume? I think you suggest this somewhere
in the book, but I strongly feel that with all this history one
needs a larger dose of philosophy proper, another *Faith for
Living* on a mightier scale. Of course all your future books are
bound to provide this, but the logic of the series now demands, I think, a volume especially adjusted to those that
precede it.[21] However, I think you must have this in mind,
the subject what you call "the organic person." (Or what
Shelley called in the phrase you quote on page 418, "the internal laws of human nature.") How wonderful, dear Lewis,
to be the chosen man of our time to be the giver of laws that
you can be. . . .

I wish I could share your habit of loafing between bouts of
work, although I have never seen you do it; but my own work
is far from strenuous at present. I just keep up a steady
routine of reading, and indeed have scarcely missed one day.
This is inescapable if I am to finish my history, which will
grow more exciting with *every* volume, for I have some thou-

21 Mumford note: *"The Conduct of Life,* already planned."

sands of books still to read; but this involves very little
nervous strain, and what a happy way of passing one's days.
We are well, on the whole, but I have grave doubts about this
house of ours as a permanent abode. As Magda Pach said, it is
really a "rich man's house" and entails a kind of living we
were not built for,—there is a constant temptation to "improve" the grounds and live on a scale that simply is not ours.
We shall make no change until after the war; then we have
another plan in view that will simplify matters, I think, and
enable us to make better use of our energies in future. We
haven't an hour to waste on the *fat* of living and I have an
increasing horror of dissipating one's forces.

Amenia, New York   June 28, 1944

Dear Van Wyck:
. . . On this hellishly hot day, the elephant has been in
parturition and has miraculously given birth to two mice. One
would have been amusing but two is a portent. Dewey *and*
Bricker: Good God! What an alternative to Roosevelt. And I
for one dearly wanted a candidate I could vote for with a good
conscience, to take the place of The Great Finagler. I was
opposed to the notion of a third term but swallowed my
objections to vote for Roosevelt in the last election; I am even
more gravely opposed to a Fourth Term, which seems to me in
every way a disaster: an event that might well be a transi-
tional move from republicanism to Caesarism, for who says
that our country is so poor in leaders that it must depend
upon a single man whose weaknesses have become colossal in
proportion to his responsibilities: precisely the opposite of
Lincoln's development.

Gladly would I have voted for Stassen: even for Willkie.
Now the only person I could vote for with a happy conscience

is Van Wyck Brooks. No need to decline: no hope of escaping. If I have anything to say about it you will leave the Grey House and go to the White House.

To comfort myself I have just read the second installment of *The Age of Washington Irving:* a chapter as broad and sunlit as the Tappan Zee: proof that writing of your quality does not have to depend upon the big people and big issues that strode through the pages of *The Flowering of New England.* You are an artist, dear Van Wyck, and nothing proves it more completely than the fact that the mere magic of your presence and style turns brick into marble and small beer into champagne. Not that I would call Irving small beer, still less Cooper. How much your chapters on the latter evokes passages of my boyhood. There was a horribly printed series of books, back around 1905, done on grey paper, pinched in type, cheap to look and definitely non-lasting; but they included a large share of the classics and cost only ten cents. That was within my purse; and on Saturdays I used to go to a small uptown department store, long since vanished, to buy Cooper, in either this or a somewhat more lasting twenty-five cent edition. *The Spy* and *The Pilot* were both favorites of mine; and among the Leatherstocking Tales I think I liked *The Pioneers* best. I had a technique for evading his long-winded descriptions and for fastening upon and re-reading his more humorous scenes. He is not perhaps a humorist, but he has, at times, a salty comic touch, an eye for quirks and revealing gestures, revealed, as with Dickens, only in his minor characters. That comic aspect of his genius is too easily overlooked; but I think that this, no less than his familiarity with the sea, must have endeared him to Melville. Someday I mean to go back to Cooper: your happy judgement of him hastens that time. But meanwhile I have another astounding book on my hands, and I wonder if you have glanced at it: Rebecca West's *Black Lamb and Grey Falcon.* I am not [an] early admirer of the lady; but after reading two hundred pages of this book I am prepared to call it a work of the highest order; a picture of the Balkans done in something of the manner of Waldo's *South American Journey;* but carried along on a long slow roll of travel, historic reflection and observation, with fewer occasional bumps in the rapids than Waldo gives. It came out in 1940 and is still, I suspect, gathering its readers.

As for *The Condition of Man,* you are entirely right in your diagnosis. This is the first part of the final volume; and Volume IV, the most difficult job of all, still lies before me. The present book ran away with me, despite my different plans for it; and I think it did this for a good reason: there is something in our long common past that we need to reason with and struggle with if we are to be strong enough to build the future. We must enter purgatory before we dare to visualize heaven; and those who resent *The Condition of Man* most are those who do not wish to make this effort, those who would like to achieve heaven simply by adding a few vitamin capsules to their present diet. With this book written, I could now die happily; because I think that once its message is digested, the reader could write his own fourth volume; indeed, there will be many fourth volumes, if the change in attitude I have tried to make possible, first of all in my own life, really takes hold.

It is both amusing and pathetic to watch the reviewers struggling with *The Condition of Man.* When I selected the photograph that is used in the publicity, six months ago, I told the people at Harcourt's that it represented me laughing at the reviewers. It has been a big bundle for them to grasp; and some of those I should have thought capable of taking at least the superficial measure of the work, people like Guérard and McKeon, the head of the philosophy department at Chicago, have shown themselves childishly weak: the bundle has dropped on their toes, through their fumbling, and they have said *Ouch* in a loud voice. More than once have I been reminded of your experience with Sam Morison: the arrogance of reviewers is almost as amazing as the triviality of their interests; and this holds for the academic world no less than for journalism.

But though the book has gotten a far more *dubious* reception than any other book of mine, it has at least been well timed; for despite the reviews, the sales have been surprisingly strong: the first five thousand were disposed of within three weeks; and Harcourt has printed 7500 more. In that respect, it has done better than *The Culture of Cities,* far better, despite all the attention that the latter got; so instead of being over $3500 in debt, as I was when I got back here in April, I am now financially in the clear, and can even see ahead for the next six months without bothering to devil at odd jobs or breaking into this blissful vacation.

Blissful is the word for these days: I garden and I read and I sleep, and haven't a serious thought about anything; when one buzzes around me I swat it, as if it were a fly or a mosquito. This won't last forever; but I intend to keep it up until I am bored; at which point I will conclude that I am likewise cured. It will take two or three years of the hardest kind of concentration to write Volume IV; and though time presses on us all, I have no intention of undertaking that final task till I am again in the pink. Outwardly I am of that now; inwardly, I am almost there, too, though reviews can annoy me unreasonably and little annoyances sometimes provoke a more irritable response than is my wont.

Westport, Connecticut July 23, 1944

Dear Lewis:

How fine to hear that the book is going so well, for the reviews have been a sad sight. This kind of book inevitably goes to professors, whereas it ought to go to MAN, who is a very different creature—though Shipley's review in the *New Leader* this week is a variation. Wait till you get your Vol. IV out,—I predict that will lead all the other best-sellers. . . .

Meanwhile I read for *Whitman and His Contemporaries,* and am getting quite excited about this subject, Whitman seems to me bigger and bigger, but I find that Melville doesn't wear so well. So much of him seems to me just rhetoric, and I find I dread going through him again. (The simple adventure books do not lose their quality, but the Melville "problem" strikes me as a bore now.) I am sure you must be right about Rebecca's book, and only wish that I could take time out for it. But I must read at least 100 more books before I can begin my own in October.

Were you not cast down by the dropping of Henry Wallace? I almost decided not to vote at all this year. My ticket for the future is Willkie and Wallace, and I think that perhaps 1948 will be the first time a third party will have a chance. How right you are about Roosevelt and Lincoln. There seems to be nothing left of R. but the husk of the politician. Yet of course we can't let Dewey get in. Did I tell you that Helen Keller lives near us now, and that we have seen her often and what a glorious person she is? Also dear old Salvemini has been here twice. Otherwise we've seen virtually nobody at all. How nice you are to say those things about my Irving and Cooper book, which I think does contain a few real discoveries. But I wish you hadn't seen it in the *Atlantic,* where it was "cut" not with a sickle but with a scythe. It is a travesty of what I have written, as you will see when I send you the book next month. We are rather up in the air about plans, but shall probably go to California early in October. . . .

Dear Van Wyck:

. . . Such a time as this may not come to me for many a year; it makes me feel youthful again, for it was when one was young that time now dutifully absorbed by articles and books used to be scattered like a drunkard's purse on letter-writing. I am reminded of a little essay on idleness by Chesterton, which Sheed and Ward published in their recent broadsheet; if I hadn't thrown it away I would copy out a few paragraphs, entirely in tune with my own state of soul at present; for Chesterton reproaches those who would *do* something with their free time or fill it with any kind of amusement. Yes: I loaf and invite my soul. Some of my ways of loafing would be called work if I were under any compulsion to follow them; such, for example, are my very idle and desultory moments in the garden, which is so rank with life, so prolific with all manner of vegetables, that my little acts of superintendance are gratuitous and have now little influence on the final garnering. So, too, I sketch: Lord! how I have been sketching the last year, ever since I found it was the only tolerable way of resting from my morning's work on my book, in the middle of last summer. I have always sketched; but now I am doing it a little more seriously, with colored crayons, and with increasing skill in the use of them. My object is simply the very old fashioned one of being able to put down what I see; for I haven't more than a vestige of the true artist's imagination which can create without seeing or create beyond what it sees. As if I needed it—with such a pleasant world to look out upon as this around me.

So the days go. No: "go" is too positive a word, it indicates a destination. So they drift, and so I bend to their slightest current, like a weed in a lake. Were I not in this mood, did I not cling to it as a stranded sailor clings to his raft, I would be making the same desperate efforts I made from 1938 to 1943,

in the hope of rousing our fellow countrymen to a state a
wakefulness and alertness in which they could save themselves,
instead of rushing like Gadarene swine after leaders who will
shout, as they fall through the air themselves, hurtling toward
the bottom, that they are at last fulfilling their purpose of
climbing the heights.

The sickening spectacle of the Democratic convention is in a
way even worse than that of the Republican convention,
because it represented a more positive betrayal of life, on the
part of those who might have known, might have felt, and
might have done better. It was bad, not merely because of
what it did, but because it was symptomatic of a more general
state. The combination of technical expertness and moral
hollowness that Roosevelt showed in his manipulation of the
convention runs all through our society; it undermines the
work of the many good men who struggle for something more
coherent in the execution of their various offices and duties,
and it brings to the top, too often, those who have Roosevelt's
infirmities, his essential division of mind, in an aggravated
state. Back in 1933 I called him Mr Facing-Both-Ways; and
the tragedy of his three administrations is that he has never
been able to make a clean choice, or do a good deed without
undermining it at the same time. The *New York Times* did
well to remind us the other day that in the very year he
delivered the splendid speech on quarantining the aggressors,
he also signed the Neutrality Bill, which succeeded only in
quarantining the United States and making it incapable of
facing its tasks. Roosevelt has already done enough good
things, as President, to earn the undying gratitude of his
country: that I think is clear. But he has already shown such a
fatal weakness in handling our international relations, combined with impenetrable complacency and cockiness, that he is
likely to leave behind him as many curses as blessings. Between him in his present state and little, *very* little Dewey, I
fear there is not such a gulf as people imagine; they are both

attracting to themselves the same forces, and neither is creating the state of mind and will out of which a true peace can grow.

Seeing all this and feeling it deeply I would now be in the thick of battle once more, at least with my pen; if I did not hold myself in tether; knowing that this time the result of my efforts would not simply be frustration, but might easily be a slightly premature disability, maybe even death. So I take to my vegetables, my flowers, my sketchpad, my Magic Mountain existence in the hope that I may thereby survive long enough to lead the counter-attack when the time comes: at the moment, there is nothing to be done until the swine have tumbled to the bottom of the cliff, the swine and the swineherds together. Whitman at least had a saintly leader's memory to console him during the bitter days that followed the Civil War; he still was close enough to the high energies on which our country drew to write the *Democratic Vistas*, bitter though some of its pages are. We have to begin to create soil again where civilization has been denuded to the bare rock.

How glad I am that you are excited by Whitman again: no experience of mine, no further reading elsewhere, has diminished his stature for me, since as a lad of 19 I began to carry him around with me on my country walks. It is only the partial views of him that make him seem prosaic or grandiose: when one really gets one's critical tape-measure around the man one finds that he has girth, and that all his proportions are noble. He is really a fresh species of man, not given by nature but created out of his own imagination: that is one of the truths which the poor professors, like Esther Shepherd,[22] can never understand: for them the difference between his original self and his ideal self only indicates the extent of his pose and the character of his charlatanism, as they call it. Certainly he had defects, but they are on a fine manly scale, too. There is nothing like his sweet sanity.

[22] Author of *Walt Whitman's Pose.*

Those last words are impossible of application to Melville; but I am a little distressed that you don't find him equally alive. After I had finished the Melville book he had done me in and I couldn't bear to go near him for three or four years; but since then I have re-read *Moby-Dick* twice; and have dipped into the other works, not least my favorite *White Jacket;* and I still find him immense. He is rhetorical in the sense that the Elizabethans were; and sometimes is strained or over-inflated; but heavens! one can say the same thing of Shakespeare; and the great pages of *Moby-Dick* are still great to me, especially the most rhetorical of them all, Father Mapple's sermon. The only book of his I regard as a complete failure now is *Mardi;* that was a big intention that didn't come off; but it was the stepping stone from *Typee* to *Moby-Dick* and as such it had a preparatory role; it showed him what he might do. The chapter on Horologicals and Chronometricals in *Pierre* I look upon as one of the best essays on morals any American has written: I would rescue that pearl though the rest of the casket fell to pieces and sank. Soon after I had finished *Melville* I saw that I had missed my real opportunity; and that was to treat Whitman and Melville together, as complementary aspects of the spirit, contrasting, antagonistic, yet united. Someday I hope to write that book. Meanwhile I owe a debt to Melville, because my wrestling with him, my efforts to plumb his own tragic sense of life, were the best preparations I could have had for facing our present world: if I have seen a little farther than the man in the street—I will not talk about the blind bats in the universities—during the last dozen years, it was because I had read Dostoyevsky and Melville and had a better notion of the real contents of the world and the works of the devil than he did!

It is good to know, dear van Wyck, that you are so close to being well: keep on with your recovery. . . .

Westport, Connecticut   September 1, 1944

Dear Lewis:

I have just reread your last letter, written more than a month ago, with so much in it that I should have answered,— enough to say that loafing has done something else for you,—it has made you a prince of letter-writers. No one else writes this way, and no one else loafs. I very much fear that I *could* not, even if I had time to spare, and I will never have time as long as there is another American author to read. I envy too your sketching. I passionately longed as a boy to do something with a pencil, but never got beyond the niggling stage, and I know it would be useless now, for I haven't that sort of seeing eye.

I hope you have forgotten what I said of Melville, which would need a lot of explaining. But I had not reread him for a dozen years, though I *had* read *The Confidence Man,* which inspired that outburst. By his "rhetoric" I meant such things as "now am I hate-shod," which you will remember from *Pierre,* and I had been building hopes on your book about him, which I think now I may realize. For I *have* read him at last again, and I agree with you—he seems more wonderful than ever. I had read your book without reading him with it, and for me good criticism is so much a thing in itself that I often lose all sight of the things it deals with. My original hope was to make my next book a sort of interweaving of darkness and light, using Melville and Whitman as my two colours, and I think it will in fact be something like this. How right you are in speaking of Whitman as so much *created by* himself. No one seems to have properly brought this out: and yet the facsimiles of his notebooks show that he was a *student* of a kind of perfection, as much as Epictetus or anyone. His "naturalness" was a conquest, not the resting on his oars that most of the writers about him have supposed. And how tiresome is all this rubbish about Rousseau. But I should never talk about subjects I am working with, for I always succeed in saying what I *don't* mean. What I really do mean I never know till I've written it out. It is what comes up from within and can't be gainsaid.

Yesterday I sent you my new book,[23] but I fear it is the thinnest of the series. Our literary beginnings *were* very thin, and I am only a little pleased that I made a book of any dimensions at all about them. The next volume should be a hundred pages longer and in texture twice as dense. The plot thickens from this point on, and the three volumes to come should steadily mount in (for me, at least) interest and excitement. I have done nothing but read since December of last year and am ready to begin writing at any time. . . .

P.S. I see in the *Times Lit. Supp.* that Secker and Warburg are bringing out at once *The Condition of Man*. Also that they are bringing out a new edition of that "standard work," *The Culture of Cities.*

Amenia, New York   September 10, 1944

Dear Van Wyck:

. . . Every since *The World of Washington Irving* came I have been devouring it; or, rather, since that seems to indicate haste, I perhaps should say that I have been munching it, slowly but eagerly and with unsated appetite. Thank you for the book, and thank you again, my public and professional thanks, so to say, for what you have done *in* the book. It is not in any sense a minor book, nor is it, as you said in your letter, thin: just the contrary, the book is packed with good things right through the chapter that I have just finished reading, that on Jefferson, and I am sure it continues to be packed right to the end. You had the poet's instinct to begin this

23 *The World of Washington Irving.*

series with the most important group of figures first, in *The Flowering of New England:* that was a right choice, and one that proves how many light-years away you are from the academic mind, which would have begun with Washington Irving, or better yet with some drab and dessicated Puritan bard, in order to march in orderly fashion from date to date. Having established the method itself and the importance of the material in the *Flowering,* you made yourself free to look before and after—without pining for what is not!—and you do this to marvellously good purpose in *The World of Washington Irving.* It is the springtime energy of the *Flowering* itself, even though you show the buds are still tightly wrapped, some of them blemished by the winter before they unfold. It is only by comparison with the characters and products of the *Flowering* that the book is in any sense thin: and that fact is a matter of natural history, not due to any lack of yours. Apart from the buried treasures you dig up and the unburied treasures that you recognize, you bring us face to face with the American scene and its history as no historian in our whole past has yet done; if one had a time-machine that would hurtle one back a hundred and fifty years, I am confident one could find one's way around, with your histories as guidebooks. That is a marvellous feat; you have made America visible, gloriously visible; with an art that is masterly, because it seems as natural as breathing, and is actually as complicated as a living organism's processes. Your magic may make the arid souls who have never been alive themselves doubt whether any such America existed: but such people don't realize that you are really a Schliemann,[24] spading away the debris that forgetfulness and academic stupidity have piled in great sand heaps over the ruins and showing at last what really existed: not dust, but living marble and honest brick. Your chapter on Jefferson is masterly: how right you are to give him a central position, to make him a pivot of all those

24 Heinrich Schliemann, explorer of ancient Greek sites.

changes which made our democracy real and our pretensions to human improvement, for a little time at least, solid. In him, you have shown the New World taking effect on one who had at least one foot still planted in the Old. Bravo! say I to that and to many other things; not least your appreciation of the Bartrams, and to all the thought that was not yet literature nor philosophy, but that had the veritable juices that one day would produce those special flowers.

I had no qualms when I wrote you as to what you would eventually say about Melville; but I am deeply thrilled over the fact that you see him as a real twin to Whitman, and so absolve me from my bad conscience of having to leave behind me at my death a work I badly wanted to write but never could get around to doing. That you were disgusted by the rhetoric of *The Confidence Man* is more than understandable. That unreadable book was a product of his madness, not a wild product like *Pierre,* which has also a great deal of brummagem eloquence in it, along with the masterly kind, but a product of dull deliberation, an *intentional* satire, written with only sand and thirst for inspiration, full of private King Charles's heads, among which was an accusation against his wife for being, as he falsely imagined, unfaithful, and for wanting to put him in an asylum, as indeed she doubtless was advised to do. The book is definitely a pathological document. I alluded to some aspects of this in my study of Melville; but Murray has brought to light more data on this period which make it conclusive. Melville sent the book to his Uncle Peter, with an affectionate or at least grateful, dedication; but Uncle Peter never cut its pages: indeed, they were not cut until I did so in the Rare Book room of the Public Library in 1927! Maybe you remember that I spent a whole chapter examining Melville's poetry, giving as favorable a verdict as I then dared: though A.E. reproached me for wasting any time on it. But I find that, on going back to it, it is better than I remembered, in many places: somewhat dated because of the inversions and strained rhymes; but often at least as good as Thomas Hardy's, both in style and in content. I will be curious to see what you find in it for yourself when you go over the ground. Maybe our final title to greatness will be the fact that we are the sole living Americans who have read *Clarel* from end to end! What you say about Whitman's deliberate naturalness can be applied to his poetry, too: certainly it was full of conscious artifice, consciously bardic, with an avoidance, more often than not, of that prosy naturalness which Wordsworth achieved in his blank verse. The poisonous influence of Yvor Winters—a dogged, stupid man who prefers waxen plums and wooden pomegranates to the real fruit—and his school has begun to pervert the judgement of a whole generation of your young professors of literature, if not a lot of other students too; and your influence is needed to redress the balance. Fancy a book like Esther Shepherd's on Whitman even getting a publisher—and worse than that, getting *my* publisher, with the aid of Cap Pearce at that. . . .

Westport, Connecticut   September 24, 1944

Dear Lewis:

I wonder if this will find you returned from Vermont, where I hope the "Secret Errand" was successful. Tuesday the 3rd I'm going to make a few remarks at the N. York Historical Society. They are putting on an exhibition to illustrate my book and are having a private view for members.

Your letter was wonderfully comforting and I am so happy you liked the book. All I can say is that the next one will be better, and I'm expecting to begin it on October 1st after almost a year of preparation. As you say, Jefferson was rightly central in my scheme and will remain so throughout the series; for I've found, what I never *suspected* before and have never seen stated anywhere else, that "the left really is the side of the American imagination." It began with the clustering of minds round Jefferson, setting the current that ran still stronger through our own League of American Writers before the Communists took it over. This to me was a major discovery and I mean to make the most of it, always aware as I am, however, that literature is not politics. But as for my "influence," as you call it, I think this is nil in the colleges. The Harvard English Dept., for one, is wholly of the Eliot–Winters persuasion and I gather that most of the others are. But I detest "English Depts." anyway and don't care overmuch what they think. You speak of Melville's *Clarel* and of us as one of its only two readers. I *hope* I read it twenty years ago and rather think I did; for if not I fear it will go unread by me. The jog-trot rhythm in connection with the subject-matter drives me mildly mad after 2 or 3 pages—but I saw the other day in the *Times Lit. Supp.*, that a new volume of Melville's poetry has been published in England.

The Simonsons, who were here 2 or 3 weeks ago, told us something about Geddes. We did not know that he was in Italy at all. May all go well as usual with him. Our Kenyon was here for a day last week. He is now 3d officer on a destroyer escort and has been assigned for the present to the *Atlantic* fleet. This was a relief to us. We have a final plan to go West on Nov. 1st if we can get the tickets—but probably only for three months.

Amenia, New York   September 25, 1944

Dear Van Wyck:

My secret mission to Vermont has not been accomplished for the saddest of reasons, namely, because my friend Curt Behrendt, with whom I was going to stay in Norwich, is now desperately ill; and today Sophy has gone up there alone to stay with his wife, while I hold the fort here. But I can tell you what it was all about, if you and Eleanor will keep the knowledge in your bosoms. We have bought a plot of land, sight unseen, overlooking the Connecticut River from a bluff, right next the Behrendt's handsome redwood house; and we were going up, gaily we thought earlier in the summer, to inspect our rash purchase. The land was not altogether unseen, for I had unsuspectingly set foot on it a couple of years ago and know in general what to expect. But I have at last concluded that since my income will never be big enough to permit me to live in New York during the next six or eight years, since Alison will soon need a good high school, not to be found in these parts, and since I need a little daily companionship, and the run of a big library, there is no place that better meets all these modest needs than Hanover; so, once restrictions were lifted, we might be able to build a house for ourselves, also modest, in that delectable if somewhat frigid spot. It was a mad, quixotic resolution, doubly mad and doubly quixotic coming from such staid overprudent people as Sophy and I are; but we didn't expect that the first act of this idyll would disclose my dear friend Behrendt—I think you and Eleanor met them both here one afternoon on a side visit from the Spingarn's—in mortal peril.

John Gould Fletcher, who is now in New York at the Hotel Wolcott sends you his very friendly greetings in a letter I just received this morning; he and I contrived to make up our absurd breach, which had been the result of no ill will on my part, only of his own exacerbation and highhandedness; but of course I haven't yet met him.

Westport, Connecticut   October 13, 1944

Dear Lewis:

Can you give me that day in New York soon?—and would
Monday the 23rd suit you. If so, could you meet me for lunch
at the Hotel Chatham where we met last year? And one
further question, would you mind if we had Jenny Ballou
with us—the author of *Spanish Prelude?* You would like her—
perhaps you know her—she is so companionable—and we
might run up after lunch to the Metropolitan Museum. I long
to see you, and now we have tickets for California on November 1st and everything settled except a place to stay there. It
will be too cold to sleep on park benches. I do grieve that we
have not seen each other this summer. Yet one feels hustled all
the time. I, perhaps foolishly, have just begun my new book—
at a very bad time, when we are going west, and I am reduced
to desperation as always with that old baffled feeling of mental
chaos. It's always so with me beginning a book—I do hope
your friend Curt Behrendt is better or well. Of course I remember him at your house. Your plan for Vermont sounds
sensible and exciting. I met Mrs. Fletcher by chance at the
Library and should like to see them. But this will be impossible now. We need that ilex tree in Purgatory under which
the philosophers sit in Doré's drawing and a few moments of
eternity, since Time it appears will never suffice.

Amenia, New York   October 15, 1944

Dear Van Wyck:

Just a few days ago I was on the point of writing you to
suggest a day for our meeting. Before I could do it we got a
telegram from the War Department saying that Geddes was
listed as missing in action since 13 September. None of the

usual sources of consolation yield any hope: all the alternatives are, in almost equal degree, terrible: still we must wait patiently, smothering our grief, till we have some further word from the army or the Red Cross. For the next week or two I would hesitate to leave Sophy even for a day: indeed I'm poor company myself for anyone but her. But let me know if you have a definite date of leaving set: for I should like to look at you and grasp your hand, if no more, before you head for the coast.

Amenia, New York   October 18, 1944

Dear Van Wyck:

Our waiting is ended. Last night we learned that Geddes was killed in action on 13 September in Italy.

Amenia, New York   November 5, 1944

Dear Van Wyck and Eleanor:

It was good to feel the warmth of your friendship in times like this: for the death of one's beloved, particularly the young with their unlived life before them, sends a chill to the marrow: there are no real consolations for that deprivation of vitality; and the imagination, no matter how vivid and sympathetic, never comes within sight of the fact itself. We both pray that you will be spared this ordeal, though I know that the undercurrent of anxiety will persist until the war is ended. Death has stalked through this village. In August young John Duffy, Geddes's oldest friend and playmate—a flying ensign— was killed in a crash. Three weeks later to a day our Geddes was killed. John was the apple of his father's eye, and Henry

Duffy, whom you perhaps remember, being already broken by overwork, was further weakened by grief. Last night he, too, died. In his delirium he called to his wife for aid: John and Geddes were sinking into a pit and his own strength did not suffice to pull them out. Our two families are linked together and Leedsville will never again be for any of us what it has been these last twenty years. . . . We are concerned over the recurrence of Eleanor's illness and trust she is now recovered. Don't be too precipitate in leaving for the West. Travel is a trial these days unless you are on a streamliner: even then, it is too much for a convalescent.

Carmel, California   December 12, 1944

Dear Lewis:

You see we are at Carmel, where we were married in 1911, for we had to disregard your suggestions, and so far things go well here—it has been continuously sunny and dry—and today, as for a week past, the air outside is like May at home. We have always known this place well, having spent three years or more here, and have always prospered physically in this atmosphere. Then we know the ropes here for work and we felt we must be near the children, for they were at least our second good reason for making such a long journey.— We found them rather surprisingly well, from any point of view, and our little grandson, now 4½, is very intelligent and winning, so that we were reassured about them all. . . .

We had only ten days in San Francisco, but I met a lot of painters especially and met some friends or acquaintances of long ago; then, fortunately coming here, we found a perfect cottage on the Dunes, although there were supposed to be none of the sort to be had. It seems to have been an unparalleled bit of luck. Now I am working well again and we are back in our old routine, trying to stick to a schedule of quiet walks, avoiding the brothers and sisters of our craft who (in Carmel) used to get on my nerves,—although we have seen Robinson Jeffers and his wife. I am taking this chance, while seeing him, to read his works complete, which I have found in the public library here. There is no doubt whatever about his genius as a writer, although he inspires me with some furious thoughts. I am not going to go off half-cocked about living writers, but in about six or eight years I expect to have something really to say about them: so I say no more at the moment. But I must tell you that almost the first persons we saw here were *G. A. and Elizabeth Borgese.* He was lecturing in Monterey and we went to hear him on the present state of affairs in Italy, and I do not need to tell you that he was magnificent on the platform. They lunched with us and spent some hours at our house—and they both spoke with a world of affection of you and Sophy, of you all. They have been somehow dispossessed from their apartment in Chicago and may take another quarter off. (They have been staying for the last quarter with the Manns at Pacific Palisades.) In that case they will return here for three months,—which we of course would immensely enjoy much as I covet our quietness and little as I long for "stimulation."

Amenia, New York   December 22, 1944

Dear Van Wyck:

. . . All the enchanting tales of Carmel cannot be false; and once the autumn fogs are over it is probably the best part of California to be in. So harried were all our days in Stanford that we never got a chance to see it. We have a cousin, Taza Grollman, who used to run a famous restaurant in Modesto, who will be in Carmel presently; she owns a cottage there, I think, and is going to settle down permanently. She won't hunt you up, because I am probably the only literary light in her life, but should you run across her by accident, you will now know who she is. She is a descendant of that part of my mother's family that went to California in 1849.

What nonsense is this about your being upset over Farrell's attack upon you in the *New Republic?* . . . I haven't read the attack itself and I don't intend to. He is not one of those enemies that one can learn from, as, for example, I have occasionally learned something from De Voto. Every once in a while God sends one out of the blue a gadfly to keep one from being lazy or complacent; some unidentifiable correspondent will discover a soft spot one had kept concealed from oneself; and one always does well to heed such messengers, because they do what they do without guile, even when they want actually to hurt the recipient. Even more rarely, one gets a real criticism of one's work from one who thoroughly understands it. This is sometimes harder to take when it probes one's weaknesses; but in the long run such criticisms are deeply encouraging and one is a stronger man for having wrestled with this particular angel of the Lord. Farrell is neither kind of critic. Turn your thoughts from such, dear van Wyck. Even the truths that such a man accidentally utters are dipped in poison and dangerous.

There is an impulse of destruction in human beings whose own development has not been satisfactory; this addresses itself particularly to those who have achieved any completeness in their work or have attained to any large success; and when the impulse manifests itself, as it does in literature, in detracting "criticisms" and reviews, every friendly hand for the moment seems to be withdrawn. One stands alone and exposed. The very things that make your mature work so solid, so broadly based, so richly saturated with the juices of life and in a positive sense so deeply healthy infuriate the thwarted souls in our midst; they would rend you for your very virtues, even as they would have excused you and defended you if you had perpetuated your mistakes! The more sure your position is the more certainly you can count on being assailed. Remember the story of Goethe's mature years, when he was the butt and laughing stock of every young poetaster Germany produced. Who knows how far Shakespeare's Timonism was his response to the very same phenomenon; one which he, with all his psychological wisdom, was still unprepared to face; since he knew in his heart that it was his best self that was being rejected.

In your literary history of our country, dear Van Wyck, you have created a new genre; and you can be judged in that performance only by the standards that you yourself have erected. It is history such as we have never had a breath or hint of before; it is a revelation of the sources of spirit such as the critics and philosophers have never taken the pains to explore. You are writing a sort of Natural History of the American Spirit, as Riehl wrote a Natural History of the German People. But your reputation as a critic, above all as a dissident critic of *America's Coming of Age,* obscures your triumph as a new kind of historian: you are reproached because you do not deal in detail with the books themselves, as subjects for critical evaluation, when the fact is that you have done something infinitely more important by distilling from the books the very flavor, perfume, and colour of America. You have laid our literature open to the sunlight and the air of common day. Henceforth, much that was seemingly buried forever will be accessible; and much that we thought we knew will be forever different, because of what you have revealed of the conditions out of which it grew. The little men will take a whole generation before they will discover your really astonishing originality of conception and treatment; they will be mourning the absence of qualities that have nothing to do with this actual work, that would only cause confusion and distraction if they were present. If your work has any imperfection, it comes out of the excess of its virtue: listening intently to the voice of each and every writer, you become, like Audubon, equally concerned with them; and the picture you paint, brilliant as Maurice Prendergast's canvases, sometimes lose a little force for lack of central points strongly brought out and defined. That was less true in *The Flowering of New England;* and it will be still less true, I am sure, in the Whitman and Melville book. In a more uneven writer than you, his own nature itself might even provide the emphasis, the boldly defined forms, the sharp contrasts of light and dark that would bring out the contours of the spiritual landscape.

Incidentally, I don't think I told you before how much I admire your treatment of Poe. It is penetrating, sympathetic, exquisitely just. I never shared Waldo's admiration for Poe; and I perhaps rate him even lower than you do. His best writing is marred by the most preposterous journalese; and his affectation of philosophic profundity is what one would expect in a precocious lad who never grew up. He is not half the writer Hawthorne was.

Day before yesterday I sneaked into New York to see my dentist who, fortunately for us, keeps an office in nearby Pine Plains over his weekends; but in January I hope to emerge by degrees from this three months of silence, loneliness, and grief; going to New York regularly and trying to throw what weight I have into the political arena; to bring pressure upon the Confidence Man in Washington, so that the administration will do belatedly what it should have done in the spring of 1942, mobilize the country for war, instead of babying the civilian population and penalizing the armed forces; who, but for the wishful thinking that has served instead of prudent calculation and courageous decision might by now have won the war, instead of being at the moment in deadly jeopardy. But I mustn't go into that now: it agitates me profoundly, because I see in the apathy of our contemporaries those signs of an inner corruption that even the bravery of our young cannot redeem, for it is those very young who will be blotted out before any redemption can take place. We are led through it all by a victim of paralysis: what a symbol!

Carmel, California   January 12, 1945

Dearest Lewis:

What a wonderful letter you sent me nearly three weeks ago,—as our friend Borgese said, you're the only living letter-writer,—and I should have written at once if our grandson had not been here and eaten up every moment of my margin of time. But I must thank you for your truly generous thought of my work, which gave me a great lift, and a needed one, for I was only upset by Farrell because for four days in succession I had received articles that attacked me. There seemed to be no end to the ways in which I was all wrong, so that I was in a mood to be unstrung, never being too sure of my virtues and merits. As for the affaire Farrell, it only ended in my having my name removed from the *New Republic,* with a few savage remarks to Bruce[25] who, as it appears, was not responsible for it in any case. Now I've forgotten the numerous other detractors. A word from you counts more than all the others, so heartening, dear Lewis, because you are the only other man who is also conducting a work on a similar scale, though your work will always outweigh mine if only because it concerns mankind and has nothing of the local or the national about it. (And I feel more strongly than ever that anything merely national is doomed and hope in my way I am serving the international.) My weaknesses are many, and I shall profit by your remark about the absence of clarity in my central points, forms boldly defined, contrasts and contours. As for the rest, I suppose that, whether large or small, we all, at a certain

25 Bruce Bliven, then Editor of the *New Republic.*

moment of our work, find ourselves under attack from every side.

Yet as for Farrell, I can't agree with you. You are right, he hasn't a grain of critical talent, but he has done something in the *Studs Lonigan* series that I am sure will be remembered as a part of our time. He had an article on you, in the *Southern Review*, was it not, that struck me as not only incompetent but really insane. But you know how I am about writers. I am as curious about them as a puppy is about other dogs and am always astonished when they bite. . . .

March. The perfect weather continues here, 70 degrees of unbroken sunshine, quiet for work and all the rest, and two men here on the peninsula, Steinbeck and Robinson Jeffers, whom we have seen something of and I should like much to tell you about. I say nothing about the larger aspects of things Californian, but there is a great increase in liberality since I first knew it thirty-four years ago. I found this really striking in San Francisco. But more of this when we meet.

Someone—Lee perhaps—has told me lately that you are collecting a volume of miscellaneous papers. If that is true, how glad I am, for you have been scattering gold on every side for thirty years, and I have always felt that you should have swept it up again at regular intervals during all this time. Besides, I like miscellanies, and I am planning to publish a book of selections this year, under the title *Essays Old and New,*—that is, if, going through my various books, I find enough that is good to collect in this fashion. About old friends, I must have told you that the Borgeses were here, and last Sunday Alfred Harcourt dropped in for a couple of hours, killing time—I don't know how—with a Dr. Hastings in Monterey (the friend after whom he named his son). Then I have had two letters from your friend Dodds at Stanford, who speaks very warmly of you and kindly invites us, though I fear we cannot get to Palo Alto. Meanwhile I did not know that you had 49er cousins and hope indeed that we shall see Taza Grollman. We have been putting everything off till our little grandson goes back to his parents. Now we hear that Kenyon is out in the Pacific, and our hearts will be in our mouths for a long time to come. . . .

P.S. By the way, at the Institute, they have made me chairman of the Committee on Awards. You know we give annually fifteen awards of $1000, and they have been going to very good people lately. Candidates are thoroughly considered. The whole committee reads all their published work. Do please send in any names that occur to you. The preference is given to writers who have published enough to prove their promise and who also need the money.

Amenia, New York   January 21, 1945

Dear Van Wyck:

While I read and re-read your heart-warming letter, I do want to respond to one suggestion: a candidate for one of the Institute awards. The writer I am thinking about is Wright Morris. I have been watching him since about 1934; and he has been growing steadily. Originally he showed almost equal capacities as a water-colorist, a photographer, and a writer; but I persuaded him to settle down to writing. His chief publication is a picaresque novel, full of salty humor and biting observation, which Harcourt published without any intervention of mine in 1942. The reviewers took this fresh piece of fantasy and tried to squeeze it into one of their pigeonholes: it didn't fit, so they concluded the book was to blame. It sold only its first printing; but today you can't get hold of it for love or money—Morris is about 34 or 35; he writes in his own idiom and thinks in his own idiom, too. That is what disconcerts the reviewers and even the publishers. Now Max Perkins has taken him over for his next book: I think he would corroborate my good opinion and high hopes. If the committee wants a copy of *Uncle Dudley* I'll loan mine!

P.S. Alas! We know the constant undercurrent of anxiety Kenyon's assignment in the Pacific brings. We pray for nothing but good news. As far as possible one must put all other thought from one's mind, lest they color your letters to him with forebodings he too must struggle with. The assurance of love is all he needs: at least it's all that will serve him.

More presently.

Carmel, California   [January 28, 1945]
                                                          Sunday

Dear Lewis:

As it happened the Committee on Grants was just on the point of meeting without me, so I have sent your suggestion on by airmail. I took the liberty of copying a good part of your letter, for it will have much more weight so. But would you mind sending me your copy of *Uncle Dudley?* I will take good care of it and guarantee that it won't be lost by promising to replace it with *my* copy. For I have one, locked up in the house at Westport. I only glanced at it when it first came to me and am recommending it solely on your recommendation. But you make it sound well worth supporting.

You speak of this anxiety we all are under. The lightning has struck three times in two months in our circle of fairly close acquaintance.

P.S. I see in the Carmel paper this week that some man here is exhibiting three of your recent books as all-round admirable specimens—of thinking, writing, printing *and* binding.

Amenia, New York   February 11, 1945

Dear Van Wyck:

. . . You almost took my breath away by the promptness
with which you acted on my suggestion about Wright Morris:
I had hardly posted the letter to you when Miss Felicia
Geffen—certainly a name drawn out of mid-nineteenth New
England, scented with rose sachet—asked me to send *My
Uncle Dudley* to Sinclair Lewis. I did so at once; and I am
now asking him to send it on to you when he is through
reading it.

I am hoping that our move to Hanover will put me into a
working mood again. At the moment I am still where I have
been for a whole year: at dead center. I know perfectly well
what I want to do; but the steam is lacking; and since I am
not a lazy man, and since I am no longer in ill health, I just
must wait patiently until the boiler gets hot, for once that
happens there will be no keeping me back. My days are
occupied but empty; even my reading for Volume IV doesn't
get forrader. The one job I have done this last month was a
very melancholy one; a job I should never have undertaken
except out of a sense of public duty; namely, an analysis of the
way in which Charles Beard has stultified himself and betrayed his enormous public by clinging obstinately to his
isolationism, and warping the facts of history in order to make
his attitude seem thoroughly justified by events. The task is all
the heavier because Beard was extremely kind to me when I
was a young man in various little ways; and though we have
drifted apart these last ten or fifteen years, for good and
natural causes, I haven't lost my memory or my sense of gratitude. Yet, when I examine Beard's doctrine and his influence,
(for he is the most powerful single figure in the teaching of
American history) I think that he probably contributed more
than any other single writer to the cynicism and defeatism
which was so characteristic of our young people in the thirties,

and which has made it impossible for the soldiers between 28 and 38, with few exceptions, to understand why they are fighting or what they are fighting for. One of the few consolations about Geddes's death that we have, incidentally, is that he didn't take part in the war as a passive victim: he knew what it was about and he gave himself to the job, going out of his way to meet it when it wouldn't meet him.

The only journal of opinion that I am able to read with equanimity or confidence, to say nothing of admiration, is the *Jewish Frontier,* an organ of the Labor Zionists, whose editor, Hayim Greenberg, is one of the ripest fruits of the Jewish Intelligentsia, and has attracted a group of extraordinarily good people to his standard. Oko was building a similar group around his monthly when, poor fellow, he died last October. Papers like the *New Republic* and the *Nation* should rejuvenate themselves completely, every five years, by taking on a new editorial board; otherwise, while apparently keeping their shape, the well-baked loaf they originally offered gets displaced by the mold that is bound to form when it has been allowed to remain too long on the shelf. As for the *New Leader,* which was the only sheet that would publish me in 1940, it has become more muddled and confused than ever; despite the amiable Will Bohn the emphasis of the sheet is becoming downright reactionary; for the tone of it is given by people who swallowed ptomaines in their original dish of communism, and now are spending the latter part of their life groaning and retching, sure that all socialist food must produce the same ill effects. Chamberlin and Eastman were originally blind in their loyalty to a poisonous variety of communism; and they are still blind now that they reject everything that savors of it. If these weekly magazines really counted for much, one would have reason to be sad over the fate of the whole lot of them; but there never was a time less propitious to good journalism; and if we have anything to say, I have by now become convinced, we ought to confine our-

selves for the most part to such statements as are durable
enough to come out six months or a year later in the form of a
book.

I wish my book of essays *were* a miscellany; but though I
probably have the materials for at least one book of that kind,
it can wait; I doubt if I shall have the patience, even if I had
the capacity, to bring together a real omnium gatherum. No:
the new volume, being on city development, is really all of a
piece: it has nothing if it has not unity: For once I have
succeeded in saying just one thing six different ways; and if
that is not the way eventually to become understood and
perhaps even popularly accepted, then my name is Mud. I do
not apologize for the essays, you understand: each, in its way,
is rather good; and the book serves the purpose of an appen-
dix to *The Culture of Cities* till I get a chance to revise that
volume. If you are coming back to Westport so soon I had
probably better be merciful to you and not send you a copy
till you return. But I am glad you are going to get out a fresh
selection of your own essays: maybe the *Times Book Review,*
having finally recognized me as a Melville authority, will now
proceed to ask me to review your book, too—particularly if
more regular reviewers go overseas; and there is nothing I had
rather do than to assay your essays in public and give some
account, to the youngsters of this generation, of their exciting
impact when they were first published. I can still remember
the trainride to Scarborough in England in 1920, when one of
your *Freeman* essays made me fall in love with America!

P.O. Box A.T., Carmel, California   **February 19, 1945**

Dearest Lewis:

I am so happy to hear that you are going to Hanover. We
have both been worried all winter about you and Sophy,

living such a lonely life among those dreary blizzards. You should have companionship, good talk and good cheer, and I know you will find them at Dartmouth. We were there four years ago, only briefly, of course, but long enough to feel its very great charm, and if you can stand the society of professors at all, I should say you would find the best selection there. So . . .

I am dictating this to Eleanor because I am having eye trouble, not too serious, I hope. I have had a haemorrhage in my right eye, which frightened me badly at first but the doctor thinks, now, that I can get back to work in a month or two. . . .

Your letter was wonderful, as all your letters are. I never cease to be surprised by the fertility of your mind, though I well understand how one's days can be, as you say, "occupied but empty." When we have no big thought filling our mind and time, it all fills up with trifles and sorrowful futilities, but perhaps this time will have proved to be fruitful for your Vol. IV, which is bound to be by far your most important work thus far. I still long for a volume of Miscellanies from you, but shall be grateful for the book on city planning, little as I know about the subject.

46 College Street, Hanover, New Hampshire   March 4, 1945

Dear Van Wyck:

. . . We are well settled by now, in a warm, cosy, if slightly inconvenient house, with the library just around the corner and friendly faces all round us; and in time, I trust, our own response to this improvement will grow more adequate. . . . I I bless the library here, if nothing else. The lack of one has kept me from taking an active part in the affairs of the world this last six months; enabled me, just the other day, to correct in half an hour a terrible howler I had committed in a critical essay I had written about Charles Beard's isolationism, in which I had imputed to his earlier self some of the sentiments he had later developed, even to the point of "remembering" that he had been kicked out of Columbia, whereas the fact is that he resigned for the most creditable reasons, and had been an advocate of entering the war since Belgium was invaded. Problem: how could a man who thought this way in 1914 picture our entry into the war, in his 1927 *History,* as due mainly to Morgan's financial interests and the proud ambitions of Woodrow Wilson? We are forgetting people; we forget too much for our own good. Perhaps Beard himself will be surprised by the quotation from an article of his in *Harper's Magazine* with which I propose to introduce the article. . . .

St. Luke's Hospital, New York, N.Y.   March 27, 1945

Dear Lewis:

Don't be worried by this address. I am here for a slight operation, now all over. I was conscious and quite enjoyed it and I expect to be out by the end of the week. It was the last of a number of small disrepairs which have finally all been attended to. My eye is entirely recovered. The doctor, out west, frightened me needlessly, my blood pressure is perfectly normal and I expect to be as good as new next week.

We are staying in town until April 11th, at 307 east 44th Street . . . the Beaux Arts where we were last year. Then we shall open the Westport house again. You may guess how eager I am to get back to my book after these unfortunate two months. . . .

How happy we were, dear Lewis, to hear of your move to Hanover. I am sure it is just the circle that you need to be in.

What you say of the library makes my mouth water. I do so need to be near an adequate library, myself, and find it so difficult to work in Westport in war time.

We came back to New York in such confusion of mind that we have looked up few of our friends, but we have seen Walter and Magda and my dear Jo Davidson has just left this hospital room half an hour ago. Then last week we snared Paul into having dinner with us. I say snared because for the last three years he seemed to take flight at the mere sight of us, but when we finally caught him he was as friendly as ever and it seemed to me that we had a very happy evening together. When I saw him the next day, at the Public Library, he was as cordial as of old and we are counting on another evening with him.

He is working on a book on the literary genres which involves much wandering in rather cloudy regions, but he has much feeling for the subject and ought to do something interesting with it. . . .

46 College Street, Hanover, New Hampshire   April 14, 1945

Dear Van Wyck:

. . . Like everyone else, I suppose, I've had forebodings about Roosevelt's health; forebodings that were quite definite when he made the tragic mistake of selecting a little man for Vice-President, instead of commandeering the best that the country could provide, against this very emergency that has now occurred. I find that the shock of his death clarifies my judgements about him; but does not make any essential revisions. He was great as a symbol: his *being* was always on a higher level than his doing. The quality of his voice in his first inauguration speech did more for the country than the actual political measures he fostered. In a sense, he was a better *king* than prime minister. He had the magic touch and presence; and this quality transcended his tragic errors in action.

My chief consolation from his death at this moment is that the qualities that made him great may be enhanced by his going: what he stood for may gain now that he himself no longer stands in the way of his own better vision. He was too divided a man ever to win a clean victory: his magnificent physical courage, perhaps unparalleled in our time except in actual warfare, was never equalled by his moral courage. The chances are that he would have fumbled and compromised the organization of peace far more pitiably than Wilson did. But as the silent monitor of those who must now organize the peace he may have a decisive influence: provided that his absence moves all of us to take up, each for himself, a little more of the daily burden of democratic action. Here is a real challenge to our whole way of life: can we strengthen the base sufficiently to compensate for the weakness at the top?

No one else in our time has so fully represented both the virtues and the vices of the American people; even his dividedness was representative of what we are at present. Perhaps, had he remained alive, we would never have had the opportunity, during these critical years, to knit ourselves together, as we will be forced to rehabilitate ourselves if we are to survive. These reflections cast the only ray of hopeful light upon what otherwise is a tragedy of the largest dimensions: a tragedy likely to be repeated in England before the war draws to a final close.

46 College Street, Hanover, New Hampshire   May 19, 1945

Dear Van Wyck:

The weather is still grim here; but, for a long bout of reading, I couldn't, privately, ask for better luck. Yesterday I sent back the books. Santayana's memories betray him: they are the petty memories of a poor old pension guest: petty and platitudinous; so that all his noble aims strike one like the gestures of a ham actor, attempting to recite Lear. William James is nobility itself: with no need to act the part because he was born to it.

Amenia, New York   June 29, 1945

What a brick you are, dear Van Wyck, to think of sending me that fine *P.M.* review: for I never see that paper unless I happen to be in New York. I am still amused at these 24 gun salutes to a little popgun of a book; and even more amused at the fact that the public is not deceived—for *City Development* is way behind *The Condition of Man* in sales for the first six weeks.

I've been back here the last three weeks: struggling with a heavy crop of hay where there once used to be a lawn, and struggling even harder with a little pamphlet the OWI asked me to do: a letter to the German people. It would be easy to write if I thought a single German ear would be open to my words; but I am afraid that the only people who might profit by my harangue are the Americans and English—who still don't know their pappenheimer. I hope to get this exasperating task done within a fortnight, so that I can go to work on my final skullcracker, Vol. IV.

I hope your *Whitman and Melville* prospers. What a theme! I predict it will outtop *The Flowering of New England* in every way—impossible though that feat would be for anyone but you—

Amenia, New York   September 16, 1945

Dear Van Wyck:

. . . All I can show for the last four months is a series of
Letters to Germans, explaining what Germany must understand about herself and do in order to recover the esteem of
decent men, which I did for the OWI, and which I plan to use
as the third part of a collection of essays on politics and
education I have gathered together for publication next
spring. *Values for Survival* will probably be the title.

As you know, I have always shied away from collections of
essays, perhaps because my own would be far too dispersed in
subject and method to be tied together as a book; but I think
that this forthcoming book, which is really three little books in
one, has a real reason for existence. . . .

Most of these essays I hadn't looked at since the year in
which they were written; and I confess I was mightily
heartened to read some of them in the perspective of four, six,
or eight years, and find out how richly events had confirmed
them. One of the best in the series is on the aims of the war,
which I wrote for the Canadian Broadcasting Company and
delivered on the radio in December 1940. I wouldn't change a
word of it today. I originally intended to preface each of the
essays with the sort of autobiographical introduction I used in
City Development; but apart from the fact that this would
have made the book too long, I found it wouldn't work out:
every personal reference became obnoxious, precisely to the
degree to which I had, at the moment, been right in my
judgements; and to have said a word would have been to turn
myself into a mammon of *self*-righteousness. Enough people
dislike me as it is without my adding to the number by such a
performance. . . .

I have been re-reading *The Brothers Karamazov.* It is an
amazing book. This is the fourth time I have read it; and each
time it makes a profound impression upon me; but each time

it is a new book; and though I do not read inattentively, I find that not a single episode has remained in my mind in the way that Dostoyevsky presented it. I love the health and sanity of Tolstoy in his prime; but I confess that Dostoyevsky wears better, year by year, because perhaps what seemed merely like perverse and wicked fantasy once upon a time has now become part of our normal and daily experience. He would be as poisonous as Hitler if he were not also as full of pity and love as Jesus: Hitler-Jesus almost defines that terrible spirit of his. . . .

[Westport, Connecticut]   September 19, 1945

Dear Lewis:

In spite of the war's ending, which ought to have lifted every heart (in spite of the horrid mess the peace turns into) , I have had the very worst summer I remember and have held my tongue in charity to you. My work goes better now, and my feelings change accordingly, but for months my intellect was like a machine without any oil, and then, most unfortunately I went through my old books with the idea of making a selection from them. It left me feeling ten years older and as if my life had been lived in vain, and of course I didn't get the book of selections. Perhaps in another three years, who knows? And in any case I am going well again. . . .

Well, at least you can read your old things without blushing,—there could never have been any doubt of that,—I am so glad you are going to collect some of your essays and I am sure this will be one of your good books. There is plenty of time for Volume IV, which I am infinitely curious about and have looked forward to as the biggest and the deepest. I saw, as perhaps you did, in an English advertisement, that *The*

Condition of Man had gone through *Four printings* in August
there. Meanwhile, we've had here two readers who swear by
you and regard you (I truly believe) as the most important
living thinker. (Rudolph Ruzicka[26] and D. G. Mason[27]) I
can well believe that your trilogy as it already exists will have
the profoundest effect all over Europe,—where everything
must be built again and people are readier for fresh affirma-
tions (I mean a good many people) than perhaps we are here.
I should expect to see you influencing Europe as the 19th
century Europeans influenced us (and as we never influenced
them before). I doubt if there is energy enough in most of the
continental countries to do the sort of thinking that you are
doing, and you should be a part of the new epoch all over the
world. But, with an atomic Future, it's no time for prophesy-
ing, and are you aware of what are called the "population
trends"? Our neighbour Leopold Godowsky told me the other
day what we must expect in this line, Russia up a hundred
million in another fifty years and the whole of Western
Europe shrunk by one half. (India, a billion, 600 million in
China, English, French, Germans, Italians, etc., 100 million
altogether.) If I didn't believe so strongly in the constancy of
certain human facts, I should feel that life had passed utterly
out of control.

I am most eager to see your *Letters to the Germans,* which
the OWI is putting out. They are translating the three
volumes of my history, though it is hard for me to believe that
the Germans will have much use for them or accept any
education at American hands. But for me the best part of my
work still lies ahead, with this book on Melville and Whitman
and the two that are to follow, if only I can keep my mental
vigour for another ten years, for the greatest difficulties too lie
ahead. Still, it opens out wonderfully in my imagination, and
I think the work improves from volume to volume.

26 Rudolph Ruzicka, illustrator.
27 Daniel Gregory Mason, composer.

When they removed the gas restrictions we were hoping we could drive up, but our tires were then worn out and we had no spare. Then Amy Spingarn invited us and I think we should have somehow managed to come if you were to be there one of those Sundays. At any rate, we keep saying, Next year it will all be different. It was lovely to see Lee in the middle of such a year for him, with a book in prose, a book of poems, a new play designed, and a fine bout of painting all at once.

[Westport, Connecticut]   October 24, 1945

Dearest Lewis:

We are setting out tomorrow, driving to Carmel by way of New Orleans and perhaps Santa Fe and I can't go without a little line to you and the hope that all is going well with you. By this time you must have begun the great Opus #4, one of the most exciting prospects the future has for me, and I have to report that my own book has at last got under way and promises to be by far the best I've done. Lee came over for a night a fortnight ago, swimming as for many months but higher than ever on the top of the wave, which always delights me for I never knew anyone who can disport himself in so many ways at once.

My *Twice a Year* has just come and I have read the poem. It is very moving, dear Lewis; you have never said so much in such a little space. How strange it is that now the killing is over we can have so little sense of katharsis and relief, no sense that a war has ended, that peace is a prospect but only the most appalling risks ahead. Yet there are so many good signs appearing too. May this winter at least go well with all of you and bring us happily together in the spring. (Kenyon is in

China and may be de-commissioned by Christmas—or his ship
may—but probably not before March or April.)

46 College Street, Hanover, New Hampshire　　October 28, 1945

Dear Van Wyck:

. . . I haven't much to show for the last two months, which
I originally had planned to devote to the first draft of Vol.
IV. Not a word of that got written: instead, I found myself preparing my political essays for the printer, and on
top of that I've had to devote myself to a spate of reading
in preparation for a revised edition of *The Culture of Cities*,
for Dutch and possibly French and German translations. In
one sense I am not sorry for this; nor for the fact that I must
also revise *Technics* for my Swedish publisher; for this forces
me to look at both books very closely, and I can now see better
what remains to be done in Vol. IV. I don't like to begin a
book in autumn; somehow, at least, I have never done so. So I
am putting off my main task till January or Feburary; and
meanwhile, I now have proofs to read on my essays, a collection which begins with my "Call to Arms" and ends, on the
political side, with a long essay on the Atomic Bomb—that
bourne to which all our thoughts inevitably are drawn, as our
bodies to the grave. This book will really be three books: for
the last section will contain my letters to the Germans.

All my energies have come back, and I am in a working and
fighting mood: ready to leave despair to the young, who have
not been toughened enough by life to face the desperate odds
that now confront us. The odds seem to be about fifty-fifty.
There are great forces in our favor, which was not true of
Greece or Rome when their civilizations went backwards; but
there are also equally great odds against us; and perhaps the
worst of our dangers lies in the fact that the very institutions

and practices which seem to the ordinary men the very acme of modern civilization are those which most need to be revised: both peoples and civilizations are more often the victims of their virtues than of their vices.

I have done a lot of random reading since coming up here, and have enjoyed it immensely: don't ask me what; all I know is that vagrancy in reading promotes good thoughts perhaps even better than the most assiduous application, and I have been ranging over all sorts of strange pastures; coming back, for example, after a long absence, to Viola Paget, with renewed regrets that I never tried to meet her when I was in England in 1920 and 1922.

I am glad to hear that your opus is well under way: I am sure that it will be equal to your very best, for the theme is a rich and generous one in every way; and if by chance it outtops the other books it will only be because the material enables you to do more ample justice to yourself. You have become a classic within your own lifetime, like the great ones you have been writing about; and I hope you occasionally look into the mirror and say to yourself: What a lucky man! . . . .

P.S. Thanks for your words on the verses in *Twice a Year*. I wish the poem could have been published where *ordinary* people could have seen it. As a poet I feel a certain kinship with Melville, for many obvious reasons.

46 College Street, Hanover, New Hampshire   December 6, 1945

Dear Van Wyck:

. . . Last week, on a return trip to New York, I stopped off at Riverside to spend the night with the Borgeses; and he was disappointed to learn that you were in California, for he had hoped to have another visit with you before he returned to Chicago in January. We spent the evening comparing notes, matching gloom with gloom and foreboding with foreboding; but since the atomic bomb apparently has converted the disdainful Mr. Hutchins to the principle of World Government, Borgese sees at least a glimmer of hope on the horizon: at least a possible field for further activity, perhaps, along the lines of *The City of Man*. As for myself, looking over the essays I am going to publish, I realize how all my work during the last half dozen years has been leading up to the resolution of the present crisis (in thought) just as the work of the atomic physicists was leading up to the Fifth Act in our modern tragedy: time has lent a solemn confirmation to views I myself was sometimes inclined to hold lightly, lest it turn out, as well it might have, that the mass of mankind was right, and the few lone voices that cried Shoals Ahead! were wrong. Whether mankind will awaken in time is another question: the only people who seem properly frightened at present are the atomic physicists themselves. We may be repeating the experience of the war all over again, though I am not so sure that we will be saved by the folly of our enemies, as we were saved from the onward march of fascism; for this situation, if we are to conquer it, demands better behavior on our part than the blind passive blundering that finally brought us into the second World War.

Tomorrow night I am giving a lecture to the college under the title, "Obstacles to Survival"; and next week I shall take part in a conference at Lebanon, organized by a few wide-awake New Hampshire yeomen, to discuss what can be done to master this force that now so direfully and absolutely threatens us; indeed, the only public talking I have done or expect to do has been on this subject. One works against time, one works with night steadily drawing on; but still, thank Heaven, I can work; for my heart has become strong and steady again and I can concentrate every beat of it on the task in hand. Looking back on the last fifty years, it is curious how often our present situation appeared to many people in the form of nightmares and forebodings, even before there were visible reasons for disquiet. I am not thinking merely of Wells's prophecies, although *The War in the Air,* and *The World Set Free,* both a decade before *The Shape of Things to Come,* certainly show him to have been a good diagnostician (No: prognostician is the word. His diagnoses were often amateurish!) but just the other day I came upon a very good book by C. B. F. Masterman, *Condition of England,* published in 1909, which, in the midst of that properous and peaceful Edwardian world, asks whether Britain and Europe are not on the verge of disintegration: whether their securities and prosperities may not presently be swept away in an upsurge of primeval violence. It must have looked like very dyspeptic writing in the first decade of this century; but today it sends the shivers up one's spine by reason of its almost prescient accuracy. This month I am embarked on a new experiment: accepting a month's appointment as visitor to the Baker Library here, which involves holding a discussion group once a week and having office hours three afternoons a week for private consultation with the students. It is a chance to resume my acquaintance with the younger generation, especially with the returned veterans, who have come back in droves and threaten to inundate all our colleges. I have already had some very keen discussions with a group or two, taking over one of my friend's classes; and I have been impressed with the quiet, self-contained maturity, the poise and inner discipline, of many of them. They are the pick of our youth, of course; not merely the ones who survived, but the ones who mastered their situation. Many of them are on the way to being responsible and reflective men; and if they don't change the country club tone of our colleges nothing on earth ever will. I had a good talk with one of them the other day who proved to be a very finely tempered spirit indeed; when we parted I was told by the professor that he was a Major, indeed the very man who had piloted the plane that rescued MacArthur from the Philippines. What I shall do this month is very much what Frost has been doing here at intervals; and if it worked out well, I might be tempted to continue it, as much for my own sake as out of any sense of duty. We saw little of Frost while he was here; we met him only once at a dinner, in fact. He was very friendly again; but I had a sense that he had become a crusty old conservative: Wordsworth all over again!

Carmel, California   December 20, 1945

Dear Lewis:

It is so good to know that you are working in such good trim and preparing for all these European translations. It is only reasonable to think that for the next generation at least this country will have to do much of the thinking for Europe, as Europe once did most of our thinking for us, and it seemed to me clear long ago that you are going to become for them what writers like Mills and Taine and Ruskin were for us in the 19th century. Probably for a long time you will mean to Europe a great deal more than you will mean at home—for reasons that are obvious enough when they are in ruins and will have to begin again largely at scratch, while we have become, alas, the most conservative of nations, and it strikes me that this is lucky for you.

You will have your posterity first before your world catches up to you at home. Then, curiously enough, *writing,* in this age, in this country, means simply fiction and poetry (and sometimes the drama) , and writing here is a cult too while it excludes from the field all the Renans and Carlyles and the Emersons of our day. Very strange, these traits of the time which I *hope* I shall be able to mark when I reach this period in my history in five or six years, when I hope to understand what you are doing in all its ramifications, whereas now I see it as partially though with a feeling of the bigness of it.

My own work—just a word about that—advances well again, and I think I am saying new things about Melville and Whitman both. I have grown to *love* them deeply and I have at least this advantage, that I have been able to read *all round them* as perhaps no writer has done before. I see them at least in their American relations as I do not think they have been seen, though that of course is a small matter beside seeing new depths *in them*. For that I can only hope and trust my stars.

I am eager to see your political essays and your notes on the atomic bomb but shall say nothing on that matter at present, except that I agree with you about the "fifty-fifty" and the feeling that we have all to gain or lose. I am struck by certain hopeful things, Mackenzie King's willingness, as the head of state, to surrender sovereignty—which may well lead to revolutionary movements in Congress—and in general the Indonesian rebellion and the rising mind of Asia, hard as it is to know a time that is moving so fast in so many directions. Here in California *all* the young people are communists apparently—at least, all we see or hear of—yet the word here doesn't properly cover the thing, and I have impressions of something deeply humane and American in them, something that brings back to the word "American" what it had in Whitman's time. I keep feeling, if only the bomb will spare us, what a glorious chance we have, and perhaps this feeling of the sword of Damocles hanging over us will have some effect in speeding us on.

Last week we drove to San Francisco and passed through Stanford, which I had never seen for 32 years, when I gave up teaching there in 1913. You can imagine my feelings going through the old haunts, seeing not a single soul we knew, but it seemed to me so "far away," so lonely, so *provincial* that I couldn't help rejoicing you were not there. This may have been a false impression, or it may have been an off-day, but the students also looked so young and callow.

Well, I am getting impressions by the bushel-basketful, though I don't know what to do with them at present. Our drive across the country was most exciting in many ways, and I'm hoping now to do it again and again, only wishing now when I am on the very verge of 60 that I had got a real start with my work thirty years before. For I only began at 45 or 50 and I feel as if life were just opening for me now.

You are right in wishing that you could sample the Southwestern country. It was astonishing—to me—the Indian aspect extraordinarily rich and alive; and I kept saying to myself, why did no one ever tell me about it? This is something for another lifetime to live into and study.

This is a scrabbly and probably wholly illegible letter, but I am eager to get it off this morning, happy that Alison's school is good—among other things I wanted to say—and that you and Sophy have found so much in Hanover to be happy over.

What you say of Frost agrees with my own last impressions when I saw him two winters ago, and found him personally so affectionate and friendly; and it rather saddens me to feel that two real men of genius—for it seems to me they are in our poetry at present—Frost and Jeffers—are enervated with conversation or worse. I would like to write of Jeffers, whom I have seen a number of times and who proves to be really humane and compassionate as a man though his view of life as a poet is wholly nihilistic. But this must wait, with so many other things.

P.S. It's a pity in a way that you couldn't lecture at the Berkeley School of Religion, which I think you would have found more rewarding than Stanford. After your words about it, I asked for *The Brothers Karamazov* for Christmas and shall be deep again.

P.O. Box 2714, Carmel, California   January 14, 1946
[From Eleanor Brooks]

Dear Lewis:

On February 16th Van Wyck will have his 60th birthday, and I do not need to tell you how he dreads the thought of it! Since we are so far from all our friends the "stag" party I always planned to give him just can't take place.

So I am being very bold and writing three of the friends dearest to him, asking them to send him just three or four lines, personal ones, on that date. I know it will make all the difference in the world to him.

With affectionate greetings to you both and a thousand good wishes for the new year.

[P.S.] Of course don't answer this, as I have said nothing of it to Van Wyck.

46 College Street, Hanover, New Hampshire February 10, 1946

Your letter of 20 December, dear Van Wyck, still awaits an answer: and it will have to wait a little longer, I am afraid; for I want this letter to reach you in time for your birthday on the sixteenth. It brings you our warmest and dearest embraces, our deepest admiration over the great achievements that have crowned the sixty good years that now lie behind you—yes, good years, even when they were full of inscrutable chastisements—and our confident anticipation of the even better years that are to come. The effect of your work, dear Van Wyck, has been cumulative; and it is not your contemporaries or even your immediate successors who will be able to estimate justly its final impact. But this I know—this America of ours, this world of which it is a part, would be [a] narrower and bleaker place if your books had not enlarged it for us and made it "home." My own personal debt to you is such a deep one that I could only make it smaller if I tried to put it in words; such a debt is a blessing that one must carry about privately, confessing it only with a secret smile. But on an occasion like your sixtieth birthday it is not enough to acknowledge private debts: I feel as if I were entrusted with a public mission, confided to me by my country-men, your readers no less than your fellow writers, to say on their behalf those words one utters to heroes who have gone through combat, have suffered, and have emerged victorious: *Well done!* No one in our time, and country, no one since Emerson himself, has worked to better purpose than you have. Guard yourself well in the days to come: we need you now more than ever, to transmute the treasures of our own life, which you have taught us to respect and understand, into that which is universal and human. I salute your past; and even more I salute your future: the best is yet to be! May you flourish as the green bay tree, that for centuries to come our descendants may live under your benign shade.

Carmel, California   March 2, 1946

Dear Lewis:

You have certainly given me heart and hope. I am much more impressed with what you have done with your fifty years than with all I have done with my sixty, and it has often occurred to me that if I am remembered at all it will be as a friend and contemporary of Lewis Mumford. I have been suspecting more and more that you are one of the world minds who are going to be recognized everywhere as a pillar of the Age of Reconstruction. As for my own work, I feel at least that I've just begun to give my measure. All the most important

part is still to come, though it will take another twenty *good*
years. You are my best pace-maker, one of the things I bless
you for, and you know there are too many of these to
count. . . .

Westport, Connecticut   April 10, 1946

Dear Lewis:
. . . Now I am desperately getting back into work again, but
with the further unsettling thought that we must really give
up this house. It is wholly out of scale with the life we have
always wanted to lead and must now be disposed of. We think
of moving for good to New York, if we can find rooms that
will make a home for us. All that remains to be seen. . . . But
I have seen fine references to you and your work lately, and I
love to think of your triumphant progress. I am eager to hear
of your plans for England. Are they connected in some way
with the rebuilding of London? . . . I am ashamed to say I
have done nothing about the petition you sent me.[28] If there
is still time I should be glad, at least, to collect signatures for
the paper you sent me. . . .

46 College Street, Hanover, New Hampshire   April 14, 1946

Dear Van Wyck:
. . . Your comments on references to my work I took with a
grim smile: for at the moment I have been having a knock-
down fight with Harcourt over the way they have handled my
book; and if they have fallen down badly, what shall I say of

---

[28] Mumford note: "To urge effective atomic disarmament."

the reviewers and editors, who have found a simple way out of their dilemma in dealing with my ideas by ignoring the book completely. I had reached a very satisfactory position, I had thought, with Harcourt: my income from my books was sufficient to my needs, and I thought I had found in Frank Morley someone who was so concerned for my work that I could leave all the problems of handling the book serenely in his hands. Unless the present breach between us is healed, it will confront me with a serious problem: one I have no wish, at this time of life, to face.

I have become a sort of exile within my own country, and though I increasingly have the ear of the young, they find me, if they do so at all, only by plunging through the thickets of misunderstanding and misrepresentation that my own contemporaries have planted between us. This moment finds me in a mood of Melvillian bitterness such as I never knew before. . . .

Don't let the petition concern you now, dear Van Wyck: there are some fifteen hundred copies in circulation, and our movement has made some headway. But I have always looked upon the petition itself merely as a means of focussing discussion; and I would not have you dream of undertaking the job of starting a mass meeting anywhere. I have spent six weeks away from my desk, engaged on getting this movement started; and if it hasn't taken on spontaneously by now, and if it is not going along on its own momentum, we both had better go back to our writings. I did try to persuade Jo Davidson to get his organization working on this scheme: in their preoccupation with the MacMahon Bill they have forgotten our immediate dangers and tensions, and mistakenly take for granted that "civilian control" is going automatically to rectify this situation. The same with the Lilienthal report. Neither the bill nor the Lilienthal report deals with the issue of achieving atomic control—and the control of all other instruments of extermination—in such a way as to prevent an

atomic war from breaking out before we have achieved a
world government capable of preventing war in any form
from coming into existence. Just in case you have an opportunity to talk this over with Davidson, I am sending you our
revised covering letter, which deals with the immediate issues
more clearly. . . .

[Westport, Connecticut]   April 22, 1946

Dear Lewis:

Two or three days ago *Values for Survival* came and I have
gone through it with the excitement I find in all your books.
It carried me along on a powerful current of thinking, and I
felt as I had felt before in reading this *phase* of your work that
no one had written with such passion since Randolph Bourne.
What a true prophet you have been, and what a teacher in the
largest way for a time that is not accustomed to Carlyles and
Ruskins, a real world-mind such as nobody else I know has in
America, as readers in Europe at present are more likely to
see. Victor von Hagen here, who has had some slight acquaintance with you, spoke of you as one whose work was far better
known abroad. That has been my impression, though I know
there are disadvantages in having this verdict of posterity
perhaps at the expense of readers at home. But how many
thousands of others must feel as I do about your work, and
your constant dwelling on the need of interiorization, the
substance of *Faith for Living* and your volume to come, as
against the shallow extroversions of the last few decades. Then
what a joy it is to read such magnificent *writing* as yours, the
finest expository prose that is appearing in this country. You
are also I suppose the chief victim of the current convention
according to which writers of expository prose are often not
even classified as "writers," perhaps because we have had so

few in this age of "scientific" history (and universal journalism) that the type has been forgotten. But this concerns only the illusions of a decade and would mean nothing of any account if you were not having these difficulties—which astonish me—with Harcourt. It is dreadful that you, at the height of your power and with your superb body of work achieved, should have this kind of anxiety to contend with. At least, as you say, and as I know, you have young readers increasingly with you, whereas most of my readers and admirers are in their dotage—as it often seems to me when letters pour in after one of my books has taken these old souls, back to the days of their youth. . . .

You bring up the insoluble question of political action on the part of a writer. It seems that you really accomplish a great deal in action, for I can't be mistaken in reading between the lines of Washington news that you have influenced public thinking there. I am not effective in action myself and have not the nervous control for it. I spoke two minutes at a Roosevelt meeting the other day in Bridgeport at the cost of two days of worry about it. I would give anything to have your composure on the platform. You have not told me what the lectures in England are to be, but we shall have time for that if you will only come here for a night when you finish in New York on May 7th after your address at City College. . . .

Aboard the "Queen Mary"   August 12, 1946

Dear Van Wyck:

The news of your own tribulations lengthened the shadow cast by Paul's and Stieglitz' death; and I trust that by now the worst of Eleanor's ordeal is over and that the healing days have begun. My own trip turned out better by far than I had dared to dream; for I had not guessed how many spiritual sons and daughters my books had begotten in England; or how keen, how thoroughly awakened the young—at least the educated young—would be. England, though she has not completely overcome the deep fatigue of the war years or the final tension produced by the V-weapons, is nevertheless more "fit"—morally I mean—than any other country; and the unexpected dynamic of the Labor Party gives legitimate ground for new hope—though as usual foreign policy, that upper class monopoly, lags.

[Westport, Connecticut]   August 16, 1946

Dear Lewis:

. . . As perhaps we told you, we are selling the house. We were lucky enough to be able to buy an apartment at 350 East 57th Street and shall be moving in about October 1st.

I enclose some clippings that S. K. Ratcliffe[29] sent me though you have probably seen them. They gave us a lot of pleasure and we showed them to Lee. . . . I hope you will find it possible to write something about England. The feeling here seems to be universally hostile to England and I tend to share the mood myself, I find. But I know there is so much to say of another kind, and I heard Gandhi's son at a luncheon praising the other day the record of the Labour govt. in Indian matters—The case for England ought to be strongly presented, although it may be difficult at present with the Palestine question.

29 S. K. Ratcliffe, English journalist who lectured frequently in America and contributed to American periodicals.

[Westport, Connecticut]   August 26, 1946

Dear Lewis:

Since I wrote to you Eleanor has taken a turn for the worse
and cannot live through September. Kenyon and I will go to
the apartment alone. I don't know what lies ahead or whether
I can work without a home, infantile as I am in so many ways
emotionally. At present I am paralyzed mentally and see no
break in the blank wall ahead. I go about methodically
packing up the house, while Eleanor lies upstairs heroically
cheerful, thinking only for me and the boys, who are both
with us. Few words I have ever read would do justice to her
spirit. Don't write, dear Lewis. There is truly nothing to say,
but I will keep you posted.

Amenia, New York   August 27, 1946

Dear Van Wyck:

. . . You have already found what I am finding out now,
that as one grows older, people become even more important
than "environment," so that if one can't have both, one is
more rewarded by the first than the second. That was Socrates'
conclusion in the *Phaedrus,* you'll remember; and I followed
that principle in England, too; giving up many a solitary
ramble among the ruins to have a glimpse of some fresh facet
of the British character.

[Westport, Connecticut]   September 11, 1946

Dear Lewis:
   You are right, and only you can say it. I have had some such
thoughts but my feelings are very unruly and I can only hope
for the kind of strength to live this way. I think I have always
had good feelings but Eleanor had the philosophy that saw us
through. . . . I am not attempting to work at my book until
we are settled in town, having many things on my hands here
and small emotional control at present. I hope I sent you some
clippings from English papers that Ratcliffe sent me—I enclose another you may not have seen. I have been feeling
strongly that you are going to mean for Europe what Europeans, like Mill and Carlyle, once meant for us here.
   I am so glad to hear you speak as you do of Eleanor. If you
could have seen her during her last weeks! There was not one
moment of faltering in her high-hearted courage. *All that* will
make it possible for me to face my memories in time.

[Westport, Connecticut]   September 16, 1946

   Your letters have meant so much to me, dear Lewis. I felt very
close to you the last time I saw you and now more than ever I
need to know that you are there. . . . We are moving to New
York about October 15th and our address will be 350 East
57th Street. I am going to try to go back to my book before
this week is over, for if it goes at all it will be a life-line; and
fortunately I have finished four-fifths of it, so that the momentum should carry me through. If one were *beginning* a
book, how different it would be. Dearest Lewis, how glad I am
that you will be coming to New York.

46 College Street
Hanover, New Hampshire   December 30, 1946

A happy New Year to you, dear Van Wyck—with an avuncular embrace for Kenyon and Charles, too! I have just finished the third draft of my biography[30] and am happy in thought that you and I will be appearing in print, more or less shoulder to shoulder, next autumn. The thought of your book[31] awakens a great appetite in me: I know in my bones it will be as decisive as *The Flowering of New England* was.
. . .

[30] *Green Memories: The Story of Geddes* (1947).
[31] *The Times of Melville and Whitman* (1947).

CHAPTER V

Values for Survival
(*1947–1952*)

During the immediate postwar period, Brooks and Mumford each brought his major work to completion; Mumford with *The Conduct of Life* in 1951 and Brooks with *The Confident Years, 1885–1915* in 1952. Brooks had at one time planned a sixth volume for the period 1915–1950, but instead he published a volume of essays on his old theme *The Writer in America* (1953), an answer to his critics, and then turned to his own personal past for a series of three volumes of reminiscences which were later collected and published as his *Autobiography;* meanwhile Mumford in 1952 published his Bampton lectures under the title *Art and Technics.* The ambitious multivolumed efforts of the two men to recapture the heritage of American cultural values and, each in his own way, make them available to modern man, were brought to gratifying completion, by individual commitment, buttressed by the moral support that each man supplied to the other during two decades of a friendship, and each by similar friendships with others. There should have been nothing but rejoicing and mutual congratulation.

Early in this period, however, cracks began to appear in the solid structure of their affectionate—the word is theirs—and essentially uncritical accord. Brooks gave the first hint of the situation when he wrote on January 11, 1947, "I feel that there is a deep literary bond between us, worlds apart as our fields of thought in certain ways seem to be," but it took a relatively unimportant incident to bring these differences to an issue: namely, the award by the Institute, on the nomination of a committee of which Brooks was chairman, of the medal of distinction to the historian Charles A. Beard. Mumford protested the award on the grounds that Beard's isolationist position was "poisonous" and that he was an unethical scholar in that he was willing to warp historical evidence to support it. Brooks's defense that he was acting for the committee rather than for himself and that he had not read Beard's recent work did not deter Mumford's resignation from the Institute. The break might have been only circumstantial had it not provoked, for the first time openly, a frank criticism of the basic differences in the philosophies and aims of the two men. Even though Mumford's criticism of Brooks's method and style in his review of the *Melville and Whitman* was accepted with his usual good will by Brooks, things had been said which could not be unsaid, and it became at least clear that Mumford felt that Brooks's lack (or perhaps deliberate rejection) of the tragic issue in experience, put his work on a more objective and hence less significant level of discourse than his own. Although both were working with the problems of cultural values, not only their fields of historical concern, but their definitions of value now appeared widely different, although perhaps supplementary rather than antagonistic. That this difference had been recognized by Mumford much earlier, although he had not allowed it to interfere with his friendship and support, is clear from an unpublished letter to a friend, dated September 11, 1933: "Brooks and I are too amicable to have the intellectual battles which always lurk under the surface of our conversations. He had seen Beard the previous week and had, I gathered defended Beard against the review I had written of his book—defended that is the notion of Progress—but both of us look so eagerly for points of contact and sympathy that we tend to understress our differences, and yet I more than half suspect that he either does not believe half the things I believe in, or is antipathetic to them."

Even though Brooks stood his ground and made the award to Beard himself when Henry Canby was unable to do so, Mumford forgave him, and by midsummer of 1948 the wound had been healed and each man again offered the uncritical support for the concluding book in the series which had meant so much to both through the years. All would probably have continued well had Brooks not decided to reread all of Mumford in preparation for a tributory essay and in the process become entangled in the same kind of recognition of basic differences that had troubled Mumford. In his letter of January 21, 1952, some impulse prompted him to explode with a criticism that unintentionally turned Mumford's attack directly back at him on both counts: that of definition of value and that of style. Feeling that, in his exploration of the past, Mumford had immersed himself too exclusively in scientific writers to the injury of both his moral humanism and his earlier direct style, Brooks recommended that his friend take a year off to read the great moralists of the past and then to synthesize their best thought in a short volume written in the style of his earlier work. Long letters from both men, here included in full, relate the consequences, and the following near-silence of almost a year marks a definite break in the friendship which, even when it was renewed, never again was as intense or as essential as it had been in earlier days. But the great works had been written and perhaps it failed because it was no longer needed.

Meanwhile Brooks had married Gladys Rice whom Mumford had known for many years, and soon bought the spacious and welcoming home in Bridgewater, Connecticut, where he lived for the rest of his life. Mrs. Brooks, a writer herself and a lover of people and places, filled these years for Brooks with the peace of love and care and the excitement of travel and new friends, while Mumford, with his permanent home still in nearby Amenia, spent an even larger part of his time lecturing at the University of Pennsylvania, where he became professor in 1951, and elsewhere. Near enough to see each other more frequently, at the same time that they shared fewer common writing interests, the need for letters became less, and the correspondence more casual.

[New York, N.Y.]   January 11, 1947

Dear Lewis:

A somewhat belated but very happy New Year to you, and a thousand thanks for your good letter. I was immensely impressed by your RBIA[1] address, which Jo Davidson has just read with enthusiasm and almost awe. He found it very exciting after the two-dimensional discussions one is accustomed to on this subject, and he thinks it most certainly ought to be published here as I have thought from the beginning. I don't know whether you were aware of the conspiracy that we arranged after you left us the night you were here with Jo and Lee Simonson. I was a conniver but not the instigator of it. Margaret Cobb called up a friend on the *Times,* who was excited to hear what you had just been saying and was to arrange to assault you in the morning with a barrage of reporters to get these views. I had a few qualms myself about how you would feel when the reporters came and hauled you out of bed. But the next day (I think it was) the Rockefeller plan was suddenly announced and this, I suppose, stole the thunder from the idea. But really these ideas of yours should not be lost in that British paper. They are magnificent and still relevant, and I think it is quite naughty of you to hide them

---

[1] Royal British Institute of Architects.

under a bushel here. All your thinking has volume, in the musical sense of the word. How quick the English are to recognize *authority* when they see it in any shape or form. I have seen it happen so often, and it's one of the qualities I've always admired in them.

It is such good news that your book advances well. Melville Cane,[2] with whom I dined the other day, spoke with great delight about it. I am happy too that we are appearing side by side, for I feel that there is a deep literary bond between us, worlds apart as our fields of thought in certain ways seem to be. I do feel that my new book is going to be important, although I still have some difficult problems to solve in it. Then, as you once reminded me, I am always in serious danger of losing a sense of the *wood* because of the *trees*. I am obliged to assemble such a mass of concrete details that there is always the danger that the main lines will not show forth. Well, in this case much depends on what I can do with the final chapter which ought to bring the book in line with the problems of our day. I am now reading for the next volume, Theo. Dreiser, etc., etc. As I approach the present the study grows constantly more exciting.

I long to see you again and trust that you will let me know when you are coming this way and can spare some time for me. I have seen several of our friends, Amy Spingarn, Waldo, etc. I spent two evenings a fortnight ago with Alfonso Reyes from Mexico, a wonderful little man, he seemed to me.

[New York, N.Y.]   March 18, 1947

Dear Lewis:

I have some news to give you—now it can be told—Gladys Billings and I are going to be married in the summer. She is

2 Melville Cane, poet and lawyer.

very fond of you and said you should be told first; and I can't help feeling that you will be pleased. I am very fortunate, for I never felt more congenial with anyone. I think we are going to make a very good team. Yesterday I told Lee, who seems to be in better spirits, and I hope we can have him here for dinner next week. Please, dearest Lewis, do not feel that you must write me a letter,—I have such a horror of letterwriting that I have a morbid dread of forcing letters out of my dearest friends.

Still, there is one other thing that I must ask for a line about. You know Jo has done a walking figure of Thoreau. The model is extremely good, quite as good as his figure of Whitman,—he made it one day in the country when Eleanor and I were there. Now we are hoping that we can get it erected perhaps in Morningside Park, partly because the people in Concord have been so indifferent to it. I think myself New York is the place for it. I am diligently acting as chairman of a committee to further the prospect and am asking a dozen others to lend their names. Helen Keller will join the committee, Henry Wallace, La Guardia perhaps, perhaps Carl Sandburg, etc. etc.—Could I include your name on it? There is no question of politics here. We want a few names to impress the Park Commission, etc., that the plan is a good one, so they will allot a site for the statue. The raising of the funds will be a simple matter and does not involve us at all.

Your friend Jimmie Stern[3] was here for dinner last night. He was anxious to write to you and I gave him your address. He is going to England and France with his wife in April.

Dear Lewis! I wish I could see you. Gladys and I will probably be married in June and may spend a good part of the summer here in New York.

[3] James Stern, Irish writer, and his wife, Tania, were friends of Mrs. Brooks.

46 College Street, Hanover, New Hampshire   March 19, 1947

Dear Van Wyck:

Your letter, with its heart-warming news, came this morning; and Sophy and I hasten to embrace you. Blessings on you both! We've always had a very special feeling for Gladys, whom I first met in Edgartown in 1927[4] when I was writing my *Melville*, and this seems an ideal match. May it bring you great happiness. If I come to town this weekend I'll phone to see if you've five minutes free.

As for the Thoreau Committee, yes: please put my name down on it. If the statue is half as good as the Whitman, we ought to build a special park for it. Thanks for letting me in on it.

Amenia, New York   July 12, 1947

Dear Van Wyck:

It was good to get your card from the Vineyard, a place for me which is associated with a host of memories, some painful and some exceedingly pleasant, including among the last my first meeting with Gladys, at Edgartown: if I remember correctly, it was on the Beach, and Emily Post was dipping in the same waters. For years I have been longing to have at least a dash of salt water in the summer time; but I am farther away from that this summer than ever, for I have just begun work on Volume Four,[5] and the mere act of getting ready to write and keeping up the mood from day to day, now demands such an act of concentration in me that I begrudge even giving an hour at night to an old friend, or time needed for an afternoon jaunt to Poughkeepsie.

4 Actually 1928. (Mumford note.)
5 *The Conduct of Life* (1951).

I usually have no difficulty in getting a book started; but this time I feel like a clumsy ocean liner, trying to sail with the tide against it, and unable even to swing round in the Hudson, though all the tugs that can be mustered are chugging and cuffing and push against her side. It will take me a little time before I am out in the channel and headed for sea; and I shan't feel right about the book till I feel the slow even swell of the ocean, as one meets it off Sandy Hook, reassuring me that my voyage has at last properly started, and that there will be no turning back. The fact is, I am beginning this book a couple of months too early, for I have hardly yet had the time to get myself clean and tidy after finishing *Green Memories*, the book about Geddes; even this week I shall still be reading page proof on it. But time presses; and though I don't expect the book to save the world, it is a point of honor to act as if it, and a thousand others, *might* save the world, until the news finally comes through, definitely, that the world is beyond salvage, and that the end is at hand. Reason tells me that this may well happen within the next decade, or even before that; but quite irrationally, I cling to my post and continue to act, almost as fatally as the rest of my contemporaries, as if nothing of a catastrophic nature was likely to happen. The irony of it is that never was my personal life in better balance, never was I more free of financial worry, more able to concentrate wholly upon my work, or even physically more deeply healthy than I am at the present moment: were it not for my underlying and persistent sense that everything is going wrong, that the captain is drunk and the mates are mad and the crew is afflicted with sleeping sickness, I could hardly hope for better days than these that have been my portion, and Sophy's, this last six weeks.

Well: enough of this. I trust that the galleys of your book are all corrected and that you are well started on the preparation of your next book. As I remember, you work well near the sea, for was it not practically in sight in Westport? But even if you find yourself succumbing to the balmy magic of wind-swept moor and sheltered cliff and are not in the mood to work at all, console your conscience with the thought that you have well earned a vacation, and will be all the richer for every idle hour that falls into your lap.

Chilmark, Massachusetts   August 1, 1947

Dear Lewis:

It was good indeed to have your letter and to hear your news about the book you have just begun and Sophy's good spirits. You both deserve a little peace of mind and I hope you may have it now for months and years to come. You have in *Green Memories* a lovely title for the book and the frame of mind you picture ought to be auspicious for the much-antici-pated Volume Four. How well I know the feeling with which you are beginning it. That is always my feeling during the first six months of a book. I look forward with a keener interest to this book of yours than I have ever felt for any other. *The Times of Melville and Whitman* ought to be out in three or four months, and I am reading now for my own Volume 5. The libraries here on the island are keeping me busy.

We have settled in at the silo where I have an airy study with six windows that overlook Menemsha Bight. Tom Benton[6] is our nearest neighbour and Caroline Pratt[7] lives near by. We see them often and they always speak most warmly *of you*. Living here is, in some ways, troublesome and rough, which takes up quite a bit of energy and time, but it has compensations and I have begun to enjoy it thoroughly, especially now that the wind has changed and we are having

6 Thomas and Rita Benton, neighbors at Chilmark.

7 Caroline Pratt, founder of the City and Country School, New York City.

bracing weather. The month of July was hot and damp, as it has been everywhere. We have had visits from my Kenyon and Gladys' son with his two children, who are with us at the moment; and in about ten days we are going to visit the George Biddles, where I am to have a portrait painted[8] and we should see Waldo Frank. Here we have a little beach at the end of a short walk over the meadows, where we can swim in deep quiet water, and for the rest, besides my reading, I am arranging a book of selections from five or six of my published volumes, to be called, perhaps, "Essays Old and New."[9]

I wonder if you have taken any further steps to spend the coming winter in New York. It is not impossible that we may go for a while to Washington. If we can arrange this it will be very good for me, for I shall have reached the stage where I ought to use the Library of Congress. Meanwhile, Gladys carries on her work as a teacher of "Remedial reading." She even has one pupil here and has become herself quite an authority on the subject. She was teaching last winter at Caroline Pratt's school, as perhaps you know.

P.S. We sailed over to Nantucket last week to spend a day with Newton Arvin. Do you know that astonishingly interesting and beautiful town?

46 College Street
Hanover, New Hampshire   September 27, 1947

Dear Van Wyck:

What I am writing you now about is the book on Paul Rosenfeld[10]; for I have just received word from Mellquist

8 Now in the Library of the University of Pennsylvania.

9 *A Chilmark Miscellany* (1948).

10 *Paul Rosenfeld: Voyager in the Arts.* Edited by Jerome Mellquist and Lucie Weise (1948).

that the Creative Age Press is going to do the book: a triumph
for Mellquist and a proof that faith actually moves mountains.
What a withered skeptic and cynic I was, thinking his cause
hopeless and his enthusiasm quixotic! Even before this letter
came I had done the first draft of a long essay on Paul, based
mainly on his letters; and in writing it, it occurred to me that
you and Waldo and I had a wonderful opportunity, in this
very book, to tell an important phase of modern literary
history from the inside, thereby correcting the false and even
poisonous reports that people like Farrell and De Voto have
given. Our essays don't have to be directly on Paul: the book
will be all the better if they range over a broader field, provided that what we say is a substantial contribution to the
history of our time. There is nobody better equipped than
you, dear Van Wyck, to tell the story of the *Seven Arts* days
and their consequences which Paul never lived to write; and I
trust you are in the mood to do it. Mellquist tells me that the
deadline is November first; and I trust that you'll presently
tell me that you're hard at work.

Chilmark, Massachusetts   October 3, 1947

Dear Lewis:

We leave the island tomorrow and shall be in New York on
Monday. . . My book is ready and I'll send you a copy next
week. How are the publishers getting on with yours?

Now about the book on Paul, the question came up last
spring, and there have been few occasions when I was sorrier
to have to say no. But I have good reasons. If I were to
attempt it, I should have to read Paul's books again. It would
take a full month—and that is not my only reason. I am
getting a little desperate about my history. The next two

volumes are the crucial ones, the two generations of our own
lifetime, 1885–1915, 1915–1950; but the number of books that
I shall have to read for them is no less than appalling. For
authors have multiplied beyond belief in the last half-century.
Now, the trouble is I can't even *begin* to write my next
volume[11] until I have read 6 or 7 hundred books, so for this
summer I have read 200, and I can't put pen to paper before
next May, at earliest. I am so afraid that something will
happen before I can do these crucial books that I am perhaps
a little unreasonable on the subject. But I have resolved not
only to do nothing else but also to do nothing until I have the
right perspective. Also it happens that I have promised to
spend October preparing a book of selections from my work
that Dutton is to publish. This latter is only a minor reason:
the major one is my desperation about the length of time that
must pass before I can begin to write. When I come to write
about Paul in my final volume, I can do him ten times better
than I could ever do him now. I may have developed a certain
rigidity in the sixteen years I have spent on this history. That
is something I dislike extremely, but it is the result of difficult
conditions. With the mass of reading I have to do, and the
slowness of my mental workings—reading every word as I do
and writing only a page a day—I have had no margin of time
for all these years. It has been for me a wonderful existence
but I have bought it at the price of many things human. I
have been having a rather extraordinary correspondence with
Ernest Bloch[12]—tremendously interesting letters—one of the
best about *Paul*. But it would not be suitable for a book of
tributes, friendly as it is in part and extremely keen.

You speak of the letters that have come to light in your
search for Paul's. I can hardly *wait* to read my boxes full, and
the books of my friends!

[11] *The Confident Years: 1885–1915* (1952).
[12] Ernest Bloch, composer.

46 College Street
Hanover, New Hampshire　　　　　　　　November 13, 1947

Dear Van Wyck:

Your letter greatly relieved me, how greatly you could not perhaps guess, unless I told you how the review came to be written. They had hoped to have the review in at the office on 15 October; but the book didn't actually reach me till the twentieth; and though I knew already what I wanted to say about the series as a whole, I still hadn't read *The Times of Melville and Whitman*. In such cases, I usually take my time, even if the review is a little late: in fact, I look with disfavor upon the current habit of trying to get all the reviews plumped into the public's lap in one week so that thereafter the book may be completely neglected. But this time I couldn't put off the writing until I had fully digested the book and ordered my own thoughts, because I knew that the weeks that would follow, including this in which I'm now writing, would be, literally, too crowded for words. So I wrote the review and sent it off hastily, so hastily that I warned young Canby solemnly that I wanted to see proofs and would be down in New York the following week to read them; indeed, I gave him my address, to make sure no time would be lost sending me proofs. When Wednesday came and no proofs appeared I went around to the office to inquire after them; and was told, to my horror, that they were already in stone; for Cousins was so taken by your book that he decided, now that the review had unexpectedly come in so soon, to tear out both the cover picture and the leading review and put your face and your book in their stead. That would have been fine; but meanwhile I had discovered on re-reading my review that it held one sentence I had inserted, as an afterthought, which seemed to me unfair to you[13]; and a passage or so of your own

---

13 *Saturday Review of Literature*, XXX (November 8, 1947), 11–13. The offending sentence probably was, ". . . the method which seemed so fresh—and actually *was* fresh—in the first published volume has now become pat" (p. 11).

words needed to be added, too, so that my review shouldn't have the same fault I found in your book! When I discovered that they simply couldn't make any correction, that a correction would in fact cost them 1300 dollars, I blew up: between Cousins' generous precipitancy and young Canby's gratuitous carelessness I was caught. That careless sentence gave me more than one bad hour; and I am glad to learn from your own generous response that it perhaps gave you less trouble than it did me. Still, if I'd had a chance to revise my proof, it would have been excised, and I should never have burdened you with this lame and long-winded explanation. At least, I can say to myself with a wry grin, the review was *timely;* and if it counteracted the poisonous *Time* review—I didn't see it, but I take for granted that all *Time–Life* products are poisonous, by nature and by positive intent—I am doubly happy.

You rightly, in the act of composition, don't worry about the usefulness of your books in English classes or in works of reference; but there is one little addition, which you might wish on some young disciple or on your publisher, which would actually make them more useful, and would even, occasionally, help the ordinary reader. This is the device used by Eric Kahler in *Man the Measure,* of giving the birth and death dates of the writers you mention after the appearance of their name in the index. Sometimes one wants to check up on such matters, though there is no reason why you should introduce them in the narrative itself except when this directly serves your purpose. While I'm on the subject, there is still another task, not for you, but for some librarian, which your work should prompt: and that is a complete bibliography of American literature on the basis of your own readings. Unless I am mistaken, there is no such work; or even an approximation to it; or am I wrong? There are one or two flyspecks of fact I remember from the text that you may want to wipe off for the great complete and definitive edition of this work. On page 142 you quote Willis's description of Melville, referring to his Spanish eyes. That was a bit of journalistic carelessness

not on your part but on Willis's: for Melville's eyes were blue
and small, which is about the last conceivable association for
Spanish. As for the massacre of beards on Page 154, it probably *did* take place, not as a result of Captain Claret's caprice,
but because it finally became necessary to tighten discipline on
nearing home and carry out the Secretary of the Navy's orders.

Incidentally, I'm giving a lecture on Melville here tomorrow; for during the last few months I've been catching up on
the literature of Melville biography and criticism; indeed, I
recommended Jean Simon's classic study, the best there is, to
Harcourt a little while ago. I am still seething with indignation over a book that came out in 1939; Anderson's study on
Melville in the South Seas. The book is an outright libel on
Melville and the meanest kind of libel, a libel on a dead man
who can't hit back. I am tempted to see what the professors
did with Anderson's work and reopen the whole discussion if
they didn't point out the nature of Anderson's dirty job. I
refer specifically to his treatment of *Typee:* for Anderson's
thesis here is not that Melville embroidered his actual experience—which he of course did—but that he claimed that he
had never read sources he had cribbed from. The passages
Anderson adduces to prove this prove just the opposite. As for
his "proof" that Melville spent four weeks, not four months,
with the Typees, it rests upon an affidavit filed by the captain
of Melville's whaling ship a year after Melville had gone; so
that an error of memory, or even an error in transcription
which would turn "June" into "July" could destroy the whole
of Anderson's fabric of surmise: yet the possibility that the
affidavit might be incorrect and that Melville might be telling
the truth never crossed Anderson's mind, apparently. So resolutely, indeed, does he hold to the position that Melville is a
brazen liar, that he cannot resist exclamations of surprise
whenever he finds, in *Omoo,* that all of Melville's observations
check with the independent testimony at Anderson's disposal.
So debased are both morals and scholarship today, however,

that Anderson probably is looked upon as a "sound authority," just as Beard is looked upon as a sound historian, though
Beard actually falsified and suppressed important facts in his
histories, from 1930 onward, and if there were a sense of honor
among scholars, he would have been read out of every scholarly society, for his betrayal of scholarship. Instead, I note
with sorrow and indignation, he is even up for a medal in
history at our revered Institute of Arts and Letters. (If he gets
the medal, I shall publicly resign.)

As to reviews of your book, dear Van Wyck, I recommend
the hygienic practice of not looking at them at all, at least
until after your book has been out a year or so. Your success
makes you a marked man: remember how disgustingly
Goethe's juniors behaved toward him, just when he had
reached the height of his powers. My countrymen have an
even more drastic method of dealing with me now, and they
make a little ironic my practice of not reading reviews by the
simple expedient of not reviewing my books, or by dismissing
them in a paragraph or two, placed so that no one will notice
it, even by accident. Sophy actually read the *Times* Book
Section twice without finding Hillyer's review of *Green Memories;* and I came upon it by accident, thinking that the coast
was clear and I could read the paper unwarily. I have no
doubt as to what I have done in *Green Memories,* though I
was full of tribulations and misgivings when writing it; for the
letters that have come to me from my friends would buoy up a
drowning man or lift a depressed one into heaven. Parts of the
book are still unwritten; in a sense, it will always be incomplete to me; but what is there is there and I have no doubt
that in time it will find an audience. But now? I have become
a pariah, except out of my own country. I had occasion to note
this the other day when Whit Burnett[14] asked me to send a
selection in for the book of the *World's Greatest Writers.* He
had already, he said, received selections from 123 Americans;

14 Whit Burnett, Editor of *Story Magazine.*

but it was not on this list that I was included; for though my
world rank was among the first sixty I was not among the first
123 in my own country. It's an old story of course. When I
look at it through historic eyes it almost is a reassuring and
happy one; for so treated they our fathers before us. But there
are moments when a Melvillian bitterness and a Melvillian
scorn, if not a Melvillian despair, seize me; and I wonder then
why I am now making so many careful plans to go back to the
city, among the very people who care so little for my work.

This is a much longer letter than I meant to write, dear Van
Wyck. But there are moments, and this is one of them, when
the heart is lonely; and to whom can one turn then except to
an old friend who has perhaps his own share of this same
loneliness. I wanted *Green Memories* to go well for Geddes's
sake; and I am disappointed at what has happened to it for
that same reason. That is the last bitter berry on his tragic
wreath.

[New York, N.Y.]   November 24, 1947

Dear Lewis:
 Gladys has just come back from Amenia, where she stayed
for a night with the Sterns[15] (on her way up to the storage
warehouse in Poughkeepsie). She was so full of the charm of
your house, its all-round rightness, not to mention the blazing
fire on the kitchen hearth—and to think I hadn't remembered
there was a hearth there—it seemed more than ever unlikely
that we shall remain in New York, and just when you and
Sophy are planning to come here. It all depends upon whether
we can have quiet enough or not, though, for my own part, I
am not too disturbed here, though of course I am not writing

---

15 The Sterns lived in the Mumford house that winter.

at the moment. We shall see our way clearer in the spring. But
Gladys made me quite homesick for Amenia.

I could not guess, in the wonderful review you wrote, what
might have been the offending sentence. The point you made
against me is one I'm well aware of, though I'm still hoping in
my next volume to redress this weakness, and the review was
so magnificent that it simply lifted me off my feet. It made me
feel I was utterly spoiled, as I feel in any case. Thank you for
the suggestions in your letter. I shall see that the slight corrections are made in time and that is a good idea about the dates
in the index, I shall follow that procedure when the set is
collected. As for the general bibliography, I think that work
has been done in connection with the new *Literary History*
that Robert Spiller is superintending. This is scheduled to
appear in 1948, in three volumes, of which one is a bibliography. It ought to be virtually complete, as such things go.

I was a little disturbed by what you said about Beard and
the Institute, and I am not surprised by your impulse to resign
from this. But don't do it, dear Lewis! . . . But if Beard does
not get the medal, who will get it? I surely do not like his
isolationism, but was he not at least sincere in this? It is hard
for me to believe that he has knowingly falsified facts. Do
reconsider, Lewis, and think what the alternative is. What
other historian, one who is likely to get the medal, would you
prefer to the Beard of *forty years?*

I have just met a man, Kenneth Lindsay, M.P., who said he
had seen you in Hanover. He spoke again of the great name
you have in England. As for the yelpers and ignorers at home,
"let the dogs bark—the caravan passes on."

46 College Street
Hanover, New Hampshire   November 26, 1947

Dear Van Wyck:

It would be better that the Institute never gave a medal to anyone than that it should bestow this honor on a man with Charles Beard's record. Can you be so wilfully blind as not to realize what he has been doing these last fifteen years, and how completely he has betrayed his trust as a scholar? When Beard's Basic History[16] came out even timid little Canby was moved to protest openly against its omissions and its distortions. I went further than that at the time: I wrote a complete analysis of Beard's lapses, not only in the Basic History but in *America in Mid-Passage;* and I showed how completely and deliberately Beard had suppressed the case for the democracies, and how favorably he had put the case for our fascist enemies. I admitted his right to preach isolation from the housetops, in his openly polemic works, though by doing so he was betraying all that gives meaning to the work of writers, scholars, and scientists: but when he allowed his bias in politics to undermine his scholarship, I pointed out, he forfeited completely all respect in his chosen vocation. The *Saturday Review* held up this long article, because friends of Beard, who had heard about it, pleaded that he was in the hospital, ill, at the time and might be unfavorably affected by it: in fact, these friends of his made a valiant effort to suppress my article altogether, and they sufficiently undermined the judgment or courage of the editors to succeed.

Don't think it was easy for me to come out and write as I did. Beard was exceedingly kind to me when I was young; for long I loved and respected him, and closed my eyes to what he was saying and doing. But today he is the friend and helper of those who would defame the human cause for which all decent

16 *History of the United States,* by Charles and Mary Beard (1921); *America in Mid-Passage* (1939).

men fought during the second World War; like an even dearer erstwhile friend, John Flynn, he is on the side of the *Chicago Tribune*[17] and exercises the authority of his putative scholarship to spread their poison. He is no longer my friend; nor should he remain the friend of any other self-respecting man. His role has been that of an intellectual Quisling,[18] no less harmful because he has worked insidiously, and because instead of being openly attacked by his peers he is shielded and cozened by them. The idea that anyone in the Institute should propose to give a Medal to him for his work in History, the thought that the Institute might actually bestow it, I find profoundly shocking. If it is innocence, it is a guilty innocence, like that of Norman Cousins'[19] bystander, who watches another human being being attacked and doesn't go to his rescue or even admit there is any obligation to do so. Don't talk to me of a sense of proportion. It is you, dear Van Wyck, who has lost a sense of proportion. Precisely because men like Beard have been exercising authority and influence, the young have become indifferent to human values, cynical, and lacking in civic courage. We who have been silent, not the young, are to blame.

[New York, N.Y.]   November 30, 1947

Dear Lewis:

Your letter has disturbed me very much. I can't bear to have a falling out with you, especially over a subject that means as little to me as Charles Beard. But I am not "wilfully blind." The difficulty with me is that I am not able to read enough of

---

[17] The *Chicago Tribune* was openly pro-German.
[18] Vidkun A. L. Quisling, German puppet governor of Norway during the occupation.
[19] Norman Cousins, Editor of the *Saturday Review*.

the books that are written in our time, because, as you know, I am buried in other reading. As for John Flynn, I scarcely even know his name, and, as for Beard, I have not read either his *Basic History* or *America in Mid-Passage*. These medals are given for a man's whole life-work, and in supporting Beard I have been thinking of all his work meant to me in the years before and during *The Rise of American Civilization*. I think he is at bottom an Indiana farmer, and that to me explained his unsympathetic isolationism; but I am astonished to hear him described as a fascist and as lacking in real integrity. I bitterly regret not having read these later books, but, having heard James Truslow Adams describe him as a dangerous radical, I never supposed he could be as you describe him. On the record of his life-work, as we knew it ten years ago, I didn't see how he could be classed below Adams or Allen Nevins. If I have been mistaken, I am sorry.

But I'm not going to fall out with you on this or any other ground, for any such ground must be based on a misunderstanding. I could scarcely disagree with you on any subject if we had a preliminary agreement in regard to terms. Meanwhile, I am really handicapped by my immersion in other reading when it comes to final decisions about contemporary writers. In any case, dear Lewis, do let me beg you once again not to resign from the Institute. Even if, from your point of view, it does make many mistakes, it is probably worth while to have such a society. It will not be any better—only worse—if you leave it; and there's always a chance of improving it by staying in.

Meanwhile, I feel very, very sorry that we should have had this partial disagreement. Won't you give me a chance to see you before Christmas?

46 College Street, Hanover, New Hampshire   December 3, 1947

You are a man with a large, forgiving heart, dear Van Wyck; and even were you not, you are the last person I would willingly hurt. But the matter that lies between us is something more than a mere misunderstanding: it goes to the very bottom of each of our lives; and I should be lacking in friendship if I did not speak to you unreservedly about every aspect of it. Whether I resign from the Institute or not is a trivial matter: certainly I *will* resign if Beard gets the gold medal, but it is an idle threat on my part to say that I will do so publicly, for even if I made my resignation known to the newspapers I am not vain enough to think that they would care any more about my position than the people who see no betrayal of trust in giving a medal of honor to Beard: they wouldn't know what I was talking about, nor could they print my explanation without risking a libel suit. My resigning won't cause a ripple; and I can't even pretend that it will be a wrench on my part, since if it hadn't been for a feeling of loyalty toward the two decent people who invited me in, Frank Mather and Paul Elmer More, I'd have resigned long ago, without waiting for the Beard provocation.

If I read your handwriting correctly, you fancy I have said that Beard is a fascist as well as one "lacking in real integrity." I have not said that he was a fascist: that is a term I never use loosely. But I have indeed said that he was lacking in scholarly integrity, for in *America in Mid-Passage* and in the Basic History he pretends to describe objectively America's relation to the fascist attack without for a moment describing fascism's aims or suggesting that the civilized world was placed in jeopardy by those aims: it is the democratic governments upon which Beard vents his spleen, and in the Basic History he goes so far as to impute our participation in the war mainly to Roosevelt. His sins in these books are very easy to annotate from the standpoint of common judgment and exact scholarship: but they are mostly sins of supression and omission, and it would be difficult, except under the cover of a book review, to point out the dishonesty of Beard's practices here without opening oneself to a suit for libel it might be impossible, on purely legal grounds, to win. Beard's errors are not of the gross and flagrant kind; but the tendency of his writing during the last seventeen years is unmistakable. Without being either a traitor or a fascist himself, Beard has served the purposes of traitors and fascists, by his manner of presenting and warping the evidence, in supposedly objective works on American history. More outright enemies of the anti-fascist cause, people like Ezra Pound or Knut Hamsun, are much less dangerous than Beard; for they openly believed in fascism, while Beard's method was to give it the utmost benefit of the doubt whilst he insidiously attacked from the rear all who were prepared— and they were and *still are* a pitiful few—to resist fascism. In this Beard was not alone: he had the company of still another old friend of mine, equally venerable, equally identified with the democratic cause, Frank Lloyd Wright; and both of them had the sympathy and support of millions of complacent and unawakened people who never took the trouble to examine what they were doing. Did not the Basic History go into the list of books that went overseas to our soldiers? Grotesquely enough, it did; and so, too, in the midst of the war the Institute welcomed to its membership with equal blandness and affability, Frank Lloyd Wright.

All this may surprise you and distress you, dear Van Wyck; but the fact that you have been too absorbed in your great work to realize what has been going on about you does not absolve you. In times like these, everyone has a great temptation to withdraw from this confused and wicked world: perhaps the only work that will last in our time is work like that of Albert Schweitzer, who had the saintly courage to separate himself from this dying civilization and to exhibit the virtues that alone will save us from utter ruin. If you, too, wish to withdraw completely, that is your right; and I would respect you for exercising it. But your present course is not so inviolable or so innocent. You are sufficiently immersed in the world to concern yourself with the Institute's selections, and to give Beard your vote, if not his original support. If you wish to participate to that degree, you must accept the responsibility that goes with such participation. The fact that Beard is an old friend, the fact that he once seemed a benign and impeccable scholar, does not justify your failure to understand the struggle that has been going on these last fifteen years: the struggle that is still going on, and is focused in the very argument we are now having. Beard was my friend, too. He never did aught but kindness to me: tenderness, love, and gratitude are the only feelings I've ever had for him as a man. But I count myself grievously to blame that I didn't push all these feelings aside, long before 1944, in order to attack him with all the critical weapons I possess; for by not doing this I permitted authority and influence and honors to go to Beard without challenge of any kind, and thousands of people who fought in this last war feel cheated, because they have read and accepted Beard's interpretations of the struggle, and not mine.

When you, in turn, dear Van Wyck, vote a gold medal for Beard you are taking sides in this war: you are aligning yourself with the Beards and extending their range of influence, and at the same time you are turning your back to the Mumfords, and saying in effect that what they stood for was not important, and that in the main, people like Beard were probably right, at least you are giving aid and comfort to those who will more explicitly draw such conclusions. It was not altogether an accident that I wrote you about the gold medal for Beard in a letter wherein I exposed to you, as one of my closest and dearest friends, the utter loneliness I felt because of the reception of *Green Memories*. Both *Values for Survival* and *Green Memories* were rejected by the editors, the critics, the reviewers, the booksellers for the very reason that the works of Beard are lauded and distributed in editions by the hundred thousand. My two books dealt with the prelude to the war and its aftermath, in terms as honest and unsparing as I can set them forth. I am willing to let my whole life as a writer and a citizen be judged by those two books. Beard's success in gaining the ear of this generation is the measure of my failure. No matter how immense your good will, how capacious your giving heart, dear Van Wyck, you can't be equally benevolent toward both of us. Whether your eyes were shut or open when you voted, by voting for Beard you voted against me. You were not above the battle at that moment. You were in the thick of it *on the wrong side*. Beard's isolationism is not a trivial matter in times like these, when everything man holds dear depends on our overcoming tribalism and isolation and creating an actively cooperative world society: at this moment in world history his attitude should be something more meaningful to you than merely "unsympathetic," as if it were a taste for a curious native dish. A man of Beard's intellectual stature should not announce himself an isolationist without making every other decent man who hears him denounce him as a betrayer of humanity. Instead, you help to give him further honor and acclaim.

If only my own feelings and my own position were involved I should not go into the matter at such length, though I am afraid I would be unable to hide my disappointment. But your own work is involved, too; for by closing your eyes to what has actually been going on around you, by refusing so amiably to take sides, you have left out the bitter tragic element in the lives of Thoreau, Melville, Whitman, and have ranged yourself with the proper "gentlemanly men," who felt that these people were barbarous, hysterical or mad, because they made inconvenient issues over matters that gentlemenly men were careful never to take a position on. What I said in praise of *The Times of Melville and Whitman* and of all the other books in the series, was entirely sincere: I will never

retract a word from it, but rather will regret that there were a
score of felicities on which I did not have the time or space to
dwell. But the tragic choices and the tragic decisions in the
lives of our great writers, all those elements that caused them
to be despised and rejected by their own countrymen, not only
in their own lifetimes but long after, have somehow escaped
you; and the reason for that is that you have not let yourself
see them when they were under your nose. It would be better
to leave your series unfinished and to produce at least one
book which, out of your sympathy and understanding for your
own period, would run the full gamut of our experience. It is
only by living in the present moment fully that one could truly
have understood the experience of Melville and Whitman; and
unless you fully interpret that experience, you will not, when
the time comes, have a key to our present generation.

You meant the words kindly, dear friend; but I am not a
"great" man: though I have had persistence, I lacked either
the original talents or the ambition to achieve greatness in any
sense that is intelligible to me. No matter: we are all sinners
and we have all fallen short of our best possibilities, and today
all of us, great and small, talented and stupid, good and bad,
are fleeing from the wrath to come. In the eyes of God, Charles
Beard and I are both sinners: perhaps indistinguishably so.
But you have long been a friend, dear Van Wyck; and in the
eyes of a friend I expect a friend's loyalty and a friend's
understanding. If I have failed you here as you have failed me,
I am sorry.

[New York, N.Y.]   December 20, 1947

Dear Lewis:

As you must have guessed it would, your last letter has made
me very unhappy. It has been a sort of nightmare, a cloud over
these last days, for I don't think you can possibly know how I

feel about you and your work and I cannot bear the thought
of a barrier between us. Then again I feel the inadequacy of
words when one must clear up, if possible, a misunderstanding
as deep as this. Or perhaps "misunderstanding" is not the
right word, any more than "distasteful" was the right word to
convey my feeling about a tolerance for the fascist line. After
all, Lewis, I am not a shallow person. I have very deep and
sincere beliefs and convictions, though they are not very much
involved in this matter of elections and medals. The idea that
by voting for Beard I was voting against you was something
that could never have entered my head. Beard is not my
friend, as he is, or was, yours, I have never known him well,
nor have I ever thought that he was a great historian. He has,
to my mind, too little insight and feeling. I voted for him, in
good faith, because of *The Rise of American Civilization*. I
had no second thought, beside this, in the matter. Otherwise, I
do not take the Institute seriously. I have small influence there
and I seldom go there. I have been to just two dinner-meetings
in a year, and then I have gone in the spirit in which most of
the others go, for the pleasure of talking with other artists and
writers. It seems to me a most innocent organization, so
innocent that I don't understand why you dislike it. But,
rather than have a breach with you, I would resign from it at
once. This is, in any case, almost certainly, my last winter in
New York, and I shall have little to do with it in future. (We
are planning to go to Santa Fe next winter and to Concord,
Mass., the winter after. We must have a much simpler life
than we can have here.)

There is much in your letter that touches me and hurts me
both on your account and my own. What you say of your
loneliness grieves me very deeply. Much of it I understand,
much of it I do not. If you happened to have seen the *Tribune
Books* there you will have seen what I felt about *Green
Memories*. It is a book that I deeply loved and one that will
mean more and more, but how, with your vast following and

your world-reputation, can you feel lonely in any but a special sense? You have a multitude behind you of the most perceptive younger minds. Two of my friends within a week have spoken of you as people used to speak of Mill and Carlyle and I have met two or three Englishmen lately who told me that in England you have more influence than any other American writer. Surely you cannot feel that you are alone spiritually or, so far as I am concerned, that my small feeling for Beard can be weighted against my lifelong feeling for you.

Of course, too, I am greatly troubled by what you say of my "present course," though I don't quite know what that is. Whether I understand my own period or not I shall not know until I write about it; but I can't feel that you are right in saying I have sided with the "gentlemanly" man against the man who took the unpopular sides. It is true that I was the first writer of my generation who had one decent word to say about Longfellow and others—true that I had two chapters about O. W. Holmes. That was because I saw him in the New England setting and before I had clearly foreseen the subsequent volumes. Then I found I could not have more than two chapters about any writer. But I introduced Whitman in so many chapters that he has twice as much space as anyone else. And I do not think that, in that case at least, I failed to comprehend the more tragic elements. I *do agree* that my treatment of Melville was very inadequate. (As for Thoreau, I don't think there was anything really tragic about him.) But I think I care deeply for spiritual decency and I know the dangers of the relative "success" that I have had, the popular acceptance of my work, etc., etc. (Though this is now on the wane. My great days of "sales" are obviously over, and meanwhile my name is a byword apparently in scholarly and avant-garde circles where I am invariably treated as the scum of the earth.) But I didn't mean to go into this. I am glad you've said what you have said, for I shall be a failure unless I can do the book you say I should do. (The one book that I stake all on my ability to do and that I hope to do the first moment I can.) You cannot guess how much, for years, I have counted on your being there, how great your work has always seemed to me and how bewildered I have felt in being accused of a kind of disloyalty because of a more or less empty gesture towards a man whom I never associate with you.

P.S. Don't answer this, dear Lewis. I have too deep a confidence in the bond between us to believe it can ever be broken or seriously strained. I send real love to you all for Christmas and the New Year.

46 College Street
Hanover, New Hampshire   December 22, 1947

Dear Van Wyck:

Your letter came this morning; and I grieve at the gap between us, which has caused us both no little pain. There is no one in America whose integrity and uprightness have had such an effect in guiding my own actions as yours; and in that sense, even at the moment of quarreling, I was still your disciple. But now we have each said our say; and though I did not loose my words lightly, and cannot recall them, I am filled with remorse over their turning into an arrow in the heart of a friend. Perhaps only time will heal the wounds we've both, alas! inflicted; but to speed that process I offer you my hand, in old friendship and love. May the New Year bring every blessing to you and yours, to Gladys, to your children, and not least, your work.

[New York, N.Y.]   December 28, 1947

Dear Lewis:

Your little letter has made me very happy—I could not bear
to have a strain between us, and yet perhaps this will have
done us both some good. I could only be happy in our friendship if you made demands on me. I want you to expect my
work to be better than it has been and to expect more of me
than I have given. Of all writing men today you are the one I
care for most, the one who gives me values for survival.

We have been seeing quite a little of Lee of late! He was
here at a little party on Christmas day, and he has asked us to
the dress-rehearsal of *Rheingold*. I wish you were to be here
for it. (In spite of my having taken an oath never again to see
a Wagner opera.) He told me that you had had four offers for
movies of *Green Memories*—I can so easily imagine the travesty that Hollywood would make of it that I think you and
Sophy were wise in refusing them. But have you thought of an
English producer? What is that man's name?—is it Rank? In
England they would give you a decent production, even
perhaps a beautiful one, almost certainly one that would be
sympathetic. Could you suggest this to Harcourt? Would it not
be a good idea?

I hope so much, dear Lewis, that 1948 will be good to you
all. Gladys sends her love with mine—

Hanover, New Hampshire   February 5, 1948

Dear Van Wyck:

If old Mather[20] is still alive, will you send this on to him? I
had a shadowy memory of seeing his obituary; but I can't find

---

[20] Frank Jewett Mather, Professor of Art and Archeology, Princeton
University; art historian.

any record here in the *New York Times Index*. I wanted to explain to him my resignation:[21] since he originally sponsored me. I've just written More[22] formally. . . . Winter is still breathing down our neck here, but with the thermometer only at zero the other morning we felt that the worst was over and spring nearly here! Poor Jimmy Stern chose the wrong winter to hole up in Amenia.

At the moment I'm writing my annual article on the Atom Bomb; but I still haven't started on my book. The revision of *The Culture of Cities* took more time than I'd counted on; and I had to re-write the whole final chapter without even a flash of fresh thought. So much for brief and abstract chronicle.

[New York, N.Y.]   February 7, 1948

Dear Lewis:

The letter to F. J. Mather has just gone off. He is now living at 3 Evelyn Place, Princeton, New Jersey—and very much alive, though he is now all of eighty. I know he will be sorry to have your news. Your letter came with the *N.Y. Times* which has you spread all over the front page. Mr. Stevens called me last evening on the telephone, since you had mentioned me in your letter. What I said was that we had disagreed and that I felt very sorry about it. I *didn't* see the phrase that I was sorry you felt so "bitterly." If you feel strongly you ought to feel bitterly, but I was thinking all the time about Beard's whole lifework. I have not yet had a chance to read the Basic History. The poor old Institute has never in its fifty years had so much attention paid to it. This will lead a lot of people to read Beard again to find out the rights and wrongs of the question. I still feel that his lifework as a whole justifies the choice.

21 From the National Institute of Arts and Letters.
22 Paul Elmer More, literary critic.

We are getting on well here, but we have to fight off *people* much as one fights off mosquitoes in the summer woods. New York will never do for me when I begin to write again and we think now we shall go to Concord, Mass., for a part of next winter. I must be near big libraries and cannot go south or west.

Lee has been here twice to dinner lately. He said his great grief was that you were not here to see the *Ring*. We went four times to dress-rehearsals—the settings were extraordinary—and it has obviously done much for Lee. He is in high feather, more brilliant in talk than I've ever known him and setting out this week for a triumphant tour of the West. I dread the after-effects this summer.

My next book should be by far the best yet. What I am looking for is the roots of the literary mind of the *present,* and finding them I think in surprising ways. But I shan't begin to write before June. I have heard you were making a long revision of *The Culture of Cities,* presumably in advance of the other volumes. I am wondering how many changes you have had to make. I long for the day when I can read you *seriatim.*

[New York, N.Y.] May 1, 1948

Dear Lewis:

I am in a peck of trouble over the C. A. Beard affair, which has developed into a horrid mess. He has published a book that appears to be monstrous and several other members threaten to follow your example. I met Dean Gauss[23] the other night at an "American Scholar" dinner. He said Beard's new book was "poisonous" and felt that you were pretty well vindicated. Then Frank Mather thinks of resigning too; so does Allen Nevins. Meanwhile, I have to present the medal,

23 Christian Gauss, Dean of Princeton University.

for Canby, who was going to do it, has now refused to do so.
Some of these protestations come with ill-grace, I think, and
simply mean that the band-wagon has turned around; for the
medal was voted by a fair majority. Still, I am sorry on behalf
of the Institute and not just on my own account. I shall have
to refer in my remarks to my total disaccord with Beard's later
tendency (of which I was unaware). Then I can only fall back
on my whole-hearted admiration of the Beard I used to know
and *The Rise of American Civilization.*

You may have heard rumors of all these matters and also of
Walter Lippmann's letter urging the Institute at any price to
get you back again. Mather also proposes to make a change in
the constitution permitting you to join the Academy without
being in the Institute. He wants you in the Academy, as,
heaven knows, I do, and will work for it if he has a chance to
do so. Meanwhile, I have resigned as secretary. Probably all
this is supremely unimportant to you, but I should like to talk
it over with you as one of a dozen more important matters.

Hanover, New Hampshire   May 3, 1948

The news in your letter, dear Van Wyck, fills me with
concern; for I had no thought, when I began my protest, that
you would have to bear the brunt of it: my first remarks to
you were as a friend and confidant, rather than a member of
the Institute. The mischief is that the Beard nomination for a
medal was not nipped in the bud in committee; which means,
really, that everyone on the committee had been wrapped in
cotton-batting the last ten years and hadn't realized for a
moment what Beard had actually been doing. I am chagrined
to think that my erstwhile colleagues had to wait for the last
poisonous opus to see that my protest was justified; for I could
assure them that there was plenty of evidence in everything

else Beard had published in history during the last ten years: indeed, in order to conceal his original misjudgements he has had to multiply them, like a desperate gambler doubling his stakes and eventually losing, as Beard has lost, his honor. The courtesy that still surrounds the old villain—for that is what he has become by now—I find singularly offensive: even Pringle in the recent *Saturday Review* does little more than shake a naughty! naughty! finger at him.

But what have you to do with all this, dear Van Wyck? It is unthinkable that you should bear the burden for the collective error of bestowing the medal: the role of scapegoat, or rather Sacrificial Lamb, doesn't become you, and what is more is quite unjust. You should not be made to hold the bag while the more cowardly members of the Institute hastily run around the corner. The only way to repair the mischief, as I see it, is for you to decide in advance that you will be officially ill, the day before the affair comes off, and run away to the country till it's over. If you don't decide on an imaginary illness you may find yourself coming down with a real one. For there is really nothing you can say at that presentation: to dissociate yourself from the Beard of the last 15 years is to add an insult to the mockery of giving the medal in the first place. Even *The Rise of American Civilization* is not impeccable; for as soon as he reaches the sequel, *America in Mid-Passage,* he plays Bluebeard to the facts and quietly disposes of the inconvenient remains. If I were in Amenia now and could turn to the proofs of my suppressed article I could give you chapter and verse.

No: the thing to do is to absent yourself; and prompt some friend of Beard's to warn him to stay away from the exercises; then the presentation of the Medal can be skipped; and the medal can be forwarded without further words to Beard. To open one's mouth on such an occasion is only to invite gryphons and hippopotamuses to walk in! All the other repercussions that you tell me about are news to me: Hanover is a long way from the center of gossip and my visits to New York are so hasty and breathless that I find myself in the midst of the vacuum formed by a whirlpool. But I will be in around the twentieth; and we must meet then. By that time, I trust, the Affair Beard will be over without any further suffering for you. If it weren't for the part you've been forced to play I should say that my resignation was well worth while: without it, the stench might have been suppressed for another decade. I saw Mather when I was down in Princeton a month ago; but I hasten to add that I did nothing to encourage him to resign from the Institute: what may have prompted him is that he began reading Beard! He is such a sweet, robust, magnanimous old soul. I hate to think of reaching the age of eighty, but if I do, I hope I meet life's buffets with half the manliness he has done; and his wife, incidentally, seems to me an angel, too.

My own work is still at a standstill; but I am not without hope for it, once I get back to Amenia, even if nothing came out of my sojourn there last summer.

Amenia, New York   May 23, 1948

Dear Van Wyck:

I trust Friday wasn't too painful an ordeal for you, if indeed that is the day you gave the medal to Beard. Tell me all the grisly details! Our plans still hold to come here as a family around 14 June; and though I have to attend a conference in New York the following week, and go to Iowa City the week after, I hope to get back in time to receive you and Gladys here before you leave the Josephson's[24] domain.

[24] Matthew Josephson, political writer.

Hanover, New Hampshire   June 4, 1948
[Postcard from Mumford]

Alyse Gregory is writing a biography of Randolph Bourne
as you probably know and can't find a copy of the *Seven Arts*
in England, not even in the British Museum. Have you any
notion of anyone there who has a set? I can't for the life of me
imagine. But perhaps she's already asked you.

Amenia, New York   August 8, 1948

The news that you are working, dear Van Wyck, was altogether happy and reassuring, almost like the sound of a clock
ticking in the house when one finds that one's own watch has
stopped. And my watch *has* been stopping this summer, quite
disconcertingly, either because the mainspring has been over-
wound, or because there is sand in the works: the sand being
partly of my own doing. . . . Now I can count on barely five
uninterrupted weeks ahead of me; and though I've written
over a hundred pages, I've still to get really started on my
book. Never has a book given me so much trouble; and it will
have to be a mighty good one, indeed a quite stupendous one,
to justify all the labor pains I've been having.

c/o E. P. Dutton & Co.
300 Fourth Avenue, New York, N.Y.   September 6, 1948

Dear Lewis:
    We are still at Chilmark and I merely use this impersonal
address because we are otherwise at sea for the winter. We are
driving down next Thursday to 350 E. 57th Street, fully
determined to sell the apartment at once (as too expensive

and as getting us in for all manner of unnecessary distractions). I hope we can find a house to rent in Connecticut on our way down, so that we can move in a few weeks. In fact, we must find one very soon.

Work has gone pretty well here, in spite of a deluge of children,—no less than *seven*, including grand-children. They were all sweet to us and the summer has been a happy one, but we have seen virtually no one else.

Now I am so sorry that your summer has not been good, though I can't take very seriously the stopping of your "watch." Your inner machinery has the power of a dynamo, but I don't doubt this involves inconvenient moments. I can believe that finding an apartment must be a ghastly business (I don't suppose you would like to *buy ours?!!*), more so than finding a house, in Connecticut, of which I already know that the supply exists.

I have just had surprising notes from Mike and Sally Robinson, surprising because I feared he could not live as long as this. They settled in the Ojai Valley, where he was too ill to go, I thought, and now they are forced to pull up stakes and come East to live again. I suspect it's because they are absolutely without money. They are coming on October 1st to live with their son Bartlett at Noroton, Conn. I mention it because Mike says "The old friend Lewis Mumford is still going strong to very good 'purpose' in *Sat. Rev. of Lit.*" etc. His writing is so cramped that I can hardly read it.—This is the scrappiest of notes but brings you our love—and I could say Tom Benton's, who speaks of you affectionately. We have had four of your books strewn over our table here this summer.

Amenia, New York   September 8, 1948

Your letter, dear Van Wyck, was very welcome; and since my last note to you was rather lugubrious, let me tell you at once that almost immediately afterward I finally got started on the book,[25] the real one, not the three or four changelings that tried to foist themselves on me the last two years; and just today I finished page 200 of the first draft; which is more than two-fifths of the whole. Though the manuscript, like all my first drafts, is uneven, it will provide a good skeleton to build on; and even now there are passages in which on very familiar themes, religion and love, I have managed to say a few things I've never said before, and which no one else had said very well. I hope to finish another chapter before I close up shop here for good.

I spend part of next week in Washington, mainly to give an address at the Centennial of the American Association for the Advancement of Science: a wicked, heretical address on Technics and the Future of Western Civilization, meant to puncture a number of swollen ideological balloons that will doubtless fill the skies during that week of celebration and organized complacency. I am now so well wrapped in the cocoon of my thoughts that I can take "interruptions" in my stride: once a book is *there*, as you well know, it provides a sort of automatic security, like that which keeps a baby uninjured in the womb. . . .

I've been in touch with the Boardman Robinsons at intervals during the past few years; and even bought a few of his pictures at one of his exhibitions a little while ago: a *Leaves of Grass* and a *Moby-Dick* illustration; so I knew about his plight; but, like you, had thought that his end was near. To think of the godlike Boardman condemned to slow, ignominious decay—that sort of thing taxes one's deepest reserves of faith. I'll write him. Alas! that even money will hardly ease his lot; though the lack of it may make it more bitter.

25 *The Conduct of Life* (1951).

Cornwall, Connecticut   October 3, 1948

Dear Lewis;

We are not there yet, but we're going up on Wednesday or Thursday. Thank goodness—I was heading here for lunacy and bankruptcy, and we found there the perfect house for $100 a month rent and the possibility of buying if we like it. More later, but you must see it—the house of the widow of a Yale professor and apparently just right for us.

What good news that your book goes well—so does mine, now that I'm well under way. I am sending you my *Chilmark Miscellany*, a few selections.

We have been rather confused here, and much excited by Kenyon's marriage to Kappo Phelan, the theatre critic of the *Commonweal*. I was rather disturbed by the R.-C. aspect of it, but Kappo is a kind of heretic, she says, at any rate, politically free and thoroughly intelligent.

Forgive this scrawl, dear Lewis! I am writing my book here with confusion all around me, as you can picture to yourself. I have seen Lee Simonson once or twice and find him in excellent condition. He has been taken over by *Harper's* and is elated thereby.

153 West 82nd Street, New York, N.Y.   February 18, 1949

Dear Van Wyck:

. . . I knew that this winter would be a broken and devastating one for me, merely because of all the travelling and lecturing I had let myself in for; and though it has been prosperous, financially, as no other year I can remember has been, that hardly makes up for the great empty spaces in the very center of one's soul. . . . I count the days till May comes, when the nightmare of travelling—I am a bad traveller, partly because I let it absorb too much of me, partly, perhaps, because I am like one of those delicate regional wines of France that don't like to be jostled in transportation—and lecturing to boot will come to an end. I have rigorously ruled out any kind of lecture or other time-consuming engagement until I finish Volume Four; and I hope finally to get down to completing the first draft of it by the middle of May. Spiritually, my contact with the New south, and especially with the fine, eager, responsible young students I have met, has not been unrewarding; and in retrospect I shall probably think well of this winter. . . . Even reading has consumed only a very little of my time. I did manage, with some relish, to go through *The Princess Casamassima,* the only long work of James's, apart from *The Americans,* that I believe I have ever finished; and I have been digging away at Albert Schweitzer, whom I know of old but had never read exhaustively. He is certainly not a writer; and perhaps not even a thinker in any rigorous sense: yet a certain greatness, the greatness of a sincere conviction, simply acted upon, shines through all his writing and redeems it from platitude. I also had a go at Thomas Mann's *Faust* and found it quite indigestible, almost repulsive esthetically, wooden and labored as even the worst pages of Joseph were not. It's the second part of *Faust* all over again. His high point was *The Magic Mountain;* and what is left is just the rubble and splinters left from that great work of fabrication. Or so it seems to me.

Have your plans for Europe matured yet? I am considerably relieved that Russia didn't force us into war this summer; and think that the outlook may actually improve for a little while before it gets worse again. Once my book is done, if we are not too broke then, I have promised Alison and Sophy that we'll visit Europe as a family, possibly in the summer of 1950, or at latest 1951. I got an invitation to sit on a UN commission, which would have met for a month *in Paris* next November; but refused, because I didn't want to be interrupted: partly that, and partly because, next time I go to Europe, I want to have more time for loafing and seeing, and be less bent on work. Since 1922 I haven't once visited Europe without having definite jobs to perform and a limited time to perform them in.

Coming back to New York now, with you moved away, I realize how empty it is of any I can properly call my friends any more: my old cronies have either moved away or died, and that is something of a problem for people in their fifties. But I must not complain.

Cornwall, Connecticut   March 18, 1949

Dear Lewis:

I shan't begin another letter with my old apologies, but it's always the same reason when I don't write to you. I have been reading my eyes out and writing straight along and the days have passed like a dream, they have whirled so silently by, not a play, not a concert, not even a movie this winter, though we are going to New Haven next week to see a new translation of *Faust*.

We have just bought a house at Bridgewater, four miles from New Milford and therefore not more than a half-hour's drive from you; and there I hope we shall spend the rest of our lives. This village existence is just the thing for both of us, and I could really wish never to see New York again, or interrupt the concentration one finds out here. We hope to move into the house, after the alterations are done, sometime about June 1st. It is an odd sort of house, the kind that no one seems to like, and therefore we were able to get it at a rather low price—and it has a lovely garden, moreover. But you will see it soon, thank goodness.

We gave up all thought of Europe when we decided to buy

this house, alter it and assemble all our possessions from storage places. We should otherwise have been so happy to turn the silo over to you—if you had wished it—for July. Now we are wondering if you were able to find a house somewhere on the Vineyard—and how much we hope so! Gladys had it much in mind and sent Sophy whatever suggestions she could. But, as you know, there are so few houses to be had there, at least at our end of the island. What fun it would be if we could be fairly close together this summer on the island, and before and after. It was good news that you're coming to Amenia about April 20th. That is only four weeks away. . . .

To think you are finishing your first draught by the middle of May! I have done only 200 pages thus far, but I make steady progress and the book is always more exciting. This time, dear Lewis, I am doing something really important. I am supplying the missing link between the present and the past—or rather hundreds of missing links of a kind that most people have never suspected. *Then* my real life-work begins! For I feel deeply inside that I'm just beginning to find out what my real work is and what I have to say. Just you wait and see! And I have a clear strong feeling that things are coming *our way,* that another generation is coming along that is much more congenial with you and me than the minds that have been dominant in the last twenty years. I gather that you are encountering them in your Southern lectures, as I find them in several writers who are going to have something to say in the future (among them, Peter Viereck). But we must compare notes about all these things. We have seen the Zimmerns— bless them—several times this winter, and are dining with them again in Hartford next week Thursday—an hour's drive away. What reassuring souls they are, however one may differ with them.

Amenia, New York   August 10, 1949

Dear Van Wyck:

. . . The days are oven-hot here, too: indeed this is the first
summer in a long time that I have had to work with an
electric fan behind me, partly to keep my body cool, partly to
keep the flies who have survived DDT, a very pertinacious lot
of creatures, from driving me frantic. The second draft has
gone well, better than I dared hope; and I am now more than
a third of the way through it; though at the rate it is expanding the book will prove to be an eleven months baby, like
Gargantua himself, and everyone will curse me for its size,
—which, for our current American taste, also means unread-
ability. I have just polished off my most important chapter,
that on religion, which ends with what will look to my
enemies like sheer journalism, an account of Albert Schweitzer,
though I planned to use him long ago and wrote the first
draft of this little essay last summer. I think I've managed to
say why religion is important and yet why none of the existing
religions is anything but provisional or Ersatz; though I
daresay Emerson said most of it, in his own inimitable way,
long before me. By the end of September I hope to have the
second draft written; and such further emendations as I do
will be in details, probably, rather than a wholesale re-writing.
I am going to try, by this method, to avoid the overcomplica-
tions and elaborations and needless qualifications that sometimes encumber my later drafts, having found recently, by a
close comparison, how much I had lost in my final version of
Herman Melville. (I had deposited the first draft with the
National Institute, and though it was returned last year, at my
request, I had just got around to glancing at it.)

As for the Institute, I love Frank Mather for his doughty
advocacy of my name, and you for wanting to bring a matter
where I had forced the issue to a more happy conclusion: but
once the deed was done, the whole business disappeared from

my own mind, leaving not a wrinkle or a rankle behind; and in that state I think it would be better to leave it. My doing this may cause me to miss a few faces at my funeral; but I should not be quite sure, in advance, that those who would thus honor me, with a sigh of relief that my cantankerous self was at last beyond the possibility of further mischief, would be those by whose presence I should feel honored: so that rather evens itself up. I have had all the honors that are good for me, in my time; and the honor of staying out of the Institute, though openly qualified for membership and once accepted, is as great, almost, as the honor of being in. My fate, like Melville's, whom I don't resemble in any other particular, is to be, despite my extravert nature (vide my Rorschach) to be a decidedly unclubby man. So, dear Van Wyck, accept this brotherly embrace and erase any trace of unhappiness over the whole affair that may remain in your own consciousness.

It is good to hear of the progress you have made on your own book: I can foresee that it will give me years of fresh reading to do, and not a little reflection, too; because I have had only half an ear cocked for the voice of our contemporaries, since we got out the last *American Caravan* in 1936; and that is almost half a generation ago. . . .

153 West 82nd Street, New York, N.Y.   October 21, 1949

Dear Van Wyck:

Don't worry about the re-writing of the book. The only book I seriously damaged by re-writing was *The Culture of Cities*. My re-writing the *Herman Melville* was bad only because it tempted me to add the sublime howler and the one or two minor errors that did a powerful lot of academic damage, outrageously out of all proportion to the sins themselves, to the book and to me. But *The Renewal of Life*, while already a fairly solid and well-composed book, does not yet fulfill my original intentions; and I am prayerfully hoping that all the fine spontaneities and creativities that (in small quantities) will bring it to life will be forthcoming in the final draft, now that my mind need no longer be concerned with facts and organization. I wish the damned book were really finished: it begins to feel as heavy as an albatross and I wonder what offense I have committed against the gods, to carry this creature twenty long years. Strange that it does not yet stink!

153 West 82nd Street, New York, N.Y.   December 31, 1949

It was good to get your Christmas messages, dear Van Wyck. At the moment I'm up to my neck in the final draft of *The Renewal of Life:* mainly a matter of wringing dry the soggy parts or adding a pinch of sunlight to the dull spots! But we've had a better winter of it in New York, so far, than we dared hope for: very vivid and exciting the first month or so before I settled back to the monastic routine of writing. Now, except for a week at Yale and a weekend at Newport (talking to the Admirals), both in January, I expect to be here, tied down to my book, till April.

And how goes *your* book? I am eager to hear of it. I've been reading Henry James recently and yesterday, at the Library waiting for a book, I turned to your *New England: Indian Summer* to recall your words about him. In your final summing up you picked out the very stories that had—and how belatedly!—stirred one. That marriage of true minds gave me great joy. . . .

Bridgewater, Connecticut   January 25, 1950

Dear Lewis:

I have been buried under proofs or I should have written long ago to tell you how exciting I found your article in the *Sunday Times*.[26] Is this in any way a summary of your present book, or is it from the book, and is there much more of it? Gladys and I have read it over and over and discussed it much. I have seen nothing for a very long time that stirred me so much, and I am becoming desperately eager to finish my history now and begin to think about things that are more important. . . .

My book goes well, I think; it is about two-thirds done, and I am only anxious now about my general conclusion. I have to review so much and to have *thought out* so much that I have not been ready to do this as it should be done.

153 West 82nd Street, New York, N.Y.   January 28, 1950

Dear Van Wyck:

I returned from Newport, last night, my old alma mater, where I lectured to the students at the Naval War College on the atomic bomb, to find your letter waiting for me. As luck would have it, we're committed to go to a dinner at the New School that night and can't well back out of it, as I am to begin a short course of lectures there the following week.

It's good to get your praise for the *Times* article; for I haven't had too many letters about it from people I can really respect, though there has been a strange and wonderful flocking to my standard from all the crackpot Messiahs who have been lurking in the walls; about which I'll tell you when we meet. I fear I must have said or implied something foolish,

26 *New York Times Book Review* (January 15, 1950).

from the response I get from *those* people. The article is no
part of my book; but I wish that my book were yet written
with anything like its brevity and compactness. Actually, I
wrote the first draft, in response to a request from Brown, the
new editor, just to prove that it could *not* be done; and then
was a little surprised to find that, if one omitted all details,
something could in fact be said in 3000 words that would
otherwise probably defy expression in anything short of a
book. The amazing thing about it is that Brown read my
Golden Day and remembered that I had written literary
criticism: a feat of memory on his part that surpasses any
records of extrasensory perception. It was that compliment
that impelled me to make the effort to meet his challenge.

Amenia, New York   June 28, 1950

Dear Van Wyck:

What a delight it is to have the gift of *Indian Summer* in an
Everyman edition. As GBS felt when *Back to Methusaleh*
came out in the World's Classics edition, it is like being
canonized in your own lifetime. All the others will be in the
same format finally, no doubt; and I trust that your other
books will keep them company for the special benefits of the
young. I salute your prospective immortality—if anything
achieves that state on this benighted planet.

Well, Korea or no Korea, I have started again on my book:
with hopeful words and a sinking heart!

Bridgewater, Connecticut   July 31, 1950

Dear Lewis:

. . . I was just on the point of asking you to bring the manuscript of your book, even if you did not intend to work
on it. I do so want to see it, or at least to hear some of it read,
as you read to us from your *Melville* more than twenty years
ago. We are already building hopes on some other arrangement in a month or two—for it is very important for me to see
more of you—especially now when I am face to face with the
question of my own conclusions. I need reinforcement from
you, probably more than from anyone else; and I really need
to see you. . . .

Bridgewater, Connecticut   January 4, 1951

Dear Lewis:

I have been thinking of you constantly since "Man as Interpreter" came, a tantalizing fragment of the great book that is
coming. I have scribbled all over the margins of it, for it set
my mind running as everything you write always does. So far
as I am concerned, only you and Bertrand Russell are saying
now the great things that must be said. Could you send me a
p. c. just saying when I am to see the whole book? I am going
to set to work on my last chapter in a week or two and I want
to read you before I finish it—if possible. . . .

153 West 82nd Street, New York, N.Y.   January 6, 1951

Dear Van Wyck:

The usual physical letdown that follows the completion of a
long book overcame me in the middle of December; I want my

mind clear, if not for my book, then for a dozen other things that should occupy my attention in a country that is going to hell so rapidly that it may be in no mood to look at such a book as mine by the time it comes out. I have been concerned by the temper of our leaders: the smallness of their minds is only equalled by the enormity of their unreason. Our people are, as usual, far sounder than Congress or the newspapers would represent them as being; but as things go now, their voice is unheard; and those of us who would speak for them, as I recently tried to do in a letter to the *Herald Tribune,* are throttled by what is fast settling down into a universal censorship. I pictured all this as happening in my 1947 article on the social consequences of the atomic bomb; but even I didn't think it would overtake us so quickly, and so fatally extirpate the surviving organs of reason. Looking at our leaders, their bad judgement, their coarse impudence, their inability to admit responsibility or accept blame, I am humiliated at being an American and ashamed at the country that bore them.

As for my promise to show you the book, I would but for the fact that I have hacked away at the manuscript so sternly that it is in no shape to be read, even in Sophy's "final" version. It should go to the printer before this month is over; and I'll be happy to send you the author's galleys as soon as they come; but it would be fair to neither of us to show you my present battered draft. The book will be the better for my hacking; for despite all my vigilance in the writing I came upon prolix or overwrought passages even in the final draft. But have patience: and be comforted by the thought that you know all I am going to say anyway, except for one or two quite original conceptions, which are probably not nearly as valuable as their inflated author now thinks! . . .

Amenia, New York   August 7, 1951

Dear Van Wyck:

You don't need any extra stimulus to begin your next book: but if you did the enclosed extract,[27] which I came upon while collecting Fletcher's letters for Pearson, would perhaps supply it. . . .

Amenia, New York   August 21, 1951

Dear Van Wyck:

The first copy of *The Conduct of Life* was waiting for me on my return and Harcourt tells me that they're sending you an advance copy in the hope of getting a few words from you.[28] *Don't pay any attention to that request!* Don't spare *me* your criticisms, at your leisure: that is another matter. I shall always be grateful for what you so generously said about *The Golden Day* in advance.

---

27 (From a letter of J. G. Fletcher's: October 2, 1927.)
   I am very glad to hear that Brooks is better—I admire deeply the truth-seeking and integrity of his criticism, his devotion to his task, and his character as a man. I owe him a great debt, and so does everyone in America who cares for the tradition of great literature.
28 Lewis Mumford's *The Conduct of Life.*
   The Conduct of Life is the wisest book we are likely to see this year. It outlines realistically the new culture that must emerge from our present chaos of regression and despair, expressing for a day of disintegration the theme of the renewal of life and man that has always marked the major American tradition. It is the master-work of a lonely thinker who will seem in retrospect one of the greatest of his time.

Van Wyck Brooks

Bridgewater, Connecticut   September 13, 1951

Dear Lewis:

I have been an unconscionably long time writing to you about your book, but I have been taking it in small doses (along with *The Condition of Man,* which I have just reread in conjunction with it). I am sure it is the wisest book we are likely to see this year, immensely impressive and moving, and what perhaps strikes me most is that it carries on the major American line of Emerson, Whitman and William James. You seem to me to be number 4 in this line of succession, and you speak with, for me, unique authority in the face of the current philosophies of regression and despair. I think I am beginning to see the real dimensions of your work, which has all sprung from one tap-root that goes down very deep; and you are having your reward for the great life you have lived in this wonderful sense you convey of human renewal. I have copied out fifty or more of my pages of notes from these two books of yours alone, hoping to read all the rest in the next month or so; and it seems to me that in this last volume you have opened up a new vein that calls for a further development in many more books. I am thinking especially of "The Way and the Life" at the end of this book, but you make so many points that are revolutionary in our time—such as the need of tenderness as a condition of renewal. Also your definition of God and your constant sense of the insurgence of life, as exciting as Emerson must have been in his time, and it is really astounding that you can feel and convey this feeling so powerfully and convincingly in this time of paralysis and decay. Your book has given me just the shock I need when I am attempting to begin another in somewhat the same line. Your name ought soon to be a "household word" here as it has become in England, for your magnificent series is obviously one of the few great literary structures of our time.

I have been wondering—would it not be possible for some

younger student to write a one-volume abridgement of these four volumes, somewhat like the Toynbee abridgement? It strikes me that such a book is called for. Meanwhile, I do hope *The Conduct of Life* will find a fraction of the readers it ought to reach. I cannot imagine anyone who would not be enthralled by it,—by its great vision, its positive message, its humane imagination, unique in our time, as far as I know.

We are still on the island, leaving tomorrow for home, and I have a little chore of editing that I must do at once. Then I'm going to resume my reading of the works of Lewis Mumford, who is more and more my favorite American author. I am sending off to Harcourt a few words which they might care to use in advertising.

Amenia, New York   September 18, 1951

Dear Van Wyck:

. . . It was a double relief and a great joy to receive your letter: full of those generous words that are good for an author —pure oriental balm—when he has published a book, whether or not they are otherwise justified. The book offers a real problem to an age of literary scanners and snatchers: the problem of anyone is giving it enough time to understand, with any fullness, its message. But at least in you, dear old friend, I have found *one reader,* and one whose good opinion outweighs for me the probable indifference of a legion. So I am well satisfied. You are right in thinking the last chapter only a beginning: what follows from it are the three chapters of *application* to education, to politics, to marriage that I finally chucked out of the ms. as too meager to do justice to the theme, yet so bulky that they would, if left in, sink the book. Granted a little further time, and what is most important some measure of response, each chapter should—and may—become a book. As for your fine suggestion of a one-volume condensation, the task would be easy if any zealous young editor came forward: provided, again, that *The Conduct of Life* does not prove, from a practical standpoint, stillborn. But the Young Editor still lurks in the bushes, if indeed he has yet been born: the thought of him, as far as I am concerned, comes under the head of "Reveries of a Bachelor!"

Bridgewater, Connecticut   September 25, 1951

Dear Lewis:

My mind has been going round in circles trying to start a new book, or I should have written to you long before this. I was disquieted by the review of *The Conduct of Life* in the *Sunday Times,* with its niggling over one point in your great book; and I was troubled by the alleged phrase of mine which they have quoted in their advertising. I *may* have said what they quote a hundred years ago, but that is not what I said when I wrote to them ten days ago and when they wrote to me to acknowledge this. I can't recall all I said, but it began: "*The Conduct of Life* is the wisest book we are likely to see this year," and it ended: "The master-work of a lonely thinker who will seem in retrospect one of the greatest of his time." There was much else between, and now it boils down in their advertising to this tepid phrase,—which must have been somebody else's! Disgusting—I am writing them in this mail to ask them what they mean by it. It is a great book, I am sure of that, and when I can escape from the chaos I am in and get out from under a new box of novels that I must read for Academy awards, I look forward (as to nothing else) to reading the whole of L. M. in preparation for writing about him, *I hope* with a little success at least.

Now to follow up what I said about a *book based on your*

series—like Toynbee's abridgement written *not* by the author —it occurs to me that the person to do it might possibly be some young Englishman and that perhaps Warburg might know who this is. I think this is the kind of work the English are very skilful at and that such an abridgement might well be popular, if done with sympathy and skill, as it might be done there, and especially as you have so many followers in England. And as you might not care to suggest it, I am wondering if *I* might write to Warburg and propose this idea to him. I think this great series of yours might lend itself to some such treatment and win a new army of readers for you that your books should have. What say you to this, or would it displease you? I was rereading *The Conduct of Life* early this morning, and I am sure that you are saying immensely significant things that a very large public should have the profit of. What also strikes me is that you have opened up a vein that should now begin to flow through a dozen new books of your own. You are rightly being called a prophet, and you are really the only man who has struck the rock like Aaron in our desert of stone. I know something of the suffering that has gone to form this message, the wealth and depth of character that lie behind it.

I am floundering so myself that I don't know what I'm doing, but what I am attempting is a sort of testament and one that owes much to you and corroborates you, or will do so, I hope, when it runs clear.

Send me a p. c. about this suggestion of a line to Warburg.

P.S. If you really have a copy to spare of the *Renewal of the Arts* lectures[29] I should love to have it!

29 "From Revolt to Renewal," by Lewis Mumford, in *The Arts in Renewal*, Benjamin Franklin Lectures of the University of Pennsylvania (1951).

153 West 82nd Street, New York, N.Y.   October 1, 1951

Dear Van Wyck:

. . . I am having a taste of quiet bachelor existence myself.
Your warm, generous, overflowing letter warmed the cockles of
my heart; and as you must know from your own experience,
there is a big lump of ice in that region when a book comes
out: particularly such a book as mine, which, if it is as good as
you think—and as I, I must immodestly add, think too—cannot hope to win any overwhelming response either from reviewers or readers at first, precisely because it demands so
much from them. As to the reviewers, they are finding an easy
way out: they are ignoring it, or patronizing it when they feel
obliged to pay attention; as the simplest and easiest way of
sending it to oblivion. Judged objectively, that is a good sign;
and it confirms my original intuition, which I must have told
you as I told ten other people last summer, that this is my
Moby-Dick. But subjectively, one cannot deny that the cold
lump gets bigger and solider when one meets with such treatment, in contrast with the way my earlier books were hailed
and hallooed about; and therefore such warm understanding
words as yours are doubly welcome.

Your suggestion about making overtures to Warburg likewise
fall upon very grateful ears; and I give you both my blessing
and my thanks for that venture—not less because it is one of
those things that will take time to consummate. . . .

I try not to read reviews of my book till six months have
passed; but I could not help noting that the *New York Times
Book Review,* chose a young *architect,* with no general background, to review the *The Conduct of Life,* on the same principle that he would have asked a stonecutter to have reviewed
a book by Socrates, or an optician to give the last word on
Spinoza's *Tractatus Theologico-Politicus.* Against such glacial
stupidity, there is no fighting. As for Harcourt's ineptitude
with your quotation, it is of a piece with all that they have
done and still more haven't done. But, forgive me for saying

it, dear Van Wyck, I think you yourself were responsible for
their not using your first sentence. Even I winced a little when I
first read it in your enthusiastic letter to me: Sophy winced so
much—I was away and she happened to read it first—that she
almost wanted to keep the letter from me, in the sensitive state
I was at the moment. I knew what you meant: how could I
doubt it? But by some accident you overlooked the actual
effect on the reader of using instead of a simple positive statement an almost comically restricted superlative. To say that
The Conduct of Life was a wise book would have been a
compliment: but to say, like a cagey reviewer, that it is "the
wisest book we will see this year" is like saying that I am the
greatest American author who lives on West 82 Street. I no
longer wince, but chortle over it: as I hope you will, too. With
Waldo I have a real account to settle; for despite his praise, I
was not in the least flattered by his review: it was a hasty,
superficial performance, which at no point showed any real
understanding of my purpose or critically came to grips with
our philosophic differences. But he, poor man, is in the
doldrums over the assinine treatment the reviewers and still
more the book editors have been giving his *Bolivar*—which
seems to me a solid and important work—and I shall have to
bide my time and wait till he has licked his wounds before I
tell him candidly how I feel about his review.

[October 21, 1951]

Bridgewater, Connecticut   Sunday morning

Dear Lewis:

As we have to go up to Lake Placid on Tuesday to see my
grandson Peter at school, I fear we cannot see you this weekend—unless, by chance you drive over here—so I am writing
this hasty line to say I have written to Warburg and much
hope that something may come of this suggestion. The English

do that sort of thing superbly well, and I can imagine a simplification of your complex series that would be immensely useful all round. Of course, however, you would have to supervise it.

Rather in the doldrums myself, trying to break into my new book, I have had a sort of blood-transfusion reading some of your earlier books. They have heartened me immensely for my own task, partly because I seem to see in them a subject that is made for me (as I hope it will prove). Then they make me feel again that we are working in the same line, as I feel very closely together; and, seeing why your work now antagonizes the reigning critical mind, I feel more convinced than ever that you will have the last word. But more, much more, of this later. I have seen no reviews of your book, aside from the *Times* and *Time,* but this latter review, which may annoy you, is the kind of review that sells books and, coming from the Luce organization, means much, I should think. (But how strange it would have seemed, a decade ago, in a magazine for the millions, that the word "secular" is used in a qualifying sense.) The "next" world is more popular than ever in contrast with this one.

I did not see Waldo's review, but I have always less sympathy with a philosophy like his that repudiates the Enlightenment.

P.S. *"The Conduct of Life* is a work of strong and imaginative conception, inspired on every page by deep anguish, conviction, horror and hope."—*Time,* October 1st

153 West 82nd Street, New York, N.Y.   November 3, 1951

Dear Van Wyck:

I am asking the Press to send you a copy of *Renewal in the*

Arts. I need an extra copy of it: so keep it as long as you like without the burden of its being a gift!

The Conduct of Life only crawls along: but its pace accelerates slightly from week to week. By 1982 it should be a best-seller—in time to ward off *1984!!*

As for consistency—I inserted a whole section from *Utopias* into *The Condition of Man,* just to underline. It fitted perfectly and not even my most devoted reader noticed it!

153 West 82nd Street, New York, N.Y.   November 28, 1951

Dear Van Wyck:

I hope you have received *The Arts in Renewal* from the University of Pennsylvania Press; and the only reason that I suspect you may not have is that they haven't sent me a bill. If by any dire chance they ignored my directions, and sent the bill to you, please pass it on to me promptly. If they haven't sent it out at all please drop me a card.

I meant to write you directly after Gladys' visit; but I haven't any memory of having done so, and probably didn't. Her report, that you had actually been reading all my books and were preparing to do an essay on me was so much flaming brandy on my Thanksgiving dessert. I have long wanted to say the same thing about you; and never more so than last summer when I was looking over my own early work—I didn't tackle the books—and saw how much, consciously and unconsciously, I was indebted to you: indeed, at this very moment I still can recall the excitement of reading you for the first time in *The Seven Arts* . . . as well as that of beholding you, in the first *Freeman* office in 58 street, after having had a lunch with Walter Fuller, heaven bless his soul! Some day I will write that essay: unless you say so many nice things about me that a similar essay from my pen would be embarrassingly suspect. So dip your pen in vitriol (watered) when you actually write.

Did you see Trilling's review of *The Conduct of Life* in the *New Yorker?* I was touched by it; by its good temper, its sincerity, its painful effort to be altogether fair. He didn't get his arms around the book: but it would be unfair to ask a member of my own generation to do that, especially at a first effort. What he saw with some justice was what concerned the past and my debts to the past: what he didn't discern was the future, the possible future, and the future's debts to me. In other words, he understood what was sound, because it was bottomed on experience; but he didn't more than faintly see what was original in it. So far you are probably the only person who has yet had a glimmer of this: though I count upon students still in their diapers to discover all that I think will be plain to them by the time they read my book. But I can't complain. Florence Cane, back from Chicago, reports that one disciple of mine, on reading the book, decided thenceforth to make his own bed; to the amusement and the pleasure of the young housewife who rents him a room. By that sign, I may be confused with Gurgiev, by those who don't read!

I am tempted to go on talking the rest of the evening, if only to put off writing Waldo and telling him, at long last, what I really think of his review of my book. He hasn't the faintest notion of what he said, I am sure, and will be so shocked and hurt that he will forget the cause of my words! I trust your work goes well and that you are beginning to have that fine shut-in feeling that winter in the country, at its best, brings with it. As for me, I am in no mood for work yet. Mine is a fallow field now, and the earth is crusty and the sky gray, with the crows spattering it with black, like blown embers from a dead fire.

153 West 82nd Street, New York, N.Y.   December 19, 1951

Dear Van Wyck:

I've just come back from a five day jaunt to Princeton, where I attended a rather footling conference, sponsored by the State Department and the Rockefeller Foundation—*you* should have been there, not your namesake, Cleanth—and speaking before a very lively group of VIP's at the Cooperative Forum in Washington, on a constructive policy for peace: a matter I previously developed at a Church Peace Union Conference at Rochester. (I'll send you the pamphlet containing this when it gets printed: so I won't go into my proposals.) And now I must spend most of the glad holidays writing a report for the UN on housing and planning: the penalty for taking seriously my duties as a world citizen!

But I didn't sit down to write about myself: what I want mainly to do is to congratulate you on *The Confident Years,* which I have been guzzling greedily ever since it came. Re-reading the parts I had read this summer, and reading many other sections for the first time, I find myself confirmed in the judgement that this is in every sense the climactic volume of the series, and that it will have the same sort of impact that *The Flowering of New England* originally had. How you have been able to embrace such a vast volume of people and books and historical incidents, still unweeded by time, is almost beyond speculation: you have set a standard of density and richness of material that will make every future historian groan as he endeavors to emulate you. And you have conveyed, perhaps even better than in the other books, a sense of the relative importance of the writers you have treated, not merely among themselves, but with reference to the whole republic of letters. I feel like the inconsolable Dickens readers who used to weep when he brought his novels to an end and dismissed his characters—and even the thought that I will find myself before the footlights in the next act doesn't comfort me.

It will take a generation before people will see what you have
done in this history, so consummately, with such an air of
effortlessness that no one has yet given you half the credit you
deserve for all the arduous labors that preceded the final result, and for the constant alertness of insight during the whole
process. No one else in our time could have done this job, even
if he had been able to conceive it.

As for your essay on my work, I feel a little the way I found
myself feeling at the end of a day at the Princeton conference—my lower lip was sore because, to keep from saying too
much, I had to bite it constantly. Hands off and mouth shut!
are the only sound prescriptions for the subject who happens
also to be a friend and by that fact alone is party to the
enterprise. Still, if I were at Amenia, I think I would be
tempted to send you one part of my work you probably
haven't looked at—even though it would be only to enrich
your background, not to serve even as subject for a sentence. I
mean my verses, beginning with the semi-autobiographical
fragment in the *Second American Caravan,* covering fragments from a novel in verse published in the *New Yorker,* and
going on to the long poem—"Admonition to those Bereaved
in War"—that came out in *Twice a Year* in 1945. As with Plato,
there is a buried poet and playwright beneath the visible
monuments of my life, whose rotting bones have perhaps made
the grass a little greener. Not a very good poet, I hasten to
add: but even bad poets may be good compost.

What a mountain of unanswered mail even a short absence
from one's desk leaves! I must take leave of you for the moment, but not before embracing you again on the completion
of your great achievement, for which all future Americans, if
not all your contemporaries, will bless you.

[Bridgewater, Connecticut] [December 27, 1951]

Dear Lewis:

Would you mind returning this[30] when you have read it—answering questions on the margins?—You will see it is unfinished—the ending is to be remodelled when I have written the chapter that follows—and perhaps the first paragraph also. The whole chapter has to be fitted into the context of the book. But I seriously wish to know if I have correctly represented you, and I *seriously want no praise*. Please consider it as a composition with reference to your work *as a subject*. When I write next I have several more things to say to you. (And I have kept out of this chapter several quotations from you, etc. to be used in other sections of the book.)

153 West 82nd Street, New York, N.Y.   December 30, 1951

What a grand Christmas present, what a hopeful New Year's greeting you sent me, dear Van Wyck: no words that I can summon will even half convey to you the deep feeling of gratitude I feel. You are the first person to have looked at my work as a whole and to have fathomed its purpose and direction: and if no one else ever added another word to this appraisal I should still die content. And though I feel as if I had had an illicit peep at my obituary, the effect of your essay is, naturally, to turn my thoughts fruitfully to further work and further efforts: so it is a stimulus to my own renewal, which offsets and counteracts the soggy reviewers' reaction to the final volume. I have answered all your queries on the ms: and here I have only one point more to bring up, on a matter of fact rather than interpretation—though perhaps this is a borderline case and I should hold my tongue. On page 10 you

[30] Probably Chapter VI from *The Writer in America* (1953).

say "he shares Thoreau's spartan austerity . . ." I think it would be more accurate to say he "admires." Young Geddes indeed *shared* it: but except for the enforced poverty of my youth, from aet. 12 to 30, my life has been almost sybaritic, it seems to me, with good food, good wine and whiskey, soft beds, no touch of real hardship.

How lucky I've been to have you as a friend: how lucky to have you, further, as interpreter and critic. My cup runneth over, dear Van Wyck: and my best wish for your own New Year is that yours may be filled in equal measure!

153 West 82nd Street, New York, N.Y.   January 4, 1952

Dear Van Wyck:

I know how heavy your heart must be at the sad news about Jo Davidson: that incarnation of Energy which Blake called "Eternal Delight." But his going, in the full tide of work, had something of the quality of his life: and that must be a consolation for us. You yourself were so close to him that I feel I must offer you my hand now as I would to a member of his immediate family. He too was one of the "makers and finders."

Bridgewater, Connecticut   January 21, 1952

Dear Lewis:

I have been bursting with things I wanted to say to you. It has seemed to me I had so many that I didn't know how to begin, especially as I am so brim-full of my own new book, with all the pressure of essential reading. Your generous letters—and Sophy's—I hope she had my postcard—moved me deeply, and all I can say again is that, in my book, you will

appear at much greater length than you appear in this paper.
But what I feel above all is the great role that you should play
during this next few years at a time when your last theme,—
the "conduct of life,"—is the one theme that ought to engross
all men. I come to feel more and more that ethics in the
largest sense is really the only matter that deserves our thinking— (as it seems to me now, on rereading it, that *Cry, the
Beloved Country*[31]—which embodies this, is possibly the greatest novel of our time), and how *clear light* is needed on this
question. If you had been reading, what I have been reading,
all, or as many as I can, of the current American novelists,
male and female, you would realize how this is needed—and
what a great place stands open for you—for who can fill this
place better, dear Lewis, than you? I long to talk to you about
the need of clarification on these great all-human questions—
marriage, sex—etc. etc.—and exploring the mysteries of the
personality which you have opened up and thrown so much
light upon already.

And here I have a word of counsel which you can take or
leave but that seems to me truly important—that you should
steep yourself for a year in all the world's great moralists and
synthesize their thinking in terms of our day. Take such a
work, for instance, as Edmund Gosse's *Three French Moralists*
—which may be superficial—I don't remember—but which
will open to you—if you do not know it—a marvellously
fertilizing world of speculation. *Morals,* in the classical sense,
is an absolutely forgotten world in our universe of common
discourse, as this is a *morally illiterate generation*—and what
a world for you to explore!—forgetting all else for a while,—to
bring back forgotten treasures to the contemporary mind.
Take merely your statement about Freud and his "unex-
amined values": It seems to me I can hardly wait for you to
examine these—and what you mean in calling Dr. Kinsey
"amiable"—what volumes for all young people are implied in

31 *Cry, the Beloved Country* by Alan Paton: a novel of South Africa.

that. There is *Unamuno*[32] on *sex*—wonderful here and there. Then you come to the question of marriage, in which I know you have great things to say—for all of which you might find suggestions in writers like Vanvenvargues, La Bruyère[33] and heaven knows how many others.

You once said (to mention another point) that you felt your *style* is somehow not as good as it used to be, and I think, reading your *Aesthetics: a Dialogue,* for instance, that there is a certain truth in this. If you'll forgive me, I must say that I think your reading has for years been too *exclusively scientific,* and that a year's saturation in the literary moralists (classical, English and French) might work wonders for you in this respect. I know the general current notion that no one believes what you say, unless you can back it up with scientific authorities. But you surely have enough of this already: and I believe a year's discipline in the style and thinking of the literary moralists might work wonders for you. Excuse me for talking as if, being older, I were wiser than you. But I have such a sense of the great message you have for the world that you will forgive me for being frank with you. What you have to say is something that all men need and want. But I won't say more—until we meet, as I hope soon. I was afraid that in my paper you might feel I was overdoing the parallel between you and the old New England writers. But I couldn't help being surprised and struck by this—or going on to think how saturated they all were in writers on "moral perfection and self-culture," etc. How sure I am that the time has come again for this and that you are the man for the work in question. A new ethical synthesis is the "one thing necessary" for our time. Don't you feel this yourself, dear Lewis? More anon.

P.S. You might even find our Amiel worth rereading!

[32] Miguel de Unamuno (1864–1936) , Spanish essayist.
[33] Vanvenvargues, Marquis de (1715–1747) ; Jean de La Bruyère (1645–1696) .

153 West 82nd Street, New York, N.Y.   January 22, 1952

Your letter came this morning, dear Van Wyck; and I have read it and re-read it at intervals throughout the day, immensely stimulated by part of it, encouraged by another part, made full of contentious thoughts by another, and finally, downright startled by one of your suggestions, so much so that I rubbed my eyes and wondered whether you could be saying what you seemed to be saying, and if so, how this could be. But whatever my reaction to it was, your counsel was disarming—how could it have been otherwise?—and such frankness as you expressed was the proof of our friendship, which I shall try to deserve by equal frankness on my own part, as I continue the discussion.

Let me begin by dealing with the problem of style; for I think you may have misunderstood something that I said about the style of my later books as compared with the morning freshness of *The Golden Day*. I admire the ease and lucidity and pith, the apparent effortlessness, of that book, just as I would admire the body of a beautiful young athlete, aged twenty, and compare my own present form, with my bald head and wrinkles, unfavorably with it. But the grace of youth, good in its day, is not necessarily to be desired in middle age, which in its strength and toughness and experience has other virtues. This, it seems to me, applies to letters as well as to bodily organs. There are parts of *Technics* or of *The Culture of Cities*, a smudgy paragraph here, an over-labored thought there, or a too-facile technical vocabulary in another passage, which call for improvement: some of this was due to fatigue at the moment of writing, or to a desire for brevity even at a sacrifice of beauty. Those passages I shall be zealous in correcting, when I come to revision. But as for the style of the series as a whole, it seems to me to be, like every genuine style, a natural and proper expression of the contents. If it is complex, it is because the thought is of the same nature, not wilfully, but because a multitude of different themes cannot be woven together without achieving a certain complexity of form—just as a symphonic form is more difficult to follow than a melody carried by a single voice. The difficulty lies less in the writing itself than in the nature of the thought. Many people who declare that I am "unreadable" really mean that I am "unthinkable"—and by that they mean that they have no desire to follow me, or at least not enough patience to do so. People who are sympathetic to what I am saying and prepared to go along with the thought often characterize as simple and even brilliant the very passages others look upon as obscure and dull; and I think that in time much of what I have said will seem elementary and plain, to a generation better prepared for the thought itself. To have achieved a different style with these books, dear Van Wyck, I would have had to approach the whole series with a different intention: that of making it a purely literary work of art along the classic lines that you commend. Whether I should have done this is an arguable matter, and I will discuss it with you presently. But by the choice I originally made, I addressed the series to those who had some learning and "background" in the field covered, who were at home in the realms of science and philosophy as well as literature, and who yet lacked certain elements of humanist discipline that I, by reason of my varied heritage, could bring to the subject. Writing for such an audience, it was inevitable that my language would be a little less "pure" than it would have been if addressed to the cultivated general reader alone: some of the technical words for example are excusable only as masonic high signs, telling those who know the literature that I am familiar with their subject and have read the same essential texts as they have. But is this altogether a defect in the twentieth century—even though some of the new words will wear thin quickly and vanish! If a writer is to win over to his cause those who are hostile, because of their specialized learning and narrowed interests, he may well try to narrow the gap between him and them, provided he doesn't thus make himself unintelligible to the general reader. Where I have in fact been unintelligible—and I don't doubt you could find such places—I have, on my own terms, sinned.

But now as to the nature of the book itself, since this is the true determinant of style. The books in this area have affiliations with the more traditional writings in these various fields; but they resemble more closely a new kind of writing that grew up first in the nineteenth century: a species represented by *Moby-Dick* and by William James's *Psychology,* in which the imaginative and subjective part is counter-balanced by an equal interest in the objective, the external, the scientifically apprehended. This is no shallow fashion; and my recourse to science is not merely an attempt to make people believe what I say, by backing it up with scientific statements, as you suggest. Far from it. What lies behind the new method is the conviction that personal experience and personal intuitions, however sound, do not carry full weight until every effort has been made to square them with what William James called "hard, irreducible facts," meaning by that, results that have proved valid for all sorts of different observers, in consequence of the application of the scientific method. I would not say that this is altogether a new attitude or discovery: Aristotle had it in his writings, though he had to do the original work in science as well, before he could use it as a confirmation of his own intuitions. But this combination of personality and individuality with impersonality and collective research is what, it seems to me, characterizes the best thought of our time; and though it demands a mighty effort in the thinker—and perhaps an equal effort in the reader—the results promise well and will ultimately justify themselves by their effect on larger issues.

You are wrong, however, dear Van Wyck, when you suggest that what offends you in my style is the result of reading scientific books too exclusively "for years." My reading has *not*

been of this one sided kind; the only period when I was immersed in scientific writers (as a result of my interchanges
with old Geddes) was back in the early twenties, when my
style, because of my more simple and superficial methods, was
much closer to the moralists whom you advise me to imitate!
The question, then, is whether my purpose in writing my
major series, for a relatively limited audience, was unsound?
Perhaps it was; but my own justification would be that, if one
has new thoughts to express, one had better get them out in
some form, even if only a handful understands them entirely,
in all their complexity and depth, than to seek to avoid complexity and depth in order to satisfy the many, but leaving the
few without the best one had to give them. This, at all events,
is the assumption on which I have written these books. What
your counsel does for me is to make me ask whether, now that
I have accomplished this part of my intellectual mission, the
time may not be at hand when I should alter the pattern and
seek more direct contact with a larger body of readers. This is
a very timely question for me because, as I may have told you,
my next book will probably be on *Love and Marriage;* and
though inertia might lead me to handle the theme as I
handled the other books, a fresh decision might create quite a
different kind of book. (There was a moment when I thought
I could handle *The Conduct of Life* only as a poem!) So in
one sense, though I reject so much of what you say in criticism
of my style, to another part I am deeply receptive—and in
both cases grateful.

Perhaps I have said enough, by now, dear Van Wyck, to
show you why I don't regard your remedy, a bath in the
ancient and modern moralists, as a "cure" for what seem to
you defects in my style. But it may be that there are fundamental literary differences between us, as to what constitutes a
good style. And my first answer would be that, since style is
organic, no single style is a good one for all occasions; from
which it follows that a style that is too definitely that of the

humorist or the serious writer, of the literary man or the scientific man, is, unless it contentedly hugs its own limited boundaries, a handicap to expression. Though I have not pleased you by my efforts, I have never been unconscious of style or careless of it: I have sought, rather, to find the right mood and accent and rhythm for each new book. For that reason a pamphlet like *Men Must Act* is different in style from *The Culture of Cities,* written a little earlier, and in *Green Memories,* returning through the subject matter itself to youth, I recovered quite naturally the properties of *The Golden Day:* a fact that must, unless I err, keep you from damning the style of my later years, as if it were cast in a single mold. For me the single mold is the sign of a bad style, even if the mold itself was, for one particular purpose, a sufficient one. You passed over *Green Memories* in your essay, I think; yet at least from the standpoint of style it deserves consideration.

But there is still another reason why I found your prescription to read the moralists a strange one, dear old friend. Whom on earth do you think I read every day of my life? And whom did I read attentively and exhaustively, day after day, in preparation for *The Condition of Man* and *The Conduct of Life,* for a period of six or eight years? Perhaps I am incapable of profiting by them sufficiently; but though I never expect to leave off reading them, there is nothing fresh for me to get from Plato, Aristotle, Lucretius, Epictetus, Marcus Aurelius, Confucius, Lao-tze, and the rest of them; while except for a few Frenchmen, like La Bruyère, I know the latter day moralists equally well. What I have gotten from them and found usable is distilled, for the most part, in *The Conduct of Life;* and all that you are doing in suggesting another book on morals is to demand that I write *The Conduct of Life* over again, in another form! It was at that point that I raised my eyebrows. They are still aloft . . .

Yet in one sense your intuition—and even this strange suggestion—is sound, and I honor you for uttering it. Now that I have written these complex, symphonic books, conceived in such a way that the reader can accompany me through the details of my demonstration and verify in his own way, with the same books I have used, my conclusions, the time has perhaps come to conceive a quite different kind of book in which, with a more untethered imagination, I can present the conclusions alone—merely pointing for authority to the body of work in another form that I have produced. Such a book could have the same sort of simplicity that *The Golden Day* had or *Aesthetics* had: every sign of effort would be removed and only the results would be presented, in a compact and more easily assimilated form. Yes: that is perhaps the next step;[34] and it will be the real test of my powers as a writer, as distinguished from those as a thinker. Since I'll be busy with the revision of the first two volumes most of this year, I'll have time to brood over this new possibility, which at previous moments I have vaguely anticipated, and see what can be done about it. And if I respond to the challenge well, it may be that the book will be, in its own way, the sort of classic document you would have me write—not because I shall have newly steeped myself in the moralists, but because, in a more organic way, the more direct I-and-Thou relation with the ordinary reader will bring about the same kind of simplicity and directness.

What a gush of words, dear Van Wyck! Forgive their crudeness, and remember the deep affection and trust that underlies all our salutary differences.

P.S. One point more: though I think I ought perhaps to wait for other letters, of which there will probably be more than one, to make such addenda. Though I know you have given yourself to a sympathetic interpretation of my writing—and I am deeply honored by all this implied—it may be that you

34 Mumford's next book was *The Transformation of Man* (1956).

have been disappointed with *The Condition of Man* and *The Conduct of Life* because, in another way from Trilling, you have been looking for the connecting links with past work of the same order; and not finding them immediately visible, have assumed that I had overlooked the traditional moralists, whereas Trilling had overstressed points of resemblance to the Victorian writers, who are only a limited part of *my* working past. In both cases, you have overlooked what is fresh and original in my own statement. If you had taken full account of the latter, you would also have accepted the esthetic fact that follows from it: namely, that it must necessarily have a different formal presentation.

Bridgewater, Connecticut January 25, 1952

Dear Lewis:

I said either too little or too much but what I at least meant to say is not at all what you suppose. How could I have written as I did about you if I had wished, seriously, to quarrel with your style, which is really your mode of thinking? and it rather hurt me when you said that your "efforts" had not "pleased" me and that I had "overlooked what was fresh and original" in your statement? I quite recognized that in your series you had established a form and style that were inevitably bound up with your subjects. But it struck me that towards the end of *The Conduct of Life* you sailed out again into the kind of style that made *Green Memories* so much more accessible (along with *The South in Architecture, American Taste,* etc.) , and I feel that, from now on, if you are writing on moral themes, that would be the natural style for you to follow. I did not mean, either, that you had not read the classical moralists, although I gathered from your bibliography that you had not been reading them lately or at least to anything like the extent that you had been reading "scientific" writers. Of course, I should have realized that in writing as you did in *The Way and the Life* you would naturally fall into the same vein when you continued to write on similar subjects. For the rest, I couldn't help thinking that a rereading of certain old moralists might lead to valuable results—if only to your revising some of their *constantly* true ideas and reinterpreting them for our generation. But what I most wanted to say, after reading you all through, was how deeply I felt the tremendous future that is yours if you follow the line at the end of your series.

That was my real point—all the rest was incidental and rather blunderingly said, as I see now. I didn't mean that you were just to rewrite *The Conduct of Life,* as you seem to feel— I meant that you have entered a *vast ocean* of thought, which isn't something that concerns the handful of readers you had in mind but inescapably concerns a larger body. You don't have to "seek" this audience or that, for you are now in the "public domain,"—no one's ears could be closed to your discussion of marriage or sex, themes that concern every sentient being. What I meant to say was how *urgent* these questions now seem, how *dark* is the contemporary mind in regard to them and what a unique chance you, and you alone, have of throwing light on them. When you write on these subjects I am certain that you will write in the appropriate vein—not in "imitation" of classical writers—but because this vein is natural to you. So I can only add the hope that you will present *the conclusions* alone, as you put it, and write this "new kind" of books (although you have written several already) . I hope this says more clearly what I meant to say before, that my feeling towards you is *all* faith and expectation.

153 West 82nd Street, New York, N.Y.   January 26, 1952

Just a line, dear Van Wyck, while I am waiting for the
postman to come, and before I plunge into the correction of
proofs of *Art and Technics,* my Bampton Lectures: a better lot
of lectures than I dared hope when I was writing them,
though alas! they show in some place now irreparable signs of
my fatigue last spring. As to our present controversy, which I
have found immensely stimulating and productive, I am sorry
if I have erred anywhere in interpreting your words or have
given you cause to err in interpreting mine. In any event, I
didn't have any doubts as to your intentions in bringing up
the matters you felt necessary: for how is one to hear the truth
or be open to it, unless it comes from a friend, who speaks it in
a spirit of love. And if, on reception, it doesn't seem to be the
truth in every respect, that certainly doesn't lessen my gratitude for the spirit in which you undertook to utter your
criticism. My old friend Behrendt used to be much more
unsparing, in his fine Prussian way, in criticism of my architectural writings; and that only more firmly cemented our
friendship. As to the moralists, there are more of them in the
bibliography of *The Condition of Man* than in *The Conduct
of Life;* but in neither case is the list of my familiars in those
departments inclusive. For two reasons: I have a habit of
leaving out of my bibliography the books that are in my own
study or that I read every day. The other reason is that I take
for granted, perhaps unwisely, that all educated men have
read them; and don't list them for the same reason I don't list
the *Bible.* So I mention Seneca and leave out Epictetus, for no
good reason; and though I value Matthew Arnold as a moral-
ist and have read him backwards and forwards, the only book
I have listed in either bibliography is *St. Paul and Protes-
tantism.* So you have a case for believing that I read scientific
writers to the exclusion of the classical moralists; and you have
convinced me that in these matters one must take nothing for

granted, since even the most sympathetic of one's friends may err.

All this of course has nothing to do with your conviction that a "year's saturation in the literary moralists (classical, English, and French) might work wonders" for me; since a lifetime spent in their company has actually failed to produce this hoped-for miracle! This is either a case of invincible ignorance or stylistic deafness on my part: beyond possible cure! I tease you here, dear Van Wyck; but at the same time I take seriously what you say, since it is obvious that if my thoughts are to have some immediate effect upon my contemporaries, instead of seeping down slowly from the few to the many, they must be written in a simpler style and presented in a more straightforward fashion than the fashion in which my big books have been cast. In that respect, though the style is the man, the man himself is not hopelessly beyond any possible conviction of sin or desire to repent and do otherwise. I admit the possibility of change, and even change for the better—which is doubtless very generous of me!

For all that, I think that there are probably real differences between us, as to what constitutes a good style, and that part of our quarrel is due, not to misunderstanding, but to the fact that we understand each other quite well and do not in fact agree. My aim has been to develop a style that would be supple and ready for use on the greatest variety of occasions: a style neither rough nor smooth, neither formal nor informal, but capable of the greatest possible variation; that would be readable over long stretches, by reasons of variations in tempo, and yet be pithy and epigrammatic when necessary. In a good style, for me, form and content are one. The only way in which *The Way and the Life* differs from the earlier parts of *The Conduct of Life* is in the content, which in turn has a direct effect on the form: but apart from that, the various parts of the book were cut out of the same cloth, which in turn was woven by the same hand; and not for a moment did I say

to myself, approaching the final chapter: Now I must throw aside my scholarly cap and gown and step down from the pulpit. Some day it might be fun, just for our self education, to compare the people whose styles we most admire, and see for what reasons we like this one and reject that one. The man who perhaps comes nearest my ideal of style is Jean Jacques Rousseau—though I cannot bear his style in his more maudlin sentimental moments for the exact reason that I cannot bear the sentiment itself. Still, the breath and variety of Rousseau's style put him above the people who have only one style, which they used on every occasion, at least from my point of view.
. . .

Amenia, New York   July 5, 1952

I forget, dear Van Wyck, the exact time you're leaving for Montana; so for safety's sake I'm sending this to Bridgewater. The end of this month I must, after all, go down to New York for my operation. Two weeks in the hospital at least and six weeks of invalidism, at best, are in order. Altogether five precious months shot to hell. Perhaps it's the only way Providence knows to give me a full rest! Your *Harper's* article has made a few people who had discarded me take me up again; so mighty is your pen! I trust you and Gladys are in fine fettle. Our love to you both.

Chilmark, Massachusetts   July 9, 1952

Dear Lewis:

I have been thinking so much about you all and wondering how your summer is going. Walter Pach turned up here yesterday (with Nikifora) and said he had recently seen you. I felt so sorry about your thwarted European trip and have wondered how the Madrid matter has gone.

I have been working rather feverishly on *The Writer in America* and think I am finishing it tomorrow or the next day. We are going back to Bridgewater for 3 or 4 days on the 15th—and then on Sunday, July 20th we are starting (by train) for Montana. I don't know quite what I am supposed to do out there but thought I might use my new book for a series of lectures. We shall be coming back toward the end of August and hope to see you then.

Did you by the way see the summer issue of the *Yale Review?* It contained a good review of your *The Conduct of Life,*—said you were the no. 1 humanist of our day or words to that effect. So you are. (I think you'll like my new book, which includes the paper on yourself.)

Amenia, New York   July 17, 1952

The crossing of letters, dear Van Wyck, is one of the special tokens of friendship; and I was delighted to find this happening after so long a gap in our correspondence. My days, despite the heat—or perhaps abetted by it—remain lazy and tranquil; and although there are half a dozen tasks on which I might be working now, in the short interval before the operation, my inclination is rather to relax and to take the world passively; and that is precisely what I have been doing.

Only one thing has recently raised my dander: an abominable piece of slander and libel uttered by a Michigan congressman, to which my sister-in-law Mathilda, a secretary of Senator Lehman's, called my attention. This ugly little fascist had me plotting with Earl Browder to found the League of American Writers!! I have decided that there is no hope that this sinister insanity, so like that of Hitler, will die down by itself; so I wrote him a blistering letter and propose to follow it through. The only difficulty is that the very atmosphere that has been created by these vultures is favorable to their cause, and has closed up or subjected to suspicion many of the channels through which one would publish one's own case.

Apart from that, I have been wholly at peace. Though *Art and Technics* has been practically boycotted in the press, for reasons that are still a little mysterious and mystifying to me, the Columbia University Press has been bravely advertising it, which means either that it has been selling in spite of everything—or that the manager of the press has gone mad. I suspect the latter: so I daren't find out.

If you see a review of *The Conduct of Life* in the London *Times Literary Supplement*, which I don't get, I wish you'd lend me the copy. I am very eager to see what the English make of my book. I saw Brogan's piece in the *Manchester Guardian:* casual but friendly. I trust that your Montana resort is far enough north to give you cool nights: at all events, don't let them kill you with hospitality. . . .

P.S. Three cheers for *The Artist in America!* I never doubted it would do well—and be good.

Bridgewater, Connecticut   October 4, 1952

Dear Lewis:

I have just had a letter from Dorothy Norman repeating her request for some sort of contribution to her *American Anthology* from Austin. As she has already left, I can't very well write to her, so, as you are co-editor, I am writing to you. I told her before that I could not write anything especially for this Anthology but that she could have, if she wished, anything from my new book, *The Writer in America*. This will be out in February, but I don't suppose that makes any difference, and I could arrange with Dutton to waive any question of a fee—in fact, I can waive that question now. There would be no charge for anything of mine in this anthology. But the question is, to whom should I send this material—in case it might seem suitable to do so. I don't want to burden you with proof-sheets, though I have them and could send them (the book is 50,000 words long). Would it be better to send them to Brom Weber? I would rather like to have them use my chapter on Lewis Mumford, but something else might be proposed. What say you to the question in general? We have signed up for the Philosophical Meeting in November. Can we count on seeing you and Sophy at the dinner, etc?

Bridgewater, Connecticut   December 4, 1952

Dear Lewis,

What must you think of me, but there is nothing wrong with us, and I had really forgotten about the Philosophical Society dinner. The trouble was we found we had to go to Boston, for the opening of the Edward Sheldon room at the Harvard Library. We couldn't do both Boston and Philadelphia, so we had to cut out the latter. The only real reason we had for going was to see Sophy and you, and now we'll look forward to seeing you at Christmas.

I wrote you about two months ago and had no answer, which I only mention because you may have had trouble with Amenia forwarding. It was only about Dorothy Norman's Indian issue of *Twice-a-Year* which you are supposed to be editing, I think. She asked for a contribution from me and I suggested my essay on you or perhaps something else from *The Writer in America*. But, as this is now coming out in February, I fear the time is too short for Dorothy's magazine. I can't write things to order and am now busy with something else. But anyway the India project seems to be very vague. I am up to the eyes in a book about my Childhood and Youth, which I really think now is coming on well. I am having fun doing it, at least. How good it will be to see you! I have been filing my old letters, and nobody will ever be able to write a biography of you without tapping my really immense collection of your letters. (I haven't had a chance yet to reread them.)

CHAPTER VI

Indian Summer of
a Friendship
(1953–1963)

The final decade shared by Brooks with Mumford had much of the warmth and late afternoon sunlight of the Indian Summer about which he had once written so vividly, even though public recognition, which had come to both so fully and yet so belatedly, took them further down their somewhat different paths.

Gladys Brooks has told the story of her life with Van Wyck so well in *If Strangers Meet* (1967) that the letters written from the Huntington Hartford Foundation in California, the American Academy in Rome, the quiet study in their new home in Bridgewater, Connecticut, or the musical, literary, and academic societies of New York, Philadelphia, Berkeley, and Cambridge serve as mere hasty footnotes to the record of a life fulfilled. The books of this period were similarly footnotes to the ambitious chronicle, now christened *Makers and Finders*, which Brooks had completed and which was now coming to be recognized for what it was: the history of the literary life in the United States from the times of Washington Irving to the times of Van Wyck Brooks, a century of vivid portraits which made a moving mosaic of the cultural growth of the nation. There were brief biographies of the painter John Sloan, of Helen Keller, of William Dean Howells, and finally the unpublished beginning of a long-postponed but deeply felt biography of Lewis Mumford, to which the latter reluctantly agreed; and there was a brief chronicle of American artists and writers in Italy, *The Dream of Arcadia* (1958) . "When I was not writing I was out of focus," Brooks had said of himself (*Autobiography,* p. 562) , "yet when I had finished a book I had an obsessive conviction that I would never be able to write another." Without a sustained task absorbing him, he could now interspace these shorter works, which gave him a sense of central purpose, with the acceptance of public homage in the forms of medals of award, honorary degrees, and fellowships to writers' and artists' colonies and foundations in this country and abroad. In this way, he was left little time to think of the increasing symptoms of age and the continuing attacks of some of his critics that at last caught up with his quietly gay spirit in 1963.

All of his friendships seemed to mellow rather than deepen in these years, including that with Mumford. Differences were forgotten, first in the sharing of the disappointments and neglect of *The Conduct of Life* and *The Times of Melville and Whitman,* and then in the gradual awakening of public acclaim after 1953. But Mumford's recognition came mainly from sources quite different from those of Brooks and was the result of his widely different interests. Embittered by what seemed to him a national moral collapse in the new age of threatened atomic destruction, he spent his days and years in his study in Amenia when he was not teaching, lecturing, and writing calls to moral awakening; and there he summoned all his deepest energies for what was to become his master-statement, *The City in History* (1961) . Almost ironically, he at last accepted membership in the National Institute of Arts and Letters once more, only to move on to the American Academy of which he was president at the time of Brooks's death. Professorships, fellowships, honorary degrees, and awards came to him at home and abroad, as they had to Brooks, but more and more for his definitive work as a philosopher of architecture and city planning rather than as a literary critic and historian. With their personal faith and affection restored, and with visits as neighbors taking the place of frequent letters, the two men went each his own way to recognition and fulfilment; and the friendship ended as it had begun with a sharing of common aims and a contrasting of personalities and gifts.

Bridgewater, Connecticut   May 24, 1953

Dear Lewis:

I miss you! and, I keep thinking, if you were here, we might be meeting every week. I'll never lose hope of a time to come when we can see you in this kind of way. But now may all go well with you in Europe!

B. Berenson writes:[1] "The Mumfords will receive a hearty welcome. We now are on the way to Sicily and do not expect to be in Florence again before June 26. We then expect to be there till July 10th, or so, after which we go to our summer home at Vallombrosa, only one hour by car from Florence." That gives the necessary details; and if you miss him at Florence he will expect you at Vallombrosa, which you should probably see in any case (I never did) and which should not be too difficult to reach. He will be expecting to hear from you when you reach Italy (i Tatti, Settignano, Florence). How I wish we might be with you!

I am on the last lap of my own story[2] (with no title as yet) and hope to finish it before July (when we go to the island, for one month, returning to Bridgewater on August 1st). All goes otherwise well, and we now have Chiang Yee[3] with us.

1 Bernard Berenson, art collector and critic.

2 *Scenes and Portraits* (1954).

3 Chiang Yee, Chinese illustrator and author of *The Silent Traveller in New York* (1950), one of a series. It had a Preface by Brooks.

Hôtel des Saints-Pères, Rue des Sts-Pères, Paris   June 7, 1953

Dear Van Wyck:

Is this not the very hotel that Oscar Wilde fled to after his imprisonment? I seem for some odd reason to follow his footsteps; for in 1946 I lectured in Reading, almost within sight of his jail. Why I should begin with this remote allusion I have no notion. Perhaps because I am in a relaxed and dreamy mood, after three strenuous weeks in England. I escaped the Coronation, thank heaven, only to be driven out of Holland and Belgium because not a hotel room was to be had in Coronation week. Europe I still find deeply exciting; and full of vitality, too, whatever it may have been from 1938–1948.

McCarthy[4] and his cowardly appeasers have caused our national reputation to sink lower than it's ever been, I believe; and that says much.

For the first time, incidentally, I am seeing France from the inside—though my French is all too rusty to take full advantage of it.

Hotel Europa e Brittania, Venice   June 23, 1953

Dear Van Wyck:

If the rest of our trip is even half as successful as the first portion we'll be in miraculous good luck. And now Venice, with its heavy exhalations of Turner and Ruskin, *The Aspern Papers* and *Tod in Venedig*,[5] beautiful and sinister, delightful and depressing—almost too much so for our child who's spent a previous afternoon sleeping it off. I've just been to see Professor U. Compagnolo, of the Société Européene de Culture: a

4 Senator Joseph McCarthy, Chairman of the Committee on Un-American Activities, whose hearings caused much concern at this time.
5 *Death in Venice*, by Thomas Mann.

man of intellect and character who is trying to rally the intellectuals of the world to a common center, for discussion and understanding. I gave him your name two months or so ago and he tells me you haven't responded. This seems to me a highly promising attempt to break down the spiritual barriers that bedevil the world, and I feel that you belong here and would know just the right people in America, beyond my limited circle, to join it. Do consider it seriously.

Bridgewater, Connecticut   June 28, 1953

Dear Lewis:

I was so happy to have a letter from you in Venice. Evidently you received the message from B. Berenson and before long you ought to be seeing him. But I'm a little disturbed that Professor Campagnolo had not heard from me. I waited until *Comprendre* appeared so that I might know what the *Society* was really all about. When this arrived and I could see how good it was I wrote most cordially accepting the invitation. I hope that by this time my letter has arrived.

I get now letters from so many countries that I have the feeling of a real planetary network developing at last. The only trouble is that we can only meet on a plane of exalted sentiment. I never know how to make any scratches in the ice. There is no doubt, however, that "one world" is really coming about. Then what's to be done? That's the question.

I know you are having most exciting impressions, but you will be lucky if they don't stun you. My first glimpse of Europe after virtually 35 years did nothing whatever to speed the action of my brain. (I think off-hand of two other names to pass on to Professor Campagnolo: John Hersey and Thornton Wilder.)

I am finishing this week, I hope, the story of my first 28

years—provisionally called *The Shores I Knew:*[6] then I shall begin to work over John Sloan's papers. We are going to Chilmark for 6 weeks next Thursday, returning here in mid-August. We were in Phila. briefly a few weeks ago. They want your letters and papers badly at the U. of Penn. Library (where mine will be) and I said I would try to work on your good will. Spiller said you had reservations about it.

Amenia, New York   January 2, 1954

Dear Van Wyck:

Did I tell you what a good time I've been having with my course on American Forms and Values?—or, *The Golden Day* revisited.[7] It's been great fun in catching up with some of the scholarly and critical work of the last thirty years. Whenever I'm in trouble I fall back on your great series—that mine of keen perceptions and wise observations. If I didn't actually have three other embryonic books demanding my life-blood, I'd be tempted to sit down and do a second *Golden Day*. (I like the first one far too well to want to alter a comma in it!) Meanwhile, we both await eagerly the opening chapters of your biography and hope that you'll carry it through.

Bridgewater, Connecticut   January 8, 1954

Dear Lewis:

I was so glad to hear of the good luck you have been having with your lectures. *Why* don't you publish them when you

6 *The Shores I Knew:* Early title for *Scenes and Portraits.*
7 Lecture course at the University of Pennsylvania, Philadelphia.

have such a title, *The Golden Day Revisited?* What can be better than that? But you have three other books in mind—so have I—and I too seem to have good things to report. I shall be sending you *Scenes and Portraits* in another month, I suppose. Meanwhile, I am having good times with *John Sloan; a Painter's Life,* which I ought to finish this coming summer. We positively have to get away to escape from the people that invade even this cross-roads hamlet—so many whom we like.

Amenia, New York   March 2, 1954

Dear Van Wyck:

. . . I can't begin to tell you of all the good things I liked in your book and am grateful to you for telling about; to do that would almost involve total recall. In some ways, the scenes you describe seem even more remote than the times of Whitman and Melville; and certainly it seems, in contrast to the miasmas of the present period, a halcyon age. How I envy you having ten extra years on the better side of the dividing line marked by 1914! Still, in my so different way and so different milieu, I have comparable memories; and your own felicitous presentation of those ancient images will perhaps some day tempt me to add to the two long accounts of my own childhood, factually embroidered but essentially true to life, that I published long ago in the *New Yorker.* For the last two months I have been working at a tremendous pace, writing and giving lectures, correcting a staggering number of examination papers, finishing up odds and ends of articles; but somewhat with the feeling of a horse on a treadmill, since no matter how hard I work I seem to stay on the same spot and haven't advanced a step nearer to writing my next book. But really I have: in a week or two, if all goes well, I hope to settle down to it and not raise my head for anything but a breath of air or a glass of whisky. . . .

P.S. I don't know how you have reacted to McCarthy's latest triumph; but I find myself spending my days almost automatically writing such things as these:

"Eisenhower shows an infinite patience and an unlimited capacity for surrender."

"We have frightened sheep in the Senate and a shorn lamb in the White House."

"If the President in the White House had been the Commander-in-Chief of the Armies in Europe, D-Day would have been the signal for our wholesale surrender."

"Eisenhower manages to remain the leader, instead of McCarthy, by doing an about face every time McCarthy approaches him."

"When Generals lack courage, civilians had better oil their guns."

"McCarthy has won the Battle of the Bilge."

Amenia, New York   June 27, 1954

Dear Van Wyck:

I was deeply touched by your ambassadorial visit and I hasten to say, in the name of both friendship and fellowship, that I'll be happy to resume membership in the Institute. My original action,[8] as I look back upon it, was ill-timed and ill-directed: once the medal was voted I should have remained silent, since I had not acted before. At all events, whatever meaning my resignation had vanished with poor Beard's death. My fellow members, above all you, are generous in their willingness to open the door again: and I would be worse than a curmudgeon if I did not offer you all my sincere thanks for having made it so easy to come back.

[8] Mumford resigned from the Institute in 1948.

Amenia, New York   August 16, 1954

With two first drafts behind me, dear Van Wyck, I've at last decided to rest for a while, even though the difficult last chapters remain to be written. In my "idleness" I've written a new preface to *Sticks and Stones*,[9] now going into a reprint series, and have even done a few poems: so my days, though unhurried, have not been empty. It is good to think that you and Gladys will be back in another fortnight—though not so pleasant to realize that *we'll* be leaving for Philadelphia a few weeks later. Lee Simonson dropt in the other day, piloting a Whisky heiress whose father wants a glass tomb for himself (Branfman) and his company (Seagrams) on Park Avenue. I haven't seen Lee in better shape in fifteen years. Thank heaven: bouncy as ever, but not dangerously so! It was a happy reunion. Our house, on various weekends, has been throbbing with young people, down from Cambridge for Tanglewood; and the place has lost some of its severe, eremitic inviolability, much to our pleasure. I hope your summer has been as happy as our last six months have, incredibly, been.

P.S. What memories of my childhood Saratoga conjures up! I must have been eight when I was there last: but it is all still very vivid: the great barnlike hotel rooms and the excitement of the races. I knew the name, colors and character of every jockey, and they still stick—Crimmins, Redfern, etc.!

Bridgewater, Connecticut   October 21, 1954

Dear Lewis:
    You have only not heard from me because for the last few weeks I have been buried alive in the most boring work,—two

9 Many of Mumford's earlier books were revised and published in paperback about this time.

sets of proofs, one a long reprint, two indexes to make and two speeches also. Horrid, and I haven't had a chance yet to read the book[10] and have had only two or three exciting glances at it. For that I must wait another week, when you will be hearing from me again, and when I hope to hear that all goes well with you in Philadelphia. This is to beg for a kindness, to wit, as follows:

My daughter-in-law Kappo Phelan, whom perhaps you recall as the really brilliant theatre critic of the *Commonweal*, has been working for two or three years on television. I doubt if anyone knows more than she about it or could discuss it with more discrimination, and what she wants is a chance to run a television column in the *New Leader,* if possible. She did so well with similar work on the *Commonweal* and the *New Freeman* that I am certain she would do well here again, and she has asked me to write to S. M. Levitas about it and (if possible) to enlist your interest to the extent of a brief note. (*If* you happen to be able to do so, if you know something about her work and would be so kind as to do so.) I think it rather an imposition, for you are probably unbearably busy, but I make the suggestion and leave it there.

Bridgewater, Connecticut   November 10, 1954

Dear Lewis:

All during these weeks when I have not been writing to you, I have been breathing the mountain air of your new book. I had thought before that *The Renewal of Life* had reached your high mark thus far, but you climb still higher in your *Caliban and Prospero*. You are the only person who can do these things in the U.S.A., and I never felt surer of your uniqueness as a genuine prophet with the true ring than I have felt in reading some of these pages. I only wanted you to

10 *In the Name of Sanity* (1954).

go on forever, convinced as I am that before you are done you will carry out the one task that seems to me absolutely necessary for our generation—a new code of ethics that will synthesize all the earlier codes in terms of our predicament in these years of crisis. You can use all the great words—uniquely—without any tinge of cant, and you understand what is necessary for the wholeness of man. Of course you might say that you have done this work in your great series, and in a sense you have already done it; but all I have in mind is a work that will bring together the insights that are scattered through the earlier volumes. Possibly that's what you have in mind at present.

With every new book you bring out, I am more and more lost in the wonder of your consistency and coherence from the very start, from your first study of Utopias through all these thirty years or more through which you have built up this great tower of thought. Some day I hope to start for myself all over again and really express what your work has meant to me.

I shan't mention the details that strike me here most movingly—your brilliant use of *Emperor Jones* as an image of the U.S. mind or your profound allusions to Dr. Kinsey (a point that ought to be amplified at great length, I think). You seem to have inexhaustible sources of strength! Gladys and I both thought your review of Toynbee was really tremendous, and your last *Skyline*[11] convinced me again that you make a great mistake not to publish this architectural chronicle every few years. If Harcourt balks, others would gladly do it.

I am struggling out of my last chores—proofs, indexes, prefaces, etc.—which have kept me down for 2 or 3 months, and hope to start a new book next Monday. We expect to leave for the West just after Christmas.

Of course it delights me that you are reading *The World of Washington Irving.* I have shuffled off the proofs of the 5th

[11] A regular department in *The New Yorker*, 1932–1962.

volume in the *Everyman Edition,* and I hope you are using this. All the volumes have been greatly revised and improved.

The Drake, Philadelphia   November 21, 1954

Dear Van Wyck:

Your generous words about *In the Name of Sanity* warmed the cockles of my heart at a moment when they badly needed warming; so my gratitude is deepened to a point where it is almost impossible for it to be expressed. The book has been politely ignored, for the most part, except where it has been condescendingly noticed. I had hoped that, by the nature of its contents, it would at least provoke discussion: but its fate has been that of the three books preceding it and I now realize that there is a barrier between me and my *literary* audience that no effort of mine can break through. The situation is strange, because it has nothing to do with my alleged difficulty, since a really difficult book like *The Conduct of Life* went three times as well as *Art and Technics:* and again it is in contrast to my current success as a speaker, especially among the young. In the long run none of these things matters, of course: except that such a failure to make an impression causes me to draw on reserve stocks of moral energy that should be devoted to the production of new work. . . .

Huntington Hartford Foundation
Pacific Palisades, California   February 7, 1955

Dear Lewis:

It is good to know that you are now able, after a long interruption, to get back to your proper work—and I was so happy to hear that you feel you are in a creative period. I am sure great results will soon be forthcoming.

Here we are having a really good time. The only drawback is that the Foundation is at the bottom of a rather deep California canyon, so that we have sunlight only about 7 hours a day. On the other hand, we have good company, George Biddle and his wife Hélène, very old and good friends, a quite good novelist Irving Fineman (whose *Dr. Addams* I have just read), a young novelist Daniel Stern, a supposedly quite good sculptor named Wien, an ex-Viennese composer Ernest Kunitz whom we like extremely, etc. etc. The director, John Vincent, is also a composer and a professor at the U.C.L.A. Of him we have grown really fond.

The great thing hereabouts (we are on the outskirts of Los Angeles) is the *astonishing architecture* that has been springing up in the last 15 years. A young art critic who knows you, Langsner by name, told me that you were here a few years ago. (I didn't know you had been) —But when I said you should come here again, he said, "Yes," but that you might be bewildered; and I think he meant that there is such richness and variety in the building that you might not be able to generalize about it. But I don't think Gladys and I can be wrong in feeling it is remarkable—original and varied to a degree. Sunset Boulevard (which leads here) is lined with most beautiful houses, and one feels here a tremendous vitality that makes it seem to be the architectural laboratory of our time. Everyone seems to be prosperous—the city is growing at the rate of 50,000 a year—and there are swarms of architects, from the son of F. Lloyd Wright, who built some of the cottages in our canyon, to men from the Bauhaus, etc.—Would you care to get the *New Yorker* to send you out to survey it all? as they commissioned you to write about London? I should think you ought to see the recent developments here, if, as I suppose, you haven't seen them. (Incidentally, we have seen no "smog" at all.)

Meanwhile, we have been taken about to see the "celebrities," and I think we are to see Stravinsky and A. Huxley next week. Also Upton Sinclair, who lives near by. The Biddles took us to see old Lion Feuchtwanger whom, with his wife, we much liked, and who has an astonishing library of 25,000 books (Shakespeare first folio, Spinoza's books with his annotations, complete Goethe, Schiller, first editions, etc., etc., etc.) Edmund G. Robinson has shown us over his wonderful collection of French pictures. We had an afternoon with Frederic March at the Paramount studios—and saw him acting, also Danny Kaye acting—also Rosalind Russell—also Walter Hampton (still going strong at 79). We have been to tea with old Mrs. MacDowell (90) : and Francis Taylor of the Metropolitan came here to lunch the other day. Robert Nathan lives nearby and we saw him yesterday. Such a whirl!

I seem to be getting along well with my little book on Helen Keller—(I sent you a day or two ago my *John Sloan: a Painter's Life*, which I hope will find you at Amenia) , and, since you speak of the "literary audience," I seem to be largely leaving this too—or being left *by it*, for, I'm planning another book, to follow *Helen Keller* but will also be ignored by the critics. Something strange has happened in the separation of *humane general* minds from *literary minds*, technically speaking—since the latter have abandoned their interest in *human contact*. That is too large a subject to bring up in a letter. But I have been greatly struck by two letters that Upton Sinclair sends me—sent to him by Einstein and C. G. Jung. Both praise immeasurably a book by him which I know to be fifth-rate from a literary point of view. But this praise ignores this entirely because of the subject-matter, which seems to them of the greatest importance. It strikes me as symptomatic of our time that these two absolutely first-rate minds can praise so highly a book which the critics would utterly (and in *this* case rightly from a literary point of view) ignore. There is something here that has to be thought out!

But I must not go on with this (I fear) illegible letter. Forgive it!

Amenia, New York   February 20, 1955

This is one of those February days, dear Van Wyck, that opened with ice on the fields and the thermometer below freezing and warmed up so fast that by now, which is mid-day, one can go out of doors without a coat. The sky is blue and the only clouds in it are the trails of vapor formed by a squadron of jet planes doing cosmic circles perhaps twenty or thirty miles away. In short, this is what would be called sugaring weather in Vermont; and the day was sweetened for me in extra measure by the fine review your book got from James Johnson Sweeney, of all persons, on the front page of the *Times* book section, crowding out Walter Lippmann's gloomy interpretation of the degradation of the democratic dogma, reviewed by the even more gloomy Niebuhr. Ironically, now that the central work of your life has appeared, a target for poisoned academic arrows and ruffianly gas-house-district bricks, your subsequent books seem fated to be crowned with praise, by the very same set of people, if not the very persons, who previously had sought only to conk you, thus proving the efficacy of Emerson's law of compensation, if not raising the status of criticism in America. Not of course that your new biography does not fully deserve this response to itself; it is only in comparison to the treatment of *The Confident Years* that the present attitude seems ironic; and all the more because what were you doing in the Sloan book, but treating the confident years all over again, in the person of your subject.

The book has given me great delight, because it tells so much and evokes so much. It places Sloan and everything he stood for better than one could have hoped, in a figure that is still so near us, and so entangled ideologically with our own attitudes and prepossessions. Your rich and generous treatment of the subordinate characters, like old Yeats and Walter Pach, is a contribution to the history of our times, which will, I hope,

not be lost on other historians and biographers; and your
analysis of the effect of the Armory show on Sloan himself I
found very illuminating. Even though you pretend to avoid
critical disquisitions, you have put all the esthetic innovations
of the period, whether they were as weak as Henri's or as
strong as Braque's, in their right relationships, and shown
them at their correct values; and what is that but the most
masterly kind of criticism? This book will, I am sure, not only
"go well" but have in addition a long life; and no one will be
able to write about the period without consulting it and
cribbing from it.

One of the things that Sophy has done for me, when she was
not doing her own special tasks, was to bring together all the
"Sky Lines" I had written during the last nine years, which, it
turns out, come to the horrifying number of sixty. But on
reading them over I see that they are more unified, and more
substantial, than I had felt, as I did them, they could be; and
so I have consented in my mind to publishing some twenty or
twenty-five of them, and the other day offered them to Harcourt. Meanwhile, I've re-read, for the second time since last
December, the first draft of the little book on *The Transformation of Man,* which I am doing for the "World Perspectives Series"; and if I can make the final chapter as sound and
as brilliant as the earlier ones, I think that the book will say
more in fifty thousand words than Toynbee has managed to
do in a million. (Not that I under-rate Toynbee's achievement, or would butcher his work to make a mumfordian
holiday!)

But as happened last year when I was about to settle down
to writing a book, life, in the form of all the unresolved
questions I had put, to such an unresponsive audience, in *In
the Name of Sanity,* has been breathing down my neck. This
time the angel who reminded me of my duties was not Edward
Murrow, but Erich Fromm, the psychiatrist, who out of a clear
sky descended on me, and told me that he thought he and I

should make a final effort to start a campaign of general protest against the policy of enlarging our weapons of extermination and preparing, if once they were used, to wipe out the
human race. This happened last Friday, when I was down in
New York: though I had read his books, I had never met him or
corresponded with him. So I felt somehow an obligation to
listen and help; and this week I shall try to draft a letter for a
few people to sign. If it goes well, we will ask for your signature; and if you don't hear from me you'll know that I was
unable to say the right words, because I had said them too
often before, to no avail, and had dumped the responsibility
back on the too frivolous shoulders of Providence. . . .

The problem you raise in connection with Upton Sinclair's
work is one of the hardest in all literature to solve; but I think
it a different one from that raised by the gap between popular
and esoteric literature today. In the great periods more was
expected of the people than we expect today: they were
expected to make more of an effort to reach the highest level,
and evidently had enough of an inward life to respect it and
reach it. Perhaps the gap was already widening in Shakespear's
time; but the man in the street nevertheless stayed through
the whole performance, even if he didn't understand it completely, instead of demanding that all of it be on the level of
the clowns; and this was true in Pepy's time, or in Hayden's,
when the chambermaids or the serfs could share the same
music, and like it.

But with Upton Sinclair's work something else is involved:
the fact that he really has a decent, but commonplace mind,
which is reflected in the quality of his prose, even in books
above the Lanny Budd level, like his book on Jesus. Because
he was once a "great" figure, and perhaps because the very
commonplaceness of expression makes him more readily
understood by a European like Einstein or Jung, he has a way
of drawing out from such people more favorable responses than
his books deserve: indeed, he extracts praise in the way a

broken down actor, known to everybody in his palmy days, extracts dollars from people who once knew him at least by reputation. His subject matter is indeed of the greatest importance and I honor him for sticking so resolutely to his guns over such a long period, but his method of treatment does not do justice to the substance and therefore doesn't work any profound changes in the reader. This is of course at the opposite end of the scale from having nothing to say and saying it exquisitely; but in the end is it not equally barren? "I and mine do not convince by arguments, we convince by our presence." Is it not just the absence of "presence" in Whitman's sense that makes Sinclair, though so virtuous, so well-meaning, so palpably on the side of the angels, a writer of minor rank?

Your publishers have probably already sent you this *Times* review; but perhaps you could make use of another. I hope that this and all the other well-deserved praise you'll get will serve only to prime you more richly for the Keller biography, which, I am sure, will not only be a good book, but a great one, on the same principle that Melville felt it took a creature as big as a whale to serve as subject for a book of commensurate dimensions. Did Helen Keller and F. D. Roosevelt ever get together? That meeting of the two heroic cripples should have had an epical quality about it, even if they did nothing but discuss the weather.

Berkeley, California　　　　　　　　　　　　March 27, 1955

Dearest Lewis:

Your glorious letter has gone so long unanswered only because we have been in such a whirl—first at Los Angeles and then up the coast, at Santa Barbara, Carmel and Berkeley. We have met all the illuminati from Feuchtwanger and Will

Durant, through Henry Miller and Robinson Jeffers, to Karl Shapiro here in Berkeley, where your old friends the Meiklejohns got us a house for two weeks to rent, and here the literary life goes on in wildest exuberance. More of this anon. Enough to say that I have just finished my "Sketch for a Portrait" of Helen Keller, a little book of 45,000 words. It could not have been written by me on a larger scale.

What good news it is now that you are collecting the "Sky Lines." Didn't I tell you, you ought to do it these many years ago? You said NO—but didn't I tell you? And I hope that by this time you are sounding away in the *Transformation of Man* and you didn't need to tell me what a book that will be. I predict that your enemies will take to the woods for shelter before this decade is finished. Meanwhile, I am quite thrilled that you've made a connection with Erich Fromm. Although I have never met the man I regard him as a friend and a brother and would like to send him, by you, an affectionate greeting.

Here we are living in a paradise of May-bloom, surrounded by endless sunlight and flowering trees. We have had a most lovely 3 months in California, every aspect of it better than one would have thought. I must repeat that you should see architectural Los Angeles again. As for Upton Sinclair, you are quite right about that good man. To make my point, I should have used another example, for I *had* a point that I fear is lost and will have to be made again.

Amenia, New York   September 16, 1955

Dear Van Wyck:

. . . For all of us, I suppose, this was, meteorologically speaking, the most hellish summer in our experience; and since part of us is a creature of the weather, it would be no wonder if it worked out bad in other ways, too. As for me, I worked on my book, in a sort of dogged compulsive way, in order to get it finished by the deadline; and after I turned it in I realized that it would take another month's work to eliminate all the stupid details that the bad weather plus my bad judgement had made me add in the final writing; since one can't hope to say anything intelligible about the whole life of man in sixty or seventy thousand words without getting rid of the details. Well, I turned in the final draft at the beginning of September and badly needed a vacation; instead I was deluged by the proofs of the anthology of my work Beacon is getting out this fall, in honor, as it were, of my sixtieth birthday. If the machinery doesn't break down—they are woefully behind schedule—I shall have a copy of it in your hands before another month is out. It is called *The Human Prospect;* and what is best about it, probably, is the fact that it is coming out in a paper edition, and its sale will prove whether I have an audience or not outside the Cadillac class. . . .

Bridgewater, Connecticut   November 23, 1955

Dear Lewis:

Felicia Geffen has just called me up to say that you have just been elected to the Academy.[12] I don't know whether it means anything to you, but it means much to me, dear Lewis—*only* they are so very anxious to see you and Sophy at the annual meeting that they have begged me to intercede with you. If you can manage it, how happy we'll be. I got your new anthology, *The Human Prospect,* in town yesterday and am feverishly reading it, brooding over a letter to you soon!

12 The American Academy of Arts and Letters.

The Drake, Philadelphia
[Postcard from Mumford]   November 26, 1955

Of course I was pleased and honored and gratified in all sorts of ways over the election: but I can't come up for the December meeting because of a long-made lecture engagement here in Philadelphia. If I hadn't been under the weather this last month, plagued by demons—now called viruses but unchanged in nature—I'd have sent out copies of *The Human Prospect* weeks ago. I'll send you yours soon anyway and you can pass the one you have on to some famished soul.

Nothing would please me more than a critical letter on *The Human Prospect!*

American Academy in Rome
Via Angelo Masina, 5 (Porta S. Pancrazio)   March 9, 1956

Dear Lewis:
What wonderful news both about your book and about your coming to this Academy next winter. I really can't wait to read *The Transformation of Man,* a subject you have been brooding over for so many years; and as for the Academy I can't tell you soon enough that, from my point of view, it is a kind of paradise. When we meet of course we'll tell you in detail all about it—but I can say now that I feel sure it could not be pleasanter for you and Sophy. The expense is almost trifling, fifteen dollars a week or so; the company is delightful; the working quarters, for me at least, just about perfect. I have had good luck with my own work here, writing about one friend of the 'twenties, *The Seven Arts, Freeman, Dial,* etc. (also Lewis Mumford, W. Pach, Hendrik, Waldo, Lee and I can't say how many others). Incidentally, we have a terrace

(which I imagine you will have) with a view overlooking all Rome. We are on the top of the highest of the 7 hills. I am *sure* that both you and Sophy will love it.— (Gladys is making good progress with her own book,[13] which promises to be *very moving*.) We see multitudes of the most interesting people— today the Sandy Calders[14] have arrived; and next week we are driving up from a 3 day visit to Berenson and a visit to Percy Lubbock at Lerici. But this is only a hasty scrawl. I am so anxious to send word about the Academy—in case you have any hesitation about it. Don't!!!

Cambridge, Massachusetts   April 8, 1956

Your note from Rome gave us great pleasure, dear Van Wyck, as well as reassurance about our prospects for next winter. It's almost too good to be true; and I resolutely tell myself that it simply won't happen, as I used to tell myself at four that I wasn't going to get any Christmas presents—not any.

I am delighted at the fine critical reception your *Helen Keller* has been getting here, and I trust that the bookstores will soon tell the same tale. I'm looking forward to a free evening or two for reading it. But meanwhile I *have* been rereading in preparation for my class at Brandeis your wonderful description of Cambridge and Boston in Howells' time. Some of the husk of the fruit still is strewn around: the other night, at the Tavern Club, I met *two* Parkmans! We eagerly wait your return—though we are loathe to leave Cambridge, which has embraced us so warmly.

13 *Three Wise Virgins* (1957).
14 Alexander Calder, sculptor and designer of mobiles.

American Academy in Rome
Via Angelo Masina, 5 (Porta S. Pancrazio)   April 12, 1956

Dear Lewis:

I should have written to tell you that I have devoured *From the Ground Up,*—such a happy title. Naturally I went first for the suspect chapters on F. L. Wright, but the whole book is an indispensable chronicle of a big phase of our life, still so little acknowledged to be so,—full of ideas, all so finely expressed and of a sort that will open my eyes in the future. You have, naturally enough, in this place of architects,—I mean the Academy—many admirers and followers. You will find yourself surrounded by friends here, and everyone seems to be delighted that you are coming. We are getting a little homesick ourselves, and not sorry to sail for home on May 8th. The Alex. Calders and Henry Schnakenberg, who have been here too, are also happily going home this month or next. It is quite lovely to see how people of this kind nowadays really feel that our part of the U.S. is the most attaching and desirable corner of the world. They are all happy to give up Rome for it. But we have had really marvellous times here.

I have been writing about you again in my new *Days of the Phoenix*—about the 1920's—trying to say how much I owe you. I brought with me an old letter of yours, of February 15th, 1953. It was the letter you wrote to me about *The Writer in America* and I recognized that you had seen some of my limitations which I have been hoping to overcome. This book is about all our friends of the period, it is the second vol. of *Scenes and Portraits*—and I may ask you to glance through the ms.—for I am extremely anxious to get this right—more anxious than ever before I go on to a third volume.

P.S. Will you let me see the proofs of *The Transformation of Man?* I have many reasons for asking this.

Cambridge, Massachusetts   Patriot's Day: April 19, 1956

Dear Van Wyck:

Your over-generous praise of *From the Ground Up*[15] naturally pleases me: but what I look for even more is your reactions to *The Transformation of Man.*[16] It will come out on
May ninth, and so will be waiting for you at Bridgewater
when you return.

What a wonderful title you've found for your own book:
The Days of the Phoenix[17] vies with *The Confident Years.* (Of
course you know that the young now have a deep nostalgia for
the venerable twenties. Compared to their own state, its disillusion was one vast iridescent soap-bubble of hope.) I'd be
proud and happy to read it in ms.: and you couldn't have
struck a better moment in my life for just that pleasant
task. . . .

Amenia, New York   December 12, 1956

Dear Van Wyck:

. . . The day after we left you I began work on a book, after a
long weary drought that, it often seemed to me, might never
end; and since that time I have been working in the same
lively, effortless fashion that had so buoyed me up all through
the summer of 1954. I don't dare say what I am writing about
yet, except to say that it isn't a long poem, nor yet a novel, nor
a drama; nor is it like any of my more usual works. But it has
been conducting me—and only since I began working—
through my old manuscripts and a mass of ancient correspon-

---

15 *From the Ground Up* (1956) .
16 *The Transformation of Man* (1956) .
17 *The Days of the Phoenix* (1957) , the second volume of the *Autobiog-*
raphy.

dence, for my files date from 1910. I find my early literary work so incredibly bad that to read any considerable amount of it, before 1919, is downright depressing, and even then, for another four years or so, there are plenty of things that make me wince, though less for their lack of style or their self-conscious clumsiness than for their wry or half-baked ideas. Occasionally, there will be a piece that shows a little promise, like a sharp-spurred young cock in a flock of moulting pullets.

But the correspondence I have kept from the early twenties I find immensely stimulating in every way, especially in restoring to memory many persons and places and incidents I had completely forgotten: I daresay you've had some of the same experience, in preparing yourself for your own recent books of reminiscences and evocations. And what good letters you were writing to me, from the very beginning! One of the things that impresses me about the literary life of the twenties was how easy it was to get things done: there was none of this futile and expensive mechanical processing, with its officious interferences and its waste of time and labor and energy. Perhaps it wasn't always quite so quick and effortless as the production of my first motion picture, which was accepted in May and released for production in mid-summer; but certainly the record of my *Story of Utopias* came close to that, for I proposed it to Liveright in February, did my reading on it during the next six weeks, signed a contract at the end of March and delivered the book to the printer by the twentieth of June, reading proof completely before I sailed on the 20th of July. It takes all the efficiencies of the jet age and automation to stall things completely, so that it takes two days for a letter to reach New York from here, and in one recent case took three weeks! When I finally come to revise *Technics and Civilization* I owe it to myself, I think, to say some scarifying words about all this.

Was it you, dear Van Wyck, who recently told me you knew Alfred Zimmern's whereabouts? If you do, I wish you'd drop me a postal with his address, for I forgot then to put it down.

Even though it has been long since he has seemed to reciprocate the feeling—and I haven't the faintest way of accounting for the change—I have a warm spot in my heart for him and Lucie and would at least like to write them a note. Going back over my files, I recalled that he had written a very appreciative review of *The Story of Utopias* in the *Saturday Review of Literature*. The chorus of praise that that book got, along with my later ones *till 1940*, has spoiled me for what has happened to me since, when far better work of mine is either brushed off or completely ignored. Among the reviewers of *The Story of Utopias* I counted these: Robert Lovett, Clarence Britten, H. W. Nevinson, H. A. L. Fisher, Alfred Zimmern, all first string people as either scholars or critics. Part of the present neglect one can lay, without any tears, to the general feeling of boredom the older generation produces, when people feel that they have been around too long: Goethe got that, and many others before and since. But there is more than this to be explained, and the situation leaves me a little puzzled. . . .

Amenia, New York   February 20, 1957

Van Wyck tells me, dear Gladys, that I mustn't write him about *Days of the Phoenix;* so even if you hadn't asked me some questions I want very much to answer, or at least talk about, I would have had to address this letter to you; for I certainly don't intend to be silent about the Phoenix, whom in this case I identify myself with, and what better ears could I have to pour my joy into than yours? Since my joy is first of all a very personal joy, and would still be vivid even if the book as a whole did not evoke all the bright colors of our common youth, as if life had never soiled or unravelled or worn bare the threads of the gay tapestry, I will first record that. Van Wyck's long article about me in *The Writer in America* was like a foretaste of my obituary; reassuring in that it promised flowers and condolences, but somehow making me feel that I had been cast in bronze, and while I might be pleased by the comments of the passersby I still couldn't change my posture. But his words in the Phoenix are like a foretaste of heaven: I feel like living five more lives, promptly, just to justify the ambrosial taste of life (Van Wyck's more than mine) that he leaves in the mouth.

My pleasure in all this would be less than it is had he not dealt with so much penetration and so much love—the kind a good wife gives her husband—with our other friends, with Paul, Lee, Waldo, Walter, Joel, Hendrik, and even with that old curmudgeon Nock, who incidentally will never forgive Van Wyck for dropping the "Jay"—I can almost see his veiled wince. Van Wyck has brought us all back to life; and we shall go on talking and arguing and painting and writing and designing, in his pages, just as if it were heaven, no matter what happens to the ashes and dust of which we are now composed. I like that prospect; and feel promptly that I mustn't spoil it by ever attempting a book of my own that would cover, or even remotely touch on, the same ground. Even if Van Wyck's words about me are over-generous, they have the result of making me feel like justifying them by some further effort, just to prove how good a critic he is, if anyone at this late date still needs that proof. Perhaps it is the close personal touch one feels with the whole scene, perhaps it is the vividness of our youth; but somehow the very writing seems to have a higher color than the first volume of Van Wyck's reminiscences, as if that portrait were dulled a little by preservative varnish, while this is the original canvas, as fresh as when it came from the hands of the artist.

And then, miracle of miracles, that final chapter, the "Season in Hell": superb in the writing and valorous in moral conception, all the more because, in the final page Van Wyck shows the deepest kind of insight into the plight of the very kind of writer whose inner tendencies, whose broken values and distorted perceptions, he has, in other moments, warned us against. If Van Wyck had never written anything else, that picture of Hell, which is the hell of our times as well as his personal Hell, would live. Not write about this book? Good heavens: why should I write about anything else? (I hope that by now, dear Gladys, Van Wyck has been looking over your shoulder.) . . .

Paris   April 26, 1957

Dear Van Wyck and Gladys:

. . . Who am I to complain? I have seen the Dutch tulip fields in full bloom and Paris, with the chestnut trees in magnificent flower, and the spring rain dripping quietly through the *allées* of a deserted Tuileries! I am glad you liked *The Golden Day* on re-reading: it's perhaps one of the purest bits of writing I've done, and has always, as far as style and form go, been my particular favorite. Like good French writing, its charm derives partly from its superficiality! But it wasn't bad for a young man—if one forgets that Melville wrote *Moby Dick* at the same age! . . . All the people I came over here to see are either ill or in other parts of the world. But for all that my days are rich: did I not see a perfect performance of the *Bourgeois Gentilhomme* at the Comedie yesterday afternoon? If only my French were not so constipated!

Bridgewater, Connecticut   May 18, 1957

Dear Lewis:

I suppose you are now on your way to Italy, and in that case will you see Berenson? We have just heard from Ruth Stephan who saw him last week that he is as wide awake as ever.

Wonderful old man of 92! He wrote to me a month ago that he was having trouble with his eyes—so easy for "one who is still so passionately interested in the world at large"!!

Here we go on with some zest. I am still deep in *The Dream of Arcadia,* as I propose to call my book on America in Italy—for that is what it was up to the world-war time. The book is perhaps half finished, and, as I see it now, I shall end with B. B.—with a postscript on the Arcadia Dreamers who have been in Italy since Ezra Pound. The only trouble is that I don't know where to stop reading—for who has not been in Italy at one time or another? Of course, we have had many other things to do. Last week in Harlem I read a paper at a public meeting in honour of the great W. E. du Bois. He is 89 and has just finished a trilogy on the history of American Negroes since the Civil War. He is also a great man, as you may know. The occasion was for the presentation of a bust of him—very fine—by Wm. Zorach.

Last week your admirer Frank Stimson sent me a cheque from Tahiti to buy and send him second-hand copies of books by Lewis Mumford. By mail I cleaned out Dauber and Pine and sent him four books "in excellent condition." Now he writes me of his great affection for you and his faith in your "integrity of spirit." He said he sent you a long letter, which I hope you received. His book *Songs of the South Seas* is being published by the Peabody Museum and I expect copies this month. . . .

Bridgewater, Connecticut   October 11, 1957

Dear Lewis:

How good to have your news that all goes well in Cambridge. We were at Wellfleet for two weeks in early September seeing much of Edmund Wilson, the Biddles and Waldo.

With the latter I had three really good afternoons, the happiest ones I have ever had with him. He seemed somehow more relaxed, less touchy, in every way more mature. I felt that we were real friends at last!—also I got on very good terms with Wilson, who is a *character* and quite 18th century.

Up there I wrote my chapter on Berenson, and in fact finished *The Dream of Arcadia.* I hope and even think it's rather good. I end with the age of Fascism—the nineteenth-century "dream" could not survive that. Now I am casting about among various subjects, longing to get into focus again. When I am not writing I am out of luck! . . .

153 West 82nd Street, New York, N.Y.   October 21, 1957

Thank you, dear Van Wyck, for sending me Warburg's reply, in addition to taking the initiative in the first place. *The Conduct of Life* has met so many "accidental" misfortunes and rebuffs, has been subject to such continual oversights and such "studied" neglect that I would almost be persuaded by this treatment alone, that it is a more important book than any other I have written. But though these sage historic reflections soothe one's vanity they do not help to fill one's pocketbook: so I am thoroughly vexed by the reception it has received. "You have diagnosed this society accurately," my friend Murray admonishes me, "why then should you think that it would behave any other way than your own diagnosis indicates?" But he is a doctor and I am an author: so my vexation remains.

14 Francis Avenue
Cambridge, Massachusetts   December 20, 1957

When your *Writer's Notebook* came day before yesterday, dear Van Wyck, I received the best of all possible Christmas presents—and Sophy will say the same as soon as she gets it out of my hands. I sat down at once and devoured it: and now, like an ox, I have gone back to it and am chewing the cud. It is a scintillating book that would do honor to La Bruyère or La Rochefoucauld; a book with sharp edges, crystalline facets, a wide spectrum, transmitting light and color at once. If only this were found in the ruins of our civilization, it would both establish you as a great writer and give a lustre to the country that produced you, perhaps making the finder think more highly of us than we deserve.

This time, if not with your last book, I can say what I feel without suspicion of a too favorable natural bias. On every page you hit the target with such effortless ease—or at least the appearance of effortlessness—as to make one look upon you as an adept at Zen archery, finding the bulls-eye blindfolded. I shall be re-reading this, dear friend, as long as I can make out print. All hail to you!

Amenia, New York   February 11, 1958

Dear Van Wyck:

There's something quixotic and pathetic—I suppose the quixotic always *is* pathetic—about Hagedorn's trying to bring to life the dead bones of T.R.: a man whose essence was energy and whose influence decreased as his energy fatally ebbed and disappeared. What is left behind is a bundle of platitudes that once, with the energy behind them, sounded forceful and almost original, but were hardly better than what came forth from, say, McKinley. I've rebuffed Hagedorn so often on Moral Rearmament that I weakly agreed, in compensation, to let him put me on his TR committee, happily buried among a hundred, if not a thousand others. But I said no, flatly, to the plea he sent you, telling him that I reserved my energies for the jobs no one else was prepared to do, and that he could find a hundred other equally patriotic people to help him on this. I don't think either of us has any obligation to serve as a caryatid to support the obvious. . . .

Hotel Continental
Cambridge, Massachusetts   February 23, 1958

Dear Lewis:

You are perfectly right about Hermann Hagedorn.[18] There is in all this much childish sentiment, along with the endemic German worship of the führer. Hermann's führer happened to be T. R. instead of Hindenberg or Hitler, but neither of us is capable of this Fraülein's hero-worship.

I hope your book has begun to go. I am more and more impressed with the Howells papers and unpublished miscellanies. He was an immensely intelligent, magnanimous and perceptive mind who has been buried under a load of ignorance and incomprehension. I'll be ready to write in April or May. You are right about Cambridge. I've scarcely ever met so many good souls before, but I'll be glad to get home again nonetheless. . . .

18 Hermann Hagedorn, author of a *Life* (1918) and many other books about Theodore Roosevelt.

Amenia, New York   March 27, 1958

Welcome home, dear Van Wyck. I hope that the white ghost of winter has vanished from your part of the world. That spook has been with us long enough! I am deep in my book:[19] no mere revision this, but something far more substantial and significant, with all sorts of fresh light in places I least suspected I might find it—or throw it. The writing of it has beguiled me and delighted me in the same fashion *The Transformation of Man* did. . . .

17 Lowell Street, Cambridge, Massachusetts   October 13, 1958

Dear Van Wyck:

Being in Cambridge, without yet even attempting a party or a formal dinner, we still have had company galore; and, as with a thirsty man starting to drink, it needed the taste of company to remind us of how desperately, this summer especially, with its confinements, we had been missing it. We've scarcely more than settled down as yet; for I had to spend a week in and about New York, at conferences, and giving a Cooper Union Lecture; and so we have hardly begun to read yet, either. But we are both by turns, at this moment, absorbed in *Gramercy Square*:[20] delighted with these early glimpses of Gladys herself, who seems so amply to have embraced and profited by both her parents; and feeling all the while that this is not so much an autobiography or a memoir of an age long put away in ribbons and sachet powder, as the beginnings of a novel: a feeling that promotes the further conviction that her next book will break the traces of fact and

19 *The City in History* (1961).
20 *Gramercy Park,* by Gladys Brooks.

be wholly a work of the imagination, with all the sparkling freedoms of a novel: one of a dozen novels she might draw from her own life and the lives of those around her, without betraying any old friendships or loves. . . . .

Bridgewater, Connecticut   October 25, 1958

Dear Lewis:

. . . You have perhaps heard that Frank Stimson died last Sunday in Tahiti—apparently from a sudden development of cancer in the lungs and the prostate gland. It quite stunned me at first, for the case was so like Eleanor's, and Frank had so much to live for! Ham Basso[21] is going down to Tahiti just the same, for *The New Yorker* has broken all precedents in contracting for him to write a three-part *posthumous* profile of this (almost) living legend (still so little known, but I think sure to be relatively famous when his ethnological papers are brought out). . . . .

Amenia, New York   February 14, 1959

The sole and only reason for this letter, dear Van Wyck, is to offer you our love and good wishes for your seventy-first birthday, even if we can't be in New York on Saturday. . . . Since Sophy and I at this moment are belatedly reading Berenson's autobiographic fragment, part of our wish for you is that you shall continue to flourish as long and as well as he—*at least* that long and if possible much longer. In my new preface to *The Golden Day* I have recorded some small part of the debt I owe to you: but that book seems as slow in coming

21 Hamilton Basso.

from the publishers as your new work, and I regret that it cannot accompany and substantiate this letter. But I have no hope of being able to say adequately how much I owe to you: how your integrity has kept before me, from my earliest days— for I knew your work before we met in 1920—the image of the true man of letters, following his mission, to stir up the creative forces in our life in defiance of all that deadens the spirit. The words you wrote in the *Freeman* called me home to America from England in 1920: and by following your lead in fields adjacent to yours I first found my own path. If my own debt to you has been continuous, ever since then, enlarging itself like a descending snowball over the years, what shall I say of our country's debt to you? Only that this land would now be a drearier and emptier place, were it not for all the good things, the books, the places, the people, that your imagination and insight have brought to light. (I say nothing of your industry, colossal though that has been, too.) You have enlarged both our past and our potentialities: and I anticipate the verdict of generations to come when I record my gratitude for all that your life-and-work has meant, and will continue to mean. With deepest thanks and love—

3414 Sansom Street, Philadelphia, Pennsylvania   April 8, 1959

Dear Van Wyck:

My silence indicates only how absorbed I've been in my book. It's an innocent infatuation: but I don't think anyone will get a tenth of the pleasure reading it that I have in writing it. It's bound to become a classic: it's so colossally *un*readable. But for the first time, so happily placed are we here, I have not found myself counting the number of days till we leave Philadelphia. On the contrary, the term will be over before either of us can say Jack Robinson. I had plans to visit

Washington in April: but I've had to abandon them because of sheer pressure of work. So I'll miss your lecture: never yet have I heard you give one!

How we envy your trip to Italy: we must wait a whole year before we entertain such plans, much as I'd like to sneak away right now. Do look at the *Saturday Evening Post* next week: issue of 18 April. My essay on war will be in it—the one I struggled with all last fall.

Bridgewater, Connecticut   April 15, 1959

Dear Lewis:

Two days ago I found myself at Hartford in the study of the Bishop of Connecticut (Episcopal). He pulled out of a shelf *The Culture of Cities* and said "This is one of my favorite books." He was astonished when I told him that you were my best friend. Next time I expect to see the book in the hands of the R. C. bishop and perhaps in those of the Chief Rabbi. But they won't enjoy it as much as I'll enjoy the new edition. Of course I'll snatch the *Sat Eve Post.* when we go through New York tomorrow (on our way to Washington). It's really my first lecture and how I dread it.

I finished my *Howells* 2 months ago and am reading proofs. This will be the third biography of him to appear within a year, and Max Geismar has written almost a book about him. That's making up for lost time with a vengeance. But we are not going back to Italy. We are going to Holland and England only. . . .

Hotel Grosvenor
35 Fifth Avenue, New York, N.Y.   July 3, 1959

Dear Lewis:
   You are in that blissful state of just gathering together your
notes before you turn on the tap and your lovely fountain will
begin to flow,—while I've finished my short book, now being
typewritten, and feel for the moment utterly lost. I'm only
working at present on a lecture to be given in April at the
Corcoran Gallery in Washington—and can't seem to get hold
of my brains. However! I know your book will be glorious,
and I think my *Howells* is at least reasonably good. At any
rate, it's lively, so the English Departments will be sure to
damn it. I'm beginning to think that that's reward enough.
   Yesterday we had a visit from a young man who is teaching
at the Univ. of Penna. He wants to see you very much, and we,
feeling that you like the young (!?), told him to go and
introduce himself to you! I hope that was right. His name is
Gerald Weales. He writes a lot for *The Reporter*—on the
theatre mostly—and we became very fond of him at Yaddo.[22]

10 St. Johns Road
Cambridge [Massachusetts]   September 27, 1959

   I came up here last Monday, dear Van Wyck, and Sophy
followed with our Lares and Penates and paraphernalia on
Thursday, bringing your *Howells* along as a special dessert.
Tired as we both were, I started reading it the very first night:
for I can't imagine a book whose subject and mood more
perfectly fitted two fly-by-nights settling down in Cambridge,
very much in the jaunty but uneasy Howells manner. His

22 A writers' colony near Saratoga, New York.

ghost must have hovered over you as you wrote, assured but self-critical, transmitting these virtues to your poetry—! a Freudian displacement for "portrait," but not an unpleasant slip. Your biography is unflaggingly good, from beginning to end: profoundly appreciative of all his excellences, yet finely discriminating. I don't like it less because you've pounced on certain passages in *Silas Lapham*. I've been holding up my sleeve in case I write a Boston "Skyline": just today Sophy and I were noting again how good the brickwork of the eighties was in Marlborough St., as well as Commonwealth Avenue. . . .

We are ensconced in a spacious modern house whose living room window faces the rear garden of the Longfellow House, separated from us by a young hedge of pines, ailanthuses and lilacs. Peace and verdure: who could ask for more? No other American city fills me so constantly with delight: the gardens, the faces, the little personal encounters on Brattle Street, the easy accessibility of all one wants to be close to. When we were young it might have ruined us: but it's the perfect urban nest for our old age: and we're both sorry this term will be our last.

Amenia, New York   February 7, 1960

What a tempter you are, dear Van Wyck: you and Gladys and Savannah, too. Rasmussen,[23] the great connoisseur of cities, regards the original layout of Savannah as one of the triumphs of eighteenth century town planning; and even now thinks well of the soiled remains. If I weren't devilled by a book, a book about towns, too, Sophy and I would take the next train down there to join you; though we'd probably find that the railroad line has just been abandoned—much as we

23 Steen Eiler Rasmussen, Danish architect, planner, and author.

found on coming back here that our own railroad station was closed. Some fine winter we'll follow you there: a fine student of cities I am, to have visited neither Charleston nor Savannah nor New Orleans!! It all proves that I am still an amateur, and not, like the good Dane, a dedicated expert. But my book is going well, once more, and with the revisions I am making on the ancient history of the city, it may even prove to be a classic contribution to that difficult subject. At least I feel buoyed up enough by it to face the task, not yet accomplished, of writing an adequate concluding chapter, without letting it become too grimly depressing. The book, from a purely literary point of view, as something to *read*, is a monstrosity: even *I* can't read it. But that makes it all the more likely to meet the needs and prejudices of this monstrous age. When the time comes to launch the book, I propose to take it to Cape Canaveral!

Once the fatigue of packing and moving was behind us, Amenia enfolded us in its arms; indeed, we've both been going about the last fortnight with idiotic grins of pleasure on our faces, all the more because our last two drab dusty summers here, marred with illness and sordid cares, had almost robbed us of our taste for the place. Now it has all come back; and the only difficulty will be to leave it at the end of March when we set off on the Queen Elizabeth. The house itself greeted us like an old family servant, with his shabby shuffle and spotted, rust-black coat, but smiling, knowing all our wants, and anticipating them in advance; practically a member of the family. Every crack and hump here became all the more precious, in contrast with the antiseptic glare of our Cambridge place, whose very spaciousness only made it seem colder, almost to the point of hostility. It was not for *that* that I've pleaded the cause of modern architecture!

Hotel de Soto, Savannah, Georgia   February 15, 1960

Dear Lewis:

. . . The Georgians need a little bucking up, quite aside from the Negro question here. It is in many ways a beautiful city, with splendid old houses on every side. From my window at night, believe it or not, it looks like a quiet corner of Paris.— Of course all these old *Southern* cities you say you have not seen survive from the day when America was European. So they are not in the picture of strictly American developments. So glad to hear the book goes well and that you can get off by the end of March. . . .

No doubt you saw in the paper that E. B. White receives the gold medal for *Essays and Criticism*. There were formidable candidates. . . . I am deep in Ernest Fenellosa and Gladys is writing a very good book.

Amenia, New York   March 6, 1960

How we blessed Gladys, dear Van Wyck, for letting us know so promptly about the success of your operation, and about your own striking evidences of vitality, even as you were emerging from the anesthetic. While blessing and thanking Gladys, I add an extra bit of gratitude for that long generation of Dutch ancestors who must have bequeathed to you some of their own immense appetitite for life, and their stubborn fighting spirit. Perhaps you even filched a little of the ancestral protoplasm—or perhaps I should say ectoplasm— when you were over in the Netherlands last year. Hold on to it: it's the best of blood transfusions. If you get back on your feet quickly, the real problem will be to keep you sufficiently occupied; and for that I am sorry I cannot transport to New Haven our new feeding stations for birds. There's nothing like bird-watching to occupy the mind: I sometimes have to pinch myself to remember that I am supposed to be finishing a book. We have a whole country club of chickadees, juncos, sparrows, woodpeckers, bluejays, and starlings: all of them perfect ladies and gentlemen, except the starlings. There is an established order of precedence, as you probably know, and a mere flutter of wings is sufficient to re-affirm this order, if any bird has the temerity to challenge it. The struggle for existence and the spectacle of nature red in tooth and claw does not exist in this corner of bird-dom; I suspect it belongs to the yellow journalism of science, not to the real world. But there is no doubt that the starlings are both greedy and belligerent; what is more, they gang up on the others and try to hog the suet, instead of taking a little and then yielding. For this kind of misbehavior, however, nature has provided a remedy: since the nasty starlings think the rest of the world just as bad-tempered and menacing as themselves, I have only to appear in the doorway to have them fly away in a panic, while the more trustful, good mannered little birds are not in the least daunted by my presence, and go about their feeding. Much of my life is now given up to seeing that the starlings are driven away often enough to give the others a chance at the food: it gives me much the same feeling of satisfaction I would get if I could, by appearing in Washington and waving my arm, get the government to abandon its weapons of genocide. The universe cannot be altogether bad if it rewards the very trustingness of the chickadee, and punishes the starling by way of his own bad character. By now—dear Gladys—Van Wyck should be asleep, shouldn't he?

Athens, Greece   May 16, 1960

We have just spent two radiant, exalted days at Delphi,
dear Van Wyck: days that have given me a deeper insight into
the Greek mind, and the circumstances under which it worked
than I had ever had before. What one finds there is incom-
municable: so no book ever even hinted of the beauty and
power and terror and mystery of that scene. All words are so
much pasteboard beside the living flesh of that experience.

Yet the whole vivid encounter with the Acropolis and
Delphic shrine has been tainted in my consciousness by the
official news that brings to a climax fifteen years of American
illusions, errors and monumental hypocrisies, all leading directly to the ultimate criminality and insanity of a "war" of
extermination. I had no peace until, last Friday, I wrote a
letter to *The New York Times* on the subject:[24] and I have
little enough peace now that it's written. The situation seems
to me so grave, and the attitude of our leaders of both parties
so pathetically stupid, so pathologically blind, that unless
somehow our countrymen can awaken sufficiently to challenge
our entire policy—not the premeditated attempt to break up
the Summit meeting or the misfortune of being caught—our
leaders will, to conceal their early errors, continue to pyramid
them. They behave, in Rebecca West's words, like "mad
babies"—and the biggest Baby, more imbecile than mad—
occupies the White House. I beg you, dear Van Wyck, to drop
your work for the moment and speak up. You occupy, with
Frost, a unique place in the minds of our countrymen: and a
demand from you for a complete overhauling of all our
aggressively psychotic plans would have an effect no one else
has produced. The Delphic Oracle commanded me to urge
you!

24 The letter was not printed.

Amenia, New York   September 11, 1960

I phoned you tonight, dear Van Wyck, just to tell you that my book was at last finished—all but ten final pages that may not be written till it's in proof. . . . My feeling of relief, I hasten to add, is only a temporary one; for though I've put together about fifty plates of illustrations I still have to collect the last fourteen, which will be the hardest; and in addition to that, must write about twenty thousand words of text to accompany them, before I start correcting proof. This is my *last* long book: one's joyous discoveries by the way don't atone for the tedium of the long weary road itself. From now on I'm going to live on my intellectual capital, and spend it riotously, without trying to accumulate anything further, and above all, without planting for a second time in a field I've already tilled. If I have any special qualification it is that which Geddes had for the army: I am a fairly courageous and venturesome scout, at my best when working over fresh ground; and though I can, with effort, accustom myself to the discipline and drudgery of life in the trenches, I don't do this job as well as those who have a natural talent for it. But I won't waste any tears over the three years I've spent on this book; for I think I've done something that no one in this generation could have done with the same material, and perhaps it will earn enough to pay for a good solid coffin— unless the madmen who are now in charge of our fate decide, on grounds of economy, to dispense with the need for coffins by using their nihilistic weapons before we have a chance to die decently. My book would be a better book if this second prospect had not stared me so constantly in the face as I approached the last chapter; and in one sense, the best part of my book, the part which will remain unwritten, was killed by U-2 Eisenhower, at the same moment that he called off the Summit Conference. By leaving out that chapter, the book will look, spiritually, like a Manx cat; but I flogged myself for six weeks trying to write that last chapter, and then threw the hundred pages into the wastebasket. But that's not what I started to write you.

Bridgewater, Connecticut   November 5, 1960

Dear Lewis:

It makes me very happy to hear that you have finished the great book. For I have no doubt it is really a great book. I am getting on towards the end of my autobiography—volume 3, the last thirty years. Now I have got up momentum it is really swimming. Then, what do you suppose? I am going to write a life of Randolph Bourne! It's about time, you will say, forty-two years after his death, but I have been suddenly deluged with a mass of papers, among them two unpublished biographies of him. You must surely remember him well, and I wonder if you have any letters from him that I can see and use. . . .

I am more excited on Kennedy's behalf than you seem to be, although I admit that my enthusiasm is mostly or largely against "Dirty-Dick," and I don't think that Eisenhower, the tiresome grinner, has any business mixing so in the campaign. I suppose most Republicans are voting for him. . . .

Bridgewater, Connecticut   January 16, 1961

Congratulations, dear Lewis. We were so happy to read in the *Times* about your new English medal. When your new book comes out, you should get all the other medals,—if there are any medals for philosophy as well as architecture. I am so eager to read *The City* and hope I shan't have to wait till September for it. That is when my own book is scheduled to come out. I am calling it *From the Shadow of the Mountain: My Post-Meridian Years.* The phrase means that one has been "looney": it's supposed to be an old Hudson River expression. The book explains my point of view and tells the story of my later life.

When will you be coming home? We are staying for the winter in Bridgewater, with a week off in New York now and then. I have just finished a preface for the short stories of William Carlos Williams, wonderfully good stories—do you know them? They are to be published in a paperback by New Directions. I quite fell in love with Williams as I read them. Now for Randolph Bourne. I have very fine new material and it may make a book or, more probably, a long essay. It's a great opportunity to do something handsome! . . .

Bridgewater, Connecticut   February 4, 1961

Dear Lewis:

How good that we are neighbours again, even though separated by the fourth blizzard of the winter (the worst since 1882, we are told). It's good too that *The City in History* is finished, and of course I am flattered pink to be quoted on the cover. I expect a great treat when the book arrives. There will be time to see you well before you sail in June. We may be going ourselves at the end of August, but we're not yet sure of this. I must wait before deciding until I have had my semi-annual "check-up" in March.

Meanwhile, I am ploughing ahead with R. Bourne. His letters at Yale and Columbia are wonderful. And to think that there have been four unpublished biographies written of him.

I turned in last week the manuscript of *From the Shadow of the Mountain,* the last volume of my recollections.

Next week I'll be 75 years old, though how I have got there I can't imagine. You know they are giving a dinner for me at the Academy. I shall have to make some kind of a speech, so I don't encourage anyone to be present!

Bridgewater, Connecticut   April 3, 1961

Dear Lewis:

Every minute I could spare since *The City in History* came, I have been reading what Arthur Pope called (over the telephone) this "magnificent" book, and it is certainly your masterpiece thus far. How ever you kept flowing in a steady stream that splendid mass of words is one of the miracles of our time, and I was astonished by the breadth of your vision, the energy you write with and your apparently universal knowledge. You seem to know Europe by heart, from Oslo to Palermo, visually, historically and every other way. I finished the book last evening, delighted from first to last not least of all by the superb illustrations, as well as by your all-seeing eyes and your always resilient style. The narrative gains immensely by your having short chapters. And how proud I was to see myself quoted under the fine photograph that Alison took! You will have to have a longer than usual rest after this prodigious effort of the last four years.

I seem to remember that you are going abroad again either in May or in June. I don't know where you are going besides England. Gladys and I are planning to go to Scandinavia at the end of July, then to Switzerland and finally to Italy, where my step-sister now lives in Rome. She is a Roman Catholic, surrounded by monsignori, a cousin in the Vatican and a nephew at the Collegio Beda. But she now leaves me alone in my heathenism. . . .

P.S. My *From the Shadow of the Mountain* is coming out in September.

5 Cambridge Terrace, London   June 29, 1961

Dear Van Wyck:

After three weeks here I feel like Henry James at the end of a busy London social season: the mood in which he wrote "The Great Good Place," though in my case mere physical exhaustion and a hoarse voice (from talking too much) take the place of desperation. We've never enjoyed England more —possibly because we spent half our time in Wales and Scotland. The royal medal now lies in our bureau, mid sundry more plebian bits of haberdashery: esthetically commonplace and too shining to be convincing, but, as Le Corbusier remarked when he received *his* medal, "heavy." Very heavy! . . . After this heavy bout of sociability and hospitality, exciting as it has been I began to long for the chaster silence of Leedsville—provided you and Gladys will be there to break it when we return.

1471 Greenwood Terrace
Berkeley, California   September 24, 1961

From the Shadow of the Mountain reached here a few days ago, dear Van Wyck, with almost the same happy effect as if you yourself had appeared in the doorway to chat for a while, while your vigilant writer's eye was silently taking in our new quarters. Almost at once I sat down and thirstily began to drink in the first two chapters; but before I had gone too far I reminded myself that, at this rate, the book would too soon be finished and your visit would be over: so I have put it aside, to be read—if I can restrain myself—a chapter a week, which should bring me to the end, I figure, by December as a sort of Christmas present. I daresay I won't keep this abstemious resolution beyond the next two weeks; but it will last till then, for I find myself having, out of courtesy, to take on all sorts of university duties I had somehow escaped at Pennsylvania, including a full dress university lecture which I am quite unprepared to do at this moment, especially since, for lack of any other general topic, I am going to deal with the way that the present crisis has developed over the last fifteen years, finding us completely unprepared, though we should in fact have gotten our minds ready for the task of controlling nuclear energy at least a whole generation ago. I am calling the lecture "An Apology to Henry Adams." . . . Our house is the luckiest of finds, which we fell into through the help of friends: a large modern redwood structure, in the vernacular manner of the Bay Region, originally developed by Bernard Maybeck—a sweet and humbler and more humane Frank Lloyd Wright—with unpainted wood within and without, overhanging eaves, windows of varied sizes and shapes, clinging to the side of a hill, with a terrace and a lush California garden inviting us perpetually outdoors. Through the clerestory windows of our great living room we can see the upper trunks and needles of quite lordly pines; and though we are surrounded by other similar houses, they are so completely hidden from us that we have actually a greater feeling of privacy and peace than we can achieve any more at Leedsville. . . . By now we are quite tired of travel, so much so that I have sternly refused the invitations that have been pouring in to lecture in other parts of the state: it is easy to be stern, for I hate lecturing! But last weekend we spent in

Monterey and had a chance one afternoon to poke our nose
into your old bailiwick, Carmel, which I fear will soon turn
into a vast suburban mélange, except at the water's edge
where the National government has stept in to protect the
precious rocks and foliage from the rapacity of the real estate
speculator and builder. You probably saw it on your last visit
here: so I won't go into details. But since we were taken there
by car—I had, in advance of my work here, let myself in for
two lectures—and went down by the horrid freeway and back
by the slower but mostly pleasanter coastal road, we got a
good cross section of coastal California. The landscape is
magnificent and the towns are scrofulous infections on it,
especially those parts where commercialism pustulates into
roadhouses, motels, tourist traps, and filling stations, or where
the highway engineer has bulldozed and blasted away a
woodland or a pleasant rise of land in order [to] maintain the
highest level of speed and monotony. The docility of our
fellow countrymen, before all these assaults on their eyes and
feelings, and even on their pocketbooks would perpetually
amaze me, did I not long ago suspect that they glory in these
destructions and regard them as inevitable sacrifices to progress, though what progress is, except in the opportunity to
make more money and keep the economy from collapsing, they
would find it hard to define. Every city in the United States
today spends more for street and highroad construction than it
does for education; even here in Berkeley, which once had the
best school system in California, if not the United States,
the standards of public education have steadily fallen during
the last decade, for lack of financial support, though the
Highway department has just opened up a new four lane road
through this quiet residential district, at a cost of half a
million dollars, for no reason whatever except to make it
uniform with the more crowded and frequented parts of the
city. This is enough to put all heaven in a rage; but the lack of
any sense of human realities which it betrays seems to me even

more ominous, for it now extends to every part of life, and not least of course to our extravagantly mad policies on nuclear weapons, moon exploration, and Berlin.

But enough of this: I sat down to this letter in the first place, dear Van Wyck, simply to thank you for your gift and recount my first effervescence of appreciation for this volume, which plainly lives up to the standard of its predecessors. What a life you have lived, and how rich in friends you have made it: it has been a sort of one-man *Flowering of New England,* or rather a flowering of America; and a hundred years hence, if we have any posterity above the level of neurotic savages, someone will, with your work before them, do a picture of the "World of Van Wyck Brooks," as you did of Irving. Incidentally, though I still think that the *Flowering* is the best of all your books, if only because it was the first to define your original contribution in both method and style, I share your admiration for *The World of Washington Irving,* for there you not merely brought to light many buried treasures but made a living synthesis of our essential democratic tradition, by establishing it as central in our literary culture as well as our political life. Sophy, who has read farther into the book than I have, tells me that you have mentioned Wijdeveld in it. I know from my own experience with *The City in History* that you would be bankrupt if you sent the book to all the living people who have a part in this pageant; and so I don't suspect that you have sent a copy to my Dutch friend. But I would just like your assurance of this before I send him a copy myself; for he is a man who has never gotten the attention he deserves; and I know he will be pleased with your having included him.

Bridgewater, Connecticut   October 8, 1961

Dear Lewis:

We are just setting out for ten days in Vermont, largely to get away from the telephone, but I must send you a line before we go. . . . No, I didn't send a book to Wijdeveld, in case you care to send one. I'm going to prepare in Vermont my paper on Fenollosa for the Philosophical Society. I am allowed 25 minutes and Chiang Yee has rehearsed my pronunciation of Japanese names. We have Glenway Wescott with us for Saturday and Sunday, and he has been reading to us this morning from his memoirs of the nineteen-twenties, really delightful recollections of F. M. Ford, Gertrude Stein, and Joyce. He is a good person to have in the house—such a contrast to our dear Lee! who was here last Sunday and actually broke the bed. . . .

2820 East 6th Street, Tucson, Arizona   March 19, 1962

Dear Lewis:

. . . Now I see that you have received the National Book Award, so evidently the U.S. is beginning to catch up with England. We are starting for home in about a week, driving by way of New Orleans and Mobile. But I don't think much nowadays of driving across the country. It used to be exciting, but now the by-passes make it impossible to see anything but filling stations and motels. It might as well be Danbury three thousand miles long. We were held up for three days at Fort Worth coming out. There was ice on the roads and we could not drive, but, being outside the town, we didn't even see Fort Worth. Going home we will, if possible, drive on small roads, so as to see some of the cities.

Tucson seems to me rather like Pompeii, as it must have been before the eruption. Miles of one-storied houses with patios but little else, though there is some very good architecture. We have seen a good many people, including J. W. Krutch, Ruth Stephan and, last night, Kenneth Rexroth. The latter, a confused and confusing man of 60, seems to have lived pretty much everywhere, in New York and Chicago, besides Venice and Viterbo, before he went to live in San Francisco. He took us to a cattleman's club last night for dinner, a very amusing place in the cellar of a hotel where they broiled everything over a fire in an open fireplace and had nothing else to eat that was not broiled. We spent two days last week in Phoenix, where the popular line seems to be Barry Goldwater's. These Arizona towns sprawl for miles over the desert. At Phoenix we were taken to see Taliesen West, an extraordinary village of a house with two theatres. . . .

Bridgewater, Connecticut   June 6, 1962

Dear Lewis:

I have been reading you so hard that I haven't answered your fine letter. I have read the 3 biographies of Geddes, but, while I don't think I'll make him out as over-influencing you, I'd rather keep the whole subject under my hat until I have finished reading you. With every book, I am more and more impressed by your work. You are literally, as Felicia Geffen says, *unique*. This month or probably next I will get through all your books, though I have to stop to read proofs of an anthology I have done: then I'll be ready to bomb you with questions. Your early life is still mysterious to me, and very important also for me to know about. (And yet I have just been reading all your letters to me in the 1920's. You were so immensely generous at the time of my breakdown! Your letters bring it all back.) I don't see *how* I can write this book, but I am determined to do it!—Don't fail to let me see your new introduction to *Herman Melville*. . . .

Amenia, New York   June 24, 1962

This rainy day, dear Van Wyck, makes this old gardener feel as happy as the first downpour of autumn makes a Californian: so in this smiling dripping mood I write you. Sophia and I have been living in a state of almost frightening euphoria: the first untrammeled relaxation we've had since 1957, before I began serious work on *The City in History*. That book has almost made up for the toll it took of our lives by providing us now with the means for this unpressured life: the release I had hoped for in 1951, when *The Conduct of Life* came out, but in vain, has come now—fortunately in time to be still enjoyable, in which matter I am luckier than was Melville. I shall use these idyllic months ahead to take a good long look at what I have been doing: for it was just such another period back in 1956–7 that got me started, quite unexpectedly, upon *The City in History*—a task I'd shrunk from for 15 years.

[Little Compton, Rhode Island]   July 8, 1962

Dear Lewis:
We are spending a month at Little Compton, Rhode Island, in a cottage belonging to the Carl Bingers—address, as usual, Bridgewater—and I am steadily reading Lewis Mumford. I shall be finished by the end of the month and ready to see you

and ask you questions. I am a little baffled in spots and by no means sure that I can write the book, but I'll try hard and hope to succeed. It is a very exciting and suggestive subject (at the moment, I am in the middle of your Columbia lecture, *Art and Technics*). Your letter came a few days before we left here, and I was so happy to hear of your fighting euphoria. You certainly deserve it. I look forward to a visit with you very early in August. This cottage is delightful, built for the Binger children who are coming in August. We look out on a great inland lake, with the ocean beyond. We are 50 feet away from it, and there are 30 or 40 swans swimming all day on the watery expanse. No swimming for us, as yet, but Gladys expects it in a day or two. Yesterday we went with the Bingers to a great barbecue in the village, with elements of a rodeo, riding feats, etc. I am writing, for pen, with a "ball-point" pencil and probably can't be read. So I'll make it short. The Bingers speak of you with the greatest affection. I hope you had a good visit from Harry Murray, who had spent a night with us.

Amenia, New York   August 5, 1962

Your gift of the "Fenollosa," dear Van Wyck, could not have come at a happier moment. . . . Your account of Fenollosa whets one's appetite again for another look at the Boston collection, or a first look at his and Mover's books. Again you make me feel what an ignoramus I am in the field of American literature: still more, what a dark continent that was till you opened it up . . . In short, though I've not finished the book yet, it makes me happy; and I congratulate you on making still another bulls-eye.

As to your proposed book about me, I fear I may be discouraging you in the very act of delaying you with personal data. This is partly the result of my having dedicated this year to a full review of my own life and work, with a view to completing the autobiography I started half a dozen years ago. I have no notion of publishing this at an early date: indeed the second volume (1935–196!) may not be published in my lifetime. So our works are in no sense competitive: they are rather complementary, in that one views the data from the inside, the other from the outside. The only danger may come from my too ebulliently presenting you with more material than you can conveniently use. So I won't *volunteer* more—though I'm ready to supply more, e.g. by annotating the autobiographic snatches in the *New Yorker* and "The Little Testament." If you find yourself baffled in trying to put the parts together, be comforted by the report on my Rorschach test—the tester said that while he was usually able to summarize the results in a few hours, he spent two whole days trying to reconcile the contradictions in mine and make them fit a single personality! If this book about me threatens to cause more trouble than it is worth, don't let any misgivings about my disappointment, dear Van Wyck, keep you from dropping it. Nothing can deprive me of the elation of knowing that you *wanted* to do it: that will remain an invisible and untarnishable gold medal!

Bridgewater, Connecticut   August 13, 1962

Dear Lewis:

I am also laid up for ten days. Can't leave my bedroom—a slight heart attack but, the doctor thinks, of little importance. But I was so glad to have your letter, and you needn't fear deluging me with too much information.[25] I have nothing

---

[25] A fragment of the proposed biography of Mumford still exists in manuscript, but is not reliable because it was never checked and confirmed.

ahead but *you* to write about, except a long introduction on Benjamin Franklin for the Limited Editions Club. I would appreciate it if you would *volunteer* any information about yourself before I come again to ask for it. I'll probably begin writing next month and I can certainly well use anything you turn up in working on your autobiography. After I have been to the Yale Library again, I'll probably be over to ask you for more. I *count* on writing about you and don't mean to drop the idea unless I am absolutely baffled (which I don't expect to be).

I'm sorry that Sophy too has a summer cold—so very hard to get rid of, as I know.

Please forgive my unintelligible handwriting—partly the result of the ball point pen, the only one I am able to use at the moment.

Amenia, New York   August 16, 1962

The disturbing news in your letter the other day, dear Van Wyck, was reassuringly contradicted by the fact that you could write a letter at all; but for all that it was nice to learn from Gladys today that you were making steady progress, and will soon be sufficiently back in health to commit again all the sins that may have brought on your indisposition. Perhaps we ought to thank Nature for these nudges, nagging though they sometimes seem, with their undertones of I-told-you-so; for they probably save us from getting harder wallops later. As for reading your writing, it's better than solving a crossword puzzle, or putting together an ancient skeleton from a few buried bones. I cut my teeth as a decoder of abbreviated scripts on the Melville mss. long ago; and once one can decipher Melville nothing else daunts one! At the moment I am waiting for the proofs of the revised Melville to come tumbling on my desk: though my corrections are few and far between, I find myself almost as eager to look at the results as if it were a new book. . . .

The scholars who chortled with glee over the Murray–Mumford howler of Melville's finding his own portrait in Ethan Brand never bothered to pick up the nugget of gold that I had dropt in committing that error; namely, that they are both myths dealing with modern man's dismemberment and detachment from the forces of life—one through an unfeeling development of intelligence, the other through an equally suicidal will-to-power. Someday I want to put all this in an essay; but at the rate of progress I have been making this last six months in getting down to my book, it looks as if I'll have to arrange for another incarnation to get this little job done.

We hope that the sales of Gladys' book[26] has been commensurate with all the fine critical notices she has been getting, and that the same will be true of yours. For once the daily *Times* reviewer went out of his way to give you your due. You have now passed safely, from the stage of undiscriminating abuse to the stage of undiscriminating praise; and that is a sign that Emerson's old law of compensation is still at work. . . .

Amenia, New York   November 21, 1962

What a mean, murky day this has been, dear Van Wyck: the kind of weather that makes me hate the country, for nothing about it draws me out of doors, and long for the city where I might stumble on a friend on Fifth Avenue, go to an art show, or if desperate find an old motion picture I wanted to see again. But some of the darkness lifted this afternoon when I decided to go through your file of letters, which Sophy has at

26 *Boston and Return* (1960).

last almost come to the end of putting in order: quite the biggest file in my not inconsiderable heap of ancient correspondence. And I came upon a letter of yours written in April 1925, which I had always remembered, and talked about to people discussing our period and your development, but had not actually read again for many years. This was the letter in which you tell how you had been exploring the darker side of the moon, and how Emerson had suddenly revealed the sunny side and given you a new sense of the mission of literature and its relation to the popular life of our time. I've written a little annotation on this letter, so that your biographer won't easily miss it. And this reminds me to ask: Who *is* your biographer? Have you selected one, or did you hope that your own reminiscences would ward off the muscle-bound Ph.D. who even now is probably laboriously following your trail, putting together the various pieces of your life, and proving to his own satisfaction that eight and seven make three. The time I myself have wasted the last few years, correcting the absurd academic conjectures that a couple of incipient American studies professors have been making about the genesis of my own work, trying to interpret it in terms of what they and their kind would do. . . .

The Biltmore, New York, N.Y.   December 6, 1962

The news of your improvement, dear Van Wyck, caused all your friends at the Academy meeting yesterday to rejoice among themselves. We missed you, but I, most of all, because but for you I know that I would never have been elected President, or have accepted the nomination when it was offered. I embrace you over the occasion with love and gratitude. . . .

Amenia, New York   February 14, 1963

I haven't stopt to count up your birthdays, dear Van
Wyck—though I know that if I subtracted ten they'd give me
mine! But this letter, whether or not it reaches you on the
sixteenth, is a birthday letter: and its sole purpose is to offer a
bouquet of love from Sophia and me. Rummaging through a
file of old letters today I came on one from Mukerji thanking
me for calling you, in 1927 or 1928, "our best critic," in some
review I'd written. I am still calling you that and you still are;
for all that you've done as a writer has added to the fullness of
American life and conveyed a sense of all its further possibilities. And what is criticism if it is not a perpetual turning over
of the soil, and a turning under of the weeds in order to make
ready for new growth? This has been your task: a task no one
else could have done with such effortless competence and such
magnanimous, even-handed judgment. In this dark period you
have been a sort of one-man Age of Confidence: and your
example may in time breed the very qualities our contemporaries now sadly lack. I'm not telling you all these nice things,
dear Van Wyck, *just* because it's your birthday: still less am I
saying them officially, as President of the Academy to the
Chancellor, as I well might. I am saying what I think because
what you are and what you have done has made such a great
difference in my own life, as it will continue to do for generations in the lives of our countrymen. If a friend may not say
such things freely, at the appropriate moment—and what is
better than a birthday?—who should? And if the President of
the Academy has been remiss on this occasion, let your old
friend take his place, without Felicia to tactfully nudge him!

Amenia, New York   April 2, 1963

It's a long time since I've written, dear Van Wyck: but the grim days of February and March somehow silenced me, and for the last month or so I haven't done a stroke of serious writing. My grievances against the winter are small, compared to those you may justly hold: so I mention them only to account for the hiatus between us. Tonight, for the first time, the sleigh-bell chorus of the spring peepers broke out; and I hope that this quickening sound can be heard in Bridgewater, too— a better tonic than any physician can prescribe! I am still reviewing my life-work and mulling over my vast correspondence files. I am impressed not only by the copiousness of the letters people wrote in the twenties, but by the generous spirit they breathe. Even mere acquaintances, like John Macy, were endlessly kind, while as for you, dear Van Wyck—well, I won't say what your letters meant then, and mean even more now. "The best," as Whitman tells us, "is that which must be left unsaid." With a loving embrace from both of us, to Gladys and yourself.   Ever,

                                                                  Lewis

Principal Works of
VAN WYCK BROOKS
and
LEWIS MUMFORD

1908
1910
1913
1914
1915
1915
1918
1920
1922 The Story of Utopias
1924 Sticks and Stones
1925
1926 The Golden Day
1927
1929 Herman Melville
1931 The Brown Decades
1932
1932
1934 Technics and Civilization (The Renewal of Life, Vol. I)
1936
1938 The Culture of Cities (The Renewal of Life, Vol. II)
1939 Men Must Act
1940 Faith for Living
1941 The South in Architecture
1941
1944 The Condition of Man (The Renewal of Life, Vol. III)
1946 Values for Survival
1947 Green Memories; The Story of Geddes
1948
1951 The Conduct of Life (The Renewal of Life, Vol. IV)
1952 Art and Technics
1953
1954 In the Name of Sanity
1955 The Human Prospect
1956 From the Ground Up
1957 The Transformation of Man
1958
1958
1959
1961 The City in History
1962
1963 The Highway and the City
1967 The Myth of the Machine

INDEX

INDEX